China Studies in South and Southeast Asia

Between Pro-China and Objectivism

Asia Research Center
Chulalongkorn University

The Asia Research Center (ARC) is a non-profit organization dedicated to contributing to the advancement of higher learning and supporting research by top scholars in Thailand. The ARC was jointly founded by Chulalongkorn University and the Korea Foundation for Advanced Studies (KFAS) on January 24, 2002.

The ARC provides financial support to researchers and research activities in the fields of Social Science and Humanities, Natural Science, Information Service and Technology and Petrochemical Engineering in Thailand. The ARC sponsors Thai scholars' research visits to South Korea, arranges academic meetings, publishes research, and manages other related activities.

CHINA STUDIES IN SOUTH AND SOUTHEAST ASIA

Between Pro-China and Objectivism

Edited by

Chih-yu Shih
National Taiwan University, Taiwan

Prapin Manomaivibool
Chulalongkorn University, Thailand

Reena Marwah
Delhi University, India

Asia Research Center
Chulalongkorn University

Published by

World Scientific Publishing Co. Pte. Ltd.
5 Toh Tuck Link, Singapore 596224
USA office: 27 Warren Street, Suite 401-402, Hackensack, NJ 07601
UK office: 57 Shelton Street, Covent Garden, London WC2H 9HE

and

The Asia Research Center
Chulalongkorn University
16th Floor, Chamchuri 10 Building
Phyathai Road, Pathumwan, Bangkok, Thailand 10330

Library of Congress Cataloging-in-Publication Data
Names: Shih, Chih-yu, 1958– editor. | Manomaivibool, Prapin, editor. |
　　Marwah, Reena, 1960– editor.
Title: China studies in South and Southeast Asia : between pro-China and objectivism /
　　edited by Chih-yu Shih, Prapin Manomaivibool, Reena Marwah.
Description: New Jersey : World Scientific, [2018] | Includes bibliographical references.
Identifiers: LCCN 2018010672| ISBN 9789813235243 (hc : alk. paper) |
　　ISBN 9789813236219 (pbk : alk. paper)
Subjects: LCSH: China--Research--South Asia. | China--Research--Southeast Asia. |
　　Learning and scholarship--Political aspects--South Asia. | Learning and scholarship--
　　Political aspects--Southeast Asia. | Objectivity.
Classification: LCC DS706 .C51117 2018 | DDC 951--dc23
LC record available at https://lccn.loc.gov/2018010672

British Library Cataloguing-in-Publication Data
A catalogue record for this book is available from the British Library.

Copyright © 2019 by World Scientific Publishing Co. Pte. Ltd.

All rights reserved. This book, or parts thereof, may not be reproduced in any form or by any means, electronic or mechanical, including photocopying, recording or any information storage and retrieval system now known or to be invented, without written permission from the publisher.

For photocopying of material in this volume, please pay a copying fee through the Copyright Clearance Center, Inc., 222 Rosewood Drive, Danvers, MA 01923, USA. In this case permission to photocopy is not required from the publisher.

For any available supplementary material, please visit
https://www.worldscientific.com/worldscibooks/10.1142/10856#t=suppl

Desk Editors: Chandrima Maitra/Lixi Dong

Typeset by Stallion Press
Email: enquiries@stallionpress.com

Printed in Singapore

About the Editors

Chih-yu Shih is currently teaching anthropology of knowledge and international relations theory at National Taiwan University. He is the author and the editor of many books, covering intellectual history of China/Chinese studies, international relations theory, and post-Chinese identities. Professor Shih is additionally Editor-in-Chief of the journal *Asian Ethnicity*. He holds an MPP from Harvard University and a PhD from University of Denver. His project on the intellectual history of China Studies is accessible at http://www.china-studies.taipei/.

Prapin Manomaivibool obtained her Ph.D. in Chinese from the University of Washington (UW), Seattle in 1967. She is Director of Asia Research Center at Chulalongkorn University (CU), Chair Professor of the Chinese Section, Faculty of Arts, CU, President of the Chinese Language Teachers' Association of Thailand under the Royal Patronage of HRH Princess Maha Chakri Sirindhorn, and Fellow of the Royal Society of Thailand.

She has extensive research experience and publications in Chinese language, linguistics, sinology, and linguistic-related fields. Her major academic papers are, "Thai and Chinese — Are they Genetically Related?" (published by Tokyo's NIURIASLC), "Early Sino-Thai Linguistic Links: Towards a Semantic and Quantitative Study" (published by Hong Kong's LISRC), "Yue-Tai Linguistic Links" (published by UW), "Chinese Language Teaching in Thailand" (published by CU), "Tracing the Meanings of Thai Disyllabic Words" (published by Arizona State University), "Intellectual Paths of Thailand's First Generation China Scholars: A Research Note on Encountering and Choices of Khien Theeravit and Sarasin Viraphol" (published by Routledge) and "泰国汉语教学现状" (published by 北京商务印书馆). Other major publications and textbooks she compiled or co-authored include *Mandarin Chinese Grammar, Chinese for Tourism, Vols. 1 and 2, Chinese for Business, Thai-Chinese Dictionary for Tourism, Chinese-Thai Dictionary: TalkingDict.*

Reena Marwah received her M.Phil. from Delhi University and Ph.D. from Himachal University, India. She is presently ICSSR Senior Fellow, affiliated with the Centre for the Study of Developing Societies. She has also been on deputation as Senior Academic Consultant, ICSSR, Ministry of Human Resource Development, Govt. of India, for three years (2012–2015). She is a permanent faculty member of Jesus and Mary College, Delhi University, India, as an Associate Professor and has been teaching Indian economy, macroeconomics, and politics of globalization. She is the recipient of several prestigious fellowships including the McNamara fellowship of the World Bank, 1999–2000 and the Asia fellowship of the Asian Scholarship Foundation 2002–2003. Among her research interests are international relations issues of China, the Philippines, Thailand, Nepal, and India, and development issues of gender, globalization, and poverty in South and Southeast Asia. In addition to several chapters and articles published in books/journals, she is co-author/co-editor of 11 books and monographs including *Contemporary India: Economy, Society and Polity* (Pinnacle 2009, 2011), co-edited volumes including *Economic and Environmental Sustainability of the Asian Region* (Routledge 2010), *Emerging China: Prospects for Partnership in Asia* (Routledge 2011), *On China by India: From a Civilization to a Nation State* (Cambria Press, USA); *Transforming South Asia: Imperatives for Action,* (Knowledge World, India 2014); *The Global Rise of Asian Transformation,* (Palgrave Macmillan 2014). She is the founding editor of *Millennial Asia,* a biannual journal on Asian Studies of the Association of Asia Scholars, published by Sage Publishers.

Contents

About the Editors v

Introduction xi

Part I Biographical Perspectives 1

1 Odysseys in China Watching: Comparative Look at the Philippines and Nepal 3
   Tina S. Clemente and Pamela G. Combinido

2 Malaysia, Nanyang, and the "Inner China" of Three Hong Kong Scholars: Huang Chih-Lien, Chang Chak Yan and Kueh Yik Yaw 29
   Chow-Bing Ngeow

3 Indonesian Intellectuals' Experiences and China: Peranakan Benny Gatot Setiono on the Balance Between Indonesian Nationalism and Chineseness 67
   Matsumura Toshio

4 A Long Journey from Chinese-Language Newspaperman to Chinese Specialist: The Oral History from Two Senior Chinese Intellectuals in Thailand 83
   Apiradee Charoensenee

Part II National Perspectives — 103

5 Sourcing Contemporary Vietnam's Intellectual History in Russia: Sciences, Arts, and Sinology — 105
Cong Tuan Dinh

6 Scholarship and Friendship: How Pakistani Academics View Pakistan–China Relations — 127
Pervaiz Ali Mahesar

7 Vietnam's Composite Agenda on the Rise of China: Power, Peace, and Party — 169
Quang Minh Pham and Hoang Giang Le

Part III Comparative Perspectives — 191

8 China Studies in South and South East Asia: A Comparative Perspective Through Sri Lanka and Thailand — 193
Reena Marwah

9 Crafting a Bridge Role Through Chinese Studies Without Sinology: Lessons of South Asian Think Tanks for Singapore — 225
Chih-yu Shih

10 South Asia's China Outlook: Reminiscing Through the Lens of Bangladesh and Nepal — 253
Sharad K. Soni

Part IV External Perspectives — 285

11 An American Perspective on Vietnam's Sinology — 287
James A. Anderson

12 The Knowledge of Vietnamese Intellectual Class
    to China: Focusing on the Seventeen Vietnamese
    Scholars Interviewed by National Taiwan University   303
    Xiangdong Yu and Sijia Cheng

13 Post-Chineseness, Sinology, and Vietnam's
    Approach to China   325
    Chih-yu Shih

Introduction

Complicating China Through China Studies

China scholars easily appear to be relatively pro-China because compared with other parts of their societies they can provide explanations of China's actions that may give the impression of being sympathetic. Where China studies receive stronger support in think tanks in the areas of security studies, regional politics, and economics, such as is the case of South Asia in general and Vietnam and the Philippines in Southeast Asia, experts are rarely the first to criticize China. Understanding China better may lead to the stereotype that they prefer a less confrontational approach when facing a rising China that is expanding its influence. For instance, in Singapore, Malaysia, Thailand and Indonesia, where "Chinese" Southeast Asians make up a significant portion of China scholars or China watchers, the humanities are often a priority on their agenda. Consequently, China scholars of the indigenous Muslim society who contrarily pay greater attention to security and contemporary China studies may not appear as pro-China.

More importantly, China's geographical proximity to South and Southeast Asia makes China studies a very practical rather than a pedagogical issue, as is the case of European Sinology. Even in the US where the Cold War used to dominate the development of China studies, China was treated by means of intellectual construction rather than through practical experience. In contrast, in South and Southeast Asia personal experiences make up a critical component of people's understandings of China as encounters with people, things, and phenomena Chinese occupy people's historical as well as social spaces. The amount of shared beliefs, diets, languages, kinships and worldviews within groups that trespass borders parallel the varieties among them. Neither the "Western" style of social science approach to China nor the pursuit of conversion of the Chinese population toward a sacred cause would guarantee scholars to enjoy popularity among the South and Southeast Asian China studies communities. Discursively as well as practically a constant factor in one's life, China represents simultaneously a real threat and a real opportunity, a component of the self and a constituent of alterity, and a bygone nostalgia and an inspiring future.

Proximity additionally invites immediate mutual influences that may obscure or even deconstruct China as a common category to those who enlist its name, regardless of the authorities of China either feeling more isolated due to self-perceived vulnerability to external intrusion or more influential during the time of its rise to major power status. In the 21st century, the rise of China has stimulated higher interests in learning the Chinese language facilitating the spread of Confucius Institutes. Indeed, this has prompted the transformation of the contour of China studies toward a linguistic turn. Both social exchanges and public diplomacy revolve institutionally around the Confucius Institutes, which find a warm reception in South and Southeast Asia, with the exception of India and Vietnam. This is apparently different from the developments in the US and Europe where the Confucius Institutes and China Studies remain separate. In fact, in contrast to those areas neighboring territorial China, where the Confucius Institutes have been incorporated as a part of China Studies, in the "West" the Confucius Institutes constitute a target of Sinological research.

However, although general patterns may have emerged from academic and policy practices at given times and sites, comparison at the national or the community level is nonetheless misleading. Due to the richness and fluidity of "China" as a category, it constitutes a useless category once out of context. Studies of China unavoidably bring different challenges to different individuals, despite that they may belong to the same national, religious or ethnic communities, not least because the approach taken to study China gives an indication of the way the scholar relates to the society and therefore reflects his or her choice of identity strategy — both at the level of self-identities and identities at a higher level of belonging. Therefore, adopting an ostensibly "European" Sinological perspective, a presumably "American" scientific approach, an allegedly classic "Chinese" worldview, or a seemingly "indigenous" agenda tells as much about the scholars and their communities as about China according to their understanding.

Although we deliberately avoid starting with a thematic agenda at the time we initiate the gathering of oral history from a vast number of senior experts in a region, we nonetheless notice that identities of scholars/experts and their relationships with their communities are relevant concerns in their production of knowledge on China. In addition, we notice that China scholars generally develop their knowledge from a variety of sources that by no means abide by national borders. Hence, the question of how to balance contending perspectives, paralleling sources, and purposes becomes an issue of varying extent to different scholars. Based on this observation, innumerable ways to compare them at different levels, each with different implications, can be thought of. It is no exaggeration to say that China as a category of either study or analysis can be so illuminating that we learn not only from scholarship but also in scholars as person, hence deepening reflections on our own scholarship as well as identities as scholars.

This book is divided into four parts. The first part, titled "biographical perspectives," contains four chapters that primarily compare selected individual scholars and analyzes how they have balanced their career paths and encounters. It argues that these have constrained as well as inspired the evolution of their scholarship on "their" China or Chineseness. Tina S. Clemente and Pamela G. Combinido's Chapter 1 traces paths of thinking of two senior China watchers — Jose Santiago "Chito" Santa Romana and Ramesh Nath Pandey — by studying the ideas and patterns of development of their ideas over a period of time. They do so based on interview transcripts collected as part of the oral history project. Chow-Bing Ngeow's Chapter 2 argues that Malaysia has done relatively well in the civilizational and ethnic perspectives on China, but not yet in the state perspective. Ngeow focuses on three scholars of Malaysian origin — Huang Chih-Lien 黃枝連, Chang Chak Yan 鄭赤琰, and Kueh Yik Yaw 郭益耀 — who moved to Hong Kong and established themselves as some of the best China scholars in Hong Kong academia. Matsumura Toshio's Chapter 3 studies the intellectual path of Benny Gatot Setionno. Setiono's thought represents the thinking of Peranakan Chinese in Indonesia, which positions itself by balancing between Indonesian nationalism and their own "Chineseness." Bitter past experiences led Peranakan Chinese to become careful about expressing outright pro-China arguments. Hence, this excessive sensitivity is a shared characteristic of ethnic Chinese in Indonesia. Finally, Apiradee Charoensenee's Chapter 4 portrays two life paths — the ones of Sawai Wisavanan and Praphruet Sukolrattanamethi — and provides an analysis of the factors that have brought both of them into the present scholastic spotlight.

The second part, titled "national perspectives," is conventional to the extent that authors basically stick with national categories and introduce how the intellectual trajectories of scholarship reproduce and reconstruct an international relations perspective that reflects the identity and the relationality of the nation in question. Cong Tuan Dinh's Chapter 5 presents some of the Soviet Union's and later Russia's positive influences on Vietnam and highlights some legacies that are reflected in Vietnam's development of Chinese studies. He argues that although Soviet Union/Russian influences are ideological and political, they are also scientific and methodological. Pervaiz Ali Mahesar's Chapter 6 offers a comparative view of China Studies in South Asia. The chapter particularly focuses on Pakistan and India and suggests to recalibrate fissures and hurdles in the interaction between Pakistan and India through China Studies in South Asia. Quang Minh Pham and Hoang Giang Le's Chapter 7 analyzes the characteristics of the Vietnam–China relationship from power, party, and peace approaches. They argue that both countries should not let realist points of view determine their relations. Instead, they promote confidence-building measures and encourage these to play proactive and responsible roles in the region.

Authors of the third part, titled "comparative perspectives," pick up two or three national communities in their comparative analyses which show how scholarship of China and Chineseness interact with national conditions embedded in religion, history, ethnicity, international relations, economics, and so on. Reena Marwah's Chapter 8 comprises a comparative analysis of China studies in South and South East Asia, both as sub-regions of Asia and through the countries of Thailand and Sri Lanka. Both these countries are pivotal to China's interests through linkages with its Belt and Road strategy. However, the chapter also shows that they encompass not only the economic and the strategic, but also the cultural (Buddhist) connection. Second, Chih-yu Shih argues in Chapter 9 that political considerations and historical practices have jointly established a mode of analysis in Singapore's think-tank methodology that operates without Chinese cultural sensibilities. This deliberately contrived the technicality of Singapore think tanks, which has fixed its intellectual resources to an external position that does not significantly differ from the analytical styles of Nepali, Bangladeshi, or even Bhutanese observers when perceiving Chinese affairs. Sharad K. Soni's Chapter 10 focuses on South Asia's China outlook, but particularly from the comparative perspectives of Bangladesh and Nepal. While language teaching centers are being established in order to increase understandings of China, there is also a great interest in understanding China's trajectory of economic progress and its expanding political significance not only as an Asian power, but also as a global leader.

The fourth and last part, titled "external perspectives," reviews what some of the external perspectives, practical as well as theoretical, can recount and evaluates local scholarship on China. James Anderson's Chapter 11 provides an American perspective. He argues that the shared literary conventions and philosophical schools of thought that circulated between China and Vietnam through the Chinese character-based writing system by a formerly unified Sino-Vietnamese scholarly tradition provides a strong foundation for modern-day Vietnamese Sinological studies. For Vietnamese Sinologists working in the modern era, this search for "common ground" in the Sino-Vietnamese relationship continues to be important, even though differences are simultaneously sought. Xiangdong Yu and Sijia Cheng's Chapter 12 argues that Vietnamese scholars' knowledge of China has the potential to influence the development of Sino-Vietnamese relations. The authors discuss their views on the formation of China. Chih-yu Shih's Chapter 13 uses the notion of post-Chineseness to analyze Vietnamese Sinology as a comparative agenda. Post-Chineseness refers to the cultural preparation and the political process of mutual acknowledgment among those who consider one another as sharing (some kind of) Chineseness. This Chineseness is practically defined according to the context and its trajectories, each time and at each site separately. Shih believes that the post-Chineseness of Vietnam therefore complicates its role-taking *vis-à-vis* China, intellectually as well as practically.

Finally, a very relevant and timely note on the project of oral history, which most authors in this book rely on to develop their comparative analyses. The project, officially titled as "Comparative Epistemology of China Studies," has as its home the Research and Educational Center for Mainland China Studies and Cross-Strait Relations, which is affiliated with the Department of Political Science at National Taiwan University. The primary mission of the project is to interview senior China experts. The project began in 2004 and has gradually extended to many parts of the world. Most relevant to this book are the following 108 interviews: 25 conducted in Vietnam, 11 in Malaysia, 2 in Indonesia, 18 in Singapore, 12 in the Philippines, 19 in India, 8 in Bangladesh, 6 in Nepal, 1 in Bhutan, 3 in Pakistan (where a few others are not open to the public at the time of publication), 2 in Thailand (where 5 more are in preparation for the public view) and 1 in Sri Lanka. In the process, international supports have come most actively from the Association of Asia Scholars based in New Delhi, the Institute of Chinese Studies at the University of Malay, the Asia Research Center at Chulalongkorn University, Vietnam National University of Social Sciences and Humanities at both Hanoi and Ho Chi Minh City as well as the Institute of China Studies at the Vietnamese Academy of Social Sciences, and the Asian Center at the University of the Philippines at Diliman. Interviews are accessible at http://politics.ntu.edu.tw/RAEC. Last but not the least, the Chinese Academy of Social Sciences and the Guangxi Academy of Social Sciences both coordinated strategic workshops to enable and encourage the continuation of the project.

Part I

Biographical Perspectives

1

Odysseys in China Watching: Comparative Look at the Philippines and Nepal

Tina S. Clemente

Asian Center, University of the Philippines Diliman, Philippines

Pamela G. Combinido

Independent Scholar

We attempt to trace paths of thinking by studying two senior China watchers, their ideas, and patterns of ideas over a period of time through their oral history as documented in interview transcripts. The transformation of the thinkers' positioning of their perceptions of China in a long view considers the influence of history and the larger contextual frames such as social struggle, institutional development, and cultural change and discourse (Gordon 2007, Harding 2014). This comparative work on narratives chooses Jose Santiago "Chito" Santa Romana (or Sta. Romana) and Ramesh Nath Pandey as fruitful sources of oral history. Santa Romana is a senior public intellectual in the Philippines, known for being in exile in China during the anti-Marcos struggle in the 1970s. At the time of writing, he was recently confirmed as Ambassador of the Philippines to China. Pandey, on the other hand, is respected as a veteran diplomat of Nepal who has witnessed and who was part of facilitating many watershed moments in China–Nepal relations.

This chapter attempts to accomplish three objectives. The first objective is to explore an oral history comparison that goes beyond the usual geopolitical boundaries. It is usual for the Philippine context to be compared with that of another country within Southeast Asia owing to the similar experiences of overseas, diasporic, or transnational Chinese and the issues that relate to the region's relationship with China. The second objective is to problematize the idea that oral histories on China knowledge are not hinged on essentialism. The notion that China knowledge may be less valid owing to the absence of essential elements such as classical Sinology and language proficiency deserves some rethinking. The third objective is to explore the concept that such a comparison underscores that flexible epistemological approaches can build the field of China studies.

Section 2 casts attention on dissecting the evolution of thinking of Santa Romana and Pandey, bringing to light the salient points of inflection in their odysseys. Section 3 focuses on how a deep interest in China elucidates the thinkers' positioning of their perceptions on China. In closing, the chapter argues how the comparative insights fill a gap, enriching the field of China studies.

Comparison of Intellectual Trajectories

We trace paths of China watching through parallel comparison of experiences, retrieved through oral history interview. Through parallel comparison of Santa Romana's and Pandey's transcripts, we generate insights into the linkages between the intellectuals and their China watching, considering the exercise of agency during the interplay of external socio-historical factors and their internal motivations. Drawing inspiration from Mallard's (2014) paired biographies approach, we embark on content analysis that aids in teasing out the internal deliberation by both intellectuals in their China watching. In a sense, akin to Mallard (2014), the problematique of this chapter, that is China watching is parametrized by particular contexts, is intrinsically borne of comparison, or as Mallard puts it, conceptually relational. Also, we avoid the issues on inter-subjectivities that Boyd (2015) raises, given that we allow the intellectual's subjectivity as a fundamental assumption in their storytelling to aid in our understanding of the nature of their China watching.

Giving importance to individual stories, Thomas Carlyle and Ralph Waldo Emerson viewed history in parallel fashion (Boorstin 1998). The former saw history as the "essence of innumerable biographies" (Carlyle 1852: 220) while the latter saw history as subjective, arguing that "there is properly no history; only biography" (Emerson 1841/1886: 40). In venturing into intellectual history, we go further by scrutinizing the journeys behind the ideas of the thinkers as these provide a better understanding of the internal negotiations that were instrumental in refining the thinkers' ideas and their identity as thinkers. Buchholz (2007) underscores this in his study of the celebrated economist, John Stuart Mill. While Mill is known for doing landmark work on enhancing utilitarianism, the achievement did not come without Mill going through an existential crisis at 20 years of age, wasting away in rationalism but later regenerating as a romantic — the messy internal negotiations registered as inflections in thinking. In his autobiography, Mill laments:

> Suppose that all your objects in life were realized; that all the changes in institutions and opinions which you are looking forward to, could be completely effected at this very instant: would this be a great joy and happiness to you?" And an irrepressible self-consciousness distinctly answered, "No!" At this my heart sank within me: the whole foundation on which my life was constructed fell down. All my happiness was to have been found in the continual pursuit of this end. The end had ceased to charm, and how could there ever again be any interest in the means? I seemed to have nothing left to live for. (Mill 1873: 132–134)

On a similar note, Bangladeshi intellectual and Nobel Laureate, Muhammad Yunus, recounts his journey as an economist and attributes part of his transformation to experiential learning through immersion among the poor, whose economic plight he studied. Yunus relates,

> Nothing in the economic theories I taught reflected the life around me. How could I go on telling my students make-believe stories in the name of economics? I wanted to become a fugitive from academic life. I needed to run away from these theories and from my textbooks and discover the real-life economics of a poor person's existence. (Yunus 2007: viii)

Yunus articulates an important vantage point of his intellectual transformation:

> I opted instead for "the worm's eye view." I hoped that if I studied poverty at close range, I would understand it more keenly. (Yunus 2007: ix)

We consider affective memory as the unit of analysis of this study on comparative intellectual history (Havel 2005). Thinkers recollect myriad of experiences in the course of articulating their oral history, but only those experiences that are emotionally encoded become significant units in the evolution of their thinking. The lived experience of individuals as manifested in personal affective memory, by definition and ontology, is central to public memory (Havel 2005). The perspective on affective memory in this chapter is informed by the caveats embedded in the intertwined web of emotion, experience, and identity and how social concerns tend to be seen as determined by an overemphasis on personal emotion. We thus recognize that the various mechanisms through which meaning is constructed also constitute their own narratives that are internalized in the intellectual's deliberation of his experiences. Identity, which is a "coherent sense of self over time" (Harding 2014: 99) and experience then, while elements in articulating one's narrative, are also outcomes of the narrative (Harding 2014).

Table 1 provides a brief academic and professional background of Chito Santa Romana and Ramesh Nath Pandey. Journalism played a significant role in the background of both Santa Romana and Pandey. Santa Romana had a long career as a journalist in China before becoming a Philippine-based public intellectual while Pandey was a journalist prior to his long career as a political figure, minister, and senior diplomat in Nepal.

Table 1. Professional Background

	Santa Romana	Pandey
Year of birth	1948	1944
Nationality	Filipino	Indian
Education	B.A. in Liberal Arts and Commerce, De La Salle University (1970) Finished 21 units in M.A. in Economics (University of the Philippines Diliman) Masters in International Relations, Tufts University in Boston (Fletcher School of Law and Diplomacy)	Politics and Economics, Tribhuvan University
Career	Journalist prior to being a public intellectual • Part-time translator and assistant researcher for the *Washington Post* in China • Producer and Former Beijing Bureau Chief, American Broadcasting Corporation • Trusted intellectual in Track 2 dialogues and in Public Diplomacy • Current Philippine Ambassador to China	Journalist prior to joining politics • Editor of *Janata, Naya Sandesh,* and *New Herald* • Former Foreign Minister; Former Minister of Tourism; Leader of UN Delegation of Nepalese delegation to the United Nations (2005) • Senior Diplomat

Aside from his media commentaries on issues about China–Philippines bilateral relations, Santa Romana engaged with the academe in the Philippines through symposia, conferences, and similar events. His work focused on the foreign relations issues between the Philippines and China, and particularly the maritime dispute. Pandey, on the one hand, published commentaries in newspapers in Nepal and India. He recently published his book, which details his involvement in Nepal's politics and its relations with other countries. He also wrote a chapter in a book edited by his son, Nishchal Nath Pandey. Table 2 lists selected scholarly works of these thinkers, which centered on the dynamics of bilateral relations with China.

Table 2. Selected Scholarly Work

Intellectual	Year	Role	Publication Type	Title	Subject
Pandey	2011	Main author	Chapter in a book	China and Japan and Nepal's Core Interest	Nepal's international relations Politics in Nepal
	2015	Main author	Book	Kuniti Ra Rajniti: An Autobiography	Politics in Nepal Nepal's international relations Autobiography
Santa Romana	2012	Co-editor	Edited book	Philippine–China Relations: Sailing Beyond Dispute Waters	China and the Philippines' territorial disputes Philippine's international relations
	2014	Presenter	Manuscript for a conference	An Analysis of China's Response to the Philippine Arbitration Case (2013–2014)	China and the Philippines' maritime disputes
	2015	Presenter	Manuscript for a conference	Philippine–China Relations: Challenges and Prospects	China and the Philippines bilateral relations
	2016	Presenter	Manuscript for a conference	The Escalating US–China Rivalry in Asia-Pacific Region: Its Implications for Philippine–China Relations	China and the Philippines' territorial disputes

Santa Romana and Pandey are important figures in their respective countries for their public discussions about bilateral relations with China. Santa Romana became a China "expert" owing to his many years of experience in China as an accidental exile and as a respected broadcast journalist. Pandey, on the other hand, held several government positions that gave him leeway in directly dealing with Chinese counterparts on bilateral projects that had material outcomes for Nepal. Table 3 presents both thinkers' roles in bilateral dealings with China.

As part of our attempt to grapple with the history–biography connection (Mills 1959), we trace the goings-on of the intellectuals

Table 3. Intellectuals' Key Roles in Country's Engagement with China

	Santa Romana	Pandey
Involvement in the country's relation with China	Liaison between the Philippines and China • As an accidental exile during Martial Law • As a public intellectual, sought by the media, government, and academe	Liaison between Nepal and China • Held government positions as Foreign Minister of Nepal, Minister of Tourism, which required engagement with China officials • Important political figure sought by the media, academe, and international organizations
Issues they confronted or pursued	China's transition from Cultural Revolution to "opening" up to other countries Socio-economic and political changes taking place in China and its relation with other countries) Implications of territorial disputes on China–Philippines bilateral relations	Strengthening bilateral relations of Nepal with China China–Nepal–India trilateral relations Stability of Nepal as a state, crucial in keeping good ties with China and India

by looking at their "lives processually in the context of the society they live in" (Brannen and Nielsen 2011: 609). As presented in Table 4, the content analysis framework paid attention to significant personal events that the intellectuals keep going back to in the interview transcripts. Personal events here are happenings they directly witnessed due to their interaction with China. Socio-historical events are the incidences related to history and politics and development of China which they related to their personal experience.

Table 5 summarizes the inflections in perspectives about understanding China. The perspective of China watching is shaped by the experiences, lessons, and hope for the prospects of China. The perspective changed over time as they directly experienced China and contemplated about future directions.

Studying China and Positioning as a China Watcher

Recollecting one's China watching brings to view a confluence of circumstances in the macroenvironment, one's particularities as a thinker, and the kind of role that one ascribes to oneself in studying China. In this section, we use the elements teased out in the previous section and focus on four major areas of the thinkers' lens in studying China and their internal and external negotiation in positioning themselves as a China watcher. In all the subsections, we consider the thinkers' positioning across gradations of affinity, objectivism, and balance regarding China as we posit no absolute boundaries in these categories. In this sense, we go beyond the ontological discomfiture in the objectivism vs. relativism discursive crevasse (McCourt 2007; Bernstein 1983). We first look at the motivations that began their interest in China, the experiment of direct experience, reflections on witnessed change, and opinions on the prospects of China.

Initial Impressions and Contact

For Santa Romana, it was the anti-martial law activism during the Marcos years that began his interest in China. He was an activist

Table 4. Biography–History Nexus in Intellectuals' China Watching

Year	Personal Events	Socio-Historical Events
August 19, 1971	Santa Romana's first visit to China as head of Filipino youth delegation for a three-week trip around China "Red tourism": visit to official places of interest in China's revolutionary history, i.e., Mao's home village, and the Party's base Visit to Tiananmen Square, Guangzhou, Shanghai Visit to the Forbidden City, the Summer Palace, and other historical places Meeting with Central Committee's leadership in Shanghai	Plaza Miranda Bombing and Martial Law declaration in the Philippines, which led to the "accidental exile" of Chito Santa Romana in China Last phase of "Cultural Revolution"; Mao's 10-year political and ideological campaign aimed at reviving revolutionary spirit US–China rapprochement; US President Richard Nixon visited China
October 1971	Santa Romana's attendance in National Day reception	Lin Biao "affair"
1971	Santa Romana's visit to Yan'an, Shaanxi Province, birthplace of revolution; met and discussed with Red Guards	Ethiopian Emperor, Haile Selassie, came and met Mao The fall of the Gang of Four; jockey for power; arrests and convictions of crimes against the state
December 1971	State farm experience of Santa Romana in Hunan	
1972	Santa Romana's return to Beijing and enrollment in formal language certificate program as universities are starting to "reopen"	Hua Guofeng leadership after Mao Emergence of Deng in 1977 Deng Xiaoping; adoption of economic reforms (his idea of socialist market economy) to steer China's economic growth
1973	Pandey's first visit to China, member of Nepalese delegation led by Nepalese King Birendra Personal meeting with PM Zhou Enlai and opportunity to invite him in Nepal	
1976	Pandey was invited by the Premier Hua Guofeng in a banquet at the Great Hall of the People	

(*Continued*)

Table 4. (*Continued*)

Year	Personal Events	Socio-Historical Events
1984–1986	While serving as Minister of Tourism, Pandey signed an agreement with China and Japan regarding Mt Everest expedition Requested Vice Premier Wan Li to open Kathmandu–Tibet airway	China's "Open-door policy" opens the country to foreign investment and encourages development of a market economy and private sector
1989	Santa Romana became Producer for ABC News in China	
2005	Pandey visited as foreign Minister of Nepal (Shaanxi Province) and was invited to visit Buddhist Monastery and give a speech Meeting with President Hu Jintao during the UN General Assembly	Anti-China protests in Tibet Beijing hosts Olympics
2006	Senior central leader of China visited Nepal	

during his university days in De La Salle University and was also the president of the student council and a part of the student paper. His active involvement in the national student union, national college editors' guild, and graduate studies at the University of the Philippines — the bastion of student activism — deepened his activism. Santa Romana, in his visit to the US, saw how student activism was a force that opposed the Vietnam War. But China got him hooked. The Cultural Revolution demonstrated student power and the Red Guards projected the expression of that power in his mind while his involvement in the leftist movement created an ideological affinity. Santa Romana started reading about China and Maoism and wanted to know about what the Philippines could learn.

In Pandey's case, interest comes from what he sees as a national environment that is generally interested in China, a setting where it

Table 5. Evolution of Thinking about China

	Pre-China Immersion	Direct Experiences of China	Post-China Immersion
Chito Santa Romana	China as a mystical place to be discovered Looks to China as a revolutionary model	"Nothing as it seems" in understanding China China watching as a habit Insider/outsider gaze of China Detached but immersed	Pragmatic learner of China based on gained lessons and experiences
Ramesh Nath Pandey	China as an interesting neighbor to read and write about	"To have experience by yourself" as a crucial element of understanding China	Unclear about future directions of China–Nepal relations

is usual for Nepalese to follow goings-on in China. As a journalist, he also found himself featuring China in his work. He recounts the anticipation he felt on seeing China for the first time, which he had only known from what he had read in dailies and books until then. As he traversed to "No Man's Land," crossing from Hong Kong to China in five minutes, what greeted him was the sight of the Chinese who had no gender distinction in the same gray garb and hairstyle that they wore.

Experiment of Experience

The thinkers depict China in varied ways. While both relate contentious accounts, Santa Romana depicts them with an investigative, analytical eye while Pandey renders them positively. This demonstrates that one's subjective perspective determines the interpretation of an experience and, likewise, it determines the knowledge that one forms about the experience (Nietzsche 1989: 12).

Santa Romana believed that "[d]irect experience teaches people" (Santa Romana 2016: 12). The experiment of experience led to discoveries of internal socio-political struggles in China. Santa Romana was able to capture the social climate in China at that time that the country was not open to outsider scrutiny. He had to learn to hear between the lines as *bu qingchu* (not clear) was a common response to deflect questions. Trying to understand was "almost like the art of reading tea leaves" (Santa Romana 2016: 3, 13).

Santa Romana was puzzled by the "formal protocol" set by the host team as a way of organizing the delegation hierarchically. In the first trips, Santa Romana felt uneasy that he had to ride a different vehicle because they wanted to separate the senior members from the rest of the delegation. "It was actually hierarchical when we were expecting it to be egalitarian," Santa Romana recalled (2016: 4–5). Then he narrated how they were treated better than the ordinary Chinese. In trains, they rode first class. They would be given delicacies as compared to the ration given to ordinary Chinese. They experienced being mobbed by Chinese locals who were amazed at how different they seemed. In response to the protectiveness of the hosts, Santa Romana felt ashamed and shared, "We were actually telling our guides not to be too rough... We would rather be mixed up with them than to keep them away" (2016: 10). As they stood in a sea of local Chinese "men and women [who] were alike: same dress, no cosmetics, no make-up," Santa Romana initially appreciated but eventually observed the gaps in the egalitarian socialist set-up in China (Santa Romana 2016: 9).

It was in China that Santa Romana experienced rural life for the first time. Due to the strife of Martial Law and the Anti-Subversion case filed against him in the Philippines, he and four other members had to stay longer in China. His experience as a foreigner trying to blend in with the locals, and the struggles and working conditions he witnessed, and to a certain extent, experienced on the ground in the Hunan farm, as well as the political tensions and changes in China's leadership that he directly observed, enriched his understanding of China. A man from the landed class in the Philippines, Santa Romana used his hands to plow in a farm in

Hunan. He interacted with workers and learned much about farming working alongside high school girls. The recollection of this experience prompted Santa Romana to relate China's rural life with that of the Philippines and observed similarities in the living conditions, but China was more egalitarian with no pronounced social disparity. It was not a paradise for workers, nonetheless. It was through this experience in a state farm in Hunan that Santa Romana saw China from the bottom.

In the caves of Yan'an, Shaanxi Province, the birthplace of the revolution, they met the Red Guards. They had an interesting exchange. Santa Romana remembered that his group asked, "How long will you stay here?" The Red Guards replied, "All our lives. Because that is the need of the revolution" (Santa Romana 2016: 7). He also remembered the statues and big pictures of Mao and Lin Biao and the Red Book — the work of Mao about the revolution. It became a turning point when they saw the Red Guards tear out the page of the book's introduction, which was written by Lin Biao, Red Army commander and supposed successor of Mao. It was this time that Chinese people began to acknowledge the issues surrounding Mao and Lin and the alleged planned assassination of Mao by Lin. What reaffirmed their speculation was when during the cancellation of the National Day Parade both Mao and Lin were absent and when during the visit of the Ethiopian Emperor the protocol of the toast was not followed. The toast should have said, "Long live the health of Chairman Mao and the health of Vice-Chairman Lin Biao" (Santa Romana 2018: 7). The political tensions became apparent, and here Santa Romana recalled,

> This is all looking back now, but at that point, it was a mystery... [I]t appears as though there was nothing happening; on the surface, it was just quiet... There was very intense internal struggle, but they kept it to themselves. (Santa Romana 2016: 7)

In the telling of his oral history, Pandey was asked about China studies in Nepal and if academics study China through language. He was unambiguous in emphasizing that direct experience is an important catalyst in learning about China, beyond the reading of books. Pandey was curious about reputed local behavior. He tested if reported Chinese honesty is true. He gathered that Chinese people followed the law and nobody lost anything to thieves. While he was visiting, he decided to purposely leave his shirt in the hotel in Beijing with a five-dollar bill in the shirt's pocket as he departed for Nanjing. When he arrived in his Nanjing hotel, he received a packet containing the shirt with the five-dollar bill in it. He asked himself if this kind of honesty was experienced by every visitor. The second experiment was inadvertent, which involved Pandey's desire to experience actual social conditions on the ground. Pandey was brought to a department store where he observed that although there were a few people, it was crowded. To his surprise, when the official who accompanied him pressed a button, the floor opened to a view a "full-village below" (Pandey 2012: 4), which one could bicycle out to reach another village. He described the space below as a "beautiful hall" that could fit a thousand people with "full provision for food and amenities," and a "small health post." Two Chinas, in this case, provides a visual of a physical bifurcation that simply reflected the geopolitical divisions. The beautiful hall where Pandey signed the visitor's book and gave his remarks existed as a remnant of the underground air raid center, which was built to protect China from external military action, like a nuclear attack (Pandey 2012: 3).

As Foreign Minister in 2005, Pandey had this experience in Shaanxi Province. The importance of this was emphasized in the backstory that he narrated while telling his oral history. Pandey told the story of Manjushree, the Buddhist saint from China, who stood on a lotus and surveyed Kathmandu valley and only sighted a large lake. Using his "magic sword," he "cut the southern wall of the hills and the water of the lake," drained, allowing the valley to be peopled (Pandey 2012: 5). Manjushree was then considered the founder of Kathmandu Valley. In Shaanxi Province, the mountain, Wu Tai Shan, was sacred to Manjushree. When Pandey reached Shaanxi Province, he intimated, "I have never ever received such a warm reception" (Pandey 2012: 5). His reference was to his amazement over the religious devotion of the people to the saint, the statue of which he transported from Nepal as a gift to the people.

Witnessed Change

Santa Romana saw the stark changes in China as it increasingly adopted economic reforms: from Mao's socialist, planned economy to Deng Xiaoping's concept of a socialist market economy. The changes became more apparent for Santa Romana as he witnessed the struggle and hardship of the Chinese people during his farming experience in Hunan and his encounters in various important places in China. From his recollection, "China was very insular and isolated… [and] not exposed to consumer goods, especially Western ones. It was very different. It was like being on a different planet… So it was very revealing when China decided to adopt changes" (Santa Romana 2016: 10–11). Nonetheless, Santa Romana believed that if not for the experimentation of China during the Cultural Revolution, its economic successes would not have been possible:

> If the Cultural Revolution did not happen, and they did not have a leadership who suffered from it with the people and who realized its negative effects, moderate and reformist leaders who succeeded Mao would not have had the same intensity and political will to steer China's transformation into a different direction. (Santa Romana 2016: 12)

After Mao's death, Santa Romana recalled that it was a very interesting time in China as people were out in the street, celebrating and presenting Hua Guofeng as the new leader. But at the same time, as China was making a sharp turn, it faced a crossroad. There was a lot of discussion on who possessed the correct path, the Gang of Four or the new group? It was also an interesting situation for Santa Romana as he tried to position himself in the debates about the direction of China: "During that time, there was a lot of questioning. It was difficult to situate yourself. It took a while before you could make sense of what was going on because debates were happening, some of it openly in newspapers" (Santa Romana 2016: 14). Chinese people were indeed serious about deliberating the future direction of China.

On the other hand, Santa Romana mentioned the changes he saw under the leadership of Deng Xiaoping. At that time when China was on the verge of collapse, Deng had to yield to the path of rapid economic growth. These economic opportunities for China became the new source of the Party's legitimacy. The increase in the wage of workers was noteworthy because even a little raise was a big deal for Chinese people according to Santa Romana. While it was not featured in newspapers, it became the talk of the town: "their pay increased under Deng" (Santa Romana 2018:14) as compared during Mao's time that economic incentive was attacked.

Pandey was able to visit China right after Mao Tse Tung's death, where he was at the Great Hall of the People where a banquet was hosted in Mao's honor. Pandey surmised that while Premier Hua Guofeng was present, the Vice Premier Deng Xiaoping was the actual leader and, to Pandey, this signaled the beginning of China's transition toward economic reforms.

In 2005, Pandey also visited China for the Boao summit. He was invited to speak at a Buddhist monastery. As an observation on social change, he took note of well-dressed young girls who were chanting but at the same time having their phones on their ears, with some effort of concealment. Pandey noted the distinction in the times — "religion has already embraced China" (Pandey 2012: 6). In the following year, Pandey received a senior Chinese official at the Nepal airport at the latter's request. Pandey also acquiesced to the further request that he accompany the official to Lumbini.[1] This visit gave Pandey another insight into comparing the change over time. His amazement over the official's Buddhist worship was due to the fact that such religiosity was untenable in the China he first encountered in 1973. He reflects that there is a keen interest among

---

[1] Lumbini is one of the sacred Buddhist pilgrimage sites in Nepal. It is located at the Nepalese town of Kapilavastu, district Rupandehi, south of Nepal near the Indian border.

both leaders and common people in the historical and religious aspects of Buddhism. He ends this recollection by saying pragmatically that the Chinese interest in Buddhism does not mean they do not pursue influence and monetary resources. It was a negotiation in perspective, appreciating the social change indicated by the practice of religion but not discounting the parallel force of the effects of the change in the material circumstances of the Chinese. The mention of Lumbini and Shaanxi Province in Pandey's oral history points to the role of Buddhism and Buddhist scholarship in foreign relations between China and South Asian countries in moderating threat impressions from China's rise (Shih 2016: vii).

He articulated what he observed as the confluence of changes during his stay in the Friendship Hotel, where he was hosted by the Deputy Foreign Minister. He described it as a good hotel and noted that a new building was added to the old one, which to him represented a "perfect combination of the past and present." He found the infrastructure development impressive and again noticed the change in people's lifestyle. He said, "Western culture had come to the youth. The environment was different. China was modernizing, and the society had become more open" (Pandey 2012: 4–5).

Drawing from a longer view, Pandey assessed the change in China's economic reforms as a systematic, consistent long-term vision. Pandey's past encounters, including particular recollections about his stay in hotels and negotiating infrastructure cooperation, contributed to his glowing assessment of how these structures express that solid vision, allowing China to exceed expectations. He acknowledges China's consistency in terms of proceeding as an economic power as well as regarding China's foreign relations with Nepal.

Prospects for China

Santa Romana and Pandey looked at China's prospects from the vantage point of their respective identities as a former journalist turned respected public intellectual and a senior minister who represents government interests, respectively. Both thinkers assert agency here in assessing matters in varying extent of criticality, infusing the subjectivities that allow them to consider the context of their nation in relation to China based on what affirms their socio-political values (Zalloua 2016:163).

While Pandey saw a systematic and optimistic future for China's economic development and the current strategies and challenges under Xi Jinping, Santa Romana applied critical scrutiny regarding the prospects of China. Santa Romana deemed it equally critical to look at Xi Jinping's navigation of China's economy considering that Deng's manufacturing-based export-led development model no longer suits China's present conditions. The dynamics have become more complex as Xi Jinping faces the need to "cater to nationalist sentiments" and establish political legitimacy while addressing economic problems and the tensions with the US. Amid this, Santa Romana is hopeful that The One Belt, One Road (OBOR) initiative "is a key" for state-owned enterprises and exporters to rise from the challenge of domestic overcapacity (Santa Romana 2016: 16–17).

Curiously, when asked if the foundations for analyzing China remain the same so much so that recent developments in China do not surprise Santa Romana anymore, he claimed:

> I am still surprised at how the pendulum is swinging back. I understand it would swing, but this story or joke of President Xi Jinping as the second coming of Mao does seem to be the way he is going. It is really serious. And it is interesting to know the counter-reaction to that. How long can this go on? And where will it end? (Santa Romana 2016: 16)

Here, Santa Romana paid attention to the deft navigation of Xi by pointing out the administration's resemblance to Mao's leadership, a seeming attempt to reverse policies by adhering to the past strategies of Mao:

> It seems that some of the old approaches are coming back to life, but we are not there yet. An example is the move from collective leadership to a strongman or strongman politics. That is one change it seems. Xi seems to be rewriting the rules of Chinese

politics by sidelining collective leadership along with the rest of the Standing Committee. (Santa Romana 2016: 16)

Santa Romana recalled the "drama" of the Mao and Lin Biao leadership and the internal struggles of their governance, and drew parallelisms with the predicaments of the Xi Jinping administration. Ruminating over the factor of unpredictability, Santa Romana looked back to *bu qingchu*, his first lesson in China watching:

> Now, with Xi, I think China is treading on some dangerous ground. It seems his leadership is becoming personalistic again. That is what makes it interesting. The drama continues and it's intriguing to see how long will the Communist Party survive… China may engage in the arms race, which they cannot sustain, and could eventually lead to collapse. Or there are also internal challenges that may lead to the country's downfall. But it is still an open question and only time will tell. (Santa Romana 2016: 17)

The curiosity and interest in China watching have been very much alive in Santa Romana as China continuously continues to navigate through economic hurdles and reforms. "It is no longer the same China. There are now other forces at work. So the joy of China watching continues," Santa Romana articulated (2016: 18). On a personal level, Santa Romana expressed that he no longer saw China as a top-down framework that could be easily applied to the context of the Philippines. He has taken a pragmatic position as a China watcher after his lessons and experience of China watching for 40 years:

> My point now is that I view myself more as someone trying to understand China better. I do not want to focus on whether we can use the Chinese model. No. In that sense, I could say that I have matured. Rather, I want to see what we could learn from China; there are lessons that can be looked into, but you cannot take them as a whole. But looking back in time, I would not call myself a Maoist. I was interested to learn. And I lived, learned and experienced China, particularly during the Cultural Revolution. (Santa Romana 2016: 15)

Santa Romana's observations of the reality in China revealed that his perspective comes from his social context (McSweeney 2004: 110) of China watching on behalf of the Philippines. In particular, his view is derived from a specific socio-political time and space (Cox 1986: 207). It is perhaps a very important time for Santa Romana to recount these lessons and experiences. The twist of events that led to his accidental exile, the lessons, and experiences should serve Santa Romana well in his new role as the Philippine's Ambassador to China.

When asked if Nepal will still be considered in great significance in the context of China as a rising power, Pandey first drew on the personal ties that were established and from that vantage point, to Pandey, Nepal's "requests" were accommodated, citing that "it was very easy to negotiate" (Pandey 2012: 7) with President Hu Jintao. Further, Pandey recollected the "personal touch" from Hu Jintao in an encounter in the UN General Assembly in New York back in 2005.

> One day, I was coming out from the Hall to the lobby. The same time President Hu Jintao was entering the Hall. I was surprised when he held my hand and took me back to the hall. He made me sit in the seat of the Chinese delegation. We started to talk while several others watched us. In Jakarta when I met the Chinese foreign minister, he too was very friendly and cordial. (Pandey 2012: 7–8)

This is consistent with an earlier memory he recollected about a meeting with Vice Premier Wan Li when Pandey was Tourism Minister in 1984–1986. Pandey proposed for the Kathmandu–Tibet airway, making Kathmandu "The Gateway of Tibet." After Wan Li had said that it would not be possible, Pandey invoked the memory of a very personal interaction in 1973 with Premier Zhou Enlai when the latter expressed his desire to cross the Himalayas to visit Nepal. Pandey then recounted that Wan Li agreed and at the time of the interview in 2012, Kathmandu was the only city outside of China with a direct flight to and from Tibet, boosting Nepal's tourism industry.

From Pandey's vantage point, his personal interaction contributed in allowing him to forge ties with China that benefited Nepal.

The personal touch, as Pandey called it, is a space that Pandey continuously explored for bilateral negotiation and as a source of insight into the tenor of relations. From a societal perspective, Pandey drew on warmth of reception during his visits as an indicator of implications the warm people-to-people diplomacy can have on China–Nepal relations. It shows how personalistic ties and leadership personality in such diplomacy can drive foreign relations beyond legalism. Pandey says:

> When Nepal established diplomatic relations, China was a poor country. It did not have diplomatic relations with many countries. The visits by world leaders were also very few. Now China is a global power and they have friends everywhere and have global interests. Nepal is just one small neighbor. The question that looms large for us in Nepal is: Will China remain the same with Nepal? Will that personal behavior continue to be as warm as it was? Will they continue to behave the same or will there be a change in their attitude? It was a model relationship between a big and small neighbor. But to be honest I do not have any answer to what the future course of our relations will be like. (Pandey 2012: 8)

In reference to Wen Jiabao's visit to Nepal, Pandey reflected that the postponement of an earlier visit had raised questions in Nepal about China's interests and if the latter "turned cold towards Nepal" (Pandey 2012: 9). Pandey asserts that Nepal is still within China's strategic interests and Wen Jiabao's 2012 visit expressed this. Interestingly, when asked about his views on the 2008 Tibetan uprising, Pandey replied briefly saying that Nepal follows a humanitarian refugee policy. While this is independently approached, it could also reflect the navigation that Nepal has to be sensitive to in light of the power relations between China and India as dominant regional players. In fact, the rest of his lengthy answer focused on China–Indian relations as global power, economic partners who coordinate but also compete strategically. On the other hand, Pandey also said that they in Nepal see themselves "as a part of a large triangle" (Pandey 2012: 9) where Nepal is situated between the two countries, with which Nepal shares important borders with, and hence "will continue to be of strategic relevance both for India and China" (Pandey 2012: 9). In the end, Pandey's position goes back to the need for Nepal to achieve internal stability, which is vital in maximizing relations with both China and India. This is an extremely important point. Pandey sharply contends that without domestic stability, both big neighbors will have the propensity to be more involved in Nepal's internal affairs to protect their national interests. Finally, when asked about China's role in the South Asian Association for Regional Cooperation, Pandey intimated that he saw China more as an observer than a member at present, and acknowledged the greater role to play by India, which has now paid greater attention to the sensitivities of its smaller South Asian neighbors.

Closing Remarks: Contribution to China Studies

This comparative work on the Santa Romana and Pandey transcripts contributes to the field of China studies in a number of ways. The comparison of the thinkers' intellectual histories demonstrates that China studies as a field or specialization can be built from varied local contexts. This is underscored by the fact that the comparison used intellectual histories from atypical geopolitical spaces, which brings to light contrasting milieus. Whether the study of China is for advancing foreign relations or for socio-political reflection of domestic utility, delving into such a comparative work enriches China studies. In particular, the comparative intellectual history of China studies is salient for both the Philippines and Nepal as there are significant historical, political, economic, social, and diplomatic national linkages with China that could benefit from critical China knowledge. In Nepal's case, China knowledge had immediate practical use as Pandey utilized his China knowledge and experiences in advancing state agenda within his purview as a minister. On the other hand, Santa Romana utilized his China knowledge in his capacity as an organic public intellectual, who came forth from a "popular movement" (Critchley 2016: 175). The utility of China knowledge in this sense is therefore in the vein of intellectual advocacy among academic, policy, and diplomacy circles. Furthermore, the linkages between the thinkers and their China-related inquiries are also important as they show how inclusive the field can be in its evolution, veering away from parameterizing the field in essentialist terms. While not discounting the utility of ethnicity and language proficiency (Santa Romana, for instance, is fluent in Mandarin), we also argue that these are not the only elements that propel the field or shape good scholarship on China. Also, identity negotiation in this essay was tackled from the vantage point of one's persona as a China watcher. Analyzing how one positions his perspectives given internal and external motivations contributes to China studies by elucidating the salience of agency on the one hand and the nuances in the macroenvironment on the other. Finally, the work gives ample attention to the reach of the field when conscious strides in interdisciplinarity are made. In particular, the limberness in approaches used in this work by engaging various disciplines argue for transcending the foci that national issues (e.g., foreign relations, Chinese integration) privilege. While these issues are important and often the first motivations in the emergence of the field, these can nevertheless potentially wall in the field, preventing the traversing of inquiries across disciplinal domains.

References

Bernstein, Richard. 1983. *Beyond Objectivism and Relativism: Science, Hermeneutics, and Praxis.* Pennsylvania: University of Pennsylvania Press.
Boorstin, Daniel. 2001. *The Seekers: The Story of Man's Continuing Quest to Understand His World.* New York: Phoenix Press.
Boyd, Jodie. 2015. His Narrative, My History: Problematising Subjectivity and the Uses of Oral History. *Oral History* 43(2), 62–69.
Buchholz, Todd. 2007. *New Ideas from Dead Economists: An Introduction to Modern Economic Thought.* New York: Penguin.
Carlyle, Thomas. 1852. *The Modern British Essayist,* Vol 5. Philadelphia: A Hart, Late Carey & Hart.

Cox, Robert. 1986. Social Forces, States and World Orders: Beyond International Relations Theory. In Robert O. Keohane (Ed.), *Neoliberalism and its Critics*. New York: Columbia University Press.

Critchley, Simon. 2016. Bringing Intellect to the Soapbox: An Exchange. In Jeffrey Di Leo and Peter Hitchcock (Eds.), *The New Public Intellectual: Politics, Theory, and the Public Sphere*. New York: Palgrave Macmillan.

Emerson, Ralph Waldo. 1886. *Essays: First Series*. New York: John B. Walden (original work published 1841).

Gordon, Peter. 2007. What is Intellectual History? A Frankly Partisan Introduction to a Frequently Misunderstood Field, http://scholar.harvard.edu/files/pgordon/files/what_is_intell_history_pgordon_mar2012.pdf. Accessed on January 2017.

Harding, Jenny. 2014. Looking for Trouble: Exploring Emotion, Memory and Public Sociology: Inaugural Lecture, 1. *Oral History* 42(2), 94–104.

Havel, Brian. 2005. In Search of a Theory of Public Memory: The State, the Individualised, and Marcel Proust. *Indian Law Journal* 80(3), 605–723.

Mallard, Gregoire. 2014. Studying Tensions Between Imaginary Spaces and Concrete Places: The Method of Paired Biographies Applies to Scientists' Laboratory Lives. *Oral History* 39(3), 115–136.

McCourt, David. 2007. The Historical Turn and International Relations: 'Beyond Objectivism and Relativism.' EUI Working Papers.

McSweeney, Bill. 2010. *Security, Identity and Interests: A Sociology of International Relations*. Cambridge: Cambridge University Press.

Mill, John Stuart. 1873. *Autobiography*. London: Longmans, Green, Reader, and Dyer.

Mills, Charles. 1959. *The Sociological Imagination*. New York: Oxford University Press.

Nietzche, Friedrich. 1989. *On the Genealogy of Morals*. New York: Vintage.

Pandey, Ramesh Nath. 2012. Interview by Reena Marwah. *Department of Political Science, National Taiwan University: For China Studies and Cross Taiwan Strait Relations*, http://politics.ntu.edu.tw/RAEC/comm2/InterviewN03.pdf. Accessed on January 27, 2017.

Santa Romana, Chito. 2016. Interview by Lucio Pitlo III. *Department of Political Science, National Taiwan University: For China Studies and Cross Taiwan Strait Relations*, April 14.

Shih, Chih-yu. 2016. Introduction: Transcending China via Buddhism. In Prapin Manomaivibool and Chih-yu Shih (Eds.), *Understanding 21st Century China in Buddhist Asia: History, Modernity, and International*

Relations. Bangkok: Asia Research Center of the Korea Foundation for Advanced Studies in Chulalongkorn University.

Wess, Robert. 1991. Burke's Dialectic of Constitutions. *Pre-text: A Journal of Rhetorical Theory* 12(1–2), 9–30.

Yunus, Muhammad. 2007. *Banker to the Poor: Micro-lending and the Battle Against World Poverty*, p. ix. New York: Public Affairs.

Zalloua, Zou. 2016. The Double Bind of the Intellectual: Toward a Hermeneutics of Skepticism. In Jeffrey Di Leo and Peter Hitchcock (Eds.), *The New Public Intellectual: Politics, Theory, and the Public Sphere.* New York: Palgrave Macmillan.

2

Malaysia, Nanyang, and the "Inner China" of Three Hong Kong Scholars: Huang Chih-Lien, Chang Chak Yan and Kueh Yik Yaw

Chow-Bing Ngeow

Institute of China Studies, University of Malaya, Malaysia

In our previous survey of the various fields of Chinese Studies in Malaysia (Ngeow, Ling and Fan 2014), we concluded that the Malaysian academia has a good tradition in the fields of Sinology and studies of ethnic Chinese in Malaysia, but has been rather weak in the field of modern and contemporary China studies. There are not many academic experts on the China that has existed since 1949 — the People's Republic of China. Despite many advantages that Malaysia enjoys, including a positive state of relationship between China and Malaysia, its sizable ethnic Chinese population, and the widespread use of the Chinese language among the ethnic Chinese community, Malaysia does not stand exceptionally well in comparison to other Southeast Asian or South Asian countries in terms of its scholarly output on the politics, economy, foreign relations, and other aspects of the post-1949 China. In other words, Malaysia has done relatively well in the civilizational and ethnic perspectives on China, but not yet in the state perspective (Shih 2014), and this probably has something to do with the domestic identity/racial politics in Malaysia.

In another article, I have pointed out (Ngeow 2014), however, that there are many excellent Chinese Studies scholars of Malaysian origin who chose to move to universities in other countries. Included were those who studied the People's Republic of China in their professional and intellectual career. They were the China scholars that Malaysia could have but never had. In this chapter, I focus on three scholars of Malaysian origin who moved to Hong Kong and established themselves as among the best China scholars in Hong Kong academia. Each of them belongs to different social science fields. Professor Huang Chih-Lien 黃枝連[1] taught sociology at Hong Kong Baptist University for more than 30 years. Professor Chang Chak Yan 鄭赤琰[2] was a senior political scientist at the Chinese University of Hong Kong (CUHK) and later at Lingnan Univeristy. Professor Kueh Yik Yaw 郭益耀,[3] an economist, was also attached for a long time first to CUHK, and later to Lingnan.

Huaqiao 華僑, Huaren 華人, Zhongguoren 中國人

In our earlier study of Chinese Studies in Malaysia (Ngeow, Ling and Fan 2014), we highlighted the career and achievement of seven scholars: Wolfgang Franke 傅吾康, Ho Peng Yoke 何丙郁, Tay Lian Soo 鄭良樹, Lim Chooi Kwa 林水檺, Yen Ching Hwang 顏清湟, Wang Gungwu 王賡武, and Tan Chee Beng 陳志明.[4] Other than Wolfgang Franke, the other six scholars were/are all Malaysians and

---

[1] Also known as Ng Kee Lian.
[2] He is more well known in the English academic circle as C. Y. Chang. This chapter will refer to him as C. Y. Chang hereafter.
[3] He is more well known in the English academic circle as Y. Y. Kueh. This chapter will refer to him as Y. Y. Kueh hereafter.
[4] Except for a few, most of these Chinese studies experts are not experts on contemporary China.

in the study we examined how the careers of these Malaysian scholars were at one point or another crossed path with political or policy developments in Malaysia and how these shaped the choices they made. With the exception of Professor Lim Chooi Kwa, all of these scholars eventually chose to leave Malaysia and continued their scholarly career in universities in Australia and Hong Kong, and some of them opted for foreign citizenship eventually. But this does not take away the fact that all of them once identified with Malaysia closely. In this sense, all of these scholars could be more appropriately considered as ethnic Chinese or Chinese overseas (*huaren* 華人).[5] Throughout their careers, they have been close to China only in a professional or intellectual sense, not in a personal sense. Many of them also worked in Hong Kong, just like the three scholars whom I study in this chapter, but they worked in Hong Kong without the sense of "returning" to China. They did not get themselves involved in the political developments within China or Hong Kong, nor did they ever express any close political identification with the political entity called the People's Republic of China. They maintained a distance. Their identities were settled, they were *huaren*/Chinese overseas/ethnic Chinese 華人.

The concept of *huaren*/Chinese overseas/ethnic Chinese is usually juxtaposed with the concept of *huaqiao*/overseas Chinese/Chinese sojourners 華僑, or whatever term that is invoked to describe the kind of Chinese who yearn for a "return" to the homeland after a non-permanent separation from it. The concept of "huaqiao" is full of political meaning. When the anti-Qing Chinese revolutionaries (and their rivals) went to appeal to and mobilize the ethnic Chinese communities outside of China in support of their causes in the early 20th century, the result was the politicized concept of "huaqiao," which in general indicated a kind of involvement in patriotic activities toward China, the motherland. Chinese schools

---

[5]There have been a lot of complications about the terms "overseas Chinese and "Chinese overseas." Traditionally, the term "overseas Chinese" is used to encompass both Chinese nationals abroad and ethnic Chinese citizens of countries other than China. "Chinese overseas" was coined to make such a difference. Still, sometimes the term "overseas Chinese" continues to be used to refer to two different groups.

and cultural institutions (for example, the Chinese press) in Nanyang/Southeast Asia[6] modernized along the line of these patriotic activities oriented toward China. China's May Fourth Movement, in particular, served as an inspiring intellectual movement for the Chinese intellectual communities in Nanyang.

Throughout the first half of the 20th century, *huaqiao* were involved in one way or another in the important processes or events within China, including the 1911 Republican Revolution, the struggle between the Kuomintang (Nationalist Party) and the Chinese Communist Party, the Anti-Japanese War, and even the construction of the New China founded in 1949. Some of them eventually settled down in China as Zhongguoren/Chinese national 中國人, no longer being an ambiguous *huaqiao*. The prime example being the Singapore-based *huaqiao* business leader Tan Kah Kee 陳嘉庚, who contributed much of his personal fortune to the cause of rebuilding China and eventually permanently returned to China after the Second World War and died in 1961 as a Chinese national.

After the Second World War, two historical processes complicated the choices of the Chinese in Southeast Asia. First was the decolonization process and the rise of indigenous nationalist political leaders, who began to question the political identity of the Chinese. Second was the communist takeover of Mainland China in 1949, which in due time meant the cutting off of direct ties between China and the Chinese in Southeast Asia, since most governments of Southeast Asia (especially maritime Southeast Asia) adopted a nationalist and anti-communist stand in the process of decolonization. *Huaqiao* no longer could function as a viable category for these Chinese. Most of them in fact opted to make the difficult but necessary transition to being *huaren*, being the ethnic Chinese citizens of a country other than the People's Republic of China or Republic of China (see Wang 2001: 63–64). Their political identity was diverted to the newly-independent countries in

---

[6]Nanyang, literally "South Seas," is traditionally the way Chinese refer to the Southeast Asian region, especially maritime Southeast Asia (today's Malaysia, Singapore, Indonesia, Brunei, and Thailand).

Southeast Asia, and their ties to China, especially to communist China, were drastically reduced, if not completely cut off.

Still, the whole process was never smooth. As mentioned earlier, Chinese cultural institutions (Chinese schools and newspapers) in Nanyang were inspired by China's patriotic May Fourth Movement, and it was not easy to completely reduce the connections of these institutions with the intellectuals, nationalism, and politics of China, before these schools and institutions were revamped to make them more in line with the indigenous national educational curricula in the 1960s and 1970s. Hence, even though most Chinese, perhaps out of pragmatism, chose to settle for being *huaren* during the post-War era, pockets of Chinese communities continued to have the meaning of their lives oriented toward China's rather than local development. They could be *huaren* legally, but their ethos was more like *huaqiao*. "Inner China," a literary concept that refers to some Malaysian Chinese intellectuals and writers' deep sense of identification and affection with a glorious China (in contrast to the existing, real China), was more likely to be found in this group of Chinese.[7]

"Inner China" 內在中國 in Literature and Social Sciences

In the early years of the development of Malaysian Chinese/Sinophone Malaysian Literature (Mahua wenxue 馬華文學) there was an intellectual debate about indigenization vs. continuity with the "mother culture" in China. On the one hand, there were those who advocated for an "indigenization" approach, an approach that stressed the literary autonomy from "mother China" so that Mahua wenxue would have merit of its own and not just a "a Nanyang branch" of China-based Chinese Literature (Fang 1986: 132–135). On the other hand, there were also Malaysian Chinese writers who continued to have deep affection of the Chinese culture and history and felt that it was unnecessary for Mahua wenxue to completely break off relationships with China, even if it was no longer possible to maintain real connections with the real China since 1949. For

---

[7] It should be noted here that Anglophile Chinese or even non-Chinese could also potentially develop "inner China."

these writers, the discrimination they felt they faced in Malaysia (because of the increased marginalization of Chinese language and culture in the government's pro-Malay policies) made it even more pointless to "indigenize." Instead, they find solace in affirming their "inner China."

A renowned scholar on Mahua wenxue, Professor Ng Kim Chew, had the following definition of "inner China":

> For (an overseas) Chinese literary writer...if s/he follows the Chinese ideographic characters in the search of the whole of Chinese cultural tradition, and to pursue this whole system of symbols, he will have to eventually encounter a China constructed by symbols, and he will be mesmerized because of the deep culture and history (of this system of symbols). This is a construct, by the (overseas) Chinese, based on their imagination, feeling, affection, knowledge and philosophy, and is contrasted with the real, with a clear geographical pinpoint, but poor and mythical, communist China. This is what I call "inner China." (Ng 2012: 117)

Ng hence uses this concept of "inner China" to describe a kind of historical and cultural consciousness among a group of Malaysian Chinese writers who deeply identified with the Chinese literature, tradition, and culture (but not the communist regime in Mainland) and went to Taiwan in order to be part of the Chinese cultural realm in the 1960s. Taiwan in the 1960s was a popular destination of these young Malaysian Chinese writers driven by a sense of affirming their "inner China" through literary works.[8] Taiwan, under the then Kuomintang rule, also stressed that it was the inheritor of the grand Chinese tradition and was the last beacon of hope for Chinese culture against the onslaught of the western-originated communism that plagued the unfortunate Mainland. This Taiwan's myth eventually busted but "inner China" persisted and remained the leitmotif that drove the creative writings of these Malaysian Chinese writers. Woon Swee Oan[9] 溫瑞安 is one example of such writers with a deep

---

[8] For Malaysia–Taiwan literary connections, see also Bernards (2016: 81–91).
[9] In Pinyin, the name is Wen Rui'an.

sense of "inner China." His creation and immersion of himself within the literary world of *wuxia* 武俠, a unique and non-existent world of Chinese chivalry and martial arts, was to affirm and bring out the "inner China" that he has close affection with (Ng 2012: 115–170).

Professors Huang Chih-Lien, C. Y. Chang and Y. Y. Kueh shared similar career paths: born in Malaysia, studied in primary and secondary Chinese schools in Malaysia, received undergraduate education in a Chinese university outside of Mainland China or Taiwan, obtained post-graduate education from a Western university, built and retired from their career in Hong Kong, focused on China in their professional/intellectual career, and became affirmative of the present Beijing government and the trajectory of China's development. Throughout their careers, Huang, Chang and Kueh showed a stronger sense of being politically concerned about developments in contemporary China, and in some instances, directly involved. They hence exemplify a kind of "return" to China (albeit a "partial return" to Hong Kong) from a Nanyang overseas Chinese background, and in this sense they could be said as *huaqiao*/overseas Chinese/Chinese sojourners. Moreover, it is contended here that in many ways, there was also "inner China" in Huang, Chang, and Kueh. Their scholarship was driven, at least partly, as a form of expressing and affirming this "inner China." However, they were trained as social scientists and were not able to construct a fictitious world of China based on imagination and affection, as in literature. They must closely examine the "real" China in the process of contrasting it with their "inner China."

Huang Chih-Lien 黃枝連: Life and Scholarship

Biographical Sketches

Professor Huang Chih-Lien was born in 1939 in Klang, Malaya, to a poor family. His father was a laborer who worked at Port Klang (called Port Swettenham). In his own words, he was truly a child of the working class (Huang 2012/2013: 8). Klang was a relatively small town about 60 kilometers south of Kuala Lumpur. The Chinese population in Klang was quite big and the town had several Chinese schools (from primary to secondary). Huang attended one of those schools and studied until junior high standard before moving to continue senior high school in Kuala Lumpur.

As a student from a poor family, Huang had to work while receiving his high school education in Kuala Lumpur. Huang worked for a student newspaper called *The Chinese Student Weekly* (Zhongguo xuesheng zhoubao 中國學生週報), an anti-communist publication published by the Union Research Institute (Youlian yanjiusuo 友聯研究所) in Hong Kong. By his own reckoning, this was the beginning of his political consciousness. Union Research Institute was an anti-communist organization (rumored to be funded by the Central Intelligence Agency) but not an anti-China outfit (*fangong bu fanhua* 反共不反華). It sent its personnel and its publication to Malaya and Singapore at that time to counter the leftist discourses among the Chinese intellectual circle in the region.

After high school, Huang attended New Asia College, one of the predecessors of modern-day CUHK. New Asia College was founded by the refugee Chinese intellectuals fleeing the communist takeover in Mainland but who also refused to go to the equally repressive Kuomintang-ruled Taiwan. Most of these intellectuals had a strong anti-communist stand. New Asia College was also the base of the New Confucian philosophers (*xin rujia* 新儒家), such as Xu Fuguan 徐復觀, Tang Junyi 唐君毅 and Mou Zongsan 牟宗三. Huang studied under these philosophers but was not necessarily impressed by the argument of the New Confucians, but from here he developed a life-long passion with the theories of Zhu Xi 朱熹, the Song-dynasty Confucian philosopher (Huang 2012/2013: 21). During his days at New Asia, he also continued to be a work-student, working at the same Union Research Institute. Hence, in his own words, he was a rather "right-wing" student during his college years.

After college, Huang went to Harvard University to pursue a Master's degree in East Asian Studies. Although he studied under Harvard star professors such as John King Fairbank, Benjamin Schwartz, Henry Kissinger, and so on, he was not necessarily influenced by them much, at least not in his worldview or ideology. Instead, his years at Harvard (1962–1964) turned him from a "rightist" into a "leftist," because at Harvard, for the first time, he had a chance to study many primary materials of Communist China, and he began to systematically read Marx, Lenin, Stalin, Mao, Zhou Enlai, and so on (Huang 2012/2013: 27–28). His own reading of these materials convinced him to become a "leftist."

By the time he returned to Hong Kong in 1965 to teach sociology at Chong Chi College (another predecessor of CUHK), Huang was a determined "leftist." He reckoned that in the 1960s many intellectuals turned "left," influenced by the anti-(Vietnam) war movement in the US and the Cultural Revolution in China. At Chong Chi, he would use a Marxist point of view in his class lectures, which incurred the wrath of his department head, who was then a Kuomintang person. Huang also began to involve in underground leftist and anti-British politics. His leftist politics finally led to the termination of his teaching contract at Chong Chi, and he left for Singapore's Nanyang University (popularly referred to as Nantah), and stayed there until 1971.

Nantah was founded by the Chinese communities in Singapore and Malaysia and attracted many local Chinese students, and at that time it was the only university to use Chinese as the main language of instruction outside of Mainland China, Taiwan, or Hong Kong. The Singapore government, under Lee Kuan Yew and his anti-communist People Action Party (PAP), however, always had a suspicious view of Nantah, seeing its Chinese education as incompatible with the Singapore national vision which is built upon the mastering of English, and suspected Nantah to be infested with leftist politics and too sympathetic toward Communist China. It was eventually closed by the PAP government in 1982.

During his Nantah years, Huang published some of the pioneering sociological studies of the Chinese communities in Malaysia/Singapore at that time (more discussion of his scholarship later). He admitted that before his Nantah career, his intellectual focus was mostly focused on China (or the West), and rarely touched upon Southeast Asia. This was the first time his scholarly attention turned to the region he was born — Nanyang (Huang 1972: 10). During his years at Nantah and Singapore, Huang continued to be interested in political activism. As a "leftist" he was also under the suspect of the PAP authorities, although at one point the PAP did attempt to co-opt him (Huang 2012/2013: 31). He got into trouble at Singapore because, after the Kissinger's secret visit to China in 1971, he made an open prediction that China would become the center of regional geopolitics in Southeast Asia following Sino-American detente, and this drew the irk of the anti-communist PAP government in Singapore (Huang 2012/2013: 32). He was expelled from Singapore in December 1971. He decided to go back to Hong Kong rather than Malaysia (he was still holding Malaysian citizenship at that time) because he foresaw that his leftist sympathies would bring him troubles again in the equally anti-communist Malaysia.

On his way to Hong Kong the ship that he boarded was also loaded with many expellees with similar leftist background. The authorities of Singapore, Malaysia, and Hong Kong all shared the same intelligence network and the British colonial authorities also knew of Huang's leftist troubles and hence Huang was only given a three-month stay in Hong Kong. Fortunately he soon secured a teaching job at the Hong Kong Baptist University that allowed him to stay long term. Huang eventually stayed at the same university for more than 30 years. In addition, on his second return he was well received by the so-called "patriotic leftist organizations" (*aiguo zuopai tuanti* 愛國左派團體), including the most determined pro-Beijing newspaper *Ta Kung Pao* 大公報, and this began Huang's long-term relationship with these organizations. Luo Fu 羅孚, who was an editor at *Ta Kung Pao* and also a famous Hong Kong writer (and also a Chinese Communist Party cadre responsible for "united front work" [*tongzhan gongzuo* 統戰工作]) became Huang's good friend.

The second return to Hong Kong was a big transition in Huang's life. Although he remained a committed leftist, he was not to engage in anymore anti-British political activities. Since his second return, he said, "I was now prepared to stay in Hong Kong in long term and immerse myself in the Chinese society in Hong Kong; I now decided that I would become a Chinese national/Zhongguoren 中國人, no longer an overseas Chinese/huaqiao 華僑. So, in the land of China, I was no longer a passerby but a true participant. I would continue to participate in politics, but I must now participate in a proper way" (Huang 2012/2013: 45).

Huang's Baptist University years were no longer marked by active political activities, although he continued to maintain close relationships with those "patriotic leftist organizations." He helped these organizations to link up with members of the Hong Kong academia, many of them remained staunchly anti-communist, but were gradually opening up to interact with these pro-Beijing organizations. In the 1980s, he was also approached by the Kuomintang in Hong Kong to liaise with the pro-Beijing groups. But overall, since joining Baptist he became more like a normal academic. After retiring from Baptist, Huang spent some years at both Macao University of Science and Technology and University of Macao. In between he was a visiting scholar to a number of academic institutions in the US, Japan, and South Korea. Afterwards he completely retired from the academia, although he is still working on some projects.

Scholarship

Professor Huang Chih-Lien is a prolific author, having written more than 20 books and countless articles and essays. All of his works, however, are published in Chinese, and this has prevented him from being more well known in the English academic circle. Overall, his scholarly output can be grouped into four areas, as shown in Table 1.

Table 1. Scholarship of Huang Chih-Lien

Areas of Study	Major Contributions	Major Works
Sociology	General Theory (the Five-Li System); Studies of the Chinese communities in Singapore and Malaysia	Huang 1971; Huang 1972; Huang 1990; Huang 2014
History	Tributary system	Huang 1992–1995
Futurology	Predictions of Great China and Chinese Economic Community; Predictions of the Belt and Road Initiative.	Huang 1989; Huang 1992a; Huang 1992b; Huang 2000; Huang 2002
Area Studies (Outside of China and Southeast Asia)	Japan and the US	Huang 1980; Huang 2003

Huang is an eclectic scholar, and even though he was Professor of Sociology for many years at Baptist, he has never been a conventional kind of sociologist. His earlier studies on the Malaysian/Singapore Chinese communities, conducted during his years at Nantah (1971, 1972, 2014), were the most sociological of his work, based on empirical data collected from field research and theoretically oriented toward Marxism. After his second return to Hong Kong and his academic appointment at Baptist, Huang seemed to have not taken again this kind of sociological-empirical research again. His academic interests shifted to general social theory and social thought, and the application of his social theory to interpreting the past and future of China, Hong Kong, and Taiwan (as well as the US and Japan).

At the risk of oversimplification, the following sentences seek to explain Huang's social theory. Huang calls his social theory the "Five-Li System" (*wuli xitong* 五理系统) theory and the theory is most comprehensively discussed in his 1990 book, *A Theory of Social Conditions* (Huang 1990).[10] In the book, he attempted to synthesize three bodies of social thought (the theories of Confucian scholar Zhu Xi, Western liberalism, and Marxism) and the result was the "Five-Li System." The "Li" here refers to the subsystems of the social–physical world (the whole System): Physiological Li/subsystem (*shengli*生理), Psychological Li/subsystem (*xinli*心理), Sociological Li/subsystem (*qunli* 群裡), Physical Li/subsystem (*wuli* 物理), and Cosmological Li/subsystem (*tianli* 天理).

In short, Huang contends that a good social system is a system that can develop the full potentials of the five subsystems. Huang divides human history into three historical epochs: the premodern (pre-western) "1.0," the modern (western) "2.0," and the future "3.0." His magnum opus, the three-volume *A Study of the Tributary Ritual Governance System* (Huang 1992–1995) is an application of this theory in examining the traditional tributary international relations system that was centered on China as being

---

[10] Although he published his theory book in 1990, Huang had already developed some of the ideas and published them prior to 1990.

the protector/hegemon of the system (the premodern "1.0"). In his final conclusion, he made the point that the traditional tributary system did not live up to the full potential of the "Five-Li" and when western modernity came in (the modern "2.0"), the traditional system was doomed to fail. Western modernity, however, has by today almost exhausted its full potential. It is time to expect a new future, the "3.0," and according to Huang, China is in the forefront of entering the futuristic epoch of "3.0."

Huang's fascination with things in future led him to earn a reputation in Hong Kong as a "futurologist." A large chunk of Huang's writings on China, Taiwan, and Hong Kong is about Huang's predictions of the future of these Chinese societies (Huang 1989, 1992a, 1992b, 2000, 2002). In the 1980s and 1990s, Huang made a series of predictions about the economic integration of these Chinese societies. Harry Harding, one of the foremost American experts on modern China, reckoned Huang as one of the earliest scholars to have predicted the formation of "Greater China" (Harding 1993). It is clear that he prefers to see Hong Kong and Taiwan remain economically integrated with China, although a high-level of autonomy and pluralism should be preserved in these societies. Another prediction that Huang made in the early 1990s that came to realization today is the present-day Belt and Road Initiative, strongly pushed by the Chinese government under Xi Jinping leadership since the announcement of the initiative in 2013. In Huang's writings in the early 1990s, he already advanced the concept of reviving two ancient silk roads and how they could interconnect with several China's regional provincial developmental strategies to bring together common development between China and its neighbors (see, for example, the articles collected in Huang 2000: 291–298, 323–327). China's recent developments made Huang confident and optimistic of the future trajectory of China — the forerunner in the "3.0" epoch. In contrast, in his studies of the US and Japan, while he recognized the great contributions made by these countries to the world (Huang 1980, 2003), he argued that too much of the "2.0 mentality" has handicapped the leaders of these countries, making them unable to appreciate China's role and cooperate with each other (and with China) in bringing the human world to the "3.0" epoch.

Finally, a major contribution Huang made to China Studies was that he designed the first curricula of a Master's in China Studies program in Hong Kong, being offered at Baptist. This was way before other Hong Kong universities started similar programs. Huang also organized a "Hong Kong Society for the 21st Century Asia Pacific," an academic society aimed to bring together experts from the academia, business, and government to explore the meaning and future of economic integration of China, Taiwan, and Hong Kong. The Society still exists today and still actively organizes academic activities.

Chang Chak-yan 鄭赤琰: Life and Scholarship

Biographical Sketches

Professor Chang Chak-yan was born in 1936 in Cheras, a suburban district in the southern part of Kuala Lumpur with many Chinese residents. His family worked in a rubber estate. Chang remembered vividly that when he was six years old (1942), the Japanese invasion of Malaya forced his family to flee to the jungle. Due to the war he did not attend schools, until the war ended in 1945. Chang recalled that on his first day at school (a Chinese school), the pupils followed the teachers in singing the song *March of the Volunteers* — today the national anthem of the People's Republic of China. "When this song became popular among the overseas Chinese, it has not yet become the national anthem of new China, but the inspiring melody and lyrics of the song made it a song of salvation for the Nanyang overseas Chinese who had to live at the edge of the sword of the Japanese army. While we were in the most hopeless situation, the greatest wish we had was that China will not perish" (Chang 2016). Chang wrote these words in the aftermath of the Occupy-Central (zhanzhong 占中) Movement, a movement he was strongly opposed to.

After the War, Chang and his family moved to Senai (in the state of Johor, in southern Peninsular Malaysia), also a small town bordering the jungle. In 1948, the Malayan communists were waging guerrilla warfare against the British authorities. Chang's family was involved. His mother was a member of the Democratic Movement (minyun 民運), which was an auxiliary support group for the Malayan communists. A number of Chang's classmates in his junior high school went to join the communists and battled the British troops. Some were killed in battle. The Japanese invasion, communists, the death of his classmates — all these made a deep imprint in the mind of Chang in his childhood. By the time he entered senior high school, he also read Chinese literary works of the May Fourth generation, such as the work of Lu Hsun 魯迅. He was deeply interested in the political critiques contained in Lu Hsun's writings. Hence, although he has had a lifelong passion in zoology, when entering the university, his first choice was political science.

In the early 1960s, Chang entered Nantah in Singapore. In the politically contentious 1960s, Nantah was also a highly politicized place; confrontations between student activists and the PAP authorities in Singapore occurred regularly. Chang was a student of political science but he stayed away from, and in fact seemed to have a distaste for, campus politics. He did not fully focus on his studies either; instead, he found a passion in writing short novels — this was later to develop into Chang's passion in writing commentaries. Nevertheless, although he did not distinguish himself in academic studies, he was still being targeted for possible grooming by the PAP authorities. It is interesting to note here that although Chang came from a family that was pro-communist or leftist and his high school environment should naturally shape him to become at least a leftist sympathizer, Chang apparently stayed away from leftist politics and actually had the opportunity to be groomed by the anti-communist PAP as a future PAP leader.

After he graduated from Nantah he was recruited by an Englishman G. G. Thompson to work at a political institute that trained Singapore's civil servants. Later he was sent to become an instructor at the National Youth Leadership Training Institute (NYLTI), a body that targeted young elite in Singapore and to train them to become future leaders. After undergoing training at NYLTI, these young leaders would be dispatched to serve at Singapore's community centers, which, until today, remain an important grassroots institution providing ground support for the PAP government. Chang excelled in his duties; he was approached by Singapore leader Lee Kuan Yew to be a PAP party member and to be in charge of the PAP's Chinese-language newspaper. Chang was henceforth involved in the PAP's consolidation of power before and after Singapore's independence (from Malaysia) in 1965, giving him the first real experience in politics (Chang 2013: 6–7).

However, Chang's real interest was never in real politics but academic studies of politics. He declined the opportunity to join PAP and instead opted to further his education overseas. Chang went on to receive a Master's degree at the University of Western Ontario (Master Thesis: *Political Violence in Malaysia*) and a Ph.D. from SUNY-Binghamton (Ph.D. Dissertation: *"Ruralia" versus "Urbania" in Chinese Political Thought*). Both topics displayed a recurring and underlying leitmotif of Chang's political science scholarship: how to deal with political conflict and violence (more about his scholarship later). After his Ph.D., he was offered a job at the National University of Singapore, but he declined and instead chose to go to CUHK, because, as he said, he "wanted to study China" (Chang 2013: 11).

However, at CUHK, he was given the task to develop studies of Southeast Asian politics (*Lianhe Maijin* 2008: 11). So his scholarship has involved, other than Chinese politics, also China–Southeast Asia relations and the studies of ethnic Chinese in Southeast Asia. He spent about 30 years at CUHK (and was nicknamed as one of the Four Elders of the Political Science Department of CUHK), and, after retiring from CUHK, another few more years at Lingnan University.

During his years at CUHK, Professor Chang was a well-known public figure through his columns in several major Hong Kong newspapers, such as *Hong Kong Economic Journal* (or known in Mandarin as Xinbao 信報) and *Ming Pao* 明報. Chang was known for his use of satirical animal metaphors in these columns to critique especially the Beijing government. During the debate on the Hong Kong political system in the 1980s, he was supportive of Hong Kong democratization and criticized those who were afraid of endorsing democracy as "mantis shrimp" (Chang 1987: 55). In another piece he had even harsher words, saying that the Chinese communist regime, by carrying out the Tiananmen killings, had "turned people into dogs" (Chang 1995: 188). He also argued that the Chinese Communist Party inherited the feudalistic tradition of "emphasis on agriculture and restraining commerce" (*zhongnong yishang* 重農抑商), and together with the anti-capitalist Marxist theory, caused Chinese massive backwardness (Chang 1987: 75–76). Although Chang never explicitly stated his ideological stand, his commentary writings displayed a strong sense of uneasiness with communism and leftist ideas in general. One could perhaps suggest that he was more aligned with a "rightist" worldview.

However, there was a remarkable turn in Chang's attitudes toward Beijing after 2000s. He continued to be a prolific writer in commentaries, and these commentaries now stand in sharp contrast to his critical views of Beijing in the 1980s and 1990s. Today, many in Hong Kong would consider him to be one of the most pro-China scholars. Chang was especially galvanized by his opposition to the Occupy-Central Movement in 2014 and was involved in organizing a pro-Beijing counter-movement called "Silent Majority for Hong Kong" (*banggang chuseng* 幫港出聲). As of today, he still continues to write against the Occupy-Central Movement, the Hong Kong pan-democrats, and the Hong Kong Independence advocates. Other than the Hong Kong issue, his stands on most issues involving China, such as the South China Sea, Taiwan, US–China relations, are generally pro-Beijing as well.

Finally, unlike Huang (and Y. Y. Kueh), Chang continued to maintain certain ties with Malaysia despite being mainly a Hong Kong academic. He has been affiliated with a small private college in Malaysia and has written two books on Malaysian Chinese leaders (a politician and a businessman) and a few commentary pieces on Malaysian politics. Overall his position is quite pro-Barisan Nasional, the conservative ruling coalition in Malaysia.

Scholarship

Like Huang, Professor C. Y. Chang is also a scholar with a wide range of interests. His scholarship can be roughly grouped into two areas of study:

Table 2. Scholarship of C. Y. Chang

Areas of Study	Major Contributions	Major Works
Political Science (Chinese Politics and Policy)	China–Southeast Asia relations; China's Overseas Chinese Policy; China–Taiwan relations; China–Hong Kong relations; Bureaucracy in China	Chang 1979; Chang 1980; Chang 1982; Chang 1983; Chang 1986; Chang 1998; Chang 1999a; Chang 2000c; Chang 2014
Ethnicity	Ritual system; Malaysian Chinese; Hakka; Indigenous inhabitants of new territories in Hong Kong	Chang 1996; Chang 1999b; Chang 2000a, 2000b; Chang 2002; Chang 2004; Chang 2005
Commentaries	Political commentaries	Chang 1987, 1995

Studies of China's policy and politics, and studies related to ethnicity. A third area, his political commentaries, can be added as his overall output but these are not strictly his academic writings (see Table 2).

Other than his Ph.D. dissertation and a book chapter analyzing the bureaucracy and administration of China's special economic zones (Chang 1986), Chang has not written much about the domestic side of Chinese politics. Chang's research into China's policy and politics, henceforth, in general focused on four sets of (Mainland) China's external relations: China–Southeast Asia relations (Chang 1979, 1983), China's policy toward the overseas Chinese/Chinese overseas (*qiaowu zhengce* 僑務政策) (Chang 1980, 2000c), China–Hong Kong relations (1982; 2014), and China–Taiwan relations (Chang 1998, 1999a). A standout work among these studies was his 1982 book *Regaining Sovereignty and the Future of Hong Kong*. This was one of the earliest books by a Hong Kong-based academic (ironically also a non-native Hong Kong scholar) to lay out the overall strategic position of Hong Kong for Beijing (in particular, Chang analyzed the importance of Hong Kong to Beijing's United Front policy), how the Southeast Asia connections of Hong Kong (i.e., common British colonial heritage and military protection, the circular ethnic Chinese capital between Hong Kong and Southeast Asia) would affect and be affected by the transfer of sovereignty, how Hong Kong could learn from the decolonization process in Southeast Asia, and the future scenarios of Hong Kong. Especially in his discussion on Hong Kong future he ruled out Hong Kong independence (Chang 1982: 88) as impossible and impractical. Instead, Chang argued that no matter what future scenario for Hong Kong turned out to be, Hong Kong must not alienate Mainland China. Chang paid particular attention to Singapore's relationship with the Malay Peninsula, such as how the Lee Kuan Yew leadership in Singapore continued to maintain a pragmatic, non-ideological relationship with the leaders of the Malay Peninsula, built up economic self-sufficiency, reduced cultural differences with the people on the Peninsula, and ensured policy coordination between the two sides (Chang 1982: 94–101). Chang proposed that a decolonized Hong Kong should model its relationship with Mainland China after Singapore–Malay Peninsula relationship. In this sense, although he was a critic of the Beijing regime in the 1980s and 1990s, he was always consistent as being against Hong Kong independence and deterioration of the relationship between Hong Kong and Mainland China, and this partly explained why he was strongly pro-Beijing in the 2014 episode involving the Occupy-Central Movement.

Another major academic interest of Chang is ethnicity. At both CUHK and Lingnan, he initiated research programs in the studies of overseas Chinese (Overseas Chinese Archive at CUHK, and the Research Programme on Ethnicity and Overseas Chinese Economics at Lingnan). The former unit received support from the Lee Foundation in Singapore while the latter was funded by Tsung Tsin Association Hong Kong 香港崇正總會, an influential Hakka-based social organization. Chang always felt that the field of overseas Chinese studies suffered from the problem of the lack of original sources, especially original archival sources, and his ambition was to collect the most complete archives relating to the overseas Chinese (Chang 2013: 19–20, 25–26). Unfortunately, his initiatives at both CUHK and Lingnan failed to survive his retirement and departure, as both programs are in an idle state now. His connection with the Tsung Tsin Association also led to his strong interests in Hakka Studies (Chang 1999b, 2000a, 2002a). Chang would later serve for many years as the President of the International Hakka Studies

Association. In addition to Hakka Studies, Chang has also been interested in the issues involving the indigenous inhabitants of Hong Kong New Territories (Xinjie yuanzhumin 新界原住民) (Chang 2000b). Finally, as mentioned earlier, Chang has maintained a somewhat active relationship with Malaysia. He has written two books on Malaysian Chinese personalities (in an approving way) — Ling Leong Shek 林良實 (Chang 2004), who is a former government minister and president of Malaysian Chinese Association[11] and Ng Teck Fong 吳德芳 (Chang 2005), a businessman/philanthropist known to be very close to the Malaysian political establishment.

Chang's interests in ethnicity are also closely related to his theoretical view of politics. As mentioned above, Chang grew up experiencing a lot of political conflict and violence. During his Ph.D. years, one of the professors who inspired and influenced him greatly was Professor Harold Nieburg, a well-known specialist in political conflict and violence. To a large extent, how to deal with political conflict and violence was a recurring leitmotif of Chang's scholarship. In developing his own theoretical view on this question, Chang was also inspired by zoology, especially by the work of Konrad Lorenz, *On Aggression* (Chang 1996: 1, 2013: 13–14). In this work, Lorenz theorized that in the animal world, a naturally developed "ritual system" exists among animals of the same species; the "ritual system" serves the purposes of intragroup communications and coherence.[12] Applied to the human society, an "ethnic group" is basically also governed by its own "ritual system." As the human being is the most complex animal, the "ritual system" developed in the human world will also be substantively more complex and involving more than just simple communications patterns. The more developed the "ritual system" for a human society, the more complete its content will be, including legal structure, political framework, ethics, education, culture, and so on. The more flexible a human society

---

[11] A political party in the ruling coalition.
[12] For instance, rats communicate through nose tips, ants through antenna. These communications allow these animals to distinguish members of their own group and their enemies. The patterns of communications and interactions hence form the "ritual system" (Chang 1996: 1).

allows its "ritual system" to become, the more resilient is such society. The western civilization is an example of a well-developed "ritual system," with its emphasis on the rational structure of society. The Chinese Confucian-based "ritual system" is also another complex, well-developed, and enduring "ritual system." Its legacy can still be seen in the complex and flexible *guanxi* network among the overseas Chinese. Chang attributed the flexibility and adaptability of the Chinese "ritual system" as a key factor in explaining the economic success of overseas Chinese businesses. In the case of Malaysia, the flexible and adaptable Confucian "ritual system" tradition also allowed the ethnic Chinese community to adapt to the government's pro-Malay New Economic Policy (Chang 1996: 7–8).

Chang has not written a comprehensive theoretical work based on this "ritual system" theory.[13] Anyhow, it can be inferred that his preoccupation with the concept of "ritual system" or "political ritualization" ("ritual system" applied in the political sphere) was because of his concern about (and real-life experience in) political conflict and violence. The most important function of politics, then, is to tame conflict and violence through ritualization. From here, it can also be inferred that Chang prefers societal orderliness, status quo and coherence (symbolizing a well-developed "ritual system" at work) and this explains his apparent "rightist" or conservative viewpoints (and opposed to radicalism and revolution). This could also be an important factor why he has taken a supportive stand of the Beijing regime — because he believes that the pan-democrats and the Hong Kong Independence advocates have become the most destabilizing factors in an otherwise orderly and pragmatic Hong Kong society.

Kueh Yak-Yeow 郭益耀: Life and Scholarship

Biographical Sketches

Professor Y. Y. Kueh was born in 1939 in Simanggang (now known as Sri Aman), a small town in the state of Sarawak, in Borneo. His

---

[13] Although, in his interview, he said that this is still a work in progress and he may yet publish his theoretical book in the future.

father was a traditional folk dentist. As in the cases of Huang and Chang, Kueh received his primary and secondary education from Chinese schools (in Simanggang, and later in Kuching, the capital city of Sarawak). As he later recalled, many teachers of his primary and secondary schools came from China and many of them were young and educated, but had to find refugee, first in Hong Kong, and later in Sarawak because of the turmoil Mainland China was experiencing then (Kueh 2016: 1–2). Naturally, these China-origin young refugee intellectuals imbued to their students a sense of Chineseness, and some of them would grow up with a deep sense of identification with the Chinese culture and history, such as Kueh.

Kueh had some memories of the years of Japanese invasion and occupation. But his greatest memory of the Japanese occupation was not about himself, but about the heroic but tragic life of his cousin, Albert Kwok 郭益南, told to him by Albert's mother. Albert Kwok was a famous guerrilla commander leading a guerrilla force of about 2,000 men against Japanese occupation. At one point, this guerrilla force was able to drive out the Japanese forces in Kota Kinabaru, only to be repelled three days later by its reinforced enemy. Albert Kwok was later captured in late 1943, and was cruelly tortured for three months and finally killed in 1944. Kueh always feels strongly about the tragic end to the life of his cousin (Kueh 2017: 28–29).

After high school Kueh won a scholarship to study at New Asia College in Hong Kong (the same college that Huang Chih-Lien attended). There he met his first mentor, Professor Tchang Pi-kai (Zhang Pijie 張丕介), a pioneering economist of China, specializing particularly in land economics. Tchang left two lasting legacies to Kueh. First, Tchang was first and foremost a patriotic Chinese intellectual. He fled communism and was a co-founder of New Asia College, together with other refugee intellectuals. Throughout his life he never failed to carry out his mission of preserving, continuing, and reviving the Chinese culture and civilization. Kueh' sense of being a Chinese was strongly reinforced under Tchang's mentorship. Second, Tchang's German-trained scholarship also heavily influenced Kueh's choice (for biographical materials of Tchang, see Song 2008).

Tchang's Ph.D. supervisor, Karl Diehl, was a leading scholar of the German "social-law" school of economics, a predecessor to today's institutional economics. An important characteristic of this school was strong reliance on empirical statistical data in combination with a deep understanding of the legal, political and historical background of particular economic issues or phenomena, which was very different from the econometric modelling prevailing in the economics discipline later. Tchang would recommend to his students major German scholars such as Max Weber, Friedrich List, Georg Simmel, and Werner Sombart, and to his Chinese students in particular, the classics in traditional Chinese economic analysis such as *The Book of Stabilization* (Pingzhunshu 平準書) and *Discourses on Salt and Iron* (Yantielun 鹽鐵論) (Kueh 2010: 245–246; 2017: 100–107). The young Kueh was taken as a protégé of Tchang. Through Tchang, Kueh would later continue his economic studies at Marburg University in West Germany, under the supervision of Professor Karl Paul Hensen, a classmate of Tchang. It was in Germany that Kueh inherited the uniquely German "phenomenology" that shaped his scholarship and his view on modern Chinese economic history (more about his scholarship later).

Kueh initially thought about doing a Ph.D. on how to use economic institutions and policies to balance the economic imbalances between the Chinese and the Malays in Malaysia (which would have been fitting to the New Economic Policy pronounced years later) but he later decided to work on economic transition in East Germany. This was to prove very beneficial to him later when he began studies of China's economic transition (Kueh 2016: 4). During his years in Germany, Kueh frequently traveled to East Berlin and other places in the socialist East Europe, including Moscow, and he was one of the few Malaysians then (in the 1960s) who had this exposure to the socialist world.[14] But his connections with Malaysia faded gradually afterwards. After receiving his Ph.D. from Marburg University (Ph.D. topic on the economic transition of East Europe), Kueh then joined the economics faculty of CUHK and stayed for about 20 years. At CUHK, he was the first to introduce

---

[14] At about the same time his younger sister was persuaded to join the communists in Sarawak. Kueh had to use all the help he could to "rescue" his younger sister from the communists (Kueh 2016: 3).

a course on the Chinese economy, and among his students some would later become well-known businessmen and bankers in Hong Kong.

In 1988, he left CUHK to join Marquette University in Australia as the director of the university's newly founded Institute of China's Political Economy. However, family circumstances forced him to leave Australia and come back to Hong Kong again (Kueh 2017: 305–320). Upon coming back, he was recruited by Lingnan University to serve as Dean of the Faculty of Social Sciences. It was during his time at Lingnan that his magnum opus, *Agricultural Instability in China (1931–1991): Weather, Technology and Institution* (Kueh 1995) was published. After retiring from Lingnan, Kueh served briefly as the Dean of the Faculty of Business at Chuhai University before completely retiring from the academia.

Unlike Huang and Chang, Kueh was never active socially and politically, either in Malaysia or Hong Kong. Also, unlike Huang and Chang, Kueh maintained very little ties (apart from family and personal friends) with Sarawak or Malaysia, although he paid attention to the current events occurring in Malaysia. Although not an activist, Kueh was quite clear in his political position. Like Chang, Kueh was strongly opposed to the Occupy Central Movement in 2014. Instead, he has high praise for the Beijing regime, saying that by being able to develop China into today's status, the Chinese Communist Party deserves all the credits it deserves.

Scholarship

Unlike Huang and Chang, Professor Y. Y. Kueh has been a less eccentric scholar. Apart from his Ph.D., throughout his professional career he had a focused academic interest: the Chinese economy. His scholarly output can be roughly grouped under two categories: Studies related to China's domestic economy, and studies related China's foreign economic relations (Table 3).

Among the economics academia in Hong Kong, Kueh (and only a few others) stood out as very different from the Western (mainly the US)-trained liberal economists, who generally dismiss China's

Table 3. Scholarship of Y. Y. Kueh

Areas of Study	Major Contributions	Major Works
Economics (Domestic economy of China)	Agricultural Economics; Economics of Mao Zedong; Economic Reforms under Deng Xiaoping; Economic Development in Southern China	Kueh 1995; Kueh 2008; Kueh 2010; Kueh, Chai and Fan 1999; Kueh and Ho 2000; Howe, Kueh, and Ash 2003
Economics (China's Foreign Economic Relations)	China's economic integration with neighbors	Kueh 1997; Kueh 2013; Chai, Kueh, and Tisdell 1997

economic performance during Mao's era and praise Deng's market-oriented economic reforms. Kueh was a rare Hong Kong economist praising both Mao's economics and Deng's economics, and the continuity of the two eras. Kueh (2008, 2010) advocated the inseparable relationship between the first 30 years of the People's Republic (the Mao years) and the second 30 years (the Deng years and after), and this preceded Xi Jinping's notion of "not using the second thirty years (of the People's Republic) to repudiate the first 30 years, and vice versa," first formulated in 2013.

Kueh came to this conclusion because of his "phenomenological" approach to the studies of China's economic development from Mao to Deng. As mentioned earlier, Kueh's Ph.D. was done under the supervision of Karl Paul Hensen, who was a disciple of Walter Eucken, the founder of an influential Post-War German economic school call "Ordo Liberalismus" (Ordoliberalism). It is not easy to characterize Ordoliberalism. Although, like all liberal schools, Ordoliberalism also preferred free market competition, it did not blindly attack any economic system that differed from the ideals of free market competition. For instance, Ordoliberals at that time were also carefully studying the Soviet economy. But unlike the mainstream American economists who were ideologically opposed to the Soviet system, Ordoliberals would treat the

Soviet system as a particular historical phenomenon; "they would analyze both its strengths and weaknesses, and include it under the research framework of 'economic morphology'" (Kueh 2016: 6). Walter Eucken, the founder of this school, came from the University of Freiburg, the home base of the thriving philosophical school of phenomenology and its founder, Edmund Husserl. Eucken was deeply influenced by Husserl's phenomenology (Kueh 2017: 158–160). Kueh was to inherit this uniquely German academic tradition.

The phenomenological way of philosophizing "emphasizes the attempt to get to the truth of matters, to describe *phenomena*, in the broadest sense as whatever appears in the manner in which it appears, that is as it manifests itself to consciousness, to the experiencer." Henceforth, "explanations are not to be imposed before the phenomena have been understood from within" (original italic, Moran 2000: 4). As the founder of this school, Husserl recommended the principle of "presuppositionlessness," which means "the claim to have discarded philosophical theorizing in favor of careful description of phenomena themselves, to be attentive only to what is *given* in intuition" (original italic, Moran 2000: 9). As a methodological procedure, Husserl proposed the "suspension of natural attitude…in order to isolate the central essential features of the phenomena under investigation." As such, "all scientific, philosophical, cultural, and everyday assumptions had to be put aside… [The] phenomena [should be attended to only] in the manner of their being given to us, in their *modes of givenness*" (original italic, Moran 2000: 11).

Therefore, a "phenomenological" approach to economic studies eschews theoretical (and essentially ideological) presuppositions and judgments. In Kueh's view, China's economic phenomena during the Mao era, such as rural collectivization, centralization of resources, heavy industrialization, deprivation of consumer products, should not be examined using standards or judgments derived from other contexts, such as profit maximization or efficiency, for these will only distort our understanding of the Chinese economy under Mao.

As Kueh wrote,

> My work (on China's economy during Mao's era) is to look at Mao era as a historicist phenomenon, and to investigate and analyze it. I do not want to morally judge the right and wrong or good or bad of the Mao phenomenon. I just want to investigate the connections and linkages of the different aspects of the phenomenon, and its internal instrumental rationality. (Kueh 2017: 148)

Kueh credits Mao with several economic achievements (Kueh 2008). First, economic growth under Mao was not really as bad as it was made out to be in the post-Mao years. Due to Mao's industrialization strategy, the living standard was kept artificially low but that did not take away the fact that China's economic growth was actually quite impressive under Mao's years. Second, the concentration in heavy industry under Mao, especially in steel and machinery, served as the foundation for other, lighter industries to growth, and would eventually allow China to have a relatively comprehensive industrial structure to support its marketization reforms during Deng's era (Kueh 2010: 28–29).

Third, even in agriculture, where Mao was consistently criticized for depriving the welfare of the rural peasants by his forced industrialization strategy, Kueh noted an important achievement made by Mao — the declining influence of weather over agricultural produce. This was the subject of his magnum opus, *Agricultural Instability in China (1931–1991): Weather, Technology and Institution* (Kueh 1995). This was a book based on more than 20 years of research. As suggested in the subtitle, Kueh argued that three factors (weather, technology, and institution) greatly influenced agricultural production. Historically, Chinese peasants were at the great mercy of weather. Whenever bad weather struck (too dry or too rainy), agriculture suffered. He compared China's agricultural production in the 1930s and 1950s, in which technological level between the two eras was similar, and found out that in the 1950s China's agricultural production was less affected by the same level of severe weather as in the 1930s. He credited this with rural collectivization (he called this "institutional hedge"). In the 1930s, rural peasants fled to the cities or other places when bad weather struck, and agricultural production would decline rapidly. In the 1950s, rural collectivization tied the peasants to their land and farm, and the peasants, because of subsistence urge, would have no choice but to work on their land, and agricultural production would still decline because of bad weather but would not decline rapidly. In other words, the weather factor was reduced. Collectivization then formed another basis of what Kueh called "technological hedge," — meaning especially the improvement in irrigation technology. Collectivization allowed the government to mobilize and centralize all resources (particularly rural labor) to build up an extensive irrigation infrastructure in the 1970s, which would not have been possible under the pre-collectivized era. "Technological hedge" was another factor that reduced weather's impact on China's agricultural production.

Both "institutional hedge" and "technological hedge" contributed much to the stabilization of China's agricultural production, and by the time Deng Xiaoping de-collectivized Chinese villages, the peasants were no longer in a position to be adversely affected by bad weather, otherwise they would have been in the same situation as in the China of 1930s, and there would have been no great stories of marketization reforms. Viewed from the liberal economic perspective, Mao's collectivization was irrational, wasteful and exploitative, but Kueh's "phenomenological" perspective allowed him to see through such distortions. Similarly, his book was solidly empirical with a lot of statistical data and documentary analysis, reflecting the emphasis on comparative, statistical, and holistic methodology of the Ordoliberalism school.

In Kueh's view, Mao's economic achievements laid the foundation for Deng's marketization reforms, and eventually, the rise of China and even the possible upcoming of a *Pax Sinica*. Deng's reforms and China's foreign economic relations were also the subjects of Kueh's economic research. By Kueh's own account, his another major book was an edited volume, *Industrial Reform and Macroeconomic Instability in China*, a book resulted from more than 10 years of collaborative research between Kueh, his colleagues and researchers from the

Chinese Academy of Social Sciences. The collaborative research was based on large-scale survey covering 300 state-owned enterprises in 6 major Chinese cities (Kueh, Chai, and Fan 1999). In addition, Kueh was involved in two major international collaborative projects — one on analyzing all major official documents of China's economic reforms (Howe, Kueh and Ash 2003), and another on empirical survey of economic development in Southern China (Kueh and Ho 2000). All these studies reflected Kueh's style of scholarship: emphasis on empirical statistical data and documentary research rather than abstract modelling and deductive reasoning. Hence, Kueh was very critical of those economists who prescribed a magical, instant solution like "privatization" to resolve all of China's problems during periods of economic transition. Kueh was more supportive of a gradual program, taking into account the overall political and social conditions: "the property right system must adjust itself according to the progress in marketization; it cannot try to achieve too much in too short a time" (Kueh 2010: 125).

Finally, Kueh also paid much attention to China's foreign economic relations, in particular China–Hong Kong economic connections and China's participation in Asian regionalism (Kueh 1997, 2013; Chai, Kueh and Tisdell 1997). For Kueh, there was no question that China benefited from the strategic position of Hong Kong during the early years of reform, but increasingly, it was Hong Kong that benefited from China's vast market and central government's support, especially since the 1997 Asian Financial Crisis. The fortune of Hong Kong's economic future certainly cannot be separated from its integration with the Mainland. Moreover, China today is embracing "open regionalism" that has vastly increased its economic connections and influences with its neighbors. Kueh's latest book (published in 2013) was titled *Pax Sinica*, but within the book he qualified that *Pax Sinica* is likely to be essentially an economic phenomenon (unlike *Pax Britannica* or *Pax America*, which were/are underpinned by military power as well), and what is likely to take shape is actually Pacific Century (or *Pax Pacifica*) rather than *Pax Sinica per se* (Kueh 2013: 371). China's economic drive, however, came to the strong geopolitical challenge, led by the US and took the shape of the so-called Trans Pacific

Partnership (TPP).[15] Kueh saw TPP more as a geopolitical initiative to exclude and contain China. However, Kueh was confident, at the end, that "the manifest economic nexus will likely continue to defy geopolitical manipulations for years to come" (Kueh 2013: 376).

Discussion and Conclusion

Table 4 is a summary of the lives and scholarships of the three senior scholars discussed in this chapter.

As can be seen in Table 4, they shared many similarities in their early lives, including childhood experiences with Japanese invasion and Cold War struggle between communism and anti-communism, early education in Chinese schools, and undergraduate education in Chinese colleges and universities (New Asia College or Nantah). Despite coming from different academic disciplines, theoretical views, and even ideologies, all of them remarkably converged on a similar position or stand regarding the Beijing regime, China's future, and China's relationship with Hong Kong. They stand out today compared to the increasing anti-Beijing sentiments among the native intelligentsia and academia in Hong Kong. In deeper reflection, perhaps what they have in common were "inner China," imbued in their heart since their childhood.

Among the three, perhaps Kueh has the strongest manifestation of this "inner China." As he himself has related in his interview:

> I was born in Sarawak as a first generation overseas Chinese/Chinese overseas, and received my primary and secondary education in Chinese schools. My university was New Asia College in Hong Kong, the center of the studies of China's national essence. Hence, it was very natural for me to love Chinese history and culture. This is the background to my specialization in the research of the Chinese economy. *I believe, that those who shared a similar background, those who were from my generation, came from Malaysia/Singapore, received early Chinese education, and studied China, they all had a similar 'sentiment' (qingcao* 情操*).* (italic added, Kueh 2016: 5)

---

[15] This was before TPP was pronounced dead upon the inauguration of Donald Trump as US President in 2017.

Table 4. Comparison of Huang Chih-Lien, C. Y. Chang and Y. Y. Kueh

	Early Life Experience Related to Politics	Education	Career Trajectory	Evolution of Political Attitudes Toward China/Beijing	Involvement in Politics in Hong Kong	Involvement in Affairs in Malaysia/Nanyang	Main Theoretical Viewpoints
Huang Chih-Lien	Distribution of Xuesheng Zhoubao	Primary and secondary Chinese schools, New Asia College (BA), Harvard (MA)	CUHK, Nantah, Baptist Univ., Macao	Right-wing during youth, left-wing and affirmative of China in the 1960s, developed close relations with the leftists/patriotic groups in HK in the 1980s and since then	Anti-British/Leftist politics, close relations with HK patriotic groups	Nantah, conflicts with PAP government, early publications on Nanyang Chinese	Five-Li system, affirm China's role in entering a new era ("3.0") that lives up to the fulfillment of Five-Li system
C. Y. Chang	Japanese invasion, communist insurgency	Primary and secondary Chinese schools, Nantah (BA) Western Ontario (MA) SUNY Binghamton (PhD)	CUHK, Lingnan	Right-wing and critical of Beijing in the 1980s/90s, gradually shifted position and now very supportive of Beijing	Involved in pro-Beijing, anti-occupy central movement activities	Nantah, possible grooming by PAP, Publications on Malaysian Chinese establishment persons.	Ritual system, affirm adaptability and flexibility in handling conflicts

(Continued)

Table 4. (*Continued*)

	Early Life Experience Related to Politics	Education	Career Trajectory	Evolution of Political Attitudes Toward China/ Beijing	Involvement in Politics in Hong Kong	Involvement in Affairs in Malaysia/ Nanyang	Main Theoretical Viewpoints
Y. Y. Kueh	Japanese invasion, communist insurgency	Primary and secondary Chinese schools, New Asia College (BA), Marburg (PhD)	CUHK, Marquatte, Lingnan	Ideologically not clear, but affirmative of the contribution made by Mao and Deng in elevating China	Very few / none	Very few /none	Phenomenology, affirm the economic achievements made by Mao

The "sentiment" that Kueh alluded to is what I mean as "inner China." To recap here, "inner China" is a literary concept that refers to the historical and cultural consciousness among certain early-generation Malaysian Chinese literary writers who see China as prosperous, mesmerizing and glorious, but this China is not to be had in the real, poor, and awful, communist China. Some of them fulfilled their "inner China" through creative literary writings.

For Huang, Chang, and Kueh, they were social scientists and could not fulfill their "inner China" by imagining a splendid but non-existent China in a literary world. Instead, they must confront the real (and for most of the time of their professional career, poor and awful) China. Their scholarly analyses, hence, had to balance between an objective examination of the Chinese society, politics, and economy, and an "inner China" that wishes to see China becoming advanced, prosperous, and powerful. For a long period of time there was this mismatch between the real China and the "inner China." The rise of China today finally brought this match.

References

Bernards, Brian. 2016. *Writing the South Seas: Imagining the Nanyang in Chinese and Southeast Asian Postcolonial Literature.* Singapore: National University of Singapore Press.

Chai, Joseph C.H., Y.Y. Kueh and Clem Tisdell (Eds.) 1997. *China and the Asia Pacific Economy.* New York: Nova Science Publishers.

Chang, C.Y. (Chak-yan) 鄭赤琰. 1979. ASEAN's Proposed Neutrality: China's Response. *Contemporary Southeast Asia* 1, 3: 249–267.

Chang, C.Y. (Chak-yan) 鄭赤琰. 1980. Overseas Chinese in China's Policy. *The China Quarterly* 82: 281–303.

Chang, C.Y. (Chak-yan) 鄭赤琰. 1982. *Shouhui zhuquan yu Xianggang qiantu* 收回主權與香港前途 (Regaining Sovereignty and the Future of Hong Kong). Hong Kong: Guangjiaojing chubanshe.

Chang, C.Y. (Chak-yan) 鄭赤琰. 1983. The Sino-Vietnam Rift: Political Impact on China's Relations with Southeast Asia. *Contemporary Southeast Asia* 4, 4: 538–564.

Chang, C.Y. (Chak-yan) 鄭赤琰. 1986. Bureaucracy and Modernization: A Case Study of the Special Economic Zones in China. In Y.C. Jao and

C.K. Leung (Eds.), *China's Special Economic Zones: Policies, Problems and Prospects*, pp. 150–121. Hong Kong: Oxford University Press.

Chang, C.Y. (Chak-yan) 鄭赤琰. 1987. *Diayu zhengzhi* 釣魚政治 (Politics of Fishing). Hong Kong: Mingbao chubanshe.

Chang, C.Y. (Chak-yan) 鄭赤琰. 1995. *Yanggou zhengzhixue* 養狗政治學 (Politics of Dog-Breeding). Taipei: Sanmin.

Chang, C.Y. (Chak-yan) 鄭赤琰. 1996. Daolun: Cong 'lihua xitong' kan huaren guanxi wangluo 導論：從'禮化系統'看華人關係網絡. (Introduction: The Chinese *Guanxi* Network from the Perspective of "Ritual System"). In Chang Chak-Yan 鄭赤琰 and Man Cheuk-Fei 文灼非 (Eds.), *Zhongguo guanxixue* 中國關係學 (Studies on Chinese *Guanxi*), pp. 1–8. Hong Kong: Overseas Chinese Archives, Chinese University of Hong Kong.

Chang, C.Y. (Chak-yan) 鄭赤琰. 1998. Taiwan Policy after Deng. In Joseph Y.S. Cheng (Ed.), *China in the Post-Deng Era*, pp. 243–271. Hong Kong: Chinese University of Hong Kong Press.

Chang, C.Y. (Chak-yan) 鄭赤琰. 1999a. You junshi kan liangan tongyi de kunjing 由軍事看兩岸統一的困境. (The Difficulty of China-Taiwan Unification from the Military Perspective) In Wong Kah-Ying 王家英 and Chang Chak-Yan 鄭赤琰 (Eds.), *Xianggang huigui yu liangan guanxi zhi zhanwang* 香港回歸於兩岸關係之展望 (Hong Kong's Return and the Future of China–Taiwan Relations), pp. 137–156. Hong Kong: Hong Kong Centre for Studies on relations Across the Taiwan Strait.

Chang, C.Y. (Chak-yan) 鄭赤琰. 1999b. Xianggang Chongzheng zonghui yu Kejiaxue kaizhan 香港崇正總會與客家學開展 (Tsung Tsin Association Hong Kong and the Development of Hakka Studies). Research Paper No. 1 for Lingnan University's Research Programme on Ethnicity and Overseas Chinese Economics.

Chang, C.Y. (Chak-yan) 鄭赤琰. 2000a. 'Minrui weijigan' yu Kejiaren de zhengzhi chengjiu "敏銳危機感"與客家人的政治成就 ("Crisis Vigilance" and Hakka's Political Achievements). Research Paper 4 for Lingnan University's Research Programme on Ethnicity and Overseas Chinese Economics.

Chang, C.Y. (Chak-yan) 鄭赤琰. 2000b. Jibenfa yu Yuanzhumin hefa chuantong quanyi 基本法與原居民合法傳統權益 (The Basic Law and the Traditional Rights of the Indigenous Inhabitants). Research Paper No. 5 for Lingnan University's Research Programme on Ethnicity and Overseas Chinese Economics.

Chang, C.Y. (Chak-yan) 鄭赤琰. 2000c. The Overseas Chinese. In Y.M. Yeung and K.Y.C. David (Eds.), *Fujian: A Coastal Province in Transition and Transformation*, pp. 67–82. Hong Kong: Chinese University of Hong Kong Press.

Chang, C.Y. (Chak-yan) 鄭赤琰. 2002. Xinmatai Fengshun zuqun de zhengzhi shiyingli: huiguan de gongneng 新馬泰豐順族群的政治適應力:會館的功能 (The Political Adaptation of the Fengshun in Singapore, Malaysia and Thailand: The Functions of Clan Houses). In Chang Chak-Yan 鄭赤琰, (Ed.), *Kejia yu Dongnanya* 客家與東南亞 (Hakka and Southeast Asia), pp. 303–316. Hong Kong: Sanlian shudian.

Chang, C.Y. (Chak-yan) 鄭赤琰. 2004. *Lin Liangshi de zhengzhi zhihui* 林良實的政治智慧 (The Political Wisdom of Ling Liong Sik). Petaling Jaya: AKIT.

Chang, C.Y. (Chak-yan) 鄭赤琰. 2005. *Wu Defang zouguo delu* 吳德芳走過的路 (The Road Walked by Ng Teck Fong). Petaling Jaya: AKIT.

Chang, C.Y. (Chak-yan) 鄭赤琰. 2013. *Interview Transcripts*, http://politics.ntu.edu.tw/RAEC/comm2/interview/malaysia/InterviewM09.pdf. Accessed on September 22, 2016.

Chang, C.Y. (Chak-yan) 鄭赤琰. 2014. 'Yiguo liangzhi' xia de sifa duli: laizi tequ sifa de tiaozhan '一國兩制'下的司法獨立：來自特區司法的挑戰 (Judicial Independence under "One Country, Two Systems": Challenges from the Judiciary of the Special Administrative Area) *Gangao yanjiu* 港澳研究 (Hong Kong and Macao Studies) 4: 18–27.

Chang, C.Y. (Chak-yan) 鄭赤琰. 2016. Renquan yu zhuquan shi mingyun gongtongti 人權與主權是命運共同體 (Human Rights and State Sovereignty Share the Same Fate) *Ta Kung Pao* 大公報, September 30, 2016, http://www.takungpao.com.hk/finance/text/2016/0930/27666.html. Accessed on January 2, 2017.

Fang, Hsiu 方修. 1986. *Mahua xinwenxue jianshi* 馬華新文學簡史 (A Brief History of New Malaysian Chinese Literature). Kuala Lumpur: Dong Zong.

Harding, Harry. 1993. The Concept of 'Greater China': Themes, Variations and Reservations. *The China Quarterly* 136: 660–686.

Ho, Samuel P.S. and Y.Y. Kueh (Eds.) 2000. *Sustainable Economic Development in South China*. London: MacMillan Press.

Howe, Christopher, Y.Y. Kueh, and Robert Ash (Eds.) 2003. *China's Economic Reforms: A Study with Documents*. London: Routledge.

Huang, Chih-Lien 黃枝連. 1971. *Mahua shehuishi daolun* 馬華社會史導論 (An Introduction to the Social History of the Malaysian Chinese). Singapore: Wanlli wenhua.

Huang, Chih-Lien 黃枝連. 1972. *Mahua lishi diaocha xulun* 馬華歷史調查緒論 (An Introduction to the Historical Investigation of the Malaysian Chinese). Singapore: Wanli wenhua.

Huang, Chih-Lien 黃枝連. 1980. *Meiguo 203 nian: dui Meiguo tixi de lishixue he weilaixue fenxi* 美國 203 年：對"美國體系"的歷史學與未來學的分析 (203 Years of the United States: A Historical and Futurological Analysis of the American System). Hong Kong: Zhongliu chubanshe.

Huang, Chih-Lien 黃枝連. 1989. *Xianggang zouxiang ershiyi shiji: Huaxia tixi he Taipingyang shidai de tansuo* 香港走向二十一世紀："華夏體系"和"太平洋時代"的探索 (Hong Kong Towards the 21st Century: Exploring the Chinese System and Pacific Era). Hong Kong: Zhonghua shuju.

Huang, Chih-Lien 黃枝連. 1990. *Shehui Qingjing lun* 社會情境論 (A Theory of Social Condition). Hong Kong: Zhonghua shuju.

Huang, Chih-Lien 黃枝連. 1992–1995. *Tianchao lizhi tixi yanjiu, shang zhong xia sanxuan* 天朝禮治體系研究，上、中、下三卷 (Studies on the Ritual-Based Tributary System, Three Volumes). Beijing: Zhongguo renmin daxue chubanshe.

Huang, Chih-Lien 黃枝連. 1992a. *Dongnanya Huazu shehui fazhanlun: tansuo zouxiang ershiyi shijie de Zhongguo yu Dongnanya guangxi* 東南亞華族社會發展論：探索走向二十一世紀的中國與東南亞關係 (On the Social Development of the Chinese in Southeast Asia: Exploring China-Southeast Asia Relations Towards the 21st Century). Shanghai: Shanghai shehui kexu chubanshe.

Huang, Chih-Lien 黃枝連. 1992b. *Zhongguo zouxiang ershiyi shiji: Zhongguo kuashiji fazhan celue de tansuo* 中國走向二十一世紀：中國跨世紀發展策略的探索 (China towards the 21st Century: Exploring China's Cross-Century Development Strategies). Hong Kong: Sanlian chubanshe.

Huang, Chih-Lien 黃枝連. 1997 (Ed.) *The Political Economy of Sino-American Relations: A Greater China Perspective.* Hong Kong: Hong Kong University Press.

Huang, Chih-Lien 黃枝連. 2000. *Zhidian tianxia: tansuo ershiyi shiji de wenxuan* 指點天下：探索二十一世紀的文選 (Pointing the Future of the World: A Collection of Articles Exploring the 21st Century). Hong Kong: Huixun chuban youxian gongsi.

Huang, Chih-Lien 黃枝連. 2002. *Dazhao Taiwan: Ershiyi shiji haixia liangan guanxi xintan* 打造台灣：二十一世紀海峽兩岸關係新探 (Building Up Taiwan: Exploring Cross-Strait Relations in the 21st Century). Hong Kong: Sanlian shudian.

Huang, Chih-Lien 黃枝連. 2003. *Xunzhao Riben: ershiyi shiji Riben neizheng waijiao yu Zhongri guanxi tansuo*尋找日本: 21世紀日本內政外交与中日關係探索 (In Search of Japan: Domestic Politics and Foreign Relations of Japan and Explorations of Sino-Japanese Relations in the 21st Century). Shanghai: Shanghai shehui kexueyuan chubanshe.

Huang, Chih-Lien 黃枝連. 2012/2013. *Interview Transcripts*, http://politics.ntu.edu.tw/RAEC/comm2/interview/malaysia/InterviewM01.pdf. Accessed on May 1, 2016.

Huang, Chih-Lien 黃枝連. 2014 (Reprint). Nanang daxue Xinjiapo huazu hangyeshi diaocha yanjiu baogao 南洋大学新加坡華族行业史调查研究報告 (Nanyang University Research Report on the History of Chinese Trades in Singapore). Singapore: World Scientific.

Kueh, Y. Y. (Yak-Yeow) 郭益耀. 1995. *Agricultural Instability in China, 1931–1991: Weather, Technology, and Institution*, Oxford: Oxford University Press.

Kueh, Y. Y. (Yak-Yeow) 郭益耀. 2008. *China's New Industrialization Strategy: Was Chairman Mao Really Necessary?* Cheltenham: Edward Elgar.

Kueh, Y. Y. (Yak-Yeow) 郭益耀. 2010. *Buke wangji Maozedong: Yiwei Xianggang jingji xuejia de linglei kanfa* 不可忘記毛澤東：一位香港經濟學家的另類看法 (Mao Should Not be Forgotten: An Unconventional View from a Hong Kong Economist). Hong Kong: Oxford University Press.

Kueh, Y. Y. (Yak-Yeow) 郭益耀. 2013. *Pax Sinica: Geopolitics and Economics of China's Ascendance*. Hong Kong: Hong Kong University Press.

Kueh, Y. Y. (Yak-Yeow) 郭益耀. 2016. *Interview Transcripts*, http://politics.ntu.edu.tw/RAEC/comm2/HK_Kuo.pdf. Accessed on March 22, 2017.

Kueh, Y. Y. (Yak-Yeow) 郭益耀. 2017. *Youxue Jiangsu liushizai: xinying, yiqu, fansi, linglei rulin waishi* 遊學江湖六十載：心影、憶趣、反思，另類儒林外史 (Being in the Scholarly World for Sixty Years: Sketches, Anecdotes, Reflections, An Alternative Unofficial History of the Literati World). Singapore: World Scientific.

Kueh, Y.Y., Joseph C.H. Chai and Gang Fan, (Eds.) 1999. *Industrial Reform and Macroeconomic Instability in China*. Oxford: Oxford University Press.

Lianhe Maijing 聯合邁進. 2008. Fang Zheng Chiyan boshi: Dongnanya zhengzhi quanwei xuezhe 訪鄭赤琰博士：東南亞政治權威學者. (Interviewing Dr. C.Y. Chang: An Authoritative Scholar on Southeast Asian Politics). *Lianhe Maijin* 聯合邁進 3: 11.

Moran, Dermont. 2000. *Introduction to Phenomenology*. New York: Routledge.

Ng, Kim Chew 黃錦樹. 2012. *Mahua wenxue yu Zhongguoxing* 馬華文學與中國性(Malaysian Chinese Literature and Chineseness). Taipei: Maitian.

Ngeow, Chow-Bing 饒兆斌. 2014. Malaixiya xueshujie de Zhongguo yanjiu 馬來西亞學術界的中國研究. (China Studies in Malaysia's Academia). *Dangdai pinglun* 當代評論 (Contemporary Review) 7: 15–24.

Ngeow, Chow-Bing, Ling Tek Soon and Fan Pik Shy. 2014. Pursuing Chinese Studies Admist Identity Politics in Malaysia. *East Asia: An International Quarterly* 31, 2: 103–122.

Shih, Chih-yu. 2014. Introduction: Humanity and Pragmatism Transcending Borders. *East Asia: An International Quarterly* 31, 2: 93–101.

Song, Xuwu 宋敘五 (ed.). 2008. *Zhang Pijie xiansheng jinianji* 張丕介先生紀念集 (Essays in Memory of Professor Tchang Pi-kai). Hong Kong: Song Xuwu.

Wang, Gungwu. 2001. *Don't Leave Home: Migration and the Chinese*. Singapore: Times Academic Press.

3

Indonesian Intellectuals' Experiences and China: Peranakan Benny Gatot Setiono on the Balance between Indonesian Nationalism and Chineseness

Matsumura Toshio

The Institute for Asia-Pacific Studies, Waseda University, Tokyo

This chapter discusses self-positioning of Peranakan Chinese in Indonesia, mainly raising an example of an activist, Mr. Benny Gatot Setiono. He wrote a bulky book entitled "Chinese Indonesians in turmoil" discussing the history of Chinese Indonesians based on various materials despite that he was originally a businessperson, not an academic. After Suharto's fall in 1998, he organized a nationwide Chinese organization. From these efforts, we can perceive his outstanding passion for social movement concerning integration of the ethnic Chinese into Indonesian society.

This passion stems from the situation of ethnic Chinese in Indonesia. The presence of ethnic Chinese was very often politicized, and Chinese were regarded as a threat for national integration and were often criticized for lack of nationalism toward the Indonesian nation.

This image of ethnic Chinese still prevails, and studying China and Chinese culture is often regarded as pro-China. Pro-China discourses sometimes provoke excessive reaction (emotional reaction, allergic), such as the pro-China attitude is against Indonesia. For this reason, in the historical and current situation of Indonesia, pro-China discourses have found it difficult to survive.

In this situation, it is mainly ethnic Chinese in Indonesia who have been forced to accept the frame of unity of Indonesia. Most of those who have led discourses concerning Indonesian nationalism and ethnic Chinese are Peranakan Chinese. They are characterized by mixed-parentage, i.e., Chinese and indigenous people, and the use of local language like Malay or Javanese. Relatively wealthy Peranakan Chinese have mainly been engaged in cultural and political activities and journalism from the time of the Dutch colonial era. After independence of Indonesia, they have been involved in the national integration and have made arguments concerning nation building.

Setiono's experience of persecution by Indonesian guerrillas because of his ethnic trait made him realize his origins during the Indonesian independence war. While he studied at the university in the 1950s, he actively committed himself to the student movement. After quitting university, he moved from Jakarta to Semarang in Central Java and then to Hong Kong from 1965 to 1974. He then worked for trade-related companies. In 1999, he established the Indonesian Chinese Association (*Perhimpunan Indonesia Tionghoa*, INTI) with several Chinese colleagues. From 2000 to 2016, he served as chairman of the Jakarta branch of the INTI, and also contributed articles to many newspapers and magazines. He is very interested in the domestic affairs of Indonesia and has made many comments on political participation of ethnic Chinese, especially from the 2000s onwards.

Meanwhile, he was anxious about excessive Chinese interference into Indonesian politics and ethnic Chinese issues. He thought that the Chinese influence could destroy the vulnerable balance between Chineseness and Indonesian nationalism.

Setiono's thought is an example of the thinking of Peranakan Chinese in Indonesia, positioning oneself in Indonesian nationalism and finding a balance between this nationalism and their "Chineseness." China to him is just a foreign country after all. However, there is a consciousness of belonging to the Chinese civilization. Apart from that, bitter experiences have led Peranakan Chinese to become careful about expressing outright Pro-China arguments. This excessive sensitiveness is the characteristic of the ethnic Chinese in Indonesia.

Introduction

The biggest difference in Southeast Asia when compared with South Asia is the existence of a large population of ethnic Chinese, as well as the fact that there is no balancer, such as India in South Asia. In Southeast Asia, the Chinese problem has been discussed in the context of nationalism and national security.

In particular in Indonesia, issues related to China have become too politicized. Ethnic Chinese in Indonesia are composed of diverse communities in various districts of Indonesia. However, in a political situation, they are regarded as a homogeneous entity having close relations with China. This image of ethnic Chinese still prevails (partly because of the lack of Chinese studies), and studying China and Chinese culture is often regarded as an indication of being pro-China. Pro-China discourses sometimes provoke excessive reaction (emotional reaction, even allergic), such as "pro-China attitude is against Indonesia." For this reason, in the historical and current situation of Indonesia, pro-China discourses have found it difficult to survive.

Furthermore, because of the lack of governmental support for academic research, in particular in Chinese studies, and because scholars do not have the ability to use materials written in Mandarin Chinese (even ethnic Chinese), there have been few scholars in this field and fewer achievements still.[1] Under these circumstances, the University of Indonesia has been the main center of Chinese studies and Sinology. In the 2000s, the Chinese studies program in the University of Indonesia became an NGO, separated from the university, but it has no constant activities because of the lack of research funding.

---

[1] Interview with Dr. Thung Ju-lan, Jakarta, February 23, 2017.

Apart from the University of Indonesia, there is no other institute in Indonesia focused on China studies, such as in Singapore. However, in the Center of Strategic International Studies (CSIS, a governmental think tank), there are some staff studying China, such as Christine Chin and Rizal Sukma. In the University of Indonesia, Tuti Muas and Hermin are studying pedagogy of Chinese language and linguistics.

Positioning of Indonesia in International Politics

Indonesia regards itself as a large and strong country. China also has the same identity. The result is that the pride of both countries makes it difficult to compromise on mutual interests, for win–win relationships and practical cooperation. Moreover, both Indonesia and China have stereotyped each other, regarding each other as a threat. This condition becomes an obstacle for mutual understanding.

For example, China has an image of Indonesia related to the persecution of ethnic Chinese that took place in 1998. Indonesia has an image of China associated with its political manipulation and interference in the 1960s. For this reason, China has been directing its efforts toward building better relationships with ethnic Chinese rather than the Indonesian government. The relationship between these countries in Asia has been trapped in a political gridlock for a long time now.[2]

This problem needs to be solved in order to build constructive relationships between both the countries and across others in the Asian region. However, Indonesia seems to be caught up its emotional reaction toward China, making it difficult for Indonesia to gain substantial advantage from the relationship. In this situation, mainly ethnic Chinese in Indonesia have been forced to accept the frame of unity of Indonesia. In this chapter, I focus on the position of ethnic Chinese in Indonesia and its implication on the entire theme.

The Situation of Ethnic Chinese in Indonesia

In Indonesia, which has the largest population of ethnic Chinese in the world, the existence of the Chinese immigrants has been a

---

[2]Interview with Yeremia Lalisang, Jakarta, February 22, 2017.

political problem in the national integration of the country. Among the ethnic Chinese, the dilemma to choose between Indonesian nationalism and psychological ties to China has always been evident. On the other hand, majority of pro-China Chinese returned to China in the 1950s–1960s and any pro-China remarks were sealed under the Suharto regime (1966–1998), so pro-China discourses itself did not exist in Indonesia. Only non-Chinese researchers centered in the University of Indonesia engaged in research on China for the purpose of national defense. However, the scale of this research was not large.

Under such circumstances, an argument that Chinese should have a certain position in the Indonesian society has often been emphasized. Even after democratization in the 2000s, the argument of outright pro-China is hard to express. Rather, business people sometimes run businesses with ties to China, but, they seldom engage in political arguments.

Peranakan Chinese

Most of those who have led discourses concerning Indonesian nationalism and ethnic Chinese are Peranakan Chinese. Who are they? The flow of Chinese immigrants to Indonesia had started since before the Dutch colonial period. Many of them were from Fujian and Guangdong Provinces, and they formed diverse Chinese societies in various districts of Indonesia. They also formed associations for each dialect group. Due to linguistic differences of original regions in China, they had a sense of belonging to the distinct language groups rather than share a national identity as Chinese.

This situation changed drastically in the beginning of the 20th century after the rise of Chinese nationalism. Ethnic Chinese in Java generally spoke local languages such as Javanese and Sundanese, and many of them did not speak Chinese dialects, such as the Hokkien dialect, despite their origins. They mainly engaged in commerce and had a consciousness that they were different from the new mass immigrants from China (most of them laborers) who flew into

Indonesia during the latter half of the 19th century. These earlier immigrants called themselves Peranakan, and they called the newcomers from China Sinkeh.

On the other hand, Chinese in Sumatra, Bangka Island, and Belitung Island are originally immigrants of the late 19th century as workers of plantations and tin deposits related to the Dutch colonial powers. They have preserved languages of southern China (mostly Hakka language) and culture of their hometowns compared with the Peranakan Chinese in Java Island. Relatively wealthy, Peranakan Chinese mainly engaged in cultural and political activities and journalism from the Dutch colonial era.

Sadayoshi's work (2016) revealed the history of Indonesia-oriented Chinese or Peranakan Chinese who have been actively involved in the national integration and have made arguments concerning nation building. From the colonial period, many Peranakan Chinese studied about China. However, they acquired knowledge of China through western languages (mainly Dutch and English), as they could not read Mandarin Chinese.

Along with the rise of Chinese nationalism at the beginning of the 20th century, under the influence of Kang You-Wei's movement, Peranakan Chinese established an educational institution (Confucianism was placed as its backbone) with emphasis on identity as Chinese nationals. This institution was called *Tiong Hoa Hwee Koan*. Based on this educational movement, activities among Peranakan intellectuals were initiated. On the other hand, the newcomers (Sinkeh) focused on improving their financial condition rather than participating in such political and cultural activities.

Peranakan Chinese took an initiative to issue newspapers and to undertake research on China. Moreover, since they were carrying out these activities mainly using Malay language, they contributed to the spread of Malay language, which later became an official Indonesian language.[3]

---

[3] Also refer Coppel (2002: 191–212). His paper is titled "Remembering, Distorting, Forgetting: Sino-Malay Literature in Independent Indonesia."

Peranakan Chinese After the Independence of Indonesia

After the independence of Indonesia in 1945, China became a model for creating a new nation. Even Pramoedya Ananta Toer (non-Chinese), a famous novelist, was interested in studying the nation-building of China. In the 1950s, many ethnic Chinese intellectuals were inspired by China. They found China to be an ideal society. They were fascinated not only because of their Chinese origins, but also because they supported China's socialist ideals (Liu 2011).

There were intellectuals who advocated social justice and equality for Indonesia's nation-building referring to China's case in the 1950s. Their arguments focused on how ethnic Chinese would compose Indonesian society. In addition, their relationship with China became a problem because China argued for Chinese nationality for the Chinese overseas based on *jus sanguinis* (right of blood). For this reason, China and Indonesia discussed this dual-nationality problem during the Asia–Africa Conference in 1955. The result of this negotiation was that the ethnic Chinese living in Indonesia were expected to acquire Indonesian nationality.

However, following that event, complicated discussions concerning nationality of ethnic Chinese continued for four years. Finally, Indonesia released a nationality law in 1958. The law was implemented in 1960, and Chinese had to choose either Chinese or Indonesian nationality.

Under these circumstances, discussions among Peranakan Chinese concerning position of ethnic Chinese in Indonesian society arose. In particular, Baperki (*Badan Permusyarawaratan Kewarganegaaan Indonesia*, the National Council for Indonesian Citizenship) saw an ideal in China's nation-building, making efforts to promote ethnic Chinese to acquire Indonesian nationality in order to be integrated into Indonesian society, just like the minorities did in China. Their argument can be summarized as follows: Siauw Giok Tjhan, the founder of Baperki, argued that ethnic Chinese should constitute a component of the Indonesian nation as other ethnic groups such as Javanese, Sundanese, and so on (Siauw 1999). The influence of this ideology was strong at that time. Many Peranakan intellectuals inherited this idea.

Siauw's ideology has become an important reference for many thinkers up to the present time in the context of nation-building and integration of ethnic Chinese. His idea was revived in the post-Suharto era where Chinese commenced to participate in politics, and played an important role in shaping thoughts concerning social status of Chinese in Indonesia. For instance, Tan Swie Ling made an argument of "synergy" of ethnic groups for Indonesian prosperity including ethnic Chinese in the 2000s (Tan 2010). Currently, it has become a widely held view in Indonesia that ethnic Chinese are an indispensable component of the Indonesian nation.

Diplomatic Relations Between Indonesia and China

Until the 1950s, in balancing with Western countries in the context of anti-colonialism, Sukarno and Indonesian intellectuals including Peranakan Chinese were interested in socialist countries, stressing solidarity of "the Third World" in Asia and Africa and connection with China. Especially after its relationships with the Western countries became worse in the 1960s, Indonesia became closer to China. China also trusted the power of the Indonesian Communist Party with three million members and the pro-China attitude of President Sukarno. Moreover, China proposed provision of nuclear weapons development technology to Indonesia (Zhou 2014).

Meanwhile, despite the Sukarno regime's inclination to the left and the Indonesian Communist Party's growth, the right wing elements of the Indonesian army strengthened their relationship with the US, and conflicts between the Communist forces and the military right wing intensified. Eventually in 1965, along with deterioration of the physical condition of Sukarno, a conflict over political powers post-Sukarno occurred (the September Thirtieth Movement). This conflict resulted in the Communist forces being defeated and destroyed by the right wing. After this incident, Sukarno lost his political power, China became an enemy of Indonesia, and the Indonesian government severed diplomatic ties with China.

During the Suharto era, there were no diplomatic ties with China. However, the University of Indonesia became a center of Chinese studies. The university has had the department of Chinese studies since the 1970s. The role of the department was the education of Chinese experts who were adept at handling domestic ethnic Chinese issues and diplomacy with China.

In 1990, Indonesia and China reestablished diplomatic relationships. During that period, along with China's economic development, China's presence in Indonesia grew drastically. In the 2000s, economic ties with China have become stronger. As a result, the number of scholars of Mandarin Chinese and research on China have increased.

A Peranakan Chinese: Benny Gatot Setiono

In this chapter, the author raises an example of a particular intellectual, Benny Gatot Setiono for his discussion of Peranakan thoughts in Indonesia.[4] Benny Gatot Setiono (許天堂) was born in West Java in 1943. As a child, he was attacked by Indonesian guerrillas during the Indonesian independence war against the Dutch (1945–1949). He studied at the University Res Publica established by Baperki, but he had to quit his studies after the turmoil of the September Thirtieth Movement, and started running a business during the Suharto era. After Suharto's fall in 1998, Setiono set up a national Chinese organization. Furthermore, he wrote a book titled *Tionghoa dalam Pusaran Politik* (Chinese in the Turmoil of Politics) (Setiono 2003).

Setiono had a typical Peranakan view. He emphasized Baperki's ideology of Chinese integration and contribution of ethnic Chinese toward Indonesian nation-building, while keeping a distance from China. Generally, Peranakan Chinese are not familiar with Mandarin Chinese or other Chinese dialects, and they think that their "motherland" is Indonesia, not China.

---

[4] Interview with Benny Gatot Setiono in March 2016.

For example, regarding food, authentic Chinese cuisine does not match their taste. It seems they prefer Indonesian food such as Indonesian style coconut flavored dishes, goat meat soup, tail soup, and so on.[5] This is also a characteristic feature of Peranakan, and that is why a unique field called Peranakan dishes (Baba Nyonya dishes in Malaya) exists.

Career

Setiono was born in the period of Japanese occupation of Indonesia. His father, Endang Sunarko or Khouw Sin Eng wrote many books on China and articles for newspapers. His grandfather, Khouw Tjauw Seng, ran a business. He was murdered by guerrilla troops during the Indonesian Revolutionary War in 1947. Following this event, the whole family fled to Jakarta.

Setiono stated in an interview, "My father, Khouw Sin Eng, wrote books in Malay language titled *Chiang Kai-shek, The Festival of Chinese People, New China: Enemy or Friend.* He was a KMT supporter." It seems that his father was also a typical Peranakan intellectual, but unfortunately this author has not acquired books published by his father.

Setiono went to Dutch elementary school in Jakarta until 1950 and then enrolled in an Indonesian national school after the Dutch transferred power to Indonesia in 1949. Then, he studied at Catholic middle school and high school. After graduating, Setiono studied at the University of Res Publica (Baperki's university), in the faculty of economics. However, he quit studies because the university was burned down in October 1965. While he studied at the university, Setiono actively committed himself to the student movement and the activities of the college student council.

After quitting university, Setiono moved from Jakarta to Semarang in Central Java, Hong Kong from 1965 to 1974. There he

---

[5]This tendency is seen not only in Setiono, but also in many Peranakan Chinese that this author has met. Moreover, many returned overseas Chinese in Hong Kong and Mainland China also frequently make candy and meals with Indonesian taste during gatherings, see Nagura (2012).

worked for trade-related companies. In 1999, he established the Indonesian Chinese Association (*Perhimpunan Indonesia Tionghoa*, INTI) with several Chinese colleagues. From 2000 to 2016, he served as Chairman of the Jakarta branch of the INTI, and also contributed articles to many newspapers and magazines.

Setiono mentioned China's influence in Indonesia, but said that it hardly affects them (especially Peranakan Chinese). He keeps a distance from China and takes a more objective path despite his Chinese origins.

It seems that Setiono is very interested in domestic affairs of Indonesia and has made many comments on political participation of ethnic Chinese, especially from 2000s onwards. Unfortunately, he passed away in January 2017. However, till he drew his very last breath he had shown a strong commitment to Indonesian politics, especially politics in Jakarta and China does not seem to have created an impact on him.

"Chineseness"

Concerning his relationship with China, more precisely, his "Chineseness," Setiono narrated a complicated story, "I would like to tell you about my childhood, because I think it will be most appropriate to express the first encounter with my 'Chineseness' or relationship with China. I was born in northern Java, in the remote countryside of Cirebon city. I was born there in 1943. In 1947, my family became a victim of the political turmoil because of my relationship with China. At that time, my family was expelled from our hometown, and we became refugees in Jakarta. In the storm of Chinese persecution in Cirebon, my grandfather was also killed. Children and women were not killed, but adult men were targeted in the crisis."

He continued, "Before the persecution of Chinese in 1947, we were rooted in the rural area and had a good relationship with *pribumi* (indigenous Indonesian, non-Chinese). Our relationship was very close. During the Dutch era, many Chinese engaged in commercial activities and had a connection with the Dutch colonial government. This relationship with the colonial powers badly affected the position of Chinese during the Indonesian Revolutionary War (1945-1949)."

Setiono's experience of encountering his Chineseness was complicated and forced as stated above. This traumatic experience is rooted in his mind, and so he has constantly argued for his "Indonesianess" during the vulnerable conditions for ethnic Chinese in Indonesia. It seems that the more they were persecuted, the more the Peranakan Chinese stress their fidelity to the Indonesian nation. Is this only a political camouflage? Considering Peranakan's disability with Mandarin Chinese and psychological distance, this would not only be a stance for political purposes, but also, a reflection of the fact that they do not have a "home" apart from Indonesia.

In addition, among people born in Indonesia and moving to China in the 1950s-1960s, the tendency of strongly recollecting Indonesia as their native home is very strong, although it is sometimes nostalgic.

Political Activities

According to Setiono, the 1960s were the heydays of political activities. The influence of Baperki and its university, Res Publica, promoted higher education for Peranakan Chinese at the time (education was conducted in Indonesian, not Chinese). Concerning Siauw Giok Tjhan, Seitono said, "He was an ardent worshiper of Sukarno. He argued the integration of Chinese into Indonesian society without being assimilated (assimilation means that Chinese lose their own cultural traits), and made efforts for the Chinese acquisition of Indonesian nationality."

Setiono also expressed his view on China, "I was interested in China because China adopted socialism as a way of national management, so naturally I was also interested in China's nation building. This was not because I had Chinese origin, but because of socialism. Many of my classmates were also attracted by China for the same reason. I was not from an affluent family, so the idea of socialism, equality and value of equity intrigued me. Again, I was interested in China because of its philosophy at that time rather than that I was Chinese. I was and am just Indonesian."

On his part, Setiono emphasized that his interest in China was not because he was of Chinese origin but because he was interested in Chinese socialism. He emphasized that he is an Indonesian rather than a Chinese.

Setiono continued, "At that time, the image of China was good. The embassy of China passed through propaganda brochures, inviting Chinese for the nation building of socialist China. He was also interested in leftist movement and participated in it. Publication in China were translated into Indonesian and prevailed in those days." He emphasized how Chinese socialism influenced them in 1950s' activities, but this was not because of their Chinese origins.

Reasons for Writing a Book

Setiono wrote a book concerning the history of Indonesian Chinese. According to him, the purpose of writing the book was to let Indonesian people know accurately the history of Indonesian Chinese, because incorrect images concerning ethnic Chinese prevail, such as not contributing to Indonesia but being active only in their own businesses and so on.

Setiono says, "Actually, Chinese have contributed greatly to the Indonesian nation building. However, this fact has remained uncovered. Moreover on the contrary, Chinese have been associated with a negative image. So, the case that John Lee, an admiral of the Indonesian army contributing to the war against the Dutch colonial powers, became the national hero of Indonesia was noteworthy. Other than that, many politicians with Chinese origin were active in those days, such as A Hok (the governor of Jakarta)."

Furthermore, Chinese business people are not involved in any political activities in general, and they seldom expressed their political opinions despite the fact they have rather strong ties with China in a practical way. Setiono condemned activities of ethnic Chinese who were not nationalistic. This is because he thought that such acts would cause the suffering of ethnic Chinese as a whole.

Activities in the 2000s

Regarding the 1998 riot, Setiono's opinion on this incident also represented a viewpoint of Peranakan Chinese. For him, this riot that targeted the Chinese was a shock, but also fortunate as this was followed by democratization, where the ethnic Chinese were able to participate in politics. Setiono, an ex-representative of INTI, was keenly aware of the necessity for Chinese to participate in politics in Indonesia.

He also thought that Chinese civilization would be useful for Indonesian people. For example, he had a project to create a new Chinese medicine school. According to him, this idea related to his thought about the ideal relationship between Indonesia and China. Its purposes are, firstly, opening the possibility of alternative medicine, secondly, promoting employment, and finally, sharing China's assets with all Indonesian people, not only the Chinese community.

Meanwhile, although Chinese culture and Chinese philosophy resonate in his thought, China is by no means Setiono's motherland. Rather, he was anxious about excessive Chinese interference into Indonesian politics and ethnic Chinese issues. He thought that Chinese influence could destroy the vulnerable balance between Chineseness and Indonesian nationalism.

China for Peranakan Chinese

Setiono stated that China's presence had a negative impact on the Chinese communities in Indonesia. For example, he referred to the Chinese diplomatic policy which made the position of Chinese communities in Indonesia more complicated such as the dual-nationality problem, or the establishment of the People's Republic of China in 1949 dividing the Chinese community into the supporters of the PRC and the supporters of KMT. This is the unique way of thought of Peranakan Chinese. As a good example, Setiono raised the experience of returned overseas Chinese from Indonesia.

After Indonesia's independence, Chinese nationality became a problem based on the Sunario (Minister for Foreign Affairs)–Zhou

Enlai agreement at the time of the Asia–Africa Conference in 1955. This agreement aimed at elimination of dual nationalities of Chinese in Indonesia. Zhou Enlai also thought that Chinese in Indonesia should acquire Indonesian nationality and be integrated into Indonesian society.

This agreement decided that all Chinese had to acquire Indonesian nationality again after forsaking Chinese nationality and clarifying their national status. Siauw Giok Tjhan objected to the Indonesian nationality acquisition system. Before this agreement, the Chinese were accepted as Indonesian nationality unless they themselves abandoned Indonesian nationality of their own accord. Siauw protested "why do the Chinese living in Indonesia for many generations have to acquire Indonesian nationality, it is quite obvious. The Indonesian government should accept such Chinese (at least Peranakan Chinese) as Indonesian nationals." However, Sunario had the opinion that Chinese have to pass more rigid procedures to get Indonesian nationality.

Other than the problem of their nationality, many Chinese encountered the nationalization of economy. Many Dutch companies and factories were confiscated by the Indonesian state, and Chinese business was also restricted strictly because Chinese were regarded as foreigners. In this period, the restriction of economic activities on foreign nationals prevailed. In particular, the presidential degree (PP10) in 1959 damaged Chinese business in local area. Chinese business in small villages was prohibited and Chinese were expelled from their home towns by military forces to the cities. In such a situation, many followers of Chinese socialism chose to go to China.

The Chinese government saw this situation as an opportunity to attract Chinese in Indonesia and sent numerous ships to help them get to China. Many Peranakan Chinese, although even their parents might not have been to China, went to China. However, the reality of China was completely different from what they had imagined and expected. Suffering in age of the Cultural Revolution in China, many of them went to Hong Kong in the 1970s.

Conclusion

Setiono's thoughts are an example of the thinking of the many Peranakan Chinese in Indonesia, positioning themselves in Indonesian nationalism while balancing this nationalism with their "Chineseness." To the Peranakan Chinese, China is just a foreign country after all. However, there is a consciousness of belonging to Chinese civilization. Apart from that, bitter experiences led Peranakan Chinese to become careful about expressing Pro-China arguments outright. This excessive sensitiveness is a characteristic of the ethnic Chinese in Indonesia.

References

Liu, Hong. 2011. *China and Shaping of Indonesia, 1949–1965*, Singapore: NUS Press.
Nagura, Kyoko. 2012. *Kikoku kakyo*, Tokyo: Fukyosha.
Peterson, Glen. 2011. *Overseas Chinese in the People's Republic of China*, Routledge.
Pramoedya, Ananta Toer. 1998. *Hoakiau di Indonesia*, Jakarta: Penerbit Garba Budaya. (Chinese in Indonesia)
Sadayoshi, Yasushi. 2016. *Kajin no indonesia gendaishi: haruka na kokumin tougou e no michi*, Tokyo: Bokutakusha.
Setiono, Benny G. 2003. *Tionghoa dalam Pusaran Politik*, Jakarta: Elkasa (Chinese in Political Turmoil).
Siauw, Giok Tjhan. 2010. *Renungan Seorang Patriot Indonesia Siauw Giok Tjhan*, Jakarta: Lembaga Kajian Sinergi Indonesia (A Reflection on an Indonesian patriot Siauw Giok Tjhan).
Siauw, Tiong Djin. 1999. *Siauw Giok Tjhan: Perjuangan Seorang Patriot Indonesia Membangun Nasion Indonesia dan Masyarakat Binneka Tunggal Ika*, Jakarta: Hasta Mitra (Siauw Giok Tjhan: The Struggle of an Indonesian patriot for the Indonesian Nation).
Zhou, Taomo. 2012. Book Review on Liu Hong, China and Shaping of Indonesia, 1949–1965, *The China Quarterly* 212: 1140–1142.
Zhou, Taomo. 2014. China and the Thirtieth of September Movement, *Indonesia* 98: 29–58.
Zhou, Taomo. 2015. Ambivalent Alliance: Chinese Policy towards Indonesia, 1960–1965, *The China Quarterly* 221: 208–228.

4

A Long Journey from Chinese-Language Newspaperman to Chinese Specialist: The Oral History from Two Senior Chinese Intellectuals in Thailand

Apiradee Charoensenee

Chinese Section, Faculty of Arts,
Chulalongkorn University, Bangkok, Thailand

This chapter is compiled from the interviews of two experts in the field of Chinese studies in Thailand who have gained their work–life experience through various fields, especially in Chinese newspaper houses where both had been involved for quite a long period of time. This served as a good base for both to enter the academic field in the later part of their lives. This chapter portrays their life paths since early childhood, their Chinese-language learning process, their access to knowledge about China, and their contributions to the academic field of Chinese studies in Thailand. The analysis of factors that brought both of them to the scholastic fields at present is also provided.

Introduction

Newspaper is the bridge to link people with the daily movement of society. Chinese newspapers also play this important role. However, the Chinese newspaper in Thailand is more than that: it not only provides the current situation and culture of Thai to overseas Chinese living in Thailand, but also brings them up-to-date political, economic, and cultural news of China. It is an important means to connect people, and people who work in the newspaper business, especially newspapermen, are an important source of news and inside information. This information directs thoughts and attitudes of Chinese people toward Thailand's existing circumstances, and also enables the overseas Chinese keep abreast with happenings in China.

The Chinese newspaper industry in Thailand has a long history. *Han Jing Yue Pao*, the first Chinese newspaper in Thailand that supported the Chinese monarchy, was formally established by a group of young overseas Chinese in 1905 (Chansiri 2006: 208). After this, the status of Chinese newspapers in Thailand changed according to the political and economic circumstances, and the relationship between Thailand and China. Disphol (2006) divided the history of Chinese newspaper in Thailand into six periods, reflecting the relationship between Thailand and China and the changing roles of Chinese newspaper in Thailand:

1. 1905–1925: The era of discord between Chinese newspapers who supported the Chinese Communists and those who supported the Chinese Republicans.
2. 1925–1938: The period of market expansion of Chinese newspapers in Thailand.
3. 1939–1943: The dark period of Chinese newspapers in Thailand, due to the concern of the spread of Chinese communism in Thailand.
4. 1944–1958: The golden years of Chinese newspaper in Thailand, with support from the Chinese overseas.

5. 1959–1970: The downturn period of Chinese newspapers in Thailand, due to the close control of the Thai government on the content printed in the newspapers and a decline in the number of people literate in Chinese language in Thailand.
6. 1970–present: A competitive period (Chansiri 2006: 209–213).

We can see that Chinese newspaper houses in Thailand confronted many changes, with distinct characteristics in each period, reflecting the changing political circumstances and the changing relations between Thailand and China. The downturn period of the Chinese newspaper industry in Thailand between 1959 and 1970 was caused by the decision to close the Chinese schools and newspaper houses in 1939 during Phibulsongkhram's reign (Suryandinata 1997: 240). This restriction led to the absence of information from China for a period. The people who were literate in Chinese language and could reach this kind of information were the Chinese-language newspapermen. When China opened its doors in 1978, this attracted much interest from all over the world. Chinese studies in Thailand gradually gained importance and popularity, but there were only few people who had in-depth knowledge of China. Chinese-language newspapermen played a very important role during this period of shortage, filling the information gap. Therefore, understanding China from the point of view of this group of people is significant, making them interesting subjects for the interview.

This chapter is based on the interviews of Sawai Wisavanan and Praphruet Sukolrattanamethi. It draws upon their encounters and choices that led to the development of their individual intellectual paths to be Chinese specialists and contributors to China studies in Thailand, by firstly presenting their life histories in chronological order, including their early childhood, education, work life, and academic contributions. The chapter then makes an analysis and comparison of the two intellectual paths of these China specialists, presenting the significant roles that each of them has played in increasing the knowledge and understanding of China in Thailand.

Life Histories of Sawai and Praphruet

Sawai Wisavanan

Early Childhood and Education. Sawai Wisavanan was born in 1932 in Bangkok, Thailand. He began his school life at Sueksawattana School in Bangkok. Since Chinese-language teaching was not allowed in Thailand during his childhood and his parents wanted their children to learn Chinese, they decided to send him and his siblings to Singapore to continue their education. Sawai was around six or seven years old at that time, and the Chinese-learning environment in Singapore provided him an opportunity to start learning the language.

After the Second World War, his house in Thailand was burnt down. His mother lived alone while his father worked as a mechanic on a Thai government ship that transported rice and plants to harbors in Singapore. This mission resulted from the agreement made between Great Britain and Thailand stating that Thailand, as the defeated country, had to pay reparations to Great Britain. When his father arrived in Singapore, he told Sawai about their family situation and wanted him, the youngest child, to go back home. So Sawai returned to Thailand when he was nearly 15 years old.

With some knowledge of Chinese, he enrolled in Chong Hua College (Thai-Chinese Chamber of Commerce) when it was founded in around 1947. He continued his Chinese-language learning in Thailand at this school. At that time, Li Tiezheng (李铁铮), the first Chinese ambassador in Thailand, requested that Chinese children in Thailand should have the opportunity to learn the Chinese language fully using the China system from the beginning and should study the Thai language only partly. Consequently, many schools of this kind appeared in Thai society, and some taught only in Chinese. The then Thai government claimed that this new kind of school was violating the Private Schools Act. While this issue was under prolonged negotiation, these schools continued their full-fledged schooling. Many Chinese children were still able to study in these kind of schools because the negotiation carried on for many years. Chinese schooling was forbidden, but the children learned the language anyway. Most of the teachers came from National Southwestern Associated University (西南联大) in Kunming, Yunnan Province. In terms of the cultural aspect, especially education, this was the first time that such an opportunity had presented itself for Chinese children who had been disconnected from Chinese cultural and educational influence. In the post-war period, Chinese-language learning spread extensively in Thailand. Intellectuals of Chinese origin, especially those who had graduated from National Southwestern Associated University, played an important role in teaching the Chinese language.[1] This was a great opportunity for Chinese descendants to learn more about China. The environment not only made Sawai and his peers excited about China-related matters, but also nurtured the spirit of Sinoism and nationalism in them. Some young people even wanted to go to China to study and do something good for their motherland.

However, after the Communist Party in China won in 1949, and the Field Marshal Plaek Phibunsongkhram led a *coup d'état* to become the Prime Minister of Thailand, Chinese schools were treated very strictly and had to comply with the Private Schools Act which required legal registration of all private schools. Chinese schools could teach Chinese language for only five hours per week (Manomaivibool 2550: 69). Some schools were even shut down because they were considered leftist or communist. After encountering pressure from the schools being closed, the Chinese teachers used the small-group teaching approach which allowed Sawai and other students to continue their Chinese studies by secretly learning in different houses. In spite of all the difficulties, the youngsters were more eager to learn about China.

Work Life, Significant Works, and Academic Contributions. Sawai completed secondary education from the Chong Hua College when he was around 20 years old. After graduation, he was trained as a Turner in Bangrak District in Bangkok. The average apprentice took three years to finish training, but, with his arithmetic ability, it took him only a year and a half. After finishing the training, he started

---

[1] From notes of Wong jongjaiharn's interview with Sawai Wisavanan.

working as a Turner at the Thai Navigation Company in the repair dock. However, he did not work there for long. When some people found out that he knew Chinese, they suggested he work at the *Guanghua Daily* (光华日报) newspaper.

At first, his duty at *Guanghua Daily* was to translate Thai news into Chinese. He did it well, and was later promoted to the Reporter position. With his interest in political news, he joined other Thai reporters to report from the Government House. Every morning, the group of reporters met at the Government Public Relations Department and was informed about the location as well as the time of the Cabinet meeting. Besides politics, Sawai was also interested in economics. After establishing a relationship with the officials in the Ministry of Commerce, he then became a part of the public relations media for the Ministry.

In addition to local news, the press circle was also interested in news about China. The newspaper tried to report the situation in Mainland China, and Sawai was the one who monitored and kept up with the news. One of the most exciting news for him was when China, as a member of the United Nations, sent their representatives to an international conference on media held by the United Nations. It was a big news that people were very interested in at that time.

After working at *Guanghua Daily* for 30 years, Sawai got an offer from the Bangkok Bank. He started his public relations career there, first as a part-timer and then as a full-time employee. His duties were to translate public relations news and deliver the reports in Chinese. While working at the bank, he also worked as a columnist. Since the Chinese newspaper stopped publishing the evening edition, he could work there one or two hours a day after his day work at the bank. The two jobs greatly benefited his China study and allowed him to apply his knowledge of the Chinese language to translate documents.

With its impressive Chinese public relations campaigns, the Bangkok Bank was recognized by several important organizations, for example, Chinese Government and Chinese Embassy. When the Bank invited experts to give presentations or when China wanted the Bank to be the middleman in dealing with the Bank of Thailand, Sawai had to act as their interpreter. He had to practice spontaneous translation in matters relating to economics and finance. Following this, many Chinese newspapers invited him to write analytical columns about economics, finance, marketing, and stock trading. Working at the Bangkok Bank allowed him to develop his Chinese studies system. While researching on China's economics and finance, which was necessary to his work, he also examined the political aspect as it was related to the others.

As Chatri Sophonphanich, the Chairman, anticipated the importance of China, he instructed the Bank to develop China-related human resources, form a working group, set up an office, and establish the department. Sawai was gradually promoted from Head of the group to Chief of the office, and then to Assistant Manager of the department. However, in practice, he handled most of the department's Chinese-language matters because the Department Manager, Chatri's secretary, had many other responsibilities. This provided Sawai a chance to contact Chulalongkorn University and get to know Professor Khien Theeravit. Professor Khien later asked Sawai, in advance, to fully assist him at the Chinese Studies Center after Sawai's retirement from the Bangkok Bank. This request, in addition to Sawai's passion for this kind of work, was the reason why he decided to work at the Center.

The Chinese Studies Center is a part of Chulalongkorn University's Asian Studies Center (Institute of Asian Studies). Since the beginning, Sawai worked there as a Senior Researcher. His duties included conducting research, attending Chinese Studies seminars, and following and collecting information about China's politics, economy, and relationship with other countries, especially those in Asia. This information would be used for writing articles to be published in the Center's newsletter, "Chinese Studies News," and publicized on the Center's website. In addition, Sawai also held roles as a Deputy Director of the Center and a member of the managing committee.

In the aspect of academic contributions, Sawai has done much research on various aspects of Chinese studies, such as in the field of economics, history, and education. One of his achievements was the research on Teochew people in Thailand, a collaborative project between the Institute of Asian Studies and the Institute for Research on SEA History at the University of Zhongshan (中山大学), China. It was the first initiative in academic relations, especially at the university level, after the Sino-Thai relationship was newly established. His first academic project series, in which he was one of the researchers and the translator, was published in the form of a research report titled "Chaochin Taechio nai prathetthai lae nai phum lamnao doem thi chaosan samai thi neung tharuea changlin 1767–1850" (The Teochiu Chinese in Thailand and in the Native Land at Chaoshan, the First Period, Zhanglin Port 1767–1850). In this report, Sawai was a translator of "Kan obphayob ma prathedthai khong chao choenghai" (The Migration to Thailand of Chenghai People). He also presented his article, "Botbat khong chaochin chuanglang tham sonthisanya baoring" (The Role of Chinese People after Signing in Bowring's Treaty), in "Chaochin Taechio nai prathedthai lae nai phum lamnao doem thi chaosan samai thi song tharuea santho 1860–1949" (The Teochiu Chinese in Thailand and in the Native Land at Chaoshan: The Second Period, Xantou Port 1860–1949). This project series was presented while he was working at Bangkok Bank.

Sawai was also a part of the research team working on the origin of Thai people in collaboration with Yunnan University. There had been many theories proposing the origin of the Thais. Some scholars said that Thai people were driven out of Tibet. Some said that they were originally Thai, and did not come from anywhere else.[2] However, the most accepted theory was that the ancient kingdom of Nanchao (present-day Dali) used to be the Thai state. This part of the history still holds and no amendment has been made.[3] Sawai translated an article about this topic, which was "Thin kamneod chonchat thai jak lakthan chin (The Origin of Thai People from Evidence in Chinese documents)."

---

[2] Interview with Sawai Wisavanan.
[3] Ibid.

The third project was the Chinese Studies Center's research on the role of Chinese in Thailand's development between 1910 and 1960. The research was conducted on a wide range of topics, for example, politics, economy, culture, and education. The output was two books titled *Mr. Xie Guang* and *Luk Chin Rak Chat*. The latter one, written by Chao Phongphichit, was about the Chinese role in Thai politics from 1910 to 1960. During that period, the Beijing government summoned their officials in Thailand to return to China to help build the new nation. The book discusses the most important issue of the period: of anti-Japanese sentiment in China when they tried to use resources in Thailand to support the resistance against Japan in their country.[4] However, it became a problem after Japan's occupation of Thailand. The anti-Japanese volunteer army was set up and joined with the Seri Thai or the Free Thai Movement.

Furthermore, Sawai also conducted research on Thai-Chinese tourism, as it was presented in "Saphab lae panha kan thongthiaw rawang thai kab chin" (Tourism Situations and its Problems between Thai and China). This research reflected the problems existing in the tourism business between Thailand and China, which needed immediate attention. Sawai wrote many articles about Chinese economy, such as "Thun thai nai krasae kan patirub setthakit chin" (Thai Funds in Economic Revolution in China), and translated many books relating to stock trading from Chinese into Thai.

In addition, Sawai also conducted the study on Chinese newspapers in Thailand supported by the Singsean newspaper fund of 100,000 Baht, and a cooperative research between Thailand and China on Chinese schooling in Thailand. Around 2011, he joined the Board of Investment's (BOI) project on Thailand's investment opportunities in the southeastern part of China, with a focus on China's food quality monitoring system and their import and export regulations.

In addition to the research projects above, Sawai was also engaged in Chinese education in Thailand. He was Deputy Chairman of a committee that wrote and compiled the textbook for

---

[4] *Ibid.*

Chinese-language for the Klai Kang Won television station for distance learning via satellite and was a special lecturer on Chinese political economics in the postgraduate classes at Rangsit University.

It is obvious that Chinese-language has always been an important tools helping Sawai make his living. Together with his eagerness to learn and seek out knowledge about China, he got many opportunities in various jobs to provide benefits to society. His experience and knowledge gathered through his work life also contribute tremendously to research on Chinese studies in academic society.

Praphruet Sukolrattanamethi

Early Childhood and Education. Praphruet Sukolrattanamethi was born in 1938 in Phetchburi Province, western part of Thailand. Since it was the period of World War II, he did not go to school until when the War was over and the situation was almost back to normal.

In 1949, Guangzhong Chinese school (光中学校) was set up, where Praphruet went for his schooling. At this time, schools were not part of any set system prescribed by the government. Once he had been there for a year, the Ministry of Education ordered schools to hold Grade 4 examinations. So the school had to find children to sit in the exams. Praphruet happened to be in the second batch of the pupils, being in the second year. The school had him study in the Grade 4 level and, luckily, he managed to pass but with fragmentary knowledge. His knowledge of the basics was not at all strong and he barely managed to pass the exams.

After Grade 4, Chinese language was no longer taught at the school. So Praphruet studied it at night. During the day he helped his father with his work at his family business, which was a brick factory.

Praphruet had had to help out at the factory since he was a little over 10 years old. This was the practice in every Chinese family during the period. The sons were put to work early on in the family trade.[5] During vacations they were not allowed to go anywhere. They had to help at home or in the shop.

---

[5] Manomaivibool's notes of interview with Praphruet Sukolrattanamethi.

Praphruet went to evening school for three years. It was a two-year syllabus, but he failed and had to repeat for one more year. As he was working during the day, he would often feel exhausted and sleepy in the evening and could not concentrate on his studies. In those days, everyone had to repeat the whole year if they failed even in one subject, even by just one mark. Praphruet was just one point short in the natural science exam. So, it took him three years to complete junior high school. He continued working with his father for another few years. His friends were going to tutorial school, so he went along with them to a temple school nearby where they were given tutorial classes for non-school education. When Matthayom 3 or Grade 9 exam was approaching, he took leave from his father's business in order to prepare for it. He studied alone for a couple of weeks, reviewing the lessons in the temple grounds and other places. He was one of the few in the province to pass the exam. After completing Grade 9, Praphruet continued to help his father at work.

Then, around 1960–1961, he got the idea of teaching Chinese. As per the rules of the Ministry of Education one had to have a certificate to teach Chinese,[6] so Praphruet took the certificate exam and qualified. But then, when he applied to become a teacher, there were some problems with the name on his certificate. So, he retook the Chinese-language exam and went on to become a Chinese-language teacher.

Praphruet's first posting as a Chinese-language teacher was at Nakhon Sawan province in central Thailand. He stayed with his uncle and taught basic Chinese to children of every age. In his second year there, the school celebrated its twentieth anniversary. They wanted to issue a Chinese magazine for which teachers had to contribute articles. And so Praphruet started to write for the first time. After working there for two semesters, his father wanted him to come home to Petchburi to help him take care of things. So Praphruet came back and taught at Guangzhong Chinese School in Petchburi for almost three years. Then, he told his parents he wanted to go back to school because he was 20 years old and his

---

[6] *Ibid.*

Grade 9 certificate was not accepted due to the wrong spelling of his name.

Praphruet then went to Bangkok and stayed at his grandfather's home at Songwat, near Chinatown, and took the Grade 9 exams right away for the second time. Then he went to tutorial schools in order to take the Matthayom 6 or Grade 12 examinations. He studied at Wat Suthat, a very famous tutorial school at that time, for quite a while. He took English classes almost everyday. After about eight months it was examination time. This meant he had had eight months altogether to learn English before he took Grade 12 level exams, and he did pass the exam. The reason why he passed the exam was very interesting. Praphruet told us he passed because he knew Chinese. He looked for Chinese books that taught English. There were a lot of Chinese scholars and professors who were very good at English and had written books on how to master the language. He just followed the instructions.

After that, he started preparing for Matthayom 8. This time he had more time, about 15 months. He developed a new tactic and decided to concentrate on English only. He studied in every possible way.

When he had passed Matthayom 8, the next step was to take the university entrance examination, which was three to four months away. He went to a tutorial school to prepare. Finally, he got into Faculty of Accountancy at Chulalongkorn University and was among the top rank-holders, too. He also got a scholarship. He studied in the Faculty for a year. But Praphruet found it awfully hard because the level of Math was a continuation of Matthayom 8, consisting of algebra and geometry, subjects he had no foundation in. Praphruet then switched and retook the entrance exam, and got into the Department of Law at the Faculty of Political Science at Chulalongkorn University instead.

In late 1950s and early 1960s, while being a Law student, Praphruet wrote four or five stories in total and published them in Chinese newspapers, such as *Tai Jing Nan Chiang* (泰京南强) and *Mangu Xinwen*, under the penname "Kongxuan (孔宣)," "Chenshan (陈珊)."

Work Life, Significant Works and Academic Contributions. When he graduated in 1970, Praphruet started working at the *Dongnan*

Daily (东南日报) newspaper in the editorial section. He translated domestic news, politics and other things into Chinese.

After a while there, he realized that he could not continue further because he was working during the day as well. He was already working in the marketing section at Southeast Insurance company. After working for two years, he left this company. Then he worked at the Bank of Asia in the Public Relations department for almost a year.

When the Law Office of Dr. Ukrit Mongkholanawin, a famous lawyer in Thailand, was about to open, they sent a few people to ask Praphruet to join them in the Chinese section. He thought it was a good idea to make use of Chinese language for law, which was his field of study.

When he joined the Law Office, he mostly did scholastic work such as writing textbooks about law, most of which were originally written in Thai. He worked there from 1970 or 1971 until the year 1977.

In the meantime, Praphruet started working for the newspapers once more. He joined *Xin Zhong Yuan*, a newly established company that began by adopting the name of its former *Zhong Yuan* newspaper. It was known as the "newly opened Xin Zhong Yuan (新中原)." He worked as a Deputy News Editor, and later on went on to become the Deputy Chief Editor at *Zhong Yuan* newspaper (中华日报).

Praphruet also assisted Thanin Kraivixien, the then Prime Minister, to start up a Thai daily newspaper, *The Chao Phraya* newspaper, but only nine issues had been published when the *coup d'état* took place in October 1977. They had to shut down the newspaper because they simply had no budget since their finance had been from the central government budget.

Much later, Praphruet set up his own attorney office with some friends. It was an independent business and lasted for more than 10 years.

In the aspect of academic contributions, Praphruet was involved in Chinese education at the higher education level. This came about one day when Praphruet went to Huachiaw University to participate in an activity there and he coincidentally met Professor Prasit Kowilaikul, the President of the university, who invited him to join the university. Praphruet has been at this university since the year 2001. In the beginning, he taught Chinese language and literature at the Chinese Department. Later, the President appointed him as the President's Assistant for Chinese Studies and also the Director of the Teocheow Studies Center. Besides teaching, Praphruet also composed a series of Chinese textbooks for Thai people in 2007, namely "Khonthai rian phasachin 1–4 (Thai people study Chinese)." This series aims to teach Mandarin Chinese to all Thai people interested in learning the language. With regards to his contribution to Chinese studies research in Thailand, Praphruet wrote many articles on various aspects. When he was part of a committee conducting a research on Thai history as was written in Chinese papers, he demonstrated his profound ability in the Chinese language through two articles. One of the two was "Phrarachasan mueangchin jorsor 1144" (The Royal Message from China, Chulasakarat 1144[7]) where he described the Chinese diplomatic words most lucidly. Furthermore, as a specialist in ancient Chinese language, he was also selected to translate "Ekkasan rachasamnak chin kiawkab rachakan Somdet Phraphuthayodfa" (Document from the Royal Court of China about the Reign of King Rama I). The two articles appeared in "Prawatsat parithat phiphit niphon choedchukiat pontho Damnoen Lekhakul nueangnai okad mi ayukhrob 84 pi" (In the Shadow of History: Essays in Honor of Lieut. Gen. Damnoen Lekhakul on the Occasion of His 84th Birth Anniversary) (Phongsiphian 1999: Preface).

Praphruet was also a member of the Committee for Chinese Studies Center, Institute of Asian Studies, Chulalongkorn University, and in 1983 when the Thailand Chinese Writers Association was established, he took the responsibility as Vice Chairman there. During his membership in the Committee for Chinese Studies Center, Praphruet, in cooperation with Duan Lisheng, a Chinese specialist in Thai history, wrote a chapter on the topic "Ekasan boran khong chin ti kiawkab prathedthai (Chinese Classical Papers about Thai History)," and also translated an article of Duan Lisheng. These two academic researches were listed in a book titled *Phlik ton trakun thai* (History of the Thai Ancestor), which is a good resource for scholars in this field.

---

[7] One kind of traditional Thai calendar system, it is year 1782. เท่ากับค.ศ. 1782.

Praphruet's present work, the one he has been involved with lately, is a great contribution to people of the next generation. As a representative of Huachiaw University, Praphruet signed a contract with Ministry of Culture to digitize the Chinese newspapers preserved in the Thai National Library. The earliest Chinese newspaper in Thailand is *Tianhan Gongbao*. It was established in 1918, almost 100 years ago. The Printing Act at that time required that two copies of all publications had to be submitted to the National Library. Chinese people always obey the law, so they submitted entirely, or almost entirely, everything they published. Praphruet thinks this is a project worth taking up, as he thinks we have to start to preserve them; otherwise, one day, all of them would be thrown away.[8] There are altogether over two million pages to scan, and the oldest issue is almost 100 years old. As of now they have finished the first phase, which is newspapers from 1918 to 1986. This is more than half of the newspapers, and the process costed millions of Baht. The scanned records will be kept in Thai National Library and also in Huachiaw University Library. He also serves Princess Maha Chakri Sirindhorn, as one of the translators of some of her books, such as *Treading the Dragon Country* and *Sra Pathum's Palace Kitchen*, as well as serving her in other tasks.

It is seen that Praphruet's profound understanding of Chinese language not only throws new light on China, but also serves to be the bridge for Chinese people to experience some quality writing pieces from Thailand.

Analysis

Sawai and Praphruet were both born in the same decade, i.e., 1930s. While Sawai was born in the early years of the decade, in 1932, Praphruet was born in the latter years of the decade, in 1938. It was the World War II period and the political situation in the world was changing dramatically, which had many effects on China's role in the world and also in Thailand. At that time, learning of Chinese

---

[8] Manomaivibool's notes of interview with Praphruet Sukolrattanamethi.

language was prohibited in Thailand, and Chinese schools were controlled by the Thai government. But nowadays, China plays a very significant role. Mandarin Chinese has already been made one of the official languages of the United Nations. The "Chinese Fever" has spread all over the world. The governments of many countries including Thailand encourage people to study Chinese. Sawai and Praphruet have experienced these changes. Their contact with Chinese language came at an early age, directly from their family backgrounds, as both of them grew up in a Chinese family, although Sawai was born in a Chinese community in Bangkok while Praphruet was born in the province of Petchburi. There were other differences, too. Sawai was sent to Singapore by his parents to begin his education there in Chinese, because Chinese language was not allowed in Thailand at that time. The Chinese learning environment in Singapore provided Sawai with a good opportunity to build a firm foundation and learn the language well. Praphruet, born in Petchburi province, began his Chinese education there. Since his family ran their own business, they wanted Praphruet to remain there to help take care of the business. When Chinese was no longer taught in Thailand, Praphruet, who had to take care of the business by day, began a self-study program on Chinese language by night. A few years later, following some problems in Sawai's family, he returned to Thailand and continued his education at Chonghua College, where he could pursue his Chinese education. As for Praphruet, he chose to go to a school following the Thai education system. When he was older, he moved to Bangkok and took many courses in a tutorial school for the university entrance examination, twice, before finally joining the Department of Law, at the Faculty of Political Science, Chulalongkorn University. From the early account of their lives, it can be seen that their family backgrounds had a direct influence on their learning of Chinese language. The fact that they were being educated in Chinese schools from their early childhood for several years helped them build a strong foundation on knowledge on China, and this proved a great asset for both of them at later stages of their lives.

When they began their work life, both chose different paths, but there were many similarities. Sawai began his career as a Turner in

Bangkok. But when people found that he knew Chinese, he was invited to work at the *Guanghua Daily* newspaper as a translator, and he was eventually promoted to the Reporter position. His 30 years of work experience in this field made him an expert in Chinese studies. When the executives at Bangkok Bank found an opportunity to invest in China, they asked Sawai to work for them in the Public Relations department. Here, Sawai used Chinese language skills and his own knowledge of China to analyze China's economic situation and to build a strategy to attract Chinese customers.

As for Praphruet, he began his work life in the newspaper industry. He was a translator at *Dongnan Daily* newspaper. Simultaneously, he was also working in the marketing section at Southeast Insurance company. Like Sawai, Praphruet even engaged in the Public Relations department at the Bank of Asia for a while. As Praphruet had graduated in the field of Law, there was a period of his life when he worked in Law offices, one of which was the Law office of Ukrit Mongkholanawin, and he also set up a Law office of his own later in life. In the meantime, Praphruet not only worked for a Chinese newspaper, but also worked for the Thai Newspaper *Chao Phraya* when Thanin Kraiwixien was the Prime Minister.

Since both these men were engaged with Chinese newspapers for a long time, especially during the period when Thai people could not access any information about China directly, they proved invaluable as sources of information about China to the Chinese living in Thailand. Both Sawai and Praphruet had good qualifications for being newspapermen. One of the qualifications needed is to be enthusiastic and very good at searching for information. With their high proficiency in Chinese language and profound knowledge on China, when they walked into the academic world and had to work on many research projects, these qualities lead them to great success. When they accepted to work for the Chinese Studies Center at Chulalongkorn University, the two intellectuals were opportunely placed to provide the overseas Chinese with the information they missed about China and lead them to new aspects of Chinese Studies in Thailand. They presented a new point of view about China, like from the research about Thailand's history from Chinese papers. This kind of research needs people who know Chinese language in depth and are interested in history. Sawai and Praphruet can present their views very well in this field, both in the form of research papers with Chinese scholars and also in the form of translations. This can broaden the view about China among Thai people.

Besides research works, Sawai and Praphruet also made great contributions to Chinese education in Thailand. They played different roles in this field. Sawai was a lecturer in the field of China's economy at Rangsit University, while Praphruet has been involved in Chinese education at Huachiaw University since 2001.

Conclusion

This chapter, based on the oral interviews of the two Chinese specialists in Thailand, analyzes the acquisition of their Chinese language and knowledge on China, their experience in Chinese Studies, and their works and contributions in academic research. Their life history is a good illustration of how Chinese language plays an important role in their work life: they began their careers in different fields, however both ended up working in Chinese newspaper houses as newspapermen and greatly contributed to China studies after their retirement. Sawai and Praphruet are Chinese descendants. They had the opportunity to learn Chinese language since their childhood. This inspired them to know more about China. Their eagerness to understand China from every aspect and their career paths have together cultivated their expertise in Chinese studies. Their contributions to the academic world after their retirement, therefore, are meaningful to the Chinese studies in Thailand. Both have delivered researches that open up new aspects of Chinese studies in Thailand, increase awareness of Chinese Studies in Thailand, and also serve as inspiration to young researchers in Thailand. As Sawai said in an interview, "the objective of my research is to establish what the Chinese Studies in Thailand should study. I have tried to show the overall picture of Chinese Studies in Thailand, so you can see the problem and how to establish your goal."[9]

---

[9] Wongjongjaiharn, "Notes of interview with Sawai Wisavanan."

References

Chansiri, Disaphol. 2006. *Overseas Chinese in Thailand: A Case Study of Chinese Émigrés in Thailand in the Twentieth Century* (Doctoral thesis). United States, Massachusetts: Tufts University.

Manomaivibool, Prapin. 2014. Unpublished notes of Interview with Praphuet Sukolrattanamethi on March 19 and April 23.

Manomaivibool, Prapin. 2007. Phattanakan khong kanrian kanson phasachinnai prathedthai. *Journal of Letters, Faculty of Arts, Chulalongkorn University* 36(2): 64–82.

Phongsiphian, Winai. 1999. *Prawatsat parithat phiphit niphon choedchukiat pontho Damnoen Lekhakul nueangnai okad mi ayukhrob* 84 pi.

Suryandinata, Leo. 1997. *Ethnic Chinese as Southeast Asians: From Siamese Chinese to Chinese-Thai*. Singapore: Institute of Southeast Asia Studies.

Wongjongjaiharn, Metta. 2012. Unpublished notes of Interview with Sawai Wisavanan on July 9–10.

Part II

National Perspectives

5

Sourcing Contemporary Vietnam's Intellectual History in Russia: Sciences, Arts, and Sinology

Cong Tuan DINH
Institute for European Studies
Vietnam Academy of Social Sciences, Vietnam

The influence of Soviet Union on Vietnamese Chinese studies is strong and impressive. It has had a significant impact on the development of Chinese studies in Vietnam. The Soviet Union influences Vietnam's development in many fields and sectors such as training, teaching and social sciences. This preliminary research shows that the Soviet Union/Russia's influence (both direct and indirect) and its unique legacy remain evident and impressive in various fields, including economic, political, cultural, and social sectors, in Vietnam society currently. In this chapter, I will focus on three main points: firstly, I make a sketch the Soviet Union/Russian Federation's influence on Vietnam's development (after the establishment of diplomatic relations since 1950 in the two countries); secondly, I highlight the influence of Soviet Union/Russia on Vietnamese Chinese Studies; and thirdly, I express the Soviet Union/Russia–Vietnam scientific cooperation and collaboration in the field of Sinology/Chinese Studies.

Introduction

Literature has not attended to the Russian influences on Vietnamese academics in general, as well as the specific influences of Russian scholarship on Vietnamese Sinology. Vietnamese Sinology is assumed to be primarily indebted to its Chinese sources in the long shared intellectual history that constitutes Chinese and Vietnamese humanities. Yet, Russian influences have comprehensively reached the science and humanities disciplines, and the Russian input in Vietnamese Sinology is significant.

Thus, this chapter first presents some of the Soviet Union/later Russia's positive influences on Vietnam's development (in politics, the socio-cultural field, education and training, social sciences, as well as humanities) during a long history and tradition of cooperation and friendship between the two countries. Then, this chapter highlights some legacies reflected in Vietnam's development on Chinese studies. The Soviet Union/Russian influences are not only ideological and political, but also scientific and methodological.

The Soviet Union/Russian Federation's Influence on Vietnam's Development (After the Establishment of Diplomatic Relations Since 1950 in the Two Countries)

Vietnam is a multi-cultural country situated in South East Asia. During different historical periods, it has undergone the acculturation of some other cultures, namely, China, France, the Soviet Union/Russia Federation, the US, and Europe.

Since the establishment of diplomatic relations (in 1950), the Soviet Union/Russian Federation has strongly supported and exerted positive multifaceted influences on Vietnam's political, economic, and socio-cultural development. In the same year (1950), the governments of Vietnam and China (PRC) also established diplomatic relations. The Soviet Union/Russian Federation has strongly supported Vietnam in the fields of education and training, natural and social sciences, scientific collaboration, academic exchanges, and research activities. Thus, Vietnam's scientific basis has been gradually established and further developed.

On the political front, since the beginning of the 1920s, President Ho Chi Minh (1890–1969), named as Nguyen Ai Quoc during the period of his revolutionary activities abroad, and the first generation of Vietnamese communists had their contacts with Russia when they attended various training courses at the Communist School for Oriental Worker Movement in Moscow (1923–1933). During this time, Nguyen Ai Quoc and his comrades had familiarized themselves with and studied the theories of Marxism–Lenism from the Russian Communist Party and obtained broad socialist revolutionary ideas and thoughts for Vietnam's national liberation and independence from the existing old feudalism and the French colonial regime. Nguyen Ai Quoc was inspired by these revolutionary ideas and thoughts and wrote many important political works. Among them is the "Brief Main Theoretical Guidelines for Vietnam's Revolution Platform." Many other contemporary comrades of Ho Chi Minh also joined these training courses and produced many historically important documents.[1]

On the cultural aspect, the Vietnam–Russia cultural contact and exchange had started as early as the 1940s. During this period, Vietnam was still under semi-feudal and French colonial regime. Moreover, many popular classical and modern cultural works written by some Russian authors had appeared in Vietnamese society through various translations into Vietnamese language from the French and Chinese versions, such as the novels *The Mother* written by Marxism Gorki, *Anna Karenina* by Lev Tolstoi, and *White Nights* by Dostoievsk.

Since Vietnam's August Revolution, in the August of 1945, and the establishment of the Democratic Republic of Vietnam, on

---

[1] Tran Phu (1904–1931), the first secretary of Vietnam's Communist Party, produced a manuscript "Theoretical political guidelines of Vietnam Communist Party." Ha Huy Tap (1906–1941) compiled a manuscript "The Action Plan of Indochina Communist Party" and "Preliminary History of Indochina Communist Party." Other famous pioneers, such as Le Hong Phong (1902–1942) and Nguyen Thi Minh Khai (1910–1941) as revolutionary activists who advocated communist course in the Communist International Organization in Moscow during 1922–1933, wrote many popular articles on the anti-fascist struggles, national salvation, and women's liberation in Vietnam.

September 2, 1946, Vietnam–Russia cultural exchange entered the mainstream and evolved as an important force. Vietnamese contemporary cultural life undergone a strong and positive influence of the Soviet Union/Russian Federation's culture. However, cultural "assimilation" in each development period has evolved with different trends and features. Close cultural exchange between two sides took different forms, ranging from the fields of education and training, literature, cinematography, art-performance, aesthetics, arts, science, and technology to publishing activities, that helped enrich and contribute to Vietnam's contemporary cultural development.

Regarding the field of literature, after the revolution and the establishment of the Democratic Republic of Vietnam, many Soviet Union/Russian Federation's books and works were introduced to a wide audience in Vietnamese society, giving them a chance to enjoy many of Russia's great books and works. These books and works, especially Russian classical literature, were translated into Vietnamese and published in Vietnam.

Owing to such active exchange activities, a wide variety of Vietnamese have had the chance to know and enjoy many of Russia's great works. Many Russian classical and contemporary writers and poets, from Lev Tolstoi, Dostoevski, Puskin, Lermontov, Trekhov, and Gogol to Solokhov, Dumbadze, and Gamzatov, have thus become popular in Vietnam.

This growing Soviet Union/Russia's literature became an important cultural and spiritual source, helping enrich Vietnamese audiences in perceiving Russia's deep beauty, nature, soul, and character. For example, the valuable heritage of the Soviet Union/Russia's literature, Marxist methodologies, and methods of research have remarkably influenced aesthetic perspectives, attitudes, and art-creation methods applied by many Vietnamese artists, scientists, researchers, poets, writers, journalists, and social activists who work in various disciplines and fields.[2]

---

[2] In the literary field, many popular works were written by Nguyen Dinh Thi, To Huu. In the field of research and criticism, various interesting works were presented by Tran Dinh Su, Vuong Tri Nhan, Pham Vinh Cu, Lai Nguyen An, and Do Lai Thuy. In field of linguistics and language research, good publications were written by Nguyen Tai Can, Nguyen Phan Canh, Truong Dong San, and Hoang Tue.

Regarding the field of cinematography and art performance, during the 1950s–1990s, Soviet Union's cinematography, drama, and art performance experts have facilitated Vietnam's cinematography development. When the Vietnam Cinematography University was established in 1959, many famous Soviet Union cinematographers and experts organized training courses for the first generation of Vietnamese students in the country through different filmmaker training projects, and their best results included some films with high distinction, such as *Two Soldiers*, *Chim Vanh Khuyen*, *Kim Dong*, *Sister Tu Hau*, and *Wind Blowing*. Their audience may feel a sense of closeness and the strong influence of the Soviet Union's cinematography style on Vietnamese work and development during that time.

Many filmmakers, especially Vietnam's third-generation filmmakers, are well trained with competencies and skills at the Soviet Union's academic institutions and later return to Vietnam; they have made tremendous progress and produced various good films, which later won prizes at many international film festivals in the Soviet Union/Russia, Germany, Czechoslovakia, France, and the US. Vietnam is proud of its many famous cinematographers, filmmakers, producers, and managers, who have worked hard to promote Vietnamese cultural image through their films to the outside world.[3]

Soviet Union/Russia's drama and art performance also left deep marks on Vietnam's drama and art performance activities. From the 1970s to the 1980s, various drama performances (Soviet Union and Russian classic drama) emerged in Vietnam's drama theaters, where artists showcased popular short classic plays on stage, written by Sekhop, or contemporary plays, such as "Kremlin's Bells," "Platon Krechew," "Khuc thu ba bi trang," and "Vong phan Capcazo."

Regarding the field of music, Tchaikovsky National Music Academy in Moscow is a popular academic institution. Many talented Vietnamese

---

[3] These famous cinematographers are Hai Ninh, Pham Van Khoa, Tran Luan Kim, Bui Dinh Hac, Luan Son, Tran Van Thuy, Le Duc Tien, Banh Chau, Bach Diep, Nguyen Thi Hong Ngat, Dang Nhat Minh, Vuong Duc, Sy Chung, Dinh Tiep, and Pham Nhue Giang.

students had the chance to be well trained and became famous singers, artists, music composers, managers, and professionals.[4]

Russian music, especially traditional music with smooth, emotional, and pleasing melodies and various multi-ethnic folk songs, is a source of inspiration for creative works of generations of Vietnamese musicians and artists. Music theorists and conductors, who were well trained at the Soviet Union/Russia's Academic Music Institution or Philharmonic orchestras, later became key instructors or leaders working at the Vietnam National Musical Academy and creative art and cultural centers throughout the country.

Regarding the field of art performance, Soviet Union/Russia has supported Vietnam to train and build many core art disciplines, such as public artwork, art performance, ballet, contemporary dance, circus, photography, kinetic art, art education, design, and architecture. Many Vietnamese painters who graduated from the Surikov Art School, and ballet or contemporary dancers and photographers trained by the Soviet Union's Academic Art Institutions during different periods, have become key persons or leaders who have actively contributed to and enriched a new image of Vietnam's contemporary art and culture since the outset of Vietnam's socialist nation-state building and through the Vietnam Resistance War against American Imperialism to present time (Shagdaryn 1982a).

Regarding the activities of publishing, printing, and distributing, since 1956, Vietnam has established a regular exchange of books, newspapers, and magazines with the Soviet Union's Books Import–Export (Mezkniga). Some of the Soviet Union's external publishing houses, such as "Progress," "Rainbow," "Peace," "Russian Language," and other culture institutions (Shagdaryn 1982b), had supported Vietnam in language translation and publishing important major anthologies, books, journals, textbooks on various subjects and topics, such as natural sciences, social sciences, humanities, politics, and philosophy, and also contributed dictionaries and

---

[4] The best artists and professionals include Dang Thai Son, Ton Nu Nguyet Minh, Ton That Chiem, Do Hong Quan, Le Dung, Trung Kien, Kieu Hung, Rơ Cham Pheng, Bui Cong Duy, and Tran Thu Ha.

encyclopedias to build a foundation for scientific and information resources, libraries, and knowledge base for Vietnam.

After Soviet Union's disintegration in 1991, the cooperation between Vietnam (SRV) and the Russian Federation faced many challenges. Cultural exchange had even been stalled during the late 1990s. The relationship between the two countries has been revitalized since with the profound changes occurring in the world upon entering the 21st century. Their relationship evolved from the old type of relationship (i.e., between the two former socialist countries with shared values and ideology, friendship, and mutual support) to a new relationship between equals. The Soviet Union and other socialist countries had strongly supported Vietnam with subsidies during the hard resistance war and the country's reunification until 1991. Since then, a new type of partnership, comprehensive strategic cooperation, and mutual benefit has been arranged in the changing context of international integration.

The post-Soviet Russia–Vietnam cultural cooperation and exchange continues to develop. Maintaining annual festivals, "Russia–Vietnam cultural days," and other relevant activities on both sides has contributed to improving the spirit of long-lasting friendship and solidarity among people in the two countries. Russia–Vietnam cultural exchange has been built and developed based on the long-lasting and close friendship between the two countries despite many challenges or difficulties. Even if this friendship was put to test, it continues to be maintained and further developed. The cultural accomplishments created by both sides are highly recognized and appraised.

Soviet Union/Russia's Influence on Vietnamese Chinese Studies

The Soviet Union/Russia Federation has supported the education and training of generations of Vietnamese students, carders, researchers, instructors, and scientists in many social sciences and humanities (i.e., philosophy, education, economics, history, literature, linguistics, ethnology, archeology, geography, sociology, journalism, communication, and international relations), which included Sinology/Chinese studies as a multi-discipline subject in Vietnam.

In the field of education and training alone, during the 50 years of bilateral cooperation (1953–2003), the Soviet Union/Russian Federation had supported the education and training of approximately 50,000 scientific, technological, and socio-cultural Vietnamese workers and officers (approximately 30,000 received a graduate degree, 3,000 received a Ph.D. degree, more than 200 persons received the Doctorate of Sciences degree), and 98,000 technicians, vocational training instructors, and apprentices received training (Nguyen 2016).

The Russian Federation annually supports the field of education and training in Vietnam. The number of annual grants given by the Russian Federation to eligible Vietnamese students has increased to 855. Moreover, approximately 5,000 students were self-financed to study in Russia's academic institutions. Like other students who travel to learn and study in the US, China, and other countries, such as the EU member states, they can learn and be equipped with new knowledge, deeply specialized skills, or modern research methods when enrolling in Russian academic institutions. The reason is that Russia has a long tradition and is popular in the fields of natural and social sciences, with ranks among the top countries in the world. Many well-trained Vietnamese students in the Soviet Union/Russia are influenced by Russia's education and training style; specifically, they often work with strong devotion when they return home. Some of them become key leaders with important positions in the Vietnamese Communist Party or the government as popular scientists and cultural and art professionals.

Since the 1950s, the Soviet Union/Russia had also supported education, opened training courses, and transferred basic knowledge and skills for Vietnamese teachers, instructors, and social sciences and humanity researchers in the field of Chinese studies (short-term and long-term courses). Owing to such strong support and cooperation in social sciences and humanities, Chinese studies have been well positioned and developed in Vietnam.

Russia is popular for its strong tradition of Sinology/Chinese studies in its research and publications. Titarenko (2012) stated that, although the history of old Russia–China relations has lasted for 400 years, the real activities of seeking mutual understanding and cooperation between the two nations only started at the beginning of the 17th century. In 1700, Russia's Tza Pie I issued a decree on the need for studying oriental languages, including China's various languages. Bisurin (1777–1853) was the first Russian scholar who laid the foundation for Chinese studies in the old Russian Empire at the end of the 18th century. Bisurin wrote more than 100 works with encyclopedic value on China. Pablovich (1818–1900) is the first Russian scholar who wrote a history of China's culture and synthesized the history of China's culture with Buddhism. Kafakov (1917–1878) together with Popov (1842–1913) compiled the Chinese–Russian dictionary, translated many exemplary works of ancient Chinese philosophy and culture into the Russian language, and described China's medical achievements and knowledge (Do Tien Sam and Titarenko 2009).

At the beginning of the 19th century, Chinese studies had become a scientific discipline in the Russia Royal Academy of Sciences. The Institute for Oriental Studies in Vladivostok was established in 1899. Other education centers for Chinese studies had been spread out in the Far East region to serve developing trading-economic ties between old Russia and China. A special collection on China is in Asia's Fine Art Museum under the Russian Royal Academy of Sciences. For more than 100 years, the field of Russia's Sinology/Chinese studies has attracted many highly distinguished intellectuals and great minds from the Royal Russia Academy of Sciences to work and research on China's history, economics, culture, medicine, and linguistics (Do Tien Sam and Titarenko 2009).

During the time of the Soviet Union, various academic institutions and research units, specializing in Oriental studies/Chinese studies, had been set up. The Institute of the Oriental Studies under the Soviet Union's Academy of Sciences, including a discipline in Chinese studies, was established in 1966. The Russian-wide Association of Chinese Studies has become an active member of the European Association of Chinese Studies and plays an active role in this field. The Soviet Union/Russia's Chinese Studies are proud of many popular scholars and their creative works.[5]

The Soviet Union's scientists from different fields of social sciences and humanities explore and apply various new scientific research methods and approaches in the area of research. Based on the basic Marxist–Leninist thoughts, theories, and methodologies (especially, dialectical materialism and historical materialism approaches, in combination with concrete specific scientific discipline methods, such as logics, statistics, system–structure, cause–effect, analysis–synthesis, making generalization, comparison, forecast, and interdisciplinary/or cross-disciplinary approaches), the Soviet Union/Russia's social scientists updated and creatively applied them into various academic disciplines, research, and education fields; consequently, various issues of interest in the changing process and concrete historical socio-cultural contexts have been explored.

The Marxist–Leninist fundamentals (philosophical, economic, and moral thoughts), theoretical and practical knowledge, and methodological basis have been passed down through generations of Vietnamese social scientists who have studied at the Soviet Union/Russia's academic institutions. They later became key instructors and researchers at various national academic institutions in Vietnam. Such continued efforts of education and training activities on both sides help obtain positive results in the fields of social science and humanities, including the field of Sinology/Chinese studies.

Some examples below illustrate the concrete evidence of the Soviet Union/Russia's legacy of research and education activities regarding Chinese studies in Vietnam. Among the first-generation social scientists in Vietnam, who trained and upgraded education on

---

[5]These scholars are Leontiev A. L. (1716), Rossokhin I. K. (1720–1770), Bisurin N. J (1777–1853), Vaxiliev V. P. (1818–1900), Kafarof P. I. (1817–1878), Alecxeiev V. M. (1885–1951), Marr. N. P. (1864–1934), Oldelburg X. P. (1863–1934), Kondrad N. L. (1891–1970), Sherbatkoi F. I. (1866–1942), Shuski L. K. (1897–1946), Vaxiliev B. A. (1899–1946), Titarenko M. L. (1926–2016), and Riphtin B. L. (1832–1912).

Chinese studies in the Soviet Union, are some famous scholars, listed as follows:

1. *Professor Academic Nguyen Khanh Toan* (1905–1993) is an outstanding educator and social scientist who made great contributions to Vietnam's education and social science development from after the Vietnam August Revolution (August 1945) to 1982. In 1929, he studied at the Soviet Union's Communist School for Oriental Workers. In 1930, the Communist International Organization awarded him a graduate degree in history studies. He later obtained his Ph.D. degree in History at Oriental Studies University in Moscow with the thesis titled "The farmers' war in Indochina during the 18th century — Tay Son uprising movement." Among his works (published and in depository), some famous popular books for Vietnam's readers include *Vietnam History, History of Vietnam Literature,* and *Some Remarks on the End of Le Dynasty to the Beginning of Nguyen Gia Long Dynasty.* He wrote a popular book, *History against Chinese Feudalism,* with Great General Vo Nguyen Giap under the nicknames "Hong Lam and Hong Linh." The books are an evidence of his deep knowledge on Chinese studies in the field of Vietnam history.
2. *Professor Dr. Nguyen Tai Can* (1926–2011) is one of the leading experts in the field of language studies who received the Ho Chi Minh Highly Honored Prize on Vietnam Science and Technology in 2000. During 1955–1960, he had been sent by the Vietnam Ministry of Education to work as Vietnam's first language expert at the Leningrad University in the Soviet Union. In 1960, he was the first person who earned the Ph.D. degree in language studies in the Soviet Union with the work titled "Types of Nouns in Vietnam language." Many of his Vietnamese language works are closely linked to Sinology/Chinese studies (Nguyen 1988, 1987, 1979).
3. *Professor D.Sc. — Nguyen Quang Hong* (1940–) conducted multi-year language research. He obtained his BA in language studies at Beijing University in the 1960s, Ph.D. degree in language studies in

the Soviet Union in 1974, and Doctor of Sciences degree in Language Studies in the Soviet Union in 1985. His published language works bear the strong mark and influence of the Soviet Union's Marxist methodology in Sinology research, with a combination of East and West viewpoints.[6]

In Vietnam's literary research, Soviet Union/Russia's research method called a "method of historical literary study (*Thi phap hoc lich su*)" was promoted by Krapchenco (1976),[7] which was later taught and passed down to students in the field of social sciences at Vietnam colleges and universities. The ideas of this study method (*Thi phap hoc lich su*) have stimulated new trends of research and innovation in the field of Vietnam's literary studies since the 1970s. During the 1970s, in the field of literary research, Vietnam's social scientists started to explore and apply this scientific method while studying the poetic styles of To Huu (Vietnam's famous contemporary poet) and the national great poet Nguyen Du in Nom language *Truyen Kieu*. A range of literary works were conducted by the author Tran Dinh Su, such as the *Poem Style of To Huu* (*Thi phap tho To Huu*) in 1985–1987, *Poem Style of Nguyen Du in the Great Work* (*Truyen Kieu*) in 1981–1982, and *Poem Style during 1850–1900 in Vietnam* (*Thi Phap thoi ki Trung Dai Vietnam*) in 1998; these works are clear examples of the Soviet Union/Russia's influence on the research method exerted on Vietnam's literary comparative research.

In the field of the ancient Sino–Nom language studies, an interdisciplinary interesting research subject, Soviet Union/Russia's markers remained, especially in the way of using the scientific method of textual reading (*Van ban hoc*) as well as the method of

---

[6]Nguyen Quang Hong's works include subjects ranging from Chinese phonetics, Yin and Yang opposite shifting in Chinese language and translation, and legacy of Sino-Nom language to Sino-Nom language in Vietnam classical literary, see also Nguyen (2015).

[7]Krapchenco made an overview on different trends of "method of literary study" (*Thi phap hoc*) reflected in different works by Vnograder, Lihachov, Ju. Manm, Friddender, Chicherin, Sokolov, and M. Poliakov.

comparison. For the past decades in Vietnam, the preservation, exploration, and research on ancient Han–Nom language treasure collections have remained critically urgent and important for national cultural heritage. Using 20-centuries-ancient Han language and 10-centuries-ancient Nom language, the Vietnamese ancestors/predecessors have left the young generations today a great and valuable database of ancient Han–Nom language records and bibliographies with various volumes and types of items. Based on the statistics of 1987, the Vietnam Institute for Han–Nom Studies has kept in its archive 4,808 ancient Han–Nom manuscripts and works, which are equivalent to 16,164 books written in ancient Han–Nom languages (Nghia 1988).

Regarding the Han–Nom documentation resources, Vietnam's Institute for Han–Nom Studies has preserved approximately 30,000 documents and records, including films, microfilms, photographs, engraving, and rubbings of different types of inscriptions on cultural relics (various inscriptions on stones, bronze bells, stone pillars, stone markers, wood cards, and block prints). These resources serve as a subject of interest to be explored for different social sciences in Vietnam, which includes history studies, philosophy, economics, law, language, art, literature, architecture, education, agriculture, and defense. The social sciences should be based on the exploration of rare books and manuscripts on the ancient Han–Nom language to understand the long historical past (Nghia 1988).

In the field of ancient Han–Nom studies, Vietnam's social scientists often use new scientific learning methods and approaches to ancient Han–Nom treasure studies to understand and preserve this national valuable heritage. Using a combination of scientific specific methods, including the Soviet Union/Russia's method of textual reading (*Van ban hoc*), social scientists presented a comparative perspective using country case studies and attempted to explore the ancient language similarities and distinction features, their links, and interrelations (e.g., among Vietnamese, Chinese, Japanese, and Korean ancient languages) (Nghia 1988). Through comparative research, Vietnam social scientists discovered some common features, such as the common use of ancient Sino text source (*Van Tu*

Chu Han), the common core of language resources, such as nouns, proverbs, case studies, and common sources of ancient classical stories (*Kho Điển tích*), including the works of creators of ancient Chinese culture, and philosophy (e.g., *Thi Thu, Dich — Le* (*Tứ Thư*); *Xuan Thu, Luan Ngu, Manh Tu, Dai hoc,* and *Trung Dung*) (*Ngũ Kinh*). The main ancient Nom language distinctions found out that the Vietnamese ancient Nom scholars used Nom language, which has elements and modes of language construction unlike those of the ancient Sino language.

Vietnam's scholars of Chinese studies learned and were influenced by the Soviet Union/Russia's method of historical textual reading in literature, which was introduced in Vietnam's academic institutions during the 1970s–1980s; Professor Ha Van Tan is a famous historian and popular scholar in the field of history studies and archeology. He had compiled and taught the main course on "Method of Textual Reading" in Hanoi National University in the 1970s–1980s and made significant contributions to the research and education in studies on ancient Han–Nom language and history studies.

According to the new demands of socio-economic changes and in the context of development, after Vietnam's Reunification in 1976 and since its renovation and opening-up process in 1986, using Ho Chi Minh's thoughts and perspectives, system of scientific methodologies, and methods in social science research and education, Vietnam's social scientists and Sinology/Chinese studies' researchers and educators constantly explore, update, or selectively apply new theoretical accounts, research methods, and approaches from the Western academic world, China, and other countries to improve the quality of their education and research practices. Those countries' best scientific achievements, knowledge, and values such as the quintessence of mankind, have been creatively applied.

Vietnam's leading social scientists, professionals, and researchers who work and teach in the field of Sinology/Chinese studies have received professional education and advanced skills training in the Soviet Union or post-Soviet Russia's academic institutions. They continue to contribute their best to research and continuously pass down their knowledge and skills to next generation of students in the fields of social sciences, humanities, and Chinese studies.[8]

Vietnam, from national to local levels, has set up and improved libraries and information and documentation systems, where archives and depositories of various books, references, documents, bibliographies, information resources, and resources on Chinese studies as a multi-discipline subject are kept. Vietnam has also developed and expanded education centers, research institutes, research units, and departments/faculties which specialize in Chinese studies. These academic institutions often organize various types of research; run collaborative projects with different scopes; compile

---

[8] In the field of economics, the notable scholars are Professor Dr. Sc Vo Dai Luoc, Associate Professor Dr. Le Van Sang, Professor Dr. Nguyen Xuan Thang, Professor Dr. Nguyen Quang Thuan, Asc. Professor Dr. Tran Dinh Thien, and Associate Professor Dr. Ha Huy Thanh.

In the field of history studies, the notable scholars are Professor Vu Duong Ninh, Professor Nguyen Quoc Hung, Professor Nguyen Van Hong, Professor Dr. Do Quang Hung, Professor Dr. Vu Minh Giang, Professor Dr. Nguyen Quang Ngoc, Professor Dr. Nguyen Van Khanh, Professor, Dr. Do Thanh Binh, and Professor Dr. Tran Thi Vinh.

In the field of literature, the notable scholars are Professor Dr. Tran Dinh Su, Professor Dr. Phuong Luu, Professor Dr. Phong Le, Associate Professor Luu Van Bong, Professor Dr. Sc Tran Ngoc Them, Professor Dr. Tran Nho Thin, Professor Dr. Tran Ngoc Vuong, Associate Professor Dr. Phan Trong Thuong, Scholar Lai Nguyen An, Vuong Tri Nhan, and Do Lai Thuy.

In the field of linguistic research, the notable scholars are Professor Dr. Hoang Tue, Professor Dr. Nguyen Huu Chau, Professor Dr. Hoang Van Hanh, Professor Dr. Luu Van Lang, Professor Dr. Ly Toan Thang, Professor Dr. Nguyen Van Khang, and Professor Dr. Nguyen Van Ton.

In the field of ethnography/anthropology, the notable scholars are Professor Dr. Phan Trong Dat, Professor Dr. Ngo Van Le, Assistant Professor Dr. Khong Dien, Assistant Professor Dr. Pham Quang Hoan, and Assistant Professor Dr. Bui Xuan Dinh.

In the field of ancient Han Nom Language studies, the notable scholars are Professor Dr. Nguyen Hue Chi, Tran Nghia, Phan van Cac, Bang Thanh, Tu Chau, Dang Duc Sieu, Nguyen Ngoc San, and Assistant Professor Dr. Trinh Khac Manh.

In the field of contemporary Chinese studies, the notable scholars are Professor Van Trong, Professor Vu Hoang Dich, Professor Nguyen Duc Su, Dr. Nguyen The Tang, Dr. Nguyen Minh Hang, Scholar Assistant Professor Dr. Le Van Sang, Assistant Professor Dr, Dinh Cong Tuan, and Professor Dr. Do Tien Sam.

textbooks and training materials; or publish various books and documents related to Chinese studies and research. Chinese studies have been highly appraised by the general public. Similarly and recently, Vietnam media agencies raised debates on the importance of teaching Han/Chinese language among other foreign languages in the school system.

The Soviet Union/Russia–Vietnam's Scientific Cooperation and Collaboration in the Field of Sinology/Chinese Studies

In the post-World War II period (1945), the Soviet Union emerged as a large and advanced socialist country and attempted to maintain a leading position in socialist countries' block[9] against the colonialism, fascism, and capitalist and imperialist aggression.

Since the bilateral relations that started in 1950, many scientific cooperation and collaboration activities between the two socialist countries, the former Soviet Union and Vietnam, have been promoted. Under social scientists' efforts on both sides, many of Soviet Union/Russia's basic social sciences and humanities resources, works, and documentations on oriental studies/Chinese studies have been translated and published for the Vietnamese. The Vietnam audience highly welcomes these publications.

During the 1960s–1970s, Soviet Union's socialist leadership and social science circles had attempted to study, raise debates, and critically highlight the ideas concerning the limitations or errors of China's incumbent leadership. Soviet Union's social scientists in the field of oriental studies/Chinese studies ran various research

---

[9]This socialist countries' block, including Vietnam, People Republic of China (PRC), and some Eastern Europe countries and other. Vietnam, the Soviet Union, and PRC signed a Treaty of Friendship and Mutual Assistance in 1950. The Soviet Union and PRC signed a Treaty of Friendship and Mutual Assistance in 1950. At the end of the 1950s, a serious conflict was found between the Soviet Union and PRC when an extreme conservatism fraction under Mao Tze Dong (Maoism) incumbent leadership sought to move out the block to the other way, which was contrary to general principles and courses of Communist International Workers Movement led by the Soviet Union's Communist Party.

projects and published highly critical works to express their objections to the limitation ideas of Maoism. Some books had been translated and published in the Vietnamese language. Some of the published books have critically highlighted Maoist narrow-minded viewpoints or distortions of the Marxist–Leninist basic principles and perspectives on the ethnicity or resolutions of ethnic issues.[10]

In the mid-1970s, Vietnam received its triumphant victory over the Resistance War against American imperialism and national reunification in April 1975. Owing to different and contradictory perspectives in the field of external relations and development course between Vietnam (SRV) and China (PRC), the extremist fraction of PRC incumbent leadership during that time followed an expression of extreme nationalist viewpoint and unilaterally used a power to block Vietnam's development in different fields (i.e., politics, economic, security, and defense), which caused much trouble in Vietnam. This extremist fraction of China's incumbent leadership tacitly supported the Pol Pot regime (the Khmer Rouge fraction in Cambodia's Tripartite Coalition government), who committed serious atrocities in Cambodia and made provocations and invasions on Vietnam's southwest borderline in 1978, which brought great suffering to the Vietnamese. In February 1979, China's incumbent leadership mobilized around 60,000 soldiers to attack Vietnam's northern borderline and seriously violated Vietnam's sovereignty. During this time, Vietnam's Chinese studies researchers had worked in close collaboration with the Soviet Union's counterparts in running research projects, organizing conferences and seminars, and producing various publications. The Chinese studies researchers on both sides made arguments and provided evidence against aggressive wrongdoing, highly criticized such extreme nationalism in Maoist viewpoints and ideology, especially the Maoist's extremism, expansionism, and hegemony of China's incumbent leadership around that time, asserted Vietnam's righteousness, and protected

---

[10]For example, some critical works done by the Soviet Union's Chinese Studies researchers have been translated and published into Vietnamese language, including the book of Tursun Rakhimov 1982; Bira 1982(a), 1982(b).

Vietnam's national sovereignty and socialism course. Some of Vietnam's research results on Chinese studies have been published during that period.[11]

After the normalization of Vietnam (SRV)–China (PRC) relationship in 1991, in the context of increasing globalization, international integration, and widespread promotion of peace, cooperation, and development, Vietnam's Chinese studies gradually shifted focus on researching, updating, and assessing China's wide socio-economic, political reforms, new trends and development aspects, and cooperation and relations with its different counterparts to contribute to building a comprehensive, objective, and valuable knowledge base and documentation on Chinese studies and promoting the two countries' friendly relations, regular dialogues, academic and cultural exchanges, education and training, and economic ties.[12]

In recent years, Vietnam–Russia's cooperation and collaboration on Chinese studies continue in various forms (i.e., annual academic exchanges, organization of conferences or seminars, joint research projects, and publication of books and documents) and have brought positive and fruitful results. For example, a published book edited by Vietnam's Professor Dr. Do Tien Sam and Russia's Professor and academician Titarenko, *China During the First Years of the 21st Century*, in 2009 is a concrete result of Russia and Vietnam's joint social science/Chinese study project on China. Another recently published book by Titarenko (2012) showed the strong efforts of maintaining collaboration on both sides in the field of Chinese studies. This book has a broad significance of providing researchers and instructors of Chinese studies and social sciences and the Vietnamese audience a good chance to update and understand the Asia-Pacific region, Russia, and China, and other countries' relations and improve further Vietnam and Russia's scientific cooperation and development.

---

[11] Some critical works done on Chinese studies published by Vietnam's scholars of Chinese studies during that time (Truong 1982, 1979).

[12] Some works done by Vietnam's scholars of Chinese studies during the 1990s–2000s include Nguyen (1991, 1995, 1997, 2003), Dinh (1998), and Vo (2004).

Concluding Remarks

The Soviet Union/Russia and Vietnam's long-standing, specific relations of comprehensive cooperation and friendship and their continuous collaborative efforts in the fields of culture, education and training, and science and technology have brought many positive accomplishments for both sides. This preliminary research shows that the Soviet Union/Russia's influence and its unique legacy have remained evident and impressive in economic, political, cultural, and social fields in the Vietnamese society. These Soviet Union/Russian legacies and values are positively reflected in education and training, which established social sciences and humanities and knowledge and information basis. The development of Chinese studies as a multi-discipline, comprehensive, complex subject is significant. Significant imprints can be found in various dimensions, including a strong and continuous support in education and training, and their effects on various generations of Vietnamese social scientists, which lays down good basic foundations for expanding Chinese study education and research units and faculties in universities, colleges, and academic graduate institutions throughout Vietnam, continuously maintaining efforts of collaboration and academic exchange between the two sides, actively contributing to improving scientific knowledge based on the issues of research interest.

Much work remains to be done to promote strong collaboration in conducting research, instructing, and exchanging academic activities. Thus, active contributions to Chinese studies and cultural and scientific development and people's mutual understanding and friendships between the two countries are needed.

References

Bira, Shagdaryn. 1982a. *Maoism and the Ethnic Issues in People Republic of China*. Hanoi: Social Sciences Publishing House.

Bira, Shagdaryn. 1982b. *The Urgent Issues in the Struggle against Maoism's Distortions in the Field of History Studies*. Hanoi: Social Sciences Publishing House.

Dinh, Cong Tuan. 1998. *The Process of Socio-economic Reform of PRC — From 1978 to Nowadays*. Hanoi: Social Sciences Publishing House.

Do Tien Sam and Titarenko, M. L. (Eds.). 2009. *China During the First Years of 21st Century*. Vietnam Academy Social Sciences — Institute For Chinese Studies, Hanoi: The Encyclopedia and Publishing House.

Nguyen, The Tang. 1997. *China's Opening External Economic Relations*. Hanoi: Social Sciences Publishing House.

Nguyen, Duc Su. 1991. *China on the Move of Reform*. Hanoi: Social Sciences Publishing House.

Nguyen, Minh Hang. 1995. *Economic Reform in PRC — A New Alternative for Development*. Hanoi: Social Sciences Publishing House.

Nguyen, Quang Hong. 2015. *Dictionary and Explanations*. Hanoi: Education Publishing House.

Nguyen, Tai Can. 1979. *Origin and Process of Formation Sino-Vietnam Language Reading*. Hanoi: Social Science Publishing House.

Nguyen, Tai Can. 1987. *Sino-Culture and Vietnam Language: The Role of Sino-origin Factors in Vietnam Modern Language* (in Japanese), Tokyo: publisher N.A.

Nguyen, Tai Can. 1988. *Sino Influence through the Nguyen Trung Ngan Poem Style of Expression in the Ly and Tran Dynasties*. Hanoi: Education Publishing House.

Nguyen, Van Hong. (Ed.) 2003. *China's Opening Reform-some Experiences and Lessons Learnt*. Hanoi: The World Publishing House.

Rakhimov, Tursun. 1982. *The Fates of Non-Han Ethnics in People Republic of China*. Hanoi: Social Publishing House.

Titarenko, M. L. 2012. *Geopolitical Significance of Far East Region, Russia, China and Other Asian Countries*. Vietnam Academy Social Sciences — Institute For Chinese Studies, in Vietnamese language, translated by Do Minh Cao, Ngo The Phuc, Nguyen Canh Toan. Hanoi: The Encyclopedia Publishing House.

Tran Nghia. 1988. Ancient Han-Nom Treasure — A Look from Literature Comparative Research Approach, *Vietnam Journal of Sino-Nom Studies*, No. 2, http://Han-Nom.org.vn Accessed on December 26, 2016.

Truong, Chinh. 1979. *The Truth of Vietnam–China Relationships During the Last 30 Years*. Hanoi: The Truth Publishing House.

Truong, Chinh. 1982. *The National Determination to Defeat China's Expansionism and Hegemony*. Hanoi: The Truth Publishing House.

Tu, Thi Loan, *Vietnam–Russia Cultural Exchange and New Posing Issues during the Integration Period*, VHH3.TB4.48 (Library document No. VHH3.T4.48, Ministry of Culture Sport and Tourism, Vietnam).

Vo, Dai Luoc. *China's Access to WTO — Opportunities and Challenges*. Hanoi: Social Sciences Publishing House.

Web References

Nguyen Le Nhung. *Depository Documents on Vietnam Russia Relations* (Quan hệ Việt — Nga qua tài liệu lưu trữ). http://vanthuluutru.com/?p=15. Accessed on July 26, 2017.

Tran Ngoc Vuong. *Chinese Studies in Contemporary Vietnam (Trung quoc hoc ngay nay o Vietnam)*. http://www.vanhoanghean.com.vn. Accessed on December 26, 2016.

6

Scholarship and Friendship: How Pakistani Academics View Pakistan–China Relations

Pervaiz Ali Mahesar

Department of International and Strategic Studies
University of Malaya, Malaysia

The global power paradigm shift from the West to the East is expected to coincide with an Asian Century, coupled with China leading from the front for the developing countries. This splendid re-emergence and transformation of the Chinese economy could trump the notion of China threat discourse in the West. Against this backdrop, there seems to be a profound interest among the China watchers in South Asia to further understand and explore China studies. In this context, this study offers a comparative view of China studies in South Asia, particularly focusing on Pakistan and India. Therefore, the roadmap for this underlined study is divided into two parts: The first part focuses on China studies in Pakistan. The second part of this study explores Indian studies on China. This chapter concludes that China studies are vigorously pursued not only in Pakistan, but also in India, yet it suggests to re-calibrate fissures and hurdles in promoting China studies in South Asia (Pakistan and India). Thus, it could contribute to the existing body of literature on China and enhance understanding of China studies in Pakistan and India.

Introduction

Pakistan and China marked their 60 years of diplomatic relations on May 17–20, 2011. The relations between two countries have transformed radically. The past 62 years of history, after the establishment of Pakistan's diplomatic ties with China, has greatly been fostered by the dynamic leaders like Mao Zedong, Zhou Enlai, and Zulfikar Ali Bhutto. The *Foreign Policy Review* reported that Xi Jinping, the Chinese President, in his landmark first state visit to Pakistan, signed an economic deal worth US$46 billion on April 20, 2015. This mega-trade deal seems to be a part of the China's Belt and Road and New Silk Road grand strategy at the global level. These two great initiatives are expected to link western China to an external world (*Foreign Policy Review* 2015).

Economically, the bilateral trade agreement between Pakistan and China was held in 1989. This agreement was expected to be a prelude for other trade agreements like FTA in 2006, Trade and Services in 2009. These trade agreements finally culminated into CPEC because both have signed around 50 MoUs under the umbrella of China–Pakistan Economic Corridor (*International Public Policy Review* 2017). Thus, there are more than 22 major projects which are launched by China in Pakistan. For instance, heavy mechanical complex, heavy electrical complex, tank rebuilding factory, aircraft rebuilding factory, machine tools, Gawadar port, and Karakoram Highway. More importantly, the recent figures indicate that there are more than 121 smaller projects and about 12,000–15,000 Chinese engineers and technicians working in Pakistan on various projects.

In 2014 and 2015, the public opinion polls conducted by the Pew Research Center at the global level, found that from 78 percent to 82 percent Pakistanis are pro-China. This ratio seems to be higher among the Southeast Asian countries opinion polls for China

(Pew Research Center 2014, 2015). More importantly, Pakistan–China friendship dates back 2000 years and the most significant point is that they are connected together by Silk Road (Lin and Shangli 2001: 13).

Politically speaking, the mutual visits of leaders of both sides, China and Pakistan, from the 1960s to 2017 show the greater transformation in bilateral relations through which several documents and joint communiques have been signed and issued.

Undeniably, Asia is reinventing itself in the 21st century. It is worth noting that, currently, 60 percent of the world population lives in Asia, out of the total 60 percent of the population of the world, 40 percent belongs to only China and India. It is also worth mentioning here that China, India and Japan comprise Asia's great civilizations in the world (Arnold 2016). However, the different cultures, traditions, and religions are what make Asia as a plural and unique region. The 56 percent of the population in the developing Asia now portrayed as a middle class who have come out of the depths of poverty and ignorance.

South Asia, once the strategic backwater for America, is now considered as the center of gravity, not only for the regional countries, but also for developed countries globally. Interestingly, the fast pace of the socio-economic development and liberalization of trade and economy and technological advancement, entails opportunities and predicts an onset of challenges in the decades to come. The close proximity of China to Pakistan and India, makes it well placed to play its significant role in the region. China, being the powerful and strong neighbor of Pakistan and India, there seems to be an overwhelming interest of China watchers on the both sides of the border. Thus, there is an extant literature/studies, either in Pakistan or India, which focuses on China, its culture, economic development, and politics.

To reiterate what is already said, this study is divided into two parts. The first part focuses on how China studies have evolved in Pakistan; it explains about China's soft power as a model of development for Pakistan; attempts to explore Pakistan's India balancing; seeks to explore how Xinjiang might complicate Pakistan–China relations. The second part of this study explores Indian studies on China; it identifies and unfolds the contemporary discourse on China among China watchers in India; explains about how India has institutionalized its China studies.

This study concludes that China studies are vigorously pursued not only in Pakistan but also in India, yet it suggests to recalibrate fissures and hurdles in promoting China studies in South Asia (Pakistan and India). This study could contribute to the existing body of literature on China and enhance understanding of China studies in Pakistan and India.

There has been a profound academic interest in understanding China from different aspects, among the Pakistani China watchers. There is no denying that Pakistan, being the natural neighbor of China has been inspired by China's peaceful rise, and strong economic dynamism, despite the Asian financial crisis and the global economic recession during 1997–1998 and 2007–2008. To expedite friendly and cordial relations with China has been the cardinal principle of Pakistan's foreign policy. The bedrock of Pakistan–China relations can be portrayed as "Iron Brothers, time tested and All-Weather Friends." According to the Chinese saying, "good neighbors cannot be traded for gold" (Hali 2015: 71). Keeping in view this context, this chapter briefly explains about how China scholarship has evolved in Pakistan.

China Studies in Pakistan

The Chinese studies are being institutionalized in Pakistan. According to this study, there are 12 China study centers in Pakistan. The purpose of the Chinese institutes is to promote language, culture, friendship, and understanding between Pakistan and China. The courses like certificate, foundation to the Master's, and Ph.D. degree programs are conducted at the Confucius Institutes in Pakistan.

According to Hanban (2016) sources, there are 110 Confucius Institutes in Asia. Country-wise data shown on Hanban website indicates that Pakistan has four Confucius Institutes. Except the

Table 1. Institutes of China Studies in Pakistan

No	Year	Name of China Study Center	Location
1	1970	Chinese Dept. at NUML Univ.	Islamabad
2	2007	Confucius Institute	Islamabad
3	2009	Pakistan–China Institute	Islamabad
4	2009	The Punjab Jiangsu Cultural Centre	Lahore
5	2010	Pakistan–China Cultural Centre	Islamabad
6	2012	Confucius Institute, Karachi Univ.	Karachi, Sindh
7	2013	China Study Centre, CIIT	Islamabad
8	2014	Centre of Excellence, China Studies, GCU Univ.	Lahore
9	2015	The Confucius Institute Faisalabad University	Faisalabad
10	2015	China Studies Corner, Sindh University, Jamshoro	Sindh
11	2015	Chinese Language Centre	UET, Lahore
12	2016	China Studies Centre	Peshawar University

Source: Compiled by the author.
Abbreviations: Dept.: Department; Univ.: University, CIIT: Comsats Institute of Information Technology; GCU: Government College University, Lahore; NUML: National University of Modern Languages, Islamabad; UET: University of Engineering and Technology, Lahore.

four Confucius Institutes, there are eight China institutes in Pakistan (Hanban 2016). Table 1 shows the upward trend toward the rising institutionalization of the China studies in Pakistan. In this context, the readymade reference with the year of its establishment, name of institute/center, and its location in Pakistan are given in Table 1.

If we look at the recent increasing growth in establishing Confucius Institutes and centers, at global level, one could be astonished to learn that in 511 Confucius Institutes and 1,073 Classrooms for 2.1 million students from 140 countries is not less than a "bridge builder" for regions. It is important to note that the fast pace of growth in China studies at global level, points to the fact that nations are advancing further to exchange and mutually learn Chinese-language and its oldest spectacular civilization. The mutual understanding among nations could lead to a deeper relations and friendship at regional and global level (http://english.hanban.org/article/2017-01/05/content_670843.htm).

Moreover, the Roots School System has introduced the teaching of the Chinese language courses at the primary and secondary level in Islamabad — the capital of Pakistan. There is a growing interest among Pakistani academics, journalists, army officers, businessman, and students to learn the Chinese language. The similar programs have been launched in other provinces in Pakistan. According to Mushahid Hussain, 2015, more than 6,000 students from Pakistan have gone to China for their higher studies in China.

However, figures vary from the 6,000 to 8,000 students enrolled in various programs in China. The good news is that the ratio of Pakistani students who are studying in China is increasing. Therefore, the Chinese language is rapidly becoming the popular foreign language among students in Pakistan. Obviously, it will leave a great impact on the Pakistani discourse and studies of China. Professor Dr. Aman Memon in his interview to the author (Pervaiz on August 12, 2016) stated:

"China studies will be helpful to understand Chinese society, its ambitions and its aspirations. That knowledge will be helpful for policy makers, intelligentsia and educated middle class forms their perceptions regarding Chinese society, state and state institutions. China studies will play a tremendous role in strengthening people to people contact." … "China and Pakistan should adopt a regional approach along with strengthening bilateral relations. People to people contact, establishing Chinese Study Centers in Pakistan and Pakistan Study Centers in China will help people of the two countries to learn from each other's experience."

These facts speak volumes about how Pakistan is embracing China not only at state to state level, but also people to people. Moreover, the friction free engagement and harmony between the two neighbors further underpins the contemporary scholarship and friendship in Pakistan on China. Consequently, three tables are shown here which reflect not only academic scholarship but also diplomats and military studies on China in Pakistan.

This chapter selects randomly from above studies on China in Pakistan. Actually, the emerging scholarship on China in Pakistan is divided here for clarity of thought, purpose, and understanding. Therefore, it focuses on previous and latest studies in Pakistan on

China that could reflect how Pakistani scholarship on China is emerging and has transformed into comprehensive strategic partnership (as shown in Tables 2 and 3).

The following review of academic studies on China in Pakistan could further develop our understanding of scholarship and friend-

Table 2.   China Analysts in Pakistan

Author/Year	Books/Articles	Published/Publisher	Academic Studies
Niloufer Wajid Ali (1975)	Communist China and South and Southeast Asia	Ferozsons Lahore	Academic
Nazir A. Mughal (1975)	China and World Powers: A Case study of Manchurian Crisis, 1931–1933	National Book Foundation Karachi	Academic
Abdul Ghani (1976)	Visit to China	Manager of Pub:, Karachi	Academic
Abu Imran (1976)	China's Policies: Other Side of the Picture	People's Publication House, Lahore	Academic
S.M. Haider (Ed.) (1976)	Administrative Reforms, Chinese Communes, and Local government: A Report on the Training of Divisional, and Tehsil level officers	Pakistan Academy for Rural Development, Peshawar.	Academic/ Journalist
Rasul Bux Rais (1977)	China and Pakistan: A Political Analysis of Mutual relations	Same	Academic
S. Nazre Hyder (1978)	Technology and Skill formation: The Chinese Experience, 1953–75	Institute of Strategic Studies, Islamabad	Academic
Samina Yasmin (1980)	Pakistan's Relations With China, 1947–1979	Institute of Strategic Studies, Islamabad	Academic
Rizvi, Hassan Askari (Summer 1994)	"China and Kashmir Problem"	Regional Studies, Vol. 12, No. 3	Academic
Dani, Ahmed Hasan (1995)	Human Records on Karakorum Highway	Lahore: Sang-e-Meel Publications	Academic
Ahmed, Mutahir (August 1997)	"China and Regional Muslim States: Challenges and Opportunities in 21st Century"	National Development and Security, Vol. 6	Academic

Source: Compiled by the author.

Table 3. Pakistani Diplomat/Think Tanks and Military Studies on China

Author/Year	Books/Articles	Published/Publisher	Diplomat/Think Tank Studies
Ali, Ahmed (1949)	Muslim China	Karachi	Diplomat
Aziz, Qutbud-Din (1964)	Relations between Pakistan and the People's Republic of China. In Foreign Policy of Pakistan — An Analysis: A Group Study	Karachi: Allies Book Corporation	Diplomat
Syed, Anwar H. (1974)	China and Pakistan: Diplomacy of an Entente Cordiale	The University of Massachusetts Press, Amherst	Diplomat (author of 10 books)
Yousaf Kamal (1977)	Rural Industrialization: A Maoist Model	Progressive Publishers, Lahore	Bureaucrat
Latif Ahmed Sherwani (1980)	Pakistan, China, and America	Karachi Council for Pakistan Studies	Think Tank Analyst worked at Pakistan Ins. of Int. Affairs
Mohammad Yunus (1986)	Reflections on China: An Ambassador's View from China	Wajidalis, Lahore	Diplomat
Bhatti, Maqbool A. (August 1996)	"Sino-Pakistan Relations: Future Prospects."	*National Development and Security*, Vol. 5, No. 1	Ambassador
Skrine, P. C. (1998)	Chinese Central Asia: An Account of Travels in Northern Kashmir and Chinese Turkestan	Karachi: Indus Publications	Sir Clarmont Skrine was British Consul-General at Kashgar during the 1920
Ahmed, Khalid. Summer (2001)	"Sino-Pak Relations: An 'All Weather' Friendship" IRS	*Inst. Of Regional Studies*, Islamabad, Vol. 19, No. 3	Think Tank Analyst IRS, Islamabad
Akhtar, Shaheen (Summer 2001)	"Pak-China Economic Relations: Forging Strategic Partnership in the 21st Century"	*Regional Studies*, Vol. 19, No. 3	Think Tank Analyst IRS, Islamabad

(*Continued*)

Table 3. (Continued)

Author/Year	Books/Articles	Published/Publisher	Diplomat/Think Tank Studies
Syed Hassan Javed (2014)	Chinese Soft Power Code	Paramount Books, Karachi	Diplomat
S.M Hali (2015)	China's Success Stories: How China Has Transformed in the Past 40 Years	Rumi Academy, Islamabad	Analyst, Journalist and Air Force Officer. Author of four books
M. Younas (2015)	Awakened China Shakes the World and is Pakistan's Mainstay: Memoirs a Diplomat	Institute of Policy Studies, Islamabad	Diplomat
M. Akram Zaki (2010, 2015)	China of Today and Tomorrow: Dynamics of Relations with Pakistan and Handbook of Pakistan–China Relations	Pakistan Institute of China, Islamabad	Diplomat and Senator
Syed Javed Hassan (2016)	Rise of China and the Asian Century	National University of Science and Technology, Islamabad, Pakistan	Ambassador
Izzat Awan (1975)	People's Republic of China as I saw it	Provincial Civil Service Academy, Peshawar	Commander Naval Force, Pakistan
K.Arif (Ed.) (1984)	China–Pakistan Relations 1947–1980	Lahore Vanguard Books	Vice Chief of Pakistan Army
Ahmed, Gulzar (1988)	Tazkara-e Sinkiang: Cheeni Turkistan [An account of Sinkiang: Chinese Turkestan]	Lahore: Idara-e Saqafat-e Islamia	Colonel in Bangladesh Army
Shafi, Iqbal M. (1989)	"Muslims in China: A Brief History"	Central Asia, Summer, Vol. 21	Brigadier in Pakistan Army

(Continued)

Table 3. (*Continued*)

Author/Year	Books/Articles	Published/Publisher	Diplomat/Think Tank Studies
Shafi, Iqbal M. (1989)	"Communication in People's Republic of China (PRC), with Special Reference to Sinkiang Autonomous Region"	*Central Asia*, Vol. 24	Brigadier in Pakistan Army
Skrine, P. C. (1998)	*Chinese Central Asia: An Account of Travels in Northern Kashmir and Chinese Turkestan*	Karachi: Indus Publications	Sir Clarmont Skrine was British Consul-General at Kashgar during the 1920
S.M Hali (2015)	*China's Success Stories: How China Has Transformed in the Past 40 Years*	Rumi Academy, Islamabad	Analyst, Journalist and Air Force Officer. Author of four books
S.M Hali (2016)	*Cheeni Saqafat Ke Tabinda Naqaush (Urdu Version) Cultural Footprints of China*	Hamza Pervez Printers, Rawalpindi	Air Force Captain and Analyst

Source: Compiled by the author.

ship between two neighbors. The first study by Pakistani academic was conducted in 1949, on *Muslim China*, by Ahmed Ali. His study was published by Pakistan Institute of International Affairs. He was visiting fellow at the National Central University, Nanking, China. He was novelist, poet, translator, critic, diplomat, and a great scholar. After joining the Foreign Service in 1950, he was posted to China. He, being a Pakistani diplomat, established relations with China in 1951. His study of China informs about the Chinese art, philosophy, calligraphy, and paintings. It also explains about how the Chinese values and culture influenced the Sadi's Gulistan and Bostan poetry. In addition, he argues that the people of China are nationalist, upholding their culture and traditions. He explains about the cultural similarity of the Chinese with Urdu in Pakistan.

Moreover, he argues that right from the Tang Dynasty to Yuan Dynasty the Muslims either Arab or Persian have enjoyed the equal rights, perks, and privileges. However, it was Manchu dynasty in which, he noted, persecuted Muslims at large scale. The study acknowledges that whatever the religion or culture of China, the people of Pakistan have deep and firm links with them; whoever ruler comes in China, China has to stay, with hope and optimism that there will be understanding and friendship between the people of Pakistan and China and the Chinese Muslims (Ahmed Ali 1949).

Whereas, in *Islam and Muslims in Red Regimes* (1970), the study by M. Rafiq Khan informs about China and Muslims interaction, briefly explains history of Turkistan and power struggle between China and Russia, the study also explains about Chinese communists anti-Muslim and anti-Islam policies. This chapter is a compilation of articles which appeared in different weekly journals, for instance, *Young Pakistan* and *Dacca*. In this section, the author focuses on China and Muslim interaction. This chapter shows that friendship can be made individually and collectively with any country. But it does not mean that they should embrace their culture, ideology, or national outlook. He suggests that strong friendship should be based on equality, mutual respect, and reciprocity. Further he said, "in many countries Muslims are living in a minority groups. If these Muslim minority groups are persecuted in any part of the world than we feel deep sympathy for them." He said, "Pakistan being a Muslim state has always taken care of such ill treatments meted out to Muslim minority groups." He believes that Pakistan is an ideological state and ideological movements have always been attracting to the general public. He argues that the "Muslims of China have always been valiant and warlike people among its population. The Muslims were persecuted and exterminated during the Manchu era. Since then, Muslims have neither submitted nor defected from their own religion. The Muslims under the Nationalist regime under Chiang Kai-Shek enjoyed their freedom. In this regime, Muslims were given high military ranks, besides political participation." The study explains that the "Muslims under the communist regime has been subjected to persecution and extermination, they were not allowed freedom either political, economic and expression." The Chinese communist regime had abolished the Waqfs, replaced the Arab script, tax levied on slaughter of animals was banned, Zakat system abolished and replaced Uighur Muslims into Han community. These steps were considered against the social, cultural, political, economic, and Islamic values of the Muslims. He argues that the "Chinese communist regime has established mosques and Mullahs as a showpiece to show the world of Muslims that it has soft corner for the Muslims. This study concludes that lack of freedom, mistreatment, persecution (Sinkiang, Kansu and Yunnan) and extermination of Uighur Muslims in Manchu regime has been widely appalling to not only Pakistan, but Malaya, Indonesia, Middle East and many Muslim countries in the world" (Khan *et al.* 1970: 6–28).

M. Akram Zaki's study of China focuses on the uniqueness of Pakistan–China friendship. His study argues that relations between two countries have radically changed in spite of different social systems, linguistic, and cultural mismatch between Pakistan and China. Further, his work indicates that there is a convergence of interests between two countries. This mutual interest has brought both of the neighbors closer to each other. It indicates about China's policy of self-reliance and asked Pakistan to follow the same.

Further, the writer explains about China's Four Modernization program that ranges from Agriculture, Industry, Science and Technology and Defense. This chapter identifies that China has adopted the policy of peaceful rise and its relations with its neighboring countries are based on non-intervention, respect for sovereignty, peace, and stability. He further argues that despite changes at regional and global politics, there has been "All weather Friendship" which has been transformed from one generation to the other. The year 2011 was celebrated as the year of friendship between two countries. The writer is influenced from the Chinese economic dynamism, peaceful rise, political stability, and more important visionary leadership which has inspired and magnetized its own people. The writer suggests that Pakistan needs to learn from the Chinese experience of development and restore the true spirit of democratic society (Zaki 2015: 1–16).

While interviewing to Professor Swaran Singh on March 10, 2012, Ambassador Shahid M. Amin, Pakistan, expressed about Pakistan–China friendship in the following words:

> China is a very well-known ancient civilization and a neighboring country of Pakistan. Even as a child, I was conscious of the fact that China is a well-known ancient civilization and a great country with its own traditions and system … Talking about the relations between Pakistan and China, in Pakistan, there is a great good will for China. In fact, China is considered as Pakistan's best friend; a friend who has been with us in good times and bad times. China is considered as a good friend by the people of Pakistan as well. China too, has been using very interesting language to describe its friendship with Pakistan as 'higher than the Himalayas' and 'deeper than the oceans'. They have helped in creating this environment of deep friendship and comradeship between the two nations …

The study on China by Syed Hasan Javed, explains about the rise of the Chinese and linked it with Asian Century. His study mainly focuses on the Chinese development, friendship with Pakistan, OBOR, and CPEC projects, introducing Civil Service reforms like in China, and his personnel memories of China visit. His study argues that the economic performance of the Chinese has significantly changed from 1980 to 2015. Moreover, the Chinese successful transition of rural-agrarian economy into a market-oriented economy has simply been remarkable. His study noted that China has uplifted millions of the youth out of the poverty trap, harnessing the full potential of its youth. This study concludes that China holds the promising and bright future not only for its neighbors, but also for the rest of the world. They desire peace, stability and prosperity in the South Asian region (Syed Hasan Javed 2016). The study suggested further that Pakistan should take steps to strengthen scholarship and friendship between two neighbors. China, with organized and well-crafted political, economic, human and resources management besides its visionary and objective oriented leadership, is imbued with the spirit of wisdom, culture, and knowledge. It reinforces the fact that how contemporary Pakistani academic studies of China have been influenced.

Moreover, another significant study done by Fazal-ur-Rahman and Hamayoun Khan's is worth mentioning here. Their studies show that economic relations between two countries are still at an evolving stage and will improve with the passage of time. It explains about trade relations with China and various projects related to investment and energy sector has been launched worth billions of dollars. It seems to be influenced by the Chinese economy, trade and investment in Pakistan. In addition to this, the Chinese acknowledgment of Pakistan's role in the region, frequent exchange of visits to each other's country by ministers, and developments related to Gawadar Deep Sea Port indicates toward strengthening Pakistani academic scholarship and friendship (Rahman and Khan 2015).

Similarly, the study on China by Sirajuddin Aziz explains about China's history and its development course. This study showed that the Chinese Great Leap Forward (1958–1960) policy and Cultural Revolution (1966–1976) have been monumental in the development of China. The economic developments in China have been eye catching for the rest of the world. His study seems to have been influenced by the Chinese five principles of peaceful coexistence, like non-intervention, nonaggression, peaceful coexistence, equality and mutual benefits. Further, it acknowledges that China has helped Pakistan in the odd hours. It showed that both the countries have shared vision, mutual interests, shared destiny, and are against imperialism, expansionism, and hegemony. This study suggests that since the Chinese are open minded and soft-hearted people, Pakistan should take it serious to promote its links not only at state to state level but also at the people to people level. In this way, one can reap the fruits of friendship (Aziz 2015).

Consequently, the study on China by Mayraj Fahim focuses on the Chinese development course in the historical perspective. His study explains that China is a unitary and the single party system. It has done wonders in decentralizing the power which is aimed at economic growth and development at the grassroots level. This study is very much influenced by the decentralization process in China that has empowered its local people. The writer suggests that Pakistan should learn lessons from how China has succeeded in introducing administrative reforms at local level in China and the similar reforms can be launched in urban areas of Pakistan (Fahim 2015).

In another significant study on China by Chaudhry Faisal Mushtaque explains about the launching of the Roots School System (RSS). The aim of this school is to impart the Chinese language to the youth of Pakistanis. Broadly speaking, by introducing the Chinese language in Pakistan, it could reduce the barrier of understanding China from different perspectives. This school system has 12 faculty members and around 3,000 students enrolled. This study noted that Pakistan and China has a unique and an exemplary friendship. The study suggests that there should be educational exchange programs at higher levels. In order to extend educational networks in Pakistan, the writer suggests that it is better in the scheme of our mutual interests that both countries extend closer collaboration not only at primary school level, but also at university level (Mushtaque 2015). Whereas, the study by Mushahid Hussain Syed on China explains about how Pakistan-China relations are resilient, time tested which have transformed into self-confidence and maturity. His study stresses on policy makers in Pakistan to learn from the Chinese development experience besides its policy of peace with its neighbors.

Historically, his study showed that natural borders, friendly exchanges and trade through Silk route through Taxila — a hub of Buddhist University and the center of attraction for the Chinese scholars, have made China Study very unique in Pakistan. It acknowledges that the relations between two countries are "friction-free," the mutual interests of peace and stability in the region, self-reliance and harmonious at domestic and external level, shared commitment have made two neighbors special and unique.

It is also noted by the study that Pakistan–China relations have assumed greater and new depth which focuses not only on strategic but also economic, cultural, language, and energy spheres. In 2014, bilateral trade was at US$12 billion, China is the biggest partner, largest importer, in which around 6,000 Pakistanis are studying. This impressive number shows that the relations between two natural neighbors are gaining momentum and importance from people to diplomatic level. This study acknowledges that in the next 50 years, the vision of China would be people friendly, peaceful, and cooperative with external countries.

The writer argues that "China does not export revolution, poverty, famine and mess around you." His study concludes that Pakistan should learn from the Chinese experience of development and peaceful rise by orienting their national objectives with development and harmony (Syed 2015). To sum up, his study of China, seems to be influenced by the Chinese peaceful rise, its journey of development, visionary leadership, peaceful domestic political transitions, desire for peace, prosperity and stability within and without and peaceful policy of coexistence. This discourse leads one to conclude that why academics in Pakistan are influenced by the scholarship and friendship discourse.

S.M. Hali, the author of five books, among them, two are worth mentioning here, like *China Stories, China's Success: How China Transformed in the past Forty years 2015*; also in Urdu, *Cheen ki kamiyabion ki kahani 2015*. His study of China shows his true friendship for China and the Chinese people. His focus of the study remained development in China, long and short term plans, and visionary leadership of China. His study indicates that he was inspired from the love and respect of the Chinese people, infrastructure developments in Shanghai, Chongqing, Hongchow, Yiwu, Qingdao, and many other places he visited. It noted that many powers in the past, like Britain, Germany, France, Netherlands, Portugal, and Spain in the 17th century to 19th century and the US in the 20th century put their foothold not only in Asia but also in Africa in order to fulfill their voracious appetite for their raw material. They plundered, looted and exploited their colonies.

China, on the contrary, which itself was also invaded and colonized by many powers in the past, is well aware of the exploitation. Moreover, his study suggested that China believes in win-win policy.

It also offers valuable solutions for resolving problems. It does not believe in exploitation and colonization. He writes in his book that his interest of China has been transferred from one generation to another. His sons and daughters have preferred to study in China than any other country in the world (Hali 2015). This study further suggests that to develop an understanding with China, Pakistan need to introduce the Chinese language in schools and harness potential of friendship as much as it can.

The study of China by Syed Javed Hassan focuses on the concept of soft power and symbols linked to it. He believes that if we want to have the Chinese wisdom, we need to understand the China linguistically and culturally. The national poet of Pakistan, Dr. Allama Iqbal, noted by author, that he predicted the rise of China and its dream. In one of his poems, he says: "Himalaya Ke Chashme Ubalne Lage, Giran Khawab Cheeni Sabhalne Lage." It means that spring of the Himalayas has begun spurting and the Chinese have woken up from deep slumber. This study indicates that China has adopted the values of soft power from one generation to the next. It acknowledged that the Chinese rise is not a new one, but it is the revival of the Middle Kingdom. This study was influenced by the Chinese wisdom and soft power throughout the decades of its development, and rise with no conflict or war. Moreover, he says that it is unique that we have a rising power as our neighbor and time tested friend (Syed Javed Hassan 2016). This study will enable new Pakistani generation to understand cultural values and wisdom of the Chinese people.

This study will enable new Pakistani generation to understand cultural values and wisdom of the Chinese people. These studies further indicate about how Pakistan is going to emulate the Chinese model of development. It is indicated in the following discussion on the Chinese soft power in the shape of an economic model that deserves to be merited and emulated. This economic model as analyzed by China watchers believes in win–win situation and enables you to prosper and develop equally.

China's Soft Power as a Model of Development for Pakistan

It is mentioned earlier that China studies have assumed a great importance among the Pakistani China watchers and this could be due to various reasons. Currently, the China's rise, its successful model for the economic development, CPEC (China–Pakistan Economic Corridor) agreement and the Chinese commitment to build pipelines, rail and road links from Kashgar to Gawader and energy-related projects in Pakistan are testimony to the fact that Pakistani watchers are deeply influenced by Chinese steps and its policies toward the region generally and Pakistan particularly. The of late investment in Pakistan on the part of China is amounting to US$46 billion. This mega investment has been hailed positive and good omen in the relation between two countries. This huge investment seems to be more than the annual US aid at global level. It is considered to be the biggest investment of China in Pakistan (Manuel 2016).

The changing geo-economic configuration in the South Asian region makes the West ambivalent on the rise of China. According to Donald Rumsfeld — the former US Secretary of Defense, "the future of China is not written, but it is being written" (Syed 2016: 17). In the Post 1978 era, China's economic opening was well orchestrated. Given the unprecedented growth rate, it greatly transformed its close looking economy into a modern, industrial and stronger one. Therefore, China's spectacular economic performance has been registered at 7.9 in 2013, and 6.7 GDP in 2016 (China GDP Annual Growth Rate Forecast 2016–2020). It indeed achieved two important milestones by undergoing a marked change from a rural agrarian economy into a modern-industrial and market based economy. It became a prelude to the development, peace and prosperity in the 20th century. With the metamorphose in the region, China's poverty alleviation programs; providing an equal employment opportunity to its people; expanding and increasing network of industrial zones have been focus of and attraction to many economists.

According to Wu Guoquan — the Director of Department of Asian Affairs, Ministry of Commerce, this unprecedented increase in the trade volume between two neighbors by 18.2 percent in fiscal year 2014–2015 that indicates mutual benefits for both countries. The surge in trade volume between the two neighbors during the fifteen years (2000–2015) and including various contracts signed in ranges from US$1.8 billion to US$150.8 billion. This trade and economic exchanges between China and Pakistan has been instrumental in understanding and strengthening cordial relations (*Dawn News* 2016).

To explain further briefly, one of the key concepts in the Chinese cultural development policy is that it is fixated with the soft power. Joseph Nye (1990), in his famous work, *Bound to Lead*, coined the term Soft power. Even his work was published in the Chinese language in 1992. Indeed, the concept of Soft power left an indelible influence on the Chinese elite groups. It also attracted the attention of the Chinese government "a new way to conceptualize and exercise power" (Wang and Lu 2008: 442). The new concept was debated and contemplated in media and Think Tanks in China. After an extensive debate, soft power was included in the highest-level policy documents on October 15, 2007. Nye (2003) believes that soft power has an ability to get one's way through the attraction and persuasion. He has identified three intangible sources of power which emanate from: culture, political values and foreign policy (Nye 2006).

It is interesting to note here that the Chinese economic model has become the talk of the town globally. The author of a book, *End of History*, Francis Fukuyama, writes in his article in Project Syndicate, "Exporting the Chinese Model," (2016), predicted that with the beginning of 2016, there seems to be an ongoing competition over the competing development models of China and USA. He believes that the upshot of these development paradigms could determine the destiny of much of Eurasia for decades to come. He further writes that there could be an external dimension to the Chinese plans. The OBOR (One Belt, One Road) as a massive initiative by the President Xi Jinping in 2013, has potential to transform the economic dynamics of Eurasia. It encapsulates not only rail links from the western China through Central Asian region to Europe, the Middle East, but also South Asia. It appears to be the first time in which China is exporting its development model to external countries. However, China intends to shift its industry to an under developed countries. By doing so, they believe that it could extend and encourage demand for the Chinese goods (Francis 2016).

As far as the Chinese soft power is concerned, it can be deciphered from four dimensions. First, the evolution of country's traditions, secondly, it reflects human progress timely, socially and technologically. It is intangible, but not a mirage. The third aspect of the Chinese soft power contains a strong capability to spread and compete. Therefore, keeping in view the different aspects of the Chinese soft power, the revolution in science and technology has made the Chinese soft power transcend the geographical boundaries ethnic makeup of the country besides the cultural difference. Consequently, it leaves a great impact on the lifestyle and behavior standards of human beings (Ramo 2004).

It is widely held that the Chinese culture besides its principles and ideas are expected to remain appealing to an external world. In this context, Voltaire and Gay (1962) has eulogized the Chinese being "the only one that has made its conquerors adopt its laws" (Voltaire and Gay 1962: 169) and the similar views were also expressed by Bertrand Russell. He expressed that if a nation in the world could ever be "too proud to fight," that nation would be China (Russell 2004: 167). These admiration aside, the Chinese Soft power is considered as a very important concept which is combined with the Chinese idea for the harmonious world. The use of the Chine Soft power and the policy of a harmonious world is said to be well crafted and well thought out approach in their foreign policy.

J. C. Ramo, the author of "*The Age of the Unthinkable*," while quoting Deng Xiaoping, said, "It doesn't matter if the cat is black or white." Therefore, in order to follow the sustainable scientific development, it was better in the scheme of things that it was essential to find a cat that was green and a cat that was transparent (Ramo 2004). It can be deciphered from an above assumption that the Chinese culture and industry located in the "green cat." There is no denying that the new "four-in-one" and "soft power" rhetoric was followed with real funding for arts and culture. The Chinese Dream, the 2008 Beijing Olympics, and the 2010 Shanghai World Expo were two unparalleled events which could showcase China in a more favorable limelight regionally and globally. Consequently, these two events further reinforce the idea that China was blended and fused into the international community.

What makes the Chinese foreign policy more important in the eyes of the world community is its strong diplomacy and economic relations. In fact, the concept of Beijing Consensus has deeper impact and is a way to export China model for promoting trade and economics. This paradigm truly contradicts with the Western led Washington Consensus. However, the government of China considers its culture and economic interaction as an instrumental factor in the global competition. The revival and rapid increase in the establishment of Confucius Institutes all over the world are known as a part of China's soft power and foreign policy. Moreover, to preserve the domestic order, well being, defending the sovereignty and territorial integrity, maintain geopolitical influence are one of the core objectives in the Chinese grand strategy (Swaine and Tellis 2000).

In the words of Nathan and Ross (1997) the Chinese foreign policy ideals have been taken from the Five Principles of Peaceful Coexistence. The FPC (Five Principles of Peaceful Coexistence) was launched in 1954. The main objective behind these golden principles was sovereignty. It means that one state has no right to get in the way of an internal affairs of another state (Nathan and Ross 1997). Having said that the FPC concept entails: mutual respect for sovereignty and territorial integrity, mutual non-aggression, non-interference, equality and mutual benefit, and peaceful coexistence.

In addition to this, in the wake of 1978 reforms, Beijing diverted its focus on economic development which was later capitalized by Deng Xiaoping in the shape of a peaceful foreign policy strategy to "hide its strength and bide its time." As time went on, the government of China issued a White Paper which is aimed at peaceful development of China. It further explains that "harmony as the building of a peaceful and prosperous world as the ultimate goal of China's development." The similar vision was also echoed at the 16th General Assemble of the United Nations in the New York 2005, in which President Hu Jintao announced his country's multilateral approach combined with mutually beneficial cooperation as indispensable in building a harmonious world (Hu 2005).

Given the wide range of reforms in China and its journey from the rags to riches points to the fact that the Chinese leadership is strong and united in its ranks. Keeping in view this context, the politicians in Pakistan are also attracted and inspired from the Chinese model of economic prosperity and modernization programs. Having said, the Prime Minister of Pakistan, Nawaz Sharif agenda aimed at roads-and-highways-heavy development agenda which is one of the key factors in the infrastructure-driven core of China's economic miracle. The similar views were also echoed by the Federal Minister of Pakistan, Ahsan Iqbal on May 27 in a seminar on China–Pakistan relations titled "Iron Brotherhood" in Islamabad, said very candidly, "We should follow the Chinese model to realize an economic boost in the country."

The Chinese model of economic growth was primarily gravitated upon its peoples' historically high saving rates. Besides that the CCP's capability to pick winners in investment, while ensuring that enough projects had 'quality of life' value for ordinary citizens. The dynamics of Pakistan's relations with China has transformed after they signed Free Trade Agreement (FTA) in November, 2003. This trade agreement basically encapsulates two important things: Goods and investment. Further, it enhanced the trade and investment in Pakistan and opened up multiple opportunities for investors on the both sides. It has potential to maximize the benefit for both of the agreeing parties. Keeping in view the Chinese policy of win-win situation, the Pakistani traders are welcoming the Chinese Foreign Direct Investment (FDI) in fruits, vegetables, seafood and livestock products, electrical and non-electrical machinery, electronics, automobiles, textile and engineering. Consequently, this will also coincide opportunities for Pakistan due to the Chinese opening up policy. The Pakistan–China economic as well development relations essentially points to an adoption of the Flying Geese Model. Besides political and economic linkages, Pakistan has always looked toward its natural, neighboring, time tested and All Weather friends like China for its safety, security, and territorial integrity. Therefore, security partnership with China was inevitable given the Pakistan's Indian dilemma.

Pakistan's India Balancing

The topography of Pakistan as a power has magnetized the global powers in the quest of their political, economic and energy interests. Pakistan's geographical proximity to India in the East, China in the Northwest, Afghanistan in the West, Iran in the Southwest and the Arabian Sea in the South provides many opportunities and challenges for Pakistan in the region. There is no doubt that Pakistan is situated at the crossroads of South Asia, West Asia, Central Asia and Western China. It is a well-known fact that Pakistan–China ties have evolved from strategic, political to military level.

Unfortunately, there happen to be a traditional and historical enmity between Pakistan and India. The post independence era in the history of Pakistan was punctuated with refugee influx, resource distribution, constitutional delays, and politico-economic woes. In such an insecurity dilemma, Pakistan looked for economic and security cooperation so that it could withstand the emerging challenges. Given the hot winds evoked in the post independence period, both Pakistan and India fought four wars against each other (1947, 1965, 1971, and 1999).

Historically speaking, K. Arif in 1984 noted that one of the compelling factors behind the embrace of Pakistan's military relations with China was the former's security dilemma from the eastern border. Therefore, keeping the sovereignty and territorial integrity was one of the foremost agenda setting in the foreign policy of Pakistan in the early decades. Although, Pakistan had made military alliance with the West in the shape of SEATO and CENTO, yet according to Arshad Hussain, the then Foreign Minister of Pakistan, "It is entirely impossible for Pakistan to preserve its security without friendship with China" (Arif 1984: 278–279).

It is widely held in Pakistan that in the wake of the 1965 war between India and Pakistan, and sanctions by the US, the only country which helped it was China (Faruqui 2003: 81). The similar views were expressed by one of the defense analyst in Pakistan, Maqbool A. Bhatty. He believes that in the midst of Western sanctions and embargoes, China happens to be a reliable source of military hardware to Pakistan. (Bhatty Winter 1999–2000: 82). The Stephen Cohen, while expressing his views on Pakistan–China ties said that the latter's policy toward Pakistan is basically to counter Indian military power (Cohen 2001: 259). Most importantly, Pakistan–China relations, as noted by Garver 2001, in his analysis, serves both Chinese and Pakistani interests by presenting India with a potential two-front theater in the wake of conflict (Garver 2001: 188). Moreover, the strategic relations between Pakistan and China were further moved in the backdrop of the military relations between the two of Indo-Soviet Treaty of Peace, Friendship, and Cooperation of August 1971 (Burke and Ziring 1990).

The threat perception in Pakistan's security establishment has traditionally remained a great predicament for its existence. Therefore, to contain and deter the security threat from its neighbors, it has adopted policy aimed at improving its defense capabilities by developing military ties with China. As Amin acknowledges that in order to counter Indian hegemony in the region, China has significantly contributed Pakistan in the shape of technology (Amin 2000: 78). Similarly, one of the experts in Pakistan on China maintains that "the preservation of Pakistan's security was the major feature of China's Afghan policy as manifest from the fact that the securities of two countries are mutually interlinked and indivisible (Fazal-ur-Rehman 1998: 72).

The Australian University expert in his article "the India–US–China–Pakistan Strategic Quadrilateral," on April 11, 2012, argues about how Pakistan has developed its defense cooperation with China were: Indian dilemma for Pakistan, Post Cold war realignments in the region, the assertive role of India in the Southeast Asia and South Asian region with the cooperation of Japan and America, the factor of the Chinese encirclement by the US (Kan and Sudhi 2009).

The similar views were reiterated by Masood Khan, the former Ambassador of Pakistan (2012); he was refereeing to air force trainers at Air Force War College: "Pakistan and China are having defense cooperation on four dimensions. These dimensions range from security, region, exchange of officers to military exchanges and exercises besides visits to each other's country" (Rasul, Bux, and Rais 1977). The military exchanges between China and Pakistan do not bode well in Washington. The latter considers China–Pakistan technological exchanges as the violation of the MTCR and NSG conventions. Nonetheless, Pakistan maintains that the development of Pakistan's nuclear technology is before even NSG existed.

There were two significant events which further provided an impetus to Pakistan–China defense: one was China-India war of 1962, second was the USA and Indian nuclear deal in 2008. The logic behind this was that "your friend's enemy is my enemy." Since America had opted for an anti-China and China-contain policy through India. So, China and Pakistan had no other option than to play the reversal. Interestingly, the US–India and China interests gravitate around South Asia and South East Asia. Apart from the US–India nexuses, either competition or rivalry, both could be the contributing factors in strengthening Pakistan's relations with the Beijing. Therefore, keeping in view the geopolitical Catch-22 situation in the region, it was an innate desire of Pakistan to maintain nukes at deterrence level.

Given the security dilemma Pakistan was faced with in its early decades of independence, the comprehensive agreement took place in 1986. After this, the Chinese Prime Minister Li-Peng Jiang Zemin- Chinese president visited Pakistan in 1996. The exchange of visits on the both sides opens up the new avenues for energy cooperation between Pakistan and China. Consequently, the two Chashma Nuclear Power Plants are currently at operational level, whereas, CHASNUPP-3-4 is under construction. However, with the collaboration of China, Pakistan has been successful in manufacturing JF-17 Thunder Aircraft, K8-Trainer Aircraft, Al-Khalid Tank, F-22 Naval Frigates, HRF (Heavy Rebuild Factory) in Taxila, PAC (Pakistan Aeronautical Complex at Kamra) KKH (Karakoram Highway) last but not the least Gawadar port. These engagements and exchanges further indicate that how Pakistan and China enjoy better relations (Pervaiz *et al.* 2016).

Nevertheless, these engagements, friendly commitments and overtures may not be without a common regional challenge. The major question is whether the Muslim-Xinjiang connections create a trouble for China–Pakistan friendship in future. The following analysis may be able to answer.

Muslim-Xinjiang Connections: How Xinjiang Might Complicate Pakistan's Relationship with China

Before this study could seek Pakistani perspective on Muslims-Xinjiang relations, it is better one understand Xinjiang. Geographically, the Chinese province-Xinjiang is a vast land that is comprised of one-sixth of what the total area of China is. Its borders too extended, like, it has around 5,600 km frontiers with Pakistan, India, Afghanistan, three Central Asian states, besides Russia and Mongolia. The figures of 1949 and 2008 shows that the proportion of Han people has significantly increased from 6.7 percent to 40 percent (Howell and Fan 2011).

However, the separatist tendencies within political and militant wings appealing more to a pan-Turkic ethnic identity. These uprisings used to demand for their rights. This demand and type of militant resistance could be appealing phenomenon for Turkistan. One of the dominant factors that could be identified as instigating Uyghurs was: Disintegration of USSR in 1991. Unfortunately, in the words of Wolfe, 2004, the militant wings of Uyghurs exploited the porous borders with Central Asian countries, including Afghanistan. They are believed to have installed their camps which seem to have been beyond the China's reach (Wolfe 2004). The matter of fact is that the Uygurs basically belong to Turkic in origin and are historically linked with Turkistan. However, China feels security threat and have branded the Uyghur separatist movement as a terrorist organization. The most important thing is that the Government of Pakistan being on the same page with its time tested friend also recognizes it as an anti-China activity.

Nevertheless, these historical interactions with Islam and Buddhism were inevitable given the natural geographic nearness. Keeping in view these religio-political and cultural exchanges in the past, the close proximity further proved to have been resulted in the minimal geographical distance. Thus, these exchanges benefited and enriched these civilizations. In the words of

Pakistan's China watchers, Butt (2007: 21–22), he explained that, Buddhist pilgrims used to visit through Northern India. The Northern India is considered as today's Pakistan. The people used to come from Kapica area to Gilgit. In addition to this, the famous and the rich Gandhara art of Pakistan could have deeply influenced the Chinese art in the 1st century. In connection to that, many of the Chinese relics have found in the Indus Valley, Hyderabad and Bhambore (today's Sindh, Pakistan). These archaeological sites are located at around thirty miles on an east side of Karachi — the former capital city of Pakistan. Therefore, it is an established fact that Pakistan enjoys not only historical but also religious and cultural relations. There is no denying too, that Pakistan has a strong trade route to China in the form of Silk Route (Butt 2007: 23–24).

What is a connecting point of Pakistan with China is from Xinjiang with Kashgar (Pakistan). The K.K.H (Karakoram Highway) is one of the adventurous places that passes from China to Pakistan. On the both sides of the border, Muslims have lived since long time (Haider 2005: 522–523). The important thing about this region is that it holds the prominent geo-economic place. It is important in a sense that there have been many historical associations and linkages in the form of culture, religion and economics. These historical exchanges were only possible due to the ancient Chinese Silk Route. Moreover, the travelers from the Chinese side believed to have contributed significantly while extending their links with Bangladesh (the former East Pakistan). Similarly, not only foreign Muslim invaders, but also Afghan and Mughal rulers happen to have developed their contacts through political and economic linkages with China (Chaudhri 1970: 77).

According to the interview taken by the author from one of the Pakistan's China watchers, while asking about the role of Pakistan in Xinjiang problem, he succinctly said:

> I see palpable sentiments among Pakistanis for Xinjiang people because common religion. They — Pakistanis and Uighur Muslims — have just one thing in common i.e., religion. However, there are lots of uncommon factors such as culture, language

and ethnic diversities. These factors should also be taken into account before analysing Uighur–Pakistani relations under the shadow of religion. By adopting this realistic approach, Pakistan would be able play positive role in helping China to achieve the objectives of national integration. (Memon 2016)

There was no denying that, in the past, has allowed the large number of Uighurs to perform their religious duty — Hajj pilgrimage. By that time Pakistan was believed to have been the major transit point for Uighurs on their way to Hajj, making it and Saudi Arabia "focal countries for Islam" in the region. It is worth to be noted here that most of the Uighur settlements that can be found in Pakistan today were established in the 1980s as transit points on the way to Mecca (www.uighuramerican.org/mediareports 2001).

In the Post 9/11 scenario and Talibanization phenomenon coupled with crisis of governance in Afghanistan and disintegration of the USSR, many issues related to militancy cropped up. These problems, no doubt, posed a grave challenge for the bilateral relations. The matter of fact was that there were an alleged link between Pakistani-based religious parties and separatist groups in China's turbulent province, Xinjiang. Some reports emerged in the media showing Pakistani religious Ulema's links with Xinjiang turmoil. What is to be noted here that at the official level, neither of the governments has approved these reports (Haider 2005: 523–526).

In spite of that, these issues could not deter Pakistan's friendship with China. In the wake of the War on Terrorism, Pakistan has institutionalized anti-terrorism dialogue with China. Therefore, both the sides have agreed to share intelligence on terrorism. With the launching of military operations in the adjacent areas of Pakistan-Afghan Durand Line in December 2003, one of the dangerous militant who was believed to have been the leader of ETIM, Hasan Mahsum was targeted. These operations were combined with wiping out remnants alleged terrorists. In connection to that China and Pakistan conducted joint military exercises in 2004, in Xinjiang, with a code name "Friendship 2004." The military operations were conducted by Pakistan Army. Having said that, it was in the national interest of two countries to carry out an anti-terrorism campaign so that the apprehensions of the Chinese side regarding support for Uighur Muslim separatists from some of Pakistani religious groups could be removed.

In connection to this, given the frequent exchange of visits on both the sides paved the way toward new dimensions and explored new areas of cooperation. For instance, the former President of Pakistan, Pevez Musharraf made a brief sojourn to China in November 2003, in which a Joint Declaration on Direction of Bilateral Relations was signed. This landmark agreement was expected to provide a big boost in framing a road map in which both countries could reap their mutual relations. It is interesting to note here that in many areas cooperation has been mechanized in such a way that could serve the interests of both states (Fazal-ur-Rehman 2006).

The year of 2005 was considered a landmark in the Pakistan-China relations. In this year a treaty of friendship and cooperation was signed in which both the countries made serious commitments in which it was agreed upon that "neither party will join any alliance or bloc, which infringed upon the sovereignty, security and territorial integrity" of either nation, while simultaneously positing that both parties "would not conclude treaties of this nature with any third party" (Ministry of Foreign Affairs 2005).

In fact, given the Islamic identity of Uighurs have at times strained Pakistan's political as well as economic links with China. Pakistan can no longer afford political or economic isolation in the region. Xinjiang holds great significance for China in terms of its broader agenda linked to China's economic developments in Eastern parts. Thus, keeping in view the abundant natural resources and strategic location as compare to Central and South Asia, China attaches great importance to the stability and prosperity of the region.

The geopolitical situation on the ground has dramatically transformed. As I have already mentioned above that there has been an increasing number of Han Chinese in Xinjiang. This factor has also created a great schism between the Pakistani businessman and the Uighurs. However, the economic and business interests of the

Pakistani traders have indeed eclipsed the impression of Islamic solidarity. The policy and approach of Pakistan toward Xinjiang gets rare attention. Consequently, Pakistan has stopped supporting the Ughurs due to the reason that China is seeking to woo Ughur minority by applying a soft power approach besides rendering/pushing them politically to embracing a Greater Chinese consciousness. The economic reforms as introduced by Deng Xioping in 1980's offers many economic opportunities and a sort of freedom to the Ughur minority. Having said that, "border minorities in general were encouraged to develop their economies through trade with neighboring countries" (June Teufel Dreyer 2000: 92).

Pakistan believes that China is investing in socio-economic, energy and education related projects. China has initiated a CPEC project, which is the part of OBOR (One Belt, One Road). This mega project is not Pakistan specific, but could link many countries in the region. Given this multi-sectoral investment on the part of China in Pakistan further indicate about how Pakistan's relations have transformed from political, strategic to economic and cultural. The range of trade and economics is so massive that it has an overwhelming impact not only on Pakistan but its future too.

Xinjiang, hitherto backward and deprived region has now become the focus of traders and the business community. The Chinese projects related to economic developments could open up new vistas for the people of Ughur community. From the Xinjiang to Kashgar, China is going to launch mega projects in the shape of pipelines, connectivity through road, industrial developments, railway lines in the region. In this context, Pakistan could be a bridge for China to access Central Asia, South Asia and Middle East. In spite of that the issues and concerns related to terrorism, political instability and security are expected to remain in bilateral relations given the geopolitical dynamics of the region.

Indian Contemporary Studies on China

In addition to studies on China in Pakistan, this study also explores Indian scholarship on China and compares their studies on China with Pakistan. There is no denying that China and India are the most populous; with the vastness of the territory; oldest civilization linkages; close proximity of borders; software and hardware powerhouses; regional competitors and regional giants having the same dream but on different beds.

Historically speaking, during the Cold War period, India remained a non-aligned power in the region. Although the period of 1950s is said to be peaceful. However, this honeymoon could not last long. The relations deteriorated in the backdrop of territorial hostilities in 1962. After the brief war over the border, the two emerging powers started exchange of visits to diffuse the tension and mistrust created after the war. These state to state visits paved the way toward rapprochement between India and China. The visit of Indian Prime Minister Rajiv Gandhi (December 19–23, 1988) to China was termed as a good omen in their bilateral relations.

The reciprocal visits were largely upheld and considered to be constructive in shaping and improving relations. In fact, much progress has been made on the border, Tibet issue, yet the atmosphere of trust deficit looms large. According to interview of Mira Sinha Bhattacharjea, by Dr. Reena Marwah, on the April 21 2012:

> ... Politics dominate everything; even if people suffer it is the state concerns that always dominate ... In fact, in my opinion, both Taiwan and Tibet could have become independent ... My fear is that there will be a greater militarization of the Tibet issue.

Moreover, Indian scholars like B.M Jain believes that the evolving trends in the region shows that both India and China would continue to compete for status and influence. In addition to this, the studies of Mohan Malik, Keshava Goha, Nitya Singh, and Jagannath P. Panda manifests that Indian studies are influenced by competition, influence and territorial factors rather than culture, religion or civilization. Some Indian scholars believe that the economic rise of China could be beneficial to India. Some others still hold that, military modernization by China and border issue are said to be the grave security concern for India (see Table 4).

Table 4. Indian Contemporary Studies of China

No.	Author/Year	Findings/Study/Key Arguments
1	B.M Jain, 2004	His study indicates that "competition and influence" are the major factors that could influence Indian studies of China in the region.
2	Mohan Malik, 2004	His study finds that "competition not cooperation" are the key factors which influences Indian study of China.
3	Rajiv Sikri, 2009	His study identifies that China studies in India are influenced by differences over the border, Tibet and Pakistan factor.
4	Abanti Bhattacharya, 2010	Her study shows that border conflict and Tibet factor are the main issues in Indian studies of China.
5	David M. Malone and Rohan Mukherjee, 2010	Their study shows that historically, Indian studies of China have almost remained "reactionary and adrift."
6	Mohan Malik, 2012	His study argues that given the asymmetric economic growth of China and India, could lead to competition. To him, this "competition," has remained the hallmark in the Indian studies of China.
7	Jagannath P. Panda, 2013	His study shows that the "Border" issue will remain the focus of China studies in India.
8	Keshava Guha, 2012	This study argues that coexistence of both China and India in an international state system is unusual, because both powers aspire for superpower status and border problem. Thus, great power ambitions and conflicting border influence Indian Studies of China.
9	Mohan Malik, 2012	His study indicates that Indian studies of China are considered as "complex" because of "historical mistrust and geographical dispute."
10	Nitya Singh, 2012	Her study acknowledges that India–China has deep cultural ties, yet Indian studies of China are widely influenced by politics, which is fraught with conflict and trust deficit.
11	Avijit Banerjee, 2012	Her study shows the historical, cultural linkages through the efforts of Cheena Bhavan between China and India, yet her study of China indicates that these ties were somehow constrained by border disputes.

(Continued)

Table 4. (*Continued*)

No.	Author/Year	Findings/Study/Key Arguments
12	B.R Deepak, 2012	His study points out that there has been rapid growth of China studies in India yet these are hamstrung by border conflict.
13	Abanti Bhattacharya, 2012	His study of Taiwan in China studies reflected that there is a dual approach among Indian scholars over one China policy besides inching toward ties with Taiwan.
14	Jagannath P. Panda, 2012	His study of China indicates that "xenophobia, personal rivalry and lack of proper trainings and skills," what mars Indian understanding of China.

Source: Compiled by the author.

In addition to that India has institutionalized studies on China through their respective higher institutions much earlier than Pakistan. In Pakistan, China studies were introduced from 1970s whereas, Indian studies of China were launched in 1943. The role of a few universities in India in disseminating the culture and language of China is worthy of applause. The institutions like JNU, Visva Bharati University and Banaras University are playing a pivotal role in introducing China studies in India. Apart from these higher learning institutions of India, there are many other institution and centers which are involved in teaching and research on China.

Some of these institutions have introduced courses at diploma and Ph.D. level. For pursuing China studies at graduate and Master level, Delhi University has been always at the center stage. The Institutes (Think Tanks) like IDS, ICS, CPR, ORF, IPCS, and Indian Council of World Affairs, have become somehow launching pads for research in language, political, economic, culture, civilization, and strategic affairs. The center of focus of these Think Tanks is internal and external affairs.

India and China have much older and closer civilizational linkages than Pakistan. Indians could realize that given the politico-economic and security factors, the Chinese studies have got wide currency, but with less understanding of China and the Chinese culture and civilization. In context to this, Professor, B.R. Deepak, in his recent study on the Chinese Studies in India, points out the various fissures and loopholes in failing to understand the Chinese culture and its civilization. Moreover, he argues that "China studies has gathered momentum not only in India but also in the world. Yet he believes that Indian Studies of China has been lopsided for a long time. He further said that there is a lack of real language expertise among China experts of India. He acknowledges that by separating language and area studies has resulted in the touch me not psychology." Keeping in view the Indian scholarship on China, India needs to revisit the history so that it could be explored about how the China studies have developed, disintegrated and reemerged under the different environment (Deepak 2012: 72).

Conclusion

The above study focused on China studies in Pakistan and India. The review on scholarship and friendship in Pakistan's context showed that there were many factors influencing Pakistani China watchers in carrying out their China studies. Indeed, China is Pakistan's traditional and time tested friend. The relations have remained unaffected even in the midst of regional, global, financial and historical upheavals. China has been the cardinal principle of Pakistan's foreign policy. Both the countries are located geographically in such a region which was cradle of an ancient civilization. It has cooperated, invested and developed many projects in Pakistan. To explore and exploit mineral resources in Pakistan, the Chinese cooperation has been remarkable.

China and Pakistan have undergone the periods of colonialism, imperialism, poverty and ignorance, war and conflicts in the region. They both share a same vision, dream and acknowledge each other's role in the region. Pakistan's China experts view the relations of both the countries as the two eyes of a man, which blink together, move together, cry together, see things together, and sleep together, even though they never see each other, their culture, ideology and civilization are poles apart. More importantly, Pakistan is geographically well placed to play a role in the peace and stability in the region. The golden five principles of peaceful policy of China have become the linchpin for Pakistan and these principles seems to become popular and of universal appeal. Non-interference and peaceful policy is really a revolutionary concept in this contemporary era.

The question is why we must conduct studies on China. For China believes in humanism, win–win relations and self-reliance. To ensure prosperity and stability in the region, China and Pakistan are fighting mutually the curse of extremism, terrorism, separatism, and militancy. Although the four decades of our relations were focused and were limited to, strategic partnership, but after the 2000, has witnessed the turning point in ties. Interestingly, "All-Weather Friendship" between China and Pakistan is likely to continue to provide a great impetus in and assistance to Pakistan in many fields. The strengthening and increasing cooperation indicates that China and Pakistan could remain an area of interest and concern to the regional and global powers. Academic studies on China in Pakistan suggest that more efforts are needed to understand China by promoting and learning the Chinese language. The enhancement in people to people cooperation could further cement a Pakistani friendship with the rising China.

Whereas, the review of Indian scholarship on China shows that China and Indian relation are not friction free, as in the context of Pakistan. Nevertheless, Indian studies seem to have been influenced by the factors like, Tibet, territorial, competition, and Pakistan. In contrast to Pakistani academic studies on China, India has established more China study centers than Pakistan. India and China are emerging powers, economic powerhouses, cooperating and competing at regional and global sphere. China is leading from the front among the developing economies in the region and poised to play an instrumental role at regional and global forums. It has fostered its peaceful relations with regions such as Latin America, Africa, Central Asia, Middle East, South East Asian countries.

The success stories about China in the world are due to its economic and technological advancement among the developing nations. The Chinese economy has obviously transformed from its waning power status to an ascending player in a regional and global system. As a regional power, China is playing an active role in addressing immediate problems and challenges which have destroyed humanity, like humanity. The steps taken by the Chinese leadership in tackling poverty and corruption are an eye opener for regional countries like Pakistan and India.

There are two dominant views among Indian China watchers: one, India sees great opportunity in the economic sphere, second, they expect a big challenge in terms of the security. In the long run, there seems to be constant fear and insecurity for they believe that their interests could be affected. The economic relations between India and China are being linked with security and politics. Therefore, China studies are seen with a less cultural and more of a security lens. India, in fact, started studies on China much earlier than Pakistan. Yet, Indian higher education institutions show a multidisciplinary approach in conducting various studies. However, this study concludes that studies on China are vigorously pursued not only in Pakistan but also in India, yet it suggests to revisit hurdles in promoting China studies in South Asia.

References

Akram, M. 2015. A Unique Partnership, China and Pakistan. In *Hand Book of Pakistan–China Relations*. Islamabad: Pakistan–China Institute, pp. 1–16.

Ali, Ahmed. 1949. *Muslim China*. Pakistan Institute of International Affairs.

Allen-Ebrahimian, Bethany. 2015. China Loves Pakistan … but Most Chinese Don't: China's Pro-Pakistan State Media Blitz May Be More about Convincing its Own People. *The Foreign Policy Review* (April 22), http://foreignpolicy.com/2015/04/22/china-pakistan-relations-trade-deal-friendship/. Accessed on March 9, 2017.

Amin, Shahid M. 2000. *Pakistan's Foreign Policy: A Reappraisal*. Oxford: Oxford University Press.

Amin, Shahid M. 2012. Interviewed by Swaran Singh March 10, 2012.

Arif, K. 1984. *Pakistan's Foreign Policy: Indian Perspectives*. Lahore: Vanguard Book Ltd.

Arnold, David D. 2016. Six Pressing Issues in Asia and How We are Adapting Our Approach to Address Them (September 6), Asian Foundation. http://asiafoundation.org/2016/09/06/six-pressing-issues-asia-adapting-approach-address/. Accessed on September 9, 2016.

Author n.a. 2000. Han Settlement Still Pouring into Western China's Xinjiang Region, August. http://www.uighuramerican.org/mediareports/2000/afpaug2400.html. Accessed on August 9, 2016.

Author n.a. 2005. Treaty of Friendship, Cooperation and Good Neighbourly Relations between the People's Republic of China and the Islamic Republic of Pakistan, Ministry of Foreign Affairs of the People's Republic of China, April 5, 2005, http://fmprc.gov.cn/Sino-eng/zilao3602/3604/default.htm. Accessed on August 5, 2016.

Author n.a. 2016. China GDP Annual Growth Rate Forecast 2016–2020, http://www.tradingeconomics.com/china/gdp-growth-annual/forecast. Accessed on September 7, 2016.

Aziz, Sirajuddin. 2015. Pakistan–China — A Withering Friendship. In *Handbook of Pakistan–China Relations*. Islamabad: Pakistan–China Institute, pp. 229–248.

Banerjee, Avijit. 2012. The Role of Cheena Bhavan. In Chih-yu Shih, Swaran Singh, and Reena Marwah (Eds.), *On China by India From Civilization to Nation State*. Amherst: Cambria Press, pp. 47–59.

Bhattacharya, Abanti. 2012. Taiwan in the Chinese Studies in India. In Chih-yu Shih, Swaran Singh, and Reena Marwah (Eds.), *On China by India From Civilization to Nation State*. Amherst: Cambria Press, pp. 145–158.

Bhatty, Maqbool Ahmad. 1999–2000. Pak–China Relations in the 21st Century. *Islamabad Regional Studies* 18(1): 420.

Burke, S. M. and Ziring, Lawrence. 1990. *Pakistan's Foreign Policy: An Historical Analysis*. Karachi: Oxford University Press.

Butt, Muhammad Ijaz. 2007. *Focus on China: Relations with Pakistan and Domestic Concern*. Lahore: Advance Publishers.

Cohen, Stephen P. 2001. *India: Emerging Power*. Washington D.C.: Brooking Institution.

Daily Times. 2016. Can Pakistan Clone the Chinese Model? http://dailytimes.com.pk/opinion/06-Jun-16/can-pakistan-clone-the-chinese-mode. Accessed on December 3, 2016.

Dawn News. April 27, 2016. Pakistan–China Trade Increases by 18.2pc to $4.4 billion, http://www.dawn.com/news/1254586. Accessed on September 6, 2016.

Deepak, B.R. 2012. The Chinese Studies in India. In Chih-yu Shih, Swaran Singh, and Reena Marwah (Eds.), *On China by India From Civilization to Nation State.* Amherst: Cambria Press, pp. 71–92.

Dreyer, June Teufel 2000. *China's Political System.* New York: Addison Wesley Longman, p. 292.

Fahim, Mayraj. 2015. The Role of Decentralization and Local Government Integration in the Chinese Economic Development and its Lessons for Pakistan. In *Handbook of Pakistan-China Relations.* Islamabad: Pakistan–China Institute, pp. 249–293.

Faruqui, Ahmad. 2003. *Rethinking National Security of Pakistan: The Price of Strategic Myopia.* Hampshire: Ashgate Publishing.

Fazal-ur-Rahman and Hamayoun Khan. 2015. Pakistan-China Economic Relations. In *Handbook of Pakistan-China Relations.* Islamabad: Pakistan–China Institute, pp. 112–158.

Fazal-ur-Rehman (1998 Winter and Spring). Pakistan's Relations with China. *Strategic Studies* 19(4–20.1): 14.

Fazal-ur-Rehman. 2006. Pak–China Economic Relations: Constraints and Opportunities, *Strategic Studies* 26(2): 53–72.

Fukuyama, Francis. 2016. Exporting the Chinese Model. Project Syndicate, https://www.project-syndicate.org/commentary/china-one-belt-one-road-strategy-byfrancis-fukuyama-2016-01#PGF36SQ2Lci55eMT.99. Accessed on September 3, 2016.

Garver, John W. 2001. *Protracted Contest: Sino-Indian Rivalry in the Twentieth Century.* Seattle: University of Washington Press.

Guha, Keshava. 2012. Sino-Indian Relations: History, Problems and Prospects. *World in Review* 34(2).

Haider, Ziad. 2005. Sino-Pakistan Relations and Xinjiang's Uighurs: Politics, Trade, and Islam along the Karakoram Highway. *Asian Survey* 45(4): 522–545.

Hali, S. M. 2015. *China's Stories China's Success How China Transformed in the Past 40 Years.* Islamabad: Rumi Academy.

Hanban Sources. Year n.a. http://english.hanban.org/node_10971.htm. Accessed on September 3, 2016.

Howell, A. and Fan C.C. 2011. Migration and Inequality in Xinjiang: A Survey of Han and Uyghur Migrants in Urumqi. *Journal of Eurasian Geography and Economics* 52(1): 119–139.

http://blogs.reuters.com/great-debate/2016/04/26/what-to-read-into-a-growing-alliance-between-china-and-pakistan/.

Hu, Jingtao. 2005. Build towards a harmonious world of lasting peace and common prosperity. Statement by H. E. Hu Jintao, President of the People's Republic of China, at the United Nations Summit, New York, September 15, 2005. http://www.un.org/webcast/summit2005/statements15/china050915eng.pdf. Accessed on September 2, 2016.

Jain, B.M. 2004. India–China relations: Issues and Emerging Trends. *The Round Table* 93(374): 253–269.

Javed, Syed Hasan. (2016). *The Rise of China and the Asian Century.* Islamabad, Pakistan: National University of Science and Technology.

Kan, Nalini. 2009. India and China after 9/11, In Search of Pragmatic Ties. In Kumar Singh Sudhi (Ed.), *Post 9/11 Indian Foreign Policy, Challenges and Opportunities.* New Delhi: Pentagon Press, pp. 164–168.

Khan, Raja M. 2010. Sino-Pak Relationship in the Historical Perspective (March 21), www.markthetruth.com/china/414-sino-pak-relationship-in-the-historical-perspective.html. Accessed on September 30, 2016.

Lin, Shangli. 2001. Pakistan–China Relations. *Pakistan Horizon* (Karachi), 54: 1–3.

Mahesar, Pervaiz Ali, Ali Khan Ghumro, Ghulam Mujtaba Khuskh, and Abdul Hameed Mahesar. 2016. Pakistan–China Relations: Thinking through an Indian lens. *International Journal of Scientific Research and Innovative Technology* 3(3).

Mahesar, Pervaiz Ali. 2017. China-Pakistan Economic Corridor: Perils and Prospects. *International Public Policy Review, Singapore,* http://www.ippreview.com/index.php/Blog/single/id/365.html. Accessed on March 4, 2017.

Malik, Mohan. 2004. *India–China Relations: Giants Stir, Cooperate and Compete.* Honolulu: Asia Pacific Center for Security Studies.

Malik, Mohan. 2012. China and India Today: Diplomats Jostle, Militaries Prepare. *The World Affairs Journal,* http://www.worldaffairsjournal.org/article/china-and-india-today-diplomats-jostle-militaries-prepare. Accessed on March 3, 2017.

Malik, Mohan. 2012. India Balances China. *Asian Politics & Policy* 4(3): 345–376.

Malone, David M. and Rohan Mukherjee. 2010. India and China: Conflict and Cooperation. *Survival* 52, 1: 137–158.

Manuel, Anja. 2016. What to Read into a Growing Alliance between China and Pakistan. (April 27), http://www.reuters.com/article/us-usa-china-pakiston-diplomacy-commenta/commentary-what-to-read-into-a-growing-alliance-between-china-and-pakistan-idUSKCN0XO2DU. Accessed on September 6, 2016.

Memon, Aman. 2016. Interviewed by Pervaiz dated 12.8.2016.

Mushtaque, Chaudhry Faisal. 2015. Education and Language Common Denominator for the Youth of Both Countries. In Handbook of *Pakistan–China Relations*. Islamabad: Pakistan–China Institute, pp. 294–305.

Nathan, Andrew and Ross, Robert. S. 1997. *The Great Wall and the Empty Fortress: China's Search for Security*. New York: W. W. Norton.

Nye, Joseph S. 1990. *Bound to Lead: The Changing Nature of American Power*. New York, NY: Basic Books.

Nye, Joseph S. 2003. Soft Power: Propaganda isn't the Way. *International Herald Tribune*, Global Edition Opinion, http://www.nytimes.com/2003/01/10/opinion/10iht-ednye_ed3_.html. Accessed on September 7, 2016.

Nye, Joseph S. 2006. "Think Again: Soft Power." *Foreign Policy*, http://www.foreignpolicy.com/story/cms.php?story_id=3393. Accessed on September 7, 2016.

Pakistan Observer. 2010. Zardari: New World Order Says China Impossible. (July 11), http/pakobserver.net/detailnews.asp?id.40699. Accessed on September 30, 2016.

Panda, Jagannath P. 2012. China Studies in Indian Think Tanks. In Chih-yu Shih, Swaran Singh, and Reena Marwah (Eds.), *On China by India From Civilization to Nation State*, 2012. Amherst: Cambria Press, pp. 159–178.

Panda, Jagannath P. 2013. Competing Realities in China–India Multilateral Discourse: Asia's Enduring Power Rivalry. *Journal of Contemporary China* 22(82): 669–690.

Pew Research Center. 2014. How Asians Rate China, India, Pakistan, Japan and the U.S, http://www.pewglobal.org/2014/07/14/global-opposition-to-u-s-surveillance-and-drones-but-limited-harm-to-americas-image/pg-2014-07-14-balance-of-power-4-01/. Accessed on March 1, 2017.

Ramo, Joshua Cooper. 2004. *The Beijing Consensus*. London: The Foreign Policy Center.

Rasul, Bux, Rais. 1977. *China and Pakistan: A Political Analysis of Mutual Relations*. New Delhi: Progressive Publishers.

Russell, B. 2004. *The Problem of China*. Charleston, SC: BiblioLife, LLC.

Sikri, Rajiv. 2009. India's Look East Policy. *Asia-Pacific Review* 16(1): 131–145.

Singh, Nitya. 2012. How to Tame Your Dragon: An Evaluation of India's Foreign Policy Toward China. *India Review* 11(3): 139–160.

Stokes, Bruce. 2015. How Asia-Pacific Publics See Each Other and Their National Leaders. The Pew Research Centre, http://www.pewglobal.org/2015/09/02/how-asia-pacific-publics-see-each-other-and-their-national-leaders/.

Swaine, Michael and Tellis, A. 2000. *Interpreting China's Grand Strategy. Past, Present, and Future*. Washington, D.C.: Rand.

Syed, Mushahid Hussain (Ed.) 2015. Pakistan and China Strategic Partners in the 21st Century. In Handbook of *Pakistan–China Relations*. Islamabad, Pakistan-China Institute: Dost Publication. pp. 306–317.

Voltaire, Francois-Marie Arouet. 1962. *Philosophical Dictionary*. New York, NY: Basic Books.

Wang, H. and Lu, Y. C. 2008. The Conception of Soft Power and its Policy Implications: A Comparative Study of China and Taiwan. *Journal of Contemporary China* 17(56): 425–447.

Wolfe Adam. 2004. China Takes the Lead in Strategic Central Asia. *Asia Times*, http://www.atimes.com. Accessed on March 2, 2017.

7

Vietnam's Composite Agenda on the Rise of China: Power, Peace, and Party

Quang Minh PHAM
Rector & International Relations
VNU University of Social Sciences and Humanities, Hanoi, Vietnam

Hoang Giang LE
International Cooperation Office
VNU University of Social Sciences and Humanities, Hanoi, Vietnam

Since the second half of the 1970s, after being confronted with external and internal changes, both China and Vietnam have carried out reforms, opened up their countries, normalized their relations, and evolved as big power and middle power, respectively. In May 2008, both sides signed the comprehensive strategic partnership making China the number one trading partner of Vietnam. However, the recent development of Vietnam–China relationship is contested and threatened by the dispute over sovereignty in the South China Sea (Bien Dong in Vietnamese), especially the Haiyang Shiyou 981 oil rig incident from May to July 2014, the reclamation of seven entities by China and the recent PCA awards on July 12, 2016. This chapter aims to analyze the characteristics of Vietnam–China relationship from power, party, and peace approaches. The first part of the chapter analyzes China's rise to power from theoretical perspectives. The second part discusses the development of Vietnam–China political relations. The third part focuses on the recent development of bilateral relations through the Haiyang Shiyou 981 oil rig incident and highlights the party factor therein. The fourth part discusses implication and recommendations for both Vietnam and China as well as for regional politics. The chapter concludes that power, party, and peace are the main factors in Vietnam–China relations, and both countries should not let the realist point of view determine their relations, but promote confidence-building measures to play proactive and responsible roles in the region.

The Rise of China from Theoretical Perspectives

In 2008, celebrating 30 years of open door policy proclaimed by Deng Xiaoping, China showed the whole world a country of long historical and cultural tradition and modern technological development through a great opening ceremony at the Beijing Summer Olympics. The importance of "Middle Kingdom" can hardly be exaggerated: With a population of 1.3 billion, China is a rising power without any discussion. Economically China is already ranked second just after the US according to purchasing power parity (PPP) calculation (see Table 1).

In September 2008, China became the third country in the world after the US and former Soviet Union to send a spacecraft with a Chinese astronaut on board into space. Politically, China is a permanent member of the United Nations Security Council. Technologically, China is a nuclear power and is ready to conquer the universe. In short, China is an economic, political, and military heavyweight in Asia. However, although China belongs to the top 10 countries in terms of economy, the process of transforming its centrally planned economic model into a market one is still ongoing. It does mean that although China can become one of the upper-income nations, it will still face social problems such as mass poverty,

Table 1. Top 10 Economies of the World in 2015

Rank	Country	GDP (Purchasing Power Parity)	Date of Information
1	China	$19,700,000,000,000	2015 Est.
2	European Union	$19,180,000,000,000	2015 Est.
3	US	$18,040,000,000,000	2015 Est.
4	India	$7,998,000,000,000	2015 Est.
5	Japan	$4,843,000,000,000	2015 Est.
6	Germany	$3,860,000,000,000	2015 Est.
7	Russia	$3,725,000,000,000	2015 Est.
8	Brazil	$3,199,000,000,000	2015 Est.
9	Indonesia	$2,848,000,000,000	2015 Est.
10	UK	$2,702,000,000,000	2015 Est.

Source: CIA (2013).

social disparity, ethnic minorities, and unequal and sustainable development, which could cause the country's collapse (Gordon Chang 2012). To some extent, the intentions of China were expressed best through a statement made by Deng Xiaoping: "Adopt a sober perspective; maintain a stable posture; be composed; conserve your strength and conceal your resources; don't aspire to be the head; do something eventually" (Wang Yusheng 2001). While China always insisted that their development is peaceful, there is a common attitude of "China's threat" existing among regional countries. Interestingly, note that the word "peaceful rise" was used for the first time in November 2003 by Zheng Bijian, the Chairman of the China Reform Forum to reassure other countries that China's development will not take the paths of Germany and Japan. Although "peaceful rise" was used frequently by President Hu Jintao and Premier Wen Jiabao in the following months, it was replaced by "peaceful development path" by President Hu Jintao in his speech at the Boao Forum on Asia on April 24, 2004 (Lampton 2008: 33). According to Zheng Bijian, China does not intend to challenge the existing international order, nor will of the order advocate undermining or overthrowing of the order by violent means (Zheng 2005). The fact was that in the beginning of the 21st century China had presented a grand strategy for development. In the political report to the 16th Party Congress on November 8, 2002, President Jiang Zemin had pointed out:

> The first decades of the 21st Century are a period of important strategic opportunities, which we must seize tightly and which offers bright prospects ... We need to concentrate on building a well-off society ... in this period ... the two decades of development will serve as an inevitable connecting link for attaining the third-step strategic objectives for our modernization drive ... A new world war is unlikely in the foreseeable future. It is realistic to bring about a fairly long period of peace in the world and a favorable environment in areas around China. (Jiang Zemin, 2002)

How can we understand the rise of China and its influence on the Vietnam–China relationship? Does the rise of China represent a threat, a chance, or a challenge for Vietnam and other countries? In the international relations studies, there are several theoretical points of view which can explain the development of China and the Vietnam–China bilateral relations, and they can be summarized by using a threefold framework of power, peace, and party.

First, in terms of *power*, the rise of China can be made sense through the theory of realism. According to realism, China's rise presents potential dangers for the regional architecture and challenges the dominant role of the US in the world. Kenneth Waltz, Stephen Walt, Robert Jervis, Michael Doyle, and others have claimed that China's growing power in the post-Cold War system reproduces a conflict within the system where the US dominates. Robert Gilpin's system-governance thesis and Organski and Kugler's power transition thesis suggested that whatever China aims to achieve, be it greater status, benefits or influence, its rise should be considered as a challenge to American hegemony (Goldstein 2003: 59). Kagan (1997) even pointed out that China intends in the near term to replace the US as the dominant power in East Asia and in the long term to challenge its position as the dominant power in the world.

The rise of China raises security dilemma not only for the US, but also for Asian countries, especially East Asian countries. The question is how the states should deal with a rising power who may challenge their *status quo*. According to Joseph Nye, Asia manages its own internal power balancing and many Asian countries will welcome the presence of the US in the region. China's military aggressiveness may also lead to the establishment of a military alliance between its neighboring countries (Nye 2010). In short, the common assumption is that China is a potential threat, and must be dealt with either by engagement or by containment. However, there are still some important questions: Would China's rise inevitably lead to a military conflict with the US? Would the rise of China mean a relative decline of the US? Does the rise of China entail increasing confrontation between the Middle Kingdom and its rivals? And would the Asian regional architecture develop into a Sino-centric hierarchy like the "tributary system" (Fairbank 1968)?

A second approach to the rise of China and China's foreign relations emphasizes the *peace* factor, and theories such as institutionalism can be applied. Different from the realist perspective, which emphasizes the struggle for power based on the principle of zero-sum game, the institutional perspective looks at the other side of international relations where a cooperative win–win situation is dominant, and a positive-sum game exists. The main assumption of the institutionalization concept is that because of globalization and economic interdependence all countries would have to consider the costs of disruptive behavior and the benefits of cooperative ones. In order to make more profit, all countries try to expand a network of international organizations and systems based on common rules and norms. In this context, any country would prefer cooperation among countries, and China is no exception. If China can become an integral part of this network or if other countries can be included into this system, the disruptive behavior of China would be constrained.

Multinational institutions would not allow any country to behave in a disruptive manner. The more a country is involved in international system, the more constructive behavior it follows. In addition, the 21st century order is also different from the past one. Ikenberry (2008) sees an interaction between these two phenomena:

> The rise of China does not have to trigger a wrenching hegemonic transition. The US-Chinese power transition can be very different from those of the past because China faces an international order that is fundamentally different from those that past rising states confronted ... Today's Western order, in short, is hard to overturn and easy to join ... Today, China can gain full access to and thrive within this system. And if it does, China will rise, but the Western order — if managed properly — will live on?

A third factor in China's emergence concerns the theory of constructivism. Identity construction is the main concern of the constructivist school of thought, and it is important to answer questions as how do other states perceive China and how does China perceive itself? The main question is about the motives behind the rise of China, whether it is the rise of a potential friend or of an enemy? Does China act as a communist state or as a developmental one? As one looks specifically into China's relations with Vietnam, the interaction between the two countries' communist parties seems to reflect that their view of each other is still strongly dominated by communist idealism; both apparently consider each other as "comrades" in the course of their diplomatic interaction (Interview of Nguyen Huy Quy — Vietnam). A unique feature of constructivism theory is that this inter-party ties touches on aspects which the realist and institutionalist approaches neglect, plays a great role in the political relations between two countries, and somewhat particularizes this bilateral relations from others in the region and the world.

In principle, the constructivists agree with the institutionalists in term of rules and norms, but try to extend it to the internationalization of the behavioral norms by the individual actors. After three decades of opening the country up, China still faces the situation of "dual identities" (Lam Peng Er and Lim Tai Wei 2009: 17). On the one side, China considers itself a victim of Western aggression, exploitation, and inequitable treatment. On the other side, China tries to show itself as a responsible member of the world. Whatever identity China would like to show, and whether it is real or not, the fact is that the Middle Kingdom is conforming itself to norms and rules which were established by the Western countries. The question is for how long, and to what extent, can China keep balancing between pursuing its national interests and committing to international norms. However, it is difficult to judge which priorities does Chinese leadership give to: search for great-power status and leadership in regional and world politics or domestic stability and economic growth (Sutter 2008: 19). There is no doubt, however, that China's perception — either of its perceived unfair treatment or its responsibility as an emerging global power — would leave profound impact on its behaviors and interaction with regional stakeholders.

A useful way to look at China's diplomatic *modus operandi* through these theoretical lenses is by using a comparative frame of unilateral, bilateral, and multilateral approaches. Unilaterally, China's increase in its share of wealth and influence, and subsequently its dramatic intensification of capacity, can be seen as a potential challenge to the current regional order, and may signify more conflict and confrontation in the future (the realist approach). Whether China's intention is to assert its territorial claim or to upset the *status quo* and affix itself as a dominant powerhouse in the region, the realists fear that it will carry severe implications for the region's stability and security nevertheless. Multilaterally, in contrast, China can be observed seeking to strengthen ties with its neighbors and at the same time demonstrating its role as a responsible international player (the institutionalist approach). Over the last decade, the Middle Kingdom has gradually sought to engage its neighbors through infrastructure projects such as the One Belt, One Road (OBOR) initiative and the Asian Infrastructure Investment Bank (AIIB), or more sophisticated dialogue platforms including the ASEAN Plus Three framework and the South Asian Association for Regional Cooperation (SAARC). Bilaterally, China has also been trying to reach out to partners through the use of direct interactions such as financial investments, cultural promotion activities, and political meetings, which take the shapes of state-level visits or, particularly in the case of Vietnam, meetings between communist party officials (see further discussion on this below).

In summary, all three theoretical approaches try to explain the rise of China and its implication for world politics, but cannot sufficiently do so. The rise of China still continues to remain questionable because of its uncertain development, mostly due to the sustainability of Chinese economic growth. The recent developments in the South China Sea seem to support the power-centric realist point of view, and the rise of China is not peaceful as it reaffirmed again and again.

The Development of Vietnam–China Political Relations

The discussion above argues that the Sino-Vietnamese interaction falls along the lines of power, peace, and party struggles. This section explores how such interaction first came into being and subsequently unfolded in the following periods. All three elements played out throughout the development, albeit at times some is more prevalent than the other(s).

The People's Republic of China was the first state to recognize the Democratic Republic of Vietnam on January 18, 1950. Initially Vietnam–China relations were characterized as "close as lips and teeth." However, it became worse during the Vietnam War, especially after its end. A number of problems made the Vietnam–China relations collapse including border security, Vietnam's policy toward oversea Chinese (Hoa Kieu), Vietnam's close relations with the Soviet Union, and the "Kampuchea problem." Responding to Vietnam's involvement in Cambodia conflict in late 1978, China decided to attack Vietnam's northern border on February 17, 1979. Influenced by a series of factors including Gorbachev's "perestroika and glasnost" in the Soviet Union, the end of the Cold War, the military situation in Cambodia, both Vietnam and China realized that the conflict could only be ended through political negotiations. In September 1989, Vietnam unilaterally withdrew its military forces from Cambodia. This put an end for both parties to begin the process of normalization of their relations at a summit of party leaders in Chengdu in southern China in September 1990. Formal normalization took place in November 1991. Both sides then exchanged high-level party and state delegations. The leaders met later to discuss their future relations continually in 1992, 1994, and 1995. Border issues were assigned to specialist groups for negotiation. Military-to-military contact was resumed. The period from 1990 to 1999 may be viewed as a transition period from "hostile asymmetry" to "normal asymmetry" (Womack 2006). Based on this beginning, bilateral political relations between Vietnam and China were formally codified by party leaders who met in Beijing from February 25 to March 3, 1999. At this summit, General Secretary Le Kha Phieu and Secretary General Jiang Zemin adopted a 16-character guideline calling for "long-term, stable, future-orientated, good-neighborly and all-round cooperative relations." In sum, party-to-party ties have been used to identify common ground between former antagonists.

In December 2000, Vietnam and China codified state-to-state relations at a summit meeting in Beijing, and signed a "Joint Statement for Comprehensive Cooperation in the New Century." According to this document, "[b]oth sides will refrain from taking any action that might complicate and escalate disputes, resorting to force or making threats with force." The 2000 Joint Statement set out the long-term framework for cooperative bilateral state-to-state relations with a provision for the regular exchange of high-level delegations led by their respective state presidents, prime ministers, other ministers, national legislatures, and other political organizations. In 2006, Vietnam and China set up a Joint Steering Committee on Bilateral Cooperation at the deputy prime ministerial level to coordinate all aspects of their relationship. The steering committee was to meet on an annual basis alternating between capital cities. On December 30, 1999 China and Vietnam signed a land border agreement during the visit to Hanoi by Premier Zhu Rongji. Both sides ratified the treaty in 2000 and the process of placing stone markers along the border was completed at the end of 2008. In December 2000, Vietnam and China signed the agreement on the Demarcation of Waters, Exclusive Economic Zones, and Continental Shelves in the Gulf of Tonkin, and the Agreement on Fishing Cooperation in the Gulf of Tonkin. The settlement of land border and Gulf of Tonkin issues set the stage for the adoption of the Vietnam–China Joint Statement for Comprehensive Cooperation in the New Century.

Vietnam's relations with China are also structured on a multilateral basis through membership in ASEAN, the ASEAN Regional Forum, and other multilateral bodies (ASEAN Plus Three and the East Asia Summit). When Vietnam joined ASEAN in 1995 it agreed to adhere to all multilateral arrangements already entered into between ASEAN and China. In 1997, ASEAN and China formalized their cooperation by establishing the ASEAN–China Joint Cooperation Committee as "the coordinator for all the ASEAN–China mechanisms at the working level." When China became an ASEAN dialogue partner, it regularly participated in the annual ASEAN Post-Ministerial Conference consultation process.

In November 2002, ASEAN and China signed three major documents: Framework Agreement on Comprehensive Economic Cooperation between ASEAN Nations and the People's Republic of China (the foundation for the China–ASEAN Free Trade Area), Joint Declaration between China and ASEAN on Cooperation in Non-Traditional Security Fields, and Declaration on the Conduct of Parties in the South China Sea (DOC). The DOC was a non-binding document that enjoined its signatories to resolve their disputes by peaceful means and "to exercise self-restraint in the conduct of activities that would complicate or escalate disputes." In early 2004, ASEAN and China set up a joint working group to implement the agreement. The most promising development, an agreement on joint seismic testing between the national oil companies of China, the Philippines, and Vietnam, signed in March 2005, however, lapsed when it expired. In October 2003, China acceded to the ASEAN Treaty of Amity and Cooperation, and China and ASEAN issued a joint declaration establishing a strategic partnership. A Five-year Plan of Action (2005–2010) was drawn up in late 2004. This plan included *inter alia* a joint commitment to increase regular high-level bilateral visits, cooperation in the field of non-traditional security, security dialogue, and military exchanges and cooperation.

In many aspects, Vietnam's use of multilateral frameworks in its relations with China is similar to how other states in the region have resorted to as a way to either enhance cooperation or assert national interests. Countries like Nepal and the Philippines have turned to multilateral institutions in such manner: Nepal, as a developing state, is currently focusing on infrastructure development and attracting Chinese investments in this field through channels like the SAARC and the AIIB, while actively seeking to engage with China's OBOR initiative (interviews of Mohan Lohani, Hiranya Lal Shreshtha, and Ramesh Nath Pandey — Nepal). The Philippines, on the other hand, has an ongoing maritime dispute with China over the Scarborough Shoal in the South China Sea, and in 2015 called upon the Permanent Court of Arbitration to peacefully settle the dispute. In both cases and as reflected by the institutionalist approach, countries with close proximity to China and who have intertwining interests with the Middle Kingdom have taken advantage of multilateral structures so as to advance their interests on the one hand while aspiring for common peace and stability on the other.

Upon closer inspection, however, certain differences between their use of multilateral frameworks and Vietnam's are evident. First of all, multilateral frameworks like ASEAN, SAARC, and the PCA are very different themselves in terms of purposes and operations, and as a result its members chose to participate in different types and levels of commitment. Nepal uses the SAARC as a framework to promote its relations with China, with some in Nepal even supporting full membership for China in the organization (interview of Ramesh Nath Pandey — Nepal), while the Philippines uses the PCA as arbitration and to assert its sovereignty claim *vis-à-vis* China. Vietnam, however, uses ASEAN-based frameworks to promote cooperation as well as to protect its core interests against Chinese assertiveness. This is due to the nature of Vietnam's relations with China — which features an equilibrium of both competition and cooperation — and the functional comprehensiveness of ASEAN. ASEAN has often proven to be a more stable platform than SAARC since the latter faces more intense intra-bloc conflicts (i.e., conflicts between its own members). While ASEAN has remained largely effective despite conflicts between some if its members including Cambodia and

Thailand, severe tensions between India and Pakistan have caused several SAARC members to withdraw from its summit (AFP 2016).

In term of dispute resolutions, the Philippines' use of the PCA and Vietnam's use of ASEAN-based platforms are also different. Although China explicitly rejected the 2016 PCA awards, it was nevertheless a major development for the Philippines' sovereignty claims. Vietnam's use of ASEAN, in contrast, only yielded limited success, due to certain limits in ASEAN's operational method that prevented it from acting as an effective arbitrator. Particularly, ASEAN's decision-making process is based on the principle of consensus of all members, so any decision concerning multilateral issues, such as the South China Sea dispute, must be agreed upon unanimously to come into effect. This commitment to the rule of consensus proved to be an obstacle for Vietnam, as in 2012 ASEAN failed to issue a joint communiqué on the South China Sea dispute for the first time. ASEAN also did not play an active arbitrary role during the Haiyang Shiyou 981 oil rig crisis in 2014, and, as a result, resolution of conflict between the two countries fell on party-to-party level (see a further discussion of this incident below), while attempts to reach a regional-based, multilateral mechanism for conflict resolution, such as the Code of Conduct (COC), has often led to a dead end.

In sum, even though Vietnam has been able to buffer its relations with China through its membership in ASEAN and other multilateral organizations, multilateralism itself has proven to be a weak reed with respect to security issues such as the South China Sea. No progress has been made to upgrade the DOC into a Code of Conduct, and when tensions arose in 2007–2008 Vietnam was essentially left on its own to deal with China. When it comes to territorial disputes, it is clear that power and party factors play a much larger role in dictating the trajectory of Vietnam–China relations, as the next section of this chapter exemplifies.

The Party Factor in Vietnam–China Relations

China's power is closely related to the peace of the region as a whole as well as of Vietnam–China relations. China's employment of "coercive, economic and ideational power across an ever-larger geographic expanse" generates concerns for the periphery (Lampton 2008: 164). But while power and peace can account for a large proportion of China's rise and behaviors unilaterally and multilaterally, it is party politics that distinguishes the relationship between China and Vietnam from those between China and other countries in South and Southeast Asia. Although as not the only channel for bilateral dialogue, party politics, as presented above, prove to be a decisive factor in laying the foundation for Sino-Vietnamese normalization in the 1990s, and, more recently, in resolving the Haiyang Shiyou 981 oil rig crisis in 2014.

The Haiyang Shiyou 981 oil rig incident which took place in early May 2014 was a turning point in Vietnam–China relationship. The incident took place within Vietnam's Economic Exclusive Zone in the South China Sea, where, in contrast to the land border and the Gulf of Tonkin issues, Vietnam and China have not been able to resolve their sovereignty disputes. It was also a surprise for many Vietnamese including their leaders because just around seven months before, during his visit to Vietnam in October 2013, China's Premier Le Keqing thoroughly discussed with Vietnam's Prime Minister Nguyen Tan Dung about the future cooperation between two countries including maritime cooperation, especially the strict implementation of the 2011 Agreement on Basic Principles Guiding the Settlement of Maritime-Related Issues. Both sides also reasserted the importance of established government-level mechanism on territory negotiations, and the so-called "step by step" and "easy first, difficult later" principles of solving problems. The key point in the 2011 Agreement to pursue "mutually acceptable fundamental solutions that do not affect each side's stance and policy" was also reconfirmed by both leaders as well. In terms of territorial disputes in the South China Sea, both leaders agreed to implement the 2002 Declaration on Conduct of Parties in the South China Sea and do their best for adopting a Code of Conduct in the South China Sea. Furthermore, both leaders agreed "to exercise tight control of maritime disputes and not to make any move that can further complicate or expand disputes." In order to remain true to their words, they even vowed that the established hot lines between their ministries of foreign affairs and ministries of agriculture will be effectively used. Two months after the visit of Premier Li, a plenary meeting of the government-level committee on border and territory issues was held. During this meeting both sides agreed to set up a Working Group to discuss cooperation for mutual development at sea with the first session scheduled for 2014.

Chinese actions were surprising and proactive because this was the first time it deployed an oil rig in the EEZ of another state without its prior notification and permission. Besides, the oil rig was accompanied by an armada of People's Liberation Army Navy warships, Coast Guard vessels, and fishing boat. The number of ships was increased from 50 to over 100 in a few days. In addition, there were also military and other aircraft. China also responded very aggressively to Vietnamese Coast Guard vessels trying to inform Chinese vessels about their violating actions and to protect Vietnam's EEZ. The situation became dangerous as Chinese ships deliberately rammed Vietnamese ships in an effort to retire them. Chinese Coast Guard vessels also deliberately targeted the radio communications antennae on Vietnamese ships with their high-powered water cannons. In some cases, China even took the wraps off the cannons and other weapons to aim them at Vietnamese Coast Guard vessels. Chinese fishing boats also joined in the intimidation. The worse case was when a Chinese fishing boat rammed and capsized a Vietnamese fishing boat. Despite facing such kinds of Chinese actions, Vietnam tried to keep a very conciliatory posture. Vietnam's attempt to maintain its hot line with China failed. Vietnam's call for hosting a special envoy to discuss how to manage the tensions got no response from China. In total, there were over 30 diplomatic overtures from Vietnam to China. China, however, set four arrogant requirements: First, Vietnam must stop its "harassment" of Chinese oil rig; second, Vietnam must drop its sovereignty claims over the Paracel archipelago; third, Vietnam must not follow legal approach against China; fourth, Vietnam must not involve third parties, e.g., the US. The Chinese actions reflected the behavior and choice of powerful actors based on their powers, and Vietnam's position was less powerful. The strategic trust that the two countries took great pains to build up, and resulted in habits of consultation and greater predictability, was lost.

It was during this seeming deadlock that the party factor, once again, proved its primary significance in the two countries' bilateral relations. On June 18, in the midst of the crisis, China's State Councilor Yang Jiechi paid a visit to Hanoi to attend the annual meeting of the Joint Steering Committee for Bilateral Cooperation. This attendance reflected that China was still interested in engaging with Vietnam. However, during the talks to Vietnamese counterpart Councilor Yang berated his "comrades" for "hyping up" the situation and warned openly that China would "take all necessary measures" to protect its oil rig. However, when he met Secretary General Nguyen Phu Trong, they agreed to continue discussing ways to ease tensions and solve sea-related issues. On July 15, China decided to withdraw the HYSD 981 oil rig from Vietnamese waters and, to release 13 Vietnamese fishermen who were arrested by China earlier. This signaled the end of confrontation at sea and a shift to diplomacy. In August, China hosted a visit of a special envoy led by senior Politburo member Le Hong Anh.

This incident prompts the question, among others, of whether party ideology and collective identity as communist states can overcome and overwhelm power politics. In the case of Vietnam–China relations, although not always the case, party politics has nevertheless proven to be an effective channel for dialogue and conflict resolution. It has played a key role since the dawn of Sino-Vietnamese interactions in the 1950s and during the Vietnam War. While *realpolitik* factors became dominant in the 1970s and 1980s when Vietnam–China relations worsened as a result of the former's rapprochement to USSR and the latter to the US, party politics later did serve as a channel for negotiation and reconciliation in the early 1990s, as it did in the 2014 incident discussed above. However, it was the South China Sea dispute that prompted the crisis in the first place, and the fact that such conflict led to a crisis is a proof that realist elements can still have severe impact on the bilateral relations. Furthermore, although the crisis had been settled, its consequences — including the deep mistrust and wariness of such an event being repeated in the future — still vibrate throughout the two countries' political landscape and will surely affect their relations in the future. Though no definitive answer can be given yet on whether power-centric considerations or party politics can overcome one another, the latter undoubtedly plays a crucial role in Vietnam–China relations, and in such context a unique feature that differentiates this interaction from other regional relations.

Implications and Recommendations for Vietnam–China Relations

This section reflects on the implications of China's foreign policy based on the analysis so far, followed by a brief recommendation for the Vietnam–China bilateral relations in the future.

It is difficult to foresee China's foreign policy for the coming time, but some observations based on the power, party, and peace approaches can be derived. Even though China has again and again emphasized its rise to be a peaceful one, its true intention remains elusive to scholars and policymakers, and recent developments such as land reclamation in the South China Sea suggest that its words does not reflect its actions. China's increased economic growth continues to worry realist observers who fear that such growth may entail military expansion (Mearsheimer 2014). However, there are signs that such economic growth is unstable and may not continue as impressively in the future, and there is no guarantee that an increase in economic might will automatically translate into military power. Meanwhile, with increasing regional engagement through ASEAN, OBOR, AIIB, and with increased investment in neighboring states, including Vietnam, Nepal, and Bangladesh, China can also be expected to assume more international responsibility. The institutionalist approach suggests that this offers a chance for peace, since it will provide more incentive for cooperation instead of confrontation while restraining disruptive behaviors. Common identities such as communist states still play a major role in Vietnam–China bilateral relationship, but when it comes to high tensions like the South

China Sea dispute it is uncertain if party politics can in fact come before realist considerations. Thus, from the current situation some observation could be derived as follows:

First, the disputes over sovereignty in the South China Sea will continue to be the most serious security threat for Vietnam in the years to come. China's assertiveness to occupy the South China Sea will constrain both sides from the so-called ideological commonalities of the two communist parties and economic interdependence. Both sides, first of all Vietnam, will reconsider their "comprehensive strategic partnership." The possibility of worsening economic relations with China also could be turned into opportunity for Vietnam to reconstruct its domestic market on the one hand, and foster closer economic ties with other countries, including more proactive negotiations in TPP on the other hand.

Second, the HYSD 981 oil rig incident has demonstrated that Vietnam was capable of standing up to China and choosing an appropriate way. Vietnam was unlikely to take legal action against China. It is in Vietnam's interest not to play this card, but to reserve it. Vietnamese leaders showed cautiousness in their relations with China. They did not show to be bowing to China on one side, but was also not ready to align with the US on the other hand. Surely Vietnam will eventually promote its comprehensive partnership with the US and strengthen ties with the Philippines, Japan, and India as part of its strategy of diversification and multilateralism of foreign relations. In this situation the choice of Vietnam is ASEAN, and it will remain fully committed to ASEAN because only ASEAN can support a binding code of conduct in the South China Sea. However, Vietnam will not and cannot rely only on ASEAN, and therefore it will attempt to re-engage with China in an attempt to repair their damaged bilateral relations and restore strategic trust.

Third, there is no doubt that China will continue to be more assertive in the South China Sea in the future, to meet its economic development and to deflect domestic discontent. This will have serious influences on fisheries, security, and freedom of navigation of the whole region. This is why it seems that the way to achieve a legally binding COC in the South China Sea will be challenged with more obstacles. Vietnam and ASEAN would fall into a dilemma between pressing China into an effective COC on the one hand, and adopting a more realist line on China on the other.

Fourth, if China National Offshore Oil Corporation could move its Haiyang Shiyou 981 oil rig into the disputed area with Vietnam in May 2014, resulting in a tensed situation lasting two and a half months, it may do the same in the future in the disputed area of South China Sea with other countries. ASEAN should avoid having to choose between the two powers. In order to do so, it should continue to play a role of catalyst and facilitator for an ASEAN-centered forum like the East Asia summit whereby all powers can consult and inform each other. In term of the South China Sea problem, ASEAN should approach the new Chinese leadership to clarify its claim by signing the code of conduct of behavior of the parties in the South China (COC). ASEAN also should understand the US dilemma in avoiding military conflict with China while maintaining its commitments to support its allies and partners. Any provocations may lead to a multiple risk for parties from both sides. In any case, ASEAN should work unitarily for not allowing the use of force or the threat thereof in the relationship between parties. ASEAN should convey its main message to all parties that their long-term interests will be guaranteed by abiding the United Nations Convention on the Law of the Sea (UNCLOS). As discussed elsewhere in this chapter, due to the reality of the region whereby the Sino-Japan rivalry, the US–Japan alliance have created the chance for ASEAN, a group of small countries, to play its centrality. Any attempts made by China, for example the AIIB, the "new security concept" that Xi Jinping spoke about at the CICA summit in Shanghai, or whoever to replace ASEAN centrality would not be accepted because they did not find a clear credibility.

Conclusion

In summary, power build-up and projection, maintaining peace through institutions, and party politics all played crucial roles in

Vietnam–China relations and are closely interrelated with each other. These three factors are denominators of a bilateral relationship. Thanks to the reform, both China and Vietnam became more powerful and confident in internal and external affairs. Thanks to reform, both the communist parties in Vietnam and China became main actors in their internal and external affairs, and the legitimation of their leadership is guaranteed by their success. Both Vietnam and China need peace for their economic development. Because of peace both the communist parties decided to negotiate. For Vietnam, peaceful approach will definitely be the solution to the dispute in the South China Sea. In response to Chinese assertiveness, Vietnam's leaders kept firmly to peaceful solution of disputes.

The recent Chinese assertiveness in the South China Sea was a turning point in Vietnam's policy toward China, and could bring them into a hostile asymmetry. In an asymmetric relationship like this, the smaller state can often observe any actions of the larger state through paranoia lens. Restrain from using military forces and peaceful resolution of conflict as well as commitment to international norms and rules are expectations of China from all countries. Faced with such behavior of China, Hanoi is reviewing all possible options including bringing China to a domestic or international court. According to Vietnam's Prime Minister Nguyen Tan Dung, it will "never barter sovereignty for an unrealizable friendship."

Facing this new context, especially the Chinese assertive policy toward the South China Sea, and the US pivot to Asia, the main strategy of Vietnam should be balancing between these two giants, and ASEAN must be a priority in Vietnam's foreign policy. However, the crucial issue of ASEAN is its principle of consensus. All members should realize that it is not the problem of only claimant states, but rather a common one.

The PCA awards in July 2016 created a good new opportunity for dealing with dispute in the South China Sea. However, the continuing assertiveness of China in the South China Sea, its uncooperative manner, and its power actually destroyed the hope for solving dispute in a just way. The visits of the Philippines President Duterte and Malaysian Prime Minister reflected a new "pivot" of these two countries to China. The election of Republican candidate Donald Trump as the 45th President of the USA would provide a good chance for China to exercise its power in East Asia.

References

AFP. 2016. Bangladesh Pulls Out of Saarc Summit as Tensions Rise. *Dawn*, https://www.dawn.com/news/1286662. Accessed on June 1, 2017.

Andaya, B.W. and L.Y. Andaya. 1982. *History of Malaysia*. London: Macmillan Publishers.

Australian Ministry of Defense. 2009. *Defense Australia in the Asia Pacific Century: Force 2030* (Defence White Paper).

British Broadcasting Company. 2012. ASEAN Nations Fail to Reach Agreement on South China Sea. *BBC News*, 13 July, http://www.bbc.com/news/world-asia-18825148. Accessed on June 1, 2017.

Brzezinski, Z. 1997. *Grand Chessboard*. New York: Basic Books.

Callick, R. 2009. Australia and China: It's Strictly Business. *The Australian*, August 20, 2009, https://uyghuramerican.org/article/australia-and-china-its-strictly-business.html. Accessed on June 1, 2017.

Central Intelligence Agency. 2015. *The World Fact Book*.

Chang, G. 2012. *The Coming Collapse of China*. London: Arrow.

Connors, M.K., R. Davison and J. Dosch. 2004. *The New Global Politics of the Asia-Pacific*. London and New York: Routledge Curzon.

Cook, M., R. Heinrichs, R. Medcalf and A. Shearer. 2010. *Power and Choice: Asian Security Futures*. New South Wales, Australia: Lowy Institute for International Policy and MacArthur Foundation.

Duiker, W. 1986. *China and Vietnam: The Roots of Conflict*. Berkeley: Institute of East Asian Studies.

Fairbank, J.K. 1968. *The Chinese World Order: Traditional Chinese Foreign Relations*. Cambridge, Mass: Harvard University Press.

Fitzgerald, C.P. 1972. *The Southern Expansion of the Chinese People*. Canberra: Australian National University Press.

Goldstein, A. 2003. An Emerging China's Emerging Grand Strategy. In J. Ikenberry and M. Mastanduno (Eds.), *International Relations Theory and the Asia Pacific*. New York: Columbia University Press.

Goodman, P.S. and P. Finn. 2007. Corruption Stains Timber Trade– Washington Post (April 1) http://www.washingtonpost.com/wp-dyn/content/article/2007/03/31/AR2007033102387.html. Accessed on August 18, 2008.

Hall, D.G.E. 1970. *A History of Southeast Asia*. London: Macmillan.
Ikenberry, J. 2008. The Rise of China and the Future of the West, *Foreign Affairs* (January/February).
Jiang, Zemin. 2002. *On the International Situation and our External Work*. XVI National Congress of the Communist Party of China (November 8), http://english.people.com.cn/200211/18/eng20021118_106985.shtml. Accessed on August 19, 2006.
Johnston, A.I. 2003. Socialization in International Institution. The ASEAN Way and International Relations Theory. In J. Ikenberry and M. Mastanduno (Eds.), *International Relations Theory and the Asia-Pacific*. New York: Columbia University Press.
Kagan, R. 1997. What China Knows that We Don't, *The Weekly Standard* (January 20).
Lam, Peng Er. and Lim Tai Wei. 2009. *The Rise of China and India — A New Asian Drama*. Singapore: World Scientific.
Lampton, D.M. 2008. *The Three Faces of Chinese Power — Might, Money, and Minds*. Berkeley: University of California Press.
Lee, Lai Too. 1981. Deng Xiaoping's ASEAN Tour: A Perspective on Sino-Southeast Asia Relation. *Contemporary Southeast Asia* 3(1): 58–75.
Logan, J.R. (Ed.) 1855. *Journal of the Indian Archipelago and Eastern Asia (JIEA)*, Singapore: Kraus Reprint.
Mearsheimer, J. 2014. *The Tragedy of Great Power Politics*. New York: W. W. Norton & Co.
Nye, J. 2010. *Con xa moi toi ky nguyen Trung Quoc* (March 5), http://www.tuanvietnam.net/2010-05-31-con-xa-moi-toi-ky-nguyen-trung-quoc.html. Accessed on June 1, 2017.
Sanjeev, G. 2017. Nepal, China sign deal on OBOR, *The Kathmandu Post*, http://kathmandupost.ekantipur.com/news/2017-05-12/nepal-china-sign-framework-deal-on-obor.html. Accessed on June 1, 2017.
Sebastian, L.C. 2000. Southeast Asian Perception of China: The Challenge of Achieving a New Strategic Accommodation. In D. da Cunha (Ed.), *Southeast Asian Perspectives on Security*. Singapore: Institute of Southeast Asian Studies.
Shearer, A. and F. Hanson. 2009. *China and the World: Public Opinion and Foreign Policy*. Sydney: Lowy Institute for International Policy.
Sun, Lixin. 2010. Chinese Maritime Concepts. Paper Presented to the International Workshop: The Baltic Sea and South China Sea Regions: Incomparable Models of Regional Integration? Singapore, Asia-Europe Foundation (ASEF) (February 18–20).

Sutter, R.G. 2008. *Chinese Foreign Relations — Power and Policy since the Cold War*. Lanham: Rowman & Littlefield Publisher.

Tarling, N. (Ed.) 1992. *The Cambridge History of Southeast Asia 1*. Cambridge: Cambridge University Press.

Thayer, C. 2009. Recent Developments in the South China Sea: Implication for Peace, Stability and Cooperation in the Region. Paper Presented to the International Conference Organized by Diplomatic Academy of Vietnam and Vietnam's Layer Association, Hanoi, November.

Wang, Yusheng. 2001. Hiding One's Capacities and Time is Weapon to Cope with Strong Enemy, *People's Daily* (August 13), http://english.people.com.cn/english/200108/10/eng20010810_77204.html. Accessed on June 7, 2006.

Womack, B. 2006. *China and Vietnam: The Politics of Asymmetry*. Cambridge: Cambridge University Press.

Zhao, Hong. 2007. India and China: Rivals or Partners in Southeast Asia? *Journal of Contemporary Southeast Asia* 29(1): 126–147.

Zheng, Bijian. 2005. Peacefully Rising China is a Firm Defender of World Peace, Speech at the International Conference on East Asia Cooperation and Sino-US Relations, Beijing (November 3).

Part III

Comparative Perspectives

8

China Studies in South and South East Asia: A Comparative Perspective Through Sri Lanka and Thailand

Reena Marwah

*Jesus and Mary College, Delhi University and
Association of Asia Scholars, New Delhi*

China has progressed to emerge as an Asian economic giant propelling the engines of growth of other countries dependent on it. In the last few years, China's interconnectedness with all continents has grown, both through continental and maritime space. China studies has also witnessed a spectacular interest among China's neighboring countries within both South and Southeast Asia. With a view to explore the perceptions of South and Southeast Asian countries about China, it is important to understand these through both secondary and primary sources of information, the latter comprising interviews of China scholars in these countries. This chapter comprises a comparative analysis of China studies in South and Southeast Asia, both as sub-regions of Asia and through the countries of Thailand and Sri Lanka. Both these countries are pivotal to China's interests not only through linkages with its Belt and Road strategy encompassing the economic and the strategic connection, but also the cultural (Buddhist) connection. This chapter is divided into three main sections. The first provides an overview of China studies in South and Southeast Asia; the second provides an overview of China's historical, civilizational, and cultural familiarity with Thailand. It also brings in some aspects of China's economic and strategic influence in Thailand. The third section focuses on China's increasing economic engagement with Sri Lanka which has spurred an increased interest in understanding China.

In conclusion, the chapter shows that while China itself is deeply embedded within the Thai society, its influence in Sri Lanka is perceptible, but disparate.

Introduction

China studies has witnessed a spectacular interest among China's neighboring countries within both South and Southeast Asia, not only because of China's expanding economic footprint both on the continental and the maritime shelf, but also because of the civilizational, demographic, and cultural connections. With a view to explore the perceptions of South and Southeast Asian countries about China, it is important to understand these through both secondary and primary sources of information. This chapter comprises a comparative analysis of China studies in South and Southeast Asia, both as sub-regions of Asia and through the countries of Thailand and Sri Lanka. The two sub-regions of Asia are distinctly different in their civilizational and cultural familiarity with China — the geographical proximity and the influence of Chinese settlers.

The *raison d'être* for identifying and comparing the two bilateral relationships of Thailand (Southeast Asia) and Sri Lanka (South Asia) through the China's lens is essentially to provide answers for compelling questions. How are the friendly and uncritical views of China related to the two bilateral relationships? Are the effects of enhanced economic connectivity and shared Buddhist legacies on the perspective on China similar nonetheless, where civilizational, demographic, and security dimensions are different? In terms of civilizational familiarity (Thailand) vs. unfamiliarity (Sri Lanka), in relation to the issue of demographic mix in Thailand vs. distinct, (Sri Lanka) are security concerns of adjacent (Thailand) and non-adjacent (Sri Lanka) more materialistic?

This chapter is divided into three main sections which discuss in more detail the above-mentioned points.

China in Asia: Comparing South and Southeast Asia

The civilizational connect of China both in South and Southeast Asia is well documented. China is Asia's largest economy and one whose growth momentum in a short span of two decades has not failed to surprise any country. With its deep pockets, China has also not failed to befriend any country, especially in South and Southeast Asia. While countries in South Asia, barring India, do not view China's assertiveness and power projection as a threat, there are countries in Southeast Asia who would prefer to see China as the economic partner, without its aggression in the maritime space. There are key points of distinction between perceptions of China and China's policies in these two sub-regions of Asia.

Firstly, according to J. Mohan Malik (2011), China's South Asia policy has been "India-centric" in its approach, in which military ties between China and India's neighbors played the dominant role. In fact in South Asia, China has been viewed as an "outsider" till a few years ago. On its part, China has defended its military ties with South Asian countries as "legitimate and normal state-to-state relations" well within the purview of the Five Principles of Peaceful Coexistence or *Panchsheel* (Garver 1992). Southeast Asia has been a key area for China, where its rise has been felt most significantly. China is engaged in weaving a close-knit ASEAN economic community through the ASEAN plus mechanism.

Secondly, boundary disputes and the Tibet issue have contributed much not only to define China's South Asia policy, especially *vis-à-vis* India, but also to shape China's relations with South Asia. It is to be noted that China has already resolved its disputed boundaries with Nepal and Pakistan, though territorial disputes with India and Bhutan are yet to be resolved. In China's point of view, "whether

China and Nepal, Sri Lanka, Bangladesh, or Pakistan wish any particular relations is exclusively for them to decide. For India to attempt to dictate or limit those relations is unacceptable" (Garver 1992). With a few Southeast Asian countries, boundary, mainly maritime disputes are recent.

Thirdly, China's relations with South Asian countries owe much to the Beijing–Islamabad "special relationship," which is part of China's grand strategy of stimulating the South Asian security environment in its favor and providing a stimulus to its One Belt One Road strategy of outreach to the Gulf countries. This "special relationship" provides a good example of using China as a counterweight to what smaller South Asian regimes perceive as India's attempts at bullying them. It demonstrates that much like Pakistan, other South Asian countries can follow an "independent" policy and need not allow India to influence their decision-making.

In Asia, the only other country that directly challenges China's interests in ASEAN countries is Japan. Although the US visualizes its Pivot to Asia strategy (announced by Hillary Clinton in 2010), in terms of greater economic cooperation and people to people contacts, there are misgivings of its real intentions, not only in China but also among countries of ASEAN.

Fourthly, China remains a major economic aid donor to countries in South Asia, *viz.* Bangladesh, Nepal, Pakistan and Sri Lanka, and "its relations with all the regional states are steadily growing with a strong underpinning on economic and trade relations" (Sami 2012: 17). Such economic ties between China and these smaller South Asian countries help strengthen its security objectives and goals in the region. In Southeast Asia, China is a major trading partner for each of the ASEAN countries. There are several bilateral FTAs and multilateral FTAs centering around ASEAN, referred to as the "noodle bowl" in Asia, (ASEAN plus 3, ASEAN plus 6, etc.). In fact, this region has seen a surge of FTAs; increasing from 4 concluded in 1990 to 123 in 2011, while altogether with those under negotiations or proposed reaching 245. In terms of connectivity and infrastructure linkages, the ties with Southeast Asia are much stronger, especially on the continental shelf.

In essence, all countries in South Asia (leaning toward China) cannot afford to ignore India, which looms large in its bilateral engagement with each neighbor (barring Pakistan). In Southeast Asia, China's sway and influence is unmatched.

The context provided herein, takes us to the next section of the chapter which seeks to understand the influence of China through country specific analyses of Sri Lanka and Thailand, belonging to different sub-regions, but engaged with China both bilaterally and through multilateral forums. Sri Lanka's significance is known to China as the Indian Ocean has assumed an increasingly critical mass in the maritime space. Maritime security affairs in relation to geo-politics and economics has transformed this region to regular global attention and focus (*Daily FT* 2015).

Thailand, as a continental neighbor of China, has close links and historical familiarity with China, and is well-known for its Chinese community of early settlers in Thailand.

China's Historical, Civilizational and Religious Familiarity with Thailand

A distinctive feature of Southeast Asia is its cultural diversity mainly because this region was exposed to different civilizations, cultures, and religions for thousands of years: Animism, Buddhism, Taoism, Confucianism, Hinduism, and Islam. In addition, culture, trade, religion, and monarchy played a significant role in the state formation of these countries.

Another feature of this region is the impact of migration. In early times, tribal groups from southern China moved into the interior areas of the mainland *via* the long river systems. Linguistically, the mainland is divided into three important families, the Austro-Asiatic (like Cambodian and Vietnamese), Tai (like Thai and Lao), and the Tibeto-Burmese (including highland languages as well as Burmese). (Languages belonging to these families can also be found in northeastern India and southwestern China.) Chinese expansion south of the Yangtze River eventually led to the colonization of Vietnam. Chinese control was permanently ended in 1427, but Confucian philosophy had a lasting influence when Vietnam became independent. Buddhism and Taoism also reached Vietnam *via* China (Andaya 2014).

The historical interface between China and Thailand is of significance. Ancient Siam (Thailand) had also been always subordinate to China as a vassal or a tributary state since the Sui dynasty until the Taiping Rebellion of the late Qing dynasty in the mid-19th century. The threat of domination by China was a key and real component of Thai history. By the middle of the 20th century, Thailand became closer ideologically to the USA. This was a relationship based on cooperation in containing the spread of communism in Southeast Asia. Thailand was viewed by the USA as a key partner in its opposition to communism in a region that was replete with political turmoil. In addition, for the Thais, communism was viewed as a threat to the Thai way of life. Northeast Thailand was vulnerable to communist guerillas. Between 1950 and 1975, the USA provided large amount of aid to Thailand — for payment of troops, construction of air bases, as well as for counter insurgency operations (Kislenko 2004).

Thailand, together with the Philippines, was a member of the anti-communist Southeast Asian Treaty Organization or SEATO. China had supported the Communist Party of Thailand's efforts to overthrow the Thai government through guerila warfare. However, US–Thailand relations got a severe jolt when America was defeated in Vietnam in April 1975. This probably shocked Thailand more than any other country in Southeast Asia, so much so that Thailand needed to come to terms with China as a new balancer. The presence of US military in Thailand (stationed to help with its war) helped the country to develop its own brand of political consciousness and nationalism, spurred on partly by anti-Americanism and advances of communists in Indochina.

The strongest basis for cooperation between China and Thailand then was common opposition to Vietnam's attempts to carve a sphere of influence over Indochina through its occupation of Cambodia. With Vietnam's occupation of Cambodia coming at a time of US' withdrawal from Indochina, China emerged as the strongest guarantor of Thailand's security (Baviera 2015: 24, 26).

Regarding Thai foreign policy, it has also often been noted that a tendency exists to seek accommodation with dominant powers based on pragmatic considerations. Contemporary relations with China are no less a reflection of this. Kukrit Pramoj and Zhou Enlai established diplomatic relations between Thailand and China in 1975, marking a shift in Thai policy to one of "peaceful coexistence" with communist states and equidistance between the superpowers (Baviera 2015: 24, 26).

China was in fact sensitive to the Thais and it did not push into Thailand too far. There was communist activity in Thailand's northeast, but this was not funded by the government in Beijing. The Chinese maintained restraint in their criticism of the influence of the USA in Thailand, although this did worry Beijing. China refrained from criticizing the Thai king or the Buddhist traditions and were extremely wary of their position *vis-a vis* the US. On its part, Thailand maintained reverence for the Thai monarchy and Buddhism and this largely contributed to the stability of its government.

During the Cold War period Thailand and China formed a military alignment against Vietnamese communists in Indochina. In the post-Cold War era, bilateral relations have remained healthy due to the absence of territorial disputes, the firm connections between Thai royal family and Chinese leadership, and the well-integrated Chinese community in Thailand (Chachavalpongpun 2015). As stated by Bangkok-based journalist Richard S. Ehrlich (2011), "There is perhaps nowhere in Southeast Asia where the growing influence of China — economically, militarily and diplomatically — is being felt more than in Thailand, long one of the US most steadfast regional allies."

Chinese in Thailand: Demography, Knowledge, and Culture

China has been regarded by Asian nations as a good neighbor and a non-threatening power. Consequently, the attempt to promote positive relations with Thailand through policies and promotions within the Confucius Institute is an extension of the Chinese government's policies to construct the norm of harmony internationally (Sydney Southeast Asia Centre Year n.a.). Owing to the influence of Chinese immigrants and close cultural ties with China over centuries, Southeast Asia is host to 25 Confucius Institutes and 19 Confucius Classrooms. With 13 institutes and 11 classrooms, Thailand is leading the development of Confucius Institutes in the region. Experienced teachers from the mainland are sent to partner Thai universities, while local teachers also have the opportunity to study in Chinese universities through scholarships offered by the Confucius Institute project.

More than 800,000 Thais have studied in these facilities. Through partnerships with universities overseas, Confucius Institutes (as those which operate in university settings are called) support Chinese studies through culture and language education (Zhao 2014). Every Confucius Institute in Thailand has a partner institute in China. Qualified teachers of relevant curriculum are sent from China to institutes in Thailand.

Director Wang who has been a Director of the Confucius Institute at Suriyan University since 2010, thinks that Chinese directors and volunteer teachers should "know that it is time to show … a good opportunity to communicate in a friendly and easy way to show a real China [and] a real Chinese."[1] At its Confucius Institute, Suan Dusit Rajabhat University also offers Chinese classes to students majoring in other fields such as hospitality and tourism, and aviation. The number of enrollees has more than doubled in the last five years, and the demand for Chinese education is still growing among Thai students.

In Suphan Buri, a Chinese-style complex called Tianlong Town has become a popular destination for local people during Thai and Chinese

---

[1] The interview with Wang revealed what he perceived as an authentic image or culture of China. In his opinion: China is rising up. You know not only the economy, but also the culture. Other countries, in his opinion, need to understand China, to accept China that it's rising. His perception of China evidently depicts a picture of a rising China that is ready to influence the world. It also shows that if people learn more about China and Chinese culture, there will be no misunderstanding and people will accept China's influence. "Director Wang believes that the Confucius Institute 'will not force someone to accept' those ideas about China but China and Thailand 'should know [about] each other so that we can mutual[ly] understand [each other] and … have better relationship."

festivals. It was established by former Thai Prime Minister Banhan Sinlapa-acha who came from an ethnic Chinese merchant family. "Local people prefer to visit the Chinese-style architectures. It is always very crowded in the little town even during holidays or even on weekends," says Zhang Xiu'e, Director of the Confucius Institute at the Suan Dusit Rajabhat University. "Now we have more Chinese students playing Chinese instruments and making Chinese food, which generates more interest among the local residents." China also benefits from the international spread of Confucius Institutes. Hundreds of thousands of Chinese teachers are sent overseas every year as volunteers. Over the past few years, Hanban — the organization under the Chinese Ministry of Education that oversees the institute has deployed more than 10,500 Chinese volunteers to Thailand; the biggest such contingent from the institute. The Confucius Institute enables young Chinese people to engage with foreign youth.

The Confucius Institute at Chulalongkorn University has opened such distinctive courses as Chinese language, calligraphy, painting, martial art and music, held various Chinese-language contests, celebrations of traditional Chinese holidays and lectures on the Chinese culture, which have drawn wide attention from the young students and all sectors of the Thai society and played an important part of deepening the traditional friendship between the two people. The Confucius Institutes are proof of the Thai government's support not only for the development of the institution, but also for the teaching of Chinese culture and language in the country. An official also said that the new institute set up at Khon Kaen University in 2013 serves as an academic center for the promotion of the Chinese heritage, including its culture and language.[2] The institute, which was set up with help from the Confucius Institute Headquarters and the China Southwest University, has more than 9,900 students as of 2014 (Women of China 2014).

The above clearly amplifies the way Chinese culture is embedded within Thai society through the educational institutions.

---

[2] Construction of the institute in Khon Kaen University, which has an area of 3,100 square meters, began in 2012 and was completed in September 2013. The structures in the center are inspired by both Chinese and Thai architectural themes.

Buddhism as a Religion in Thailand and Buddhist Activities in Non-religious Chinese Temples

An estimated 95 percent of Thais are Buddhist, making Thailand one of the world's largest Buddhist nations. Buddhism in Thailand is always presented as if it were a cultural tradition of the Thai people. In actual fact, the composition of "Buddhist society" is far more complex and the Theravada faith is but one of the religious traditions that appear as Buddhism in the state records (Gethin 1998).

The Chinese of Thailand form an inseparable part of this complexity, but unfortunately, with only a few exceptions, discussions on the Chinese and their culture in Thailand seem to have paid little attention to this issue — Buddhism as viewed from the Chinese perspective. In Thailand, most of the Chinese temples (called *sanchao* in Thai) are not recognized as "religious places" by the religious administration (namely the Department of Religious Affairs), since they come under the supervision of the Ministry of the Interior. In Phuket, Chinese temples as "non-religious" places (of worship) outnumber officially recognized Buddhist temples and they offer occasions for the worship of Buddhist deities. One of the unique features of the "Buddhist" activities of the Chinese temples in Phuket is that they are conducted without monks. Chinese temples being placed outside the state protection of "religion," they are not institutionalized as belonging to any state-approved religion. This is beneficial to the Chinese temples as they do not have to compete with "state Buddhism"; and in such temples different belief systems prevail. This implies that all these activities lying outside of "religion" actually occupy an important part of "Buddhism" in Thailand. Thus, the framework of "Buddhism" and "religion" in Thailand requires reconsideration (Kataoka 2012).

Chinese Buddhism, as a part of the anonymous Chinese religion in a broader sense, is in complete contrast to the Theravada Sangha protected by the state. In this way Buddhism in Thailand, which shifts from the state Sangha as the sole organization representing Buddhism, further contributes to the indeterminate status of Chinese temples, resulting in a puzzling state in which Chinese temples are "non-religious" but their followers are Buddhists.

Table 1. Number of Buddhist Temples According to Sects

Branch	Sect	Private	Royal	Total
Theravada	Mahanikai	28,982	199	29,181
	Thammayut	1,433	52	1,485
Mahayana	Chin (Chinese)	8	0	8
	Annam (vietnamese)	11	0	11
Grand total		30,434	251	30,685

Source: https://englishkyoto-seas.org/wp-content/uploads/0103kataoka_table2.jpg (Krom Kansatsana 1998: 84).

Yang's classical model of traditional Chinese religion could apply to the situation of the Chinese temples in Thailand. He uses the term "diffused religion" to explain the special character of traditional Chinese religion as compared to "institutionalized religion." Diffused religion according to him is a religion scattered and rooted in various secular social institutions with no significant independent and separate existence (Yang 1991: 294–295).

> People visited a particular temple, worshipped a particular spirit, called on a particular priest, all in accordance with the practical function of religion for the particular occasion. To what religion a temple or a god belonged might be a puzzle to scholars, but such questions had no functional significance in the religious life of the common people. (Yang 1991: 340)

Table 1 clearly shows that it is the Theravada Buddhist temples which are preponderant. It is Theravada Buddhism which connects Sri Lanka with Thailand. Majority of these are privately owned, with only 251 belonging to the royalty.

Spread of Buddhism from Sri Lanka to Thailand in the 13th Century

In Thailand, Sinhalese Buddhism made major inroads initially in the peninsula in South Thailand, Nakhon Si Thammarat (NST) (across the Bay of Bengal), whose monks had gone to Sri Lanka for study. In the 13th century, Parakramabahu II of Dambadeniya (Sri Lanka) sent the much revered Sihinga (Sinhala) Buddha image to King Rama Khamheng of Sukhothai, the first kingdom of Thailand. Thai rulers fought wars to own this Sinhalese image. Another "Sinhala origin" image, the Emerald Buddha located in the Royal Palace is the national palladium of Thailand. It was King Lothai (1317–1347), the son of Rama Khamheng, who too became a great admirer of Sinhala Bhikkhus. He requested Udumbara Mahasami, then resident in lower Myanmar to send a monk to perform *upasampada*. Udumbara Mahasami's disciple established the Sinhala Sangha sect in Sukhothai, Thailand's first capital. Subsequently, Udumbara Mahasami's disciples established the Sinhala Sangha in Chiangmai, Lamphun and in Sajjanalaya — all in Northern Thailand (Hema 2010).

Buddha relics brought from Sri Lanka were enshrined all over Thailand in Sri Lankan style *chaitya*.[3] In the 14th century, branches of the sacred Bodhi tree from Anuradhapura were also planted with respect by the Thai royalty. An inscription of King Luthai (1347–1368) records that his artisans made several copies of the Buddha's Footprint from Sri Lanka. Luthai also being a great patron of the Sinhala Sangha[4] received with major celebrations, Sangharaja Medhankara, a well-known monk, from Sri Lanka and a group of Sinhala sect monks. The King offered this Sinhalese Sangharaja a specially built monastery. The King studied under this Sinhala monk, and at the end of the *vassa* season, which is the three-month annual retreat observed by Theravada practitioners, received temporary ordination from him.

Buddhist Schools and Dalai Lama

A pertinent question to be considered here pertains to the Dalai Lama, the Tibetan religious leader. The reason that the Dalai Lama is very popular in the West but not to the same extent in the countries

---

[3] A *chaitya* is a Buddhist shrine or prayer hall with a *stupa* at one end.
[4] In Buddhism, Sangha refers to the monastic community of *bhikkhus* (monks) and *bhikkhunis* (nuns).

of Thailand, Sri Lanka and Myanmar where the Theravada form of Buddhism prevails is that Buddhist history shows that Theravada is not only different from Mahayana, but is strongly opposed to the other (Dalai Lama is a Mahayanist). While Mahayana is believed to be very accommodating in its collection, composition, compilation, and interpretation of Buddhist doctrines, Theravada continues to be the hardcore and traditional form of Buddhism even today. The Thai people revere the Dalai Lama, but the polity will not let him come to Thailand.

Herein lies the answer to the compelling question of the Thai Government subscribing to the One China Policy, "His Holiness the Dalai Lama last visited Thailand in 1993 when a group of Nobel Peace laureates held a solidarity meeting for fellow Nobel laureate Aung San Suu Kyi," Tenzin Taklha said, "Since then, His Holiness has not been able to visit Thailand because of the refusal of the necessary visa from the Thai government, for reasons known to them." A visit would infuriate China, one of Thailand's largest trading partners, as well as trade and diplomatic relations. The Dalai Lama's entry has not been officially banned, said Chavanond Intarakomalyasut, Secretary to the Minister of Foreign Affairs. "Of course, we would consider it case by case," he said. "But, generally, we don't allow anyone to use Thailand as a base country to do any political activities or instigate violence in other countries" (Winn 2010).

This section delineates clearly the following: (a) The Thai royalty embraced the Sinhala monks and Theravada Buddhism; (b) Theravada Buddhists in Thailand do not view the Dalai Lama with the same level of admiration as is done in the Western world, as their image of him, is also that of a politician (given the influence of China in Thailand); and (c) It is nearly impossible that the Dalai Lama would ever be given an official invitation by the Thai government.

It is China's sway over the economy and polity of Thailand that connects the next section to this narrative.

China's Economic and Strategic Diplomacy in Thailand

As the second largest economy of ASEAN, Thailand is an important country for China — both in terms of trade (China provides a market for 14 percent of all exports from Thailand and its share in Thai imports constitutes 18 percent) as well as in terms of its growing clout both internally and externally. Internally, as explained by several interviewees including Indian businessmen (Satish Sehgal, D.K. Bakshi, Mr. Bajaj), many major Thai businesses are owned by the Chinese (44 percent of all businesses are owned by Chinese, having taken on Chinese names and the latter have integrated seamlessly into the Thai society.[5]

Since 2012, China has been Thailand's largest trade partner but this is a recent phenomenon. Previously, Japan held this position since at least 1993. In 2015, trade volume with China was around 2 percent higher than that with Japan. After a Free Trade Agreement was struck in 2003, Thailand–China trade began to significantly increase, along with a widening trade deficit which rose almost three-fold within a year of enactment (from $428 million to $1.26 billion). This trade deficit reached $17 billion in 2014. In contrast, Thailand runs a trade surplus with the US (one of its top three trade partners) of between $6 billion and $10 billion a year. China only replaced the US as top importer of Thai products during 2010–2014.

With the implementation of the Belt and Road Initiative, China and Thailand launched an 845-km railway project linking the Thai capital Bangkok with the northeastern city of Nong Khai near Laos, part of a Pan-Asia railway network, in late 2015. The project would be connected to the China–Laos railway which connects Laos with the vast railway system in China. It will only take 18 hours approx. To send rice to China by train, with the freight cost lowered to about one-third of that of road or sea transport (Globalsecurity.org Year n.a.).

However, there are some issues too. Within the BRI, problems are being encountered in Southeast Asia. China is planning a 3,000

---

[5] Interviews of Indian and Chinese businessmen by Dr. Reena Marwah in Bangkok in July 2014.

km (1,900-mile) high-speed rail line from Kunming, in its southwest, to Singapore. But in June 2016, talks with Thailand over its section of the line broke down; the Thais said they would build only part of the project, and would finance it themselves (Editorial 2016). There have been many other such failures. There are other difficult issues too, such as not yet having enough viable projects for the huge amount of funds that are being allocated. The Silk Road Fund was set up to invest in infrastructure abroad. But two of its first investments were in initial public offerings by Chinese firms in Hong Kong (Editorial 2016).

Another investment project, which has not yet materialized, but which China has been keen on is the Kra Canal or the Thai Canal. This proposal, to cut through Thailand in its south, was first made by the Chinese in the 18th century and continues to find traction with China. It was even reported in the media in May 2015 that this proposal had been accepted by the Thai Government. However, till date it is on hold. Undoubtedly, this represents a huge opportunity for China as it would not only provide an alternative to transit through the Strait of Malacca but also shorten transit distance by 1,200 km. China refers to it as part of its 21st Century Maritime Silk Road. China is keen on the Kra Canal project partly for strategic reasons (Forever Vagabond 2016). Thailand is also an integral partner in the Bay of Bengal Initiative for Multi-Sectoral Technical and Economic Cooperation (BIMSTEC), which includes India, Bangladesh, Bhutan, Nepal, Myanmar, Thailand and Sri Lanka. China seeks to bring within its ambit all these countries through the Belt and Road Initiative (BRI) rather than through BIMSTEC, which sees limited progress on account of India's reluctance to join the larger initiative of China.

This section amplifies the pace and possibilities of the contours of China's Belt and Road initiative which engages Thailand both on the continental and maritime space. (The South China Sea issue is not discussed here, because although this has been discussed at the level of ASEAN, the bilateral relationship between Thailand and China is not directly impacted.)

Sri Lanka: A Small yet Strategic Partner for China

There is a long tradition of friendship between China and Sri Lanka. Historical records suggest that the two countries have had strong commercial and cultural linkages from the very early time. Sri Lanka's socialist "march" did not ever quite catch up with China's, but since the first Rubber-Rice Pact was signed in 1952 China–Sri Lankan relations have been a source of unity and continue on an upward trajectory today (Gordman 2014).

This section discusses China studies in Sri Lanka as an off shoot of the rapidly growing influence of China as well as the One China policy for a country that subscribes largely to Buddhism.

Sri Lanka's Maritime Centricity

As China's economic power has grown, investing overseas has been a tool of economic policy used across the world by China to help bolster its national interest. Its financial foreign policy rests on two strategies: "accumulating foreign currency reserves and sending money abroad in the form of FDI, aid, assistance and loans," as stated by the US economic advisor Ken Miller in *Foreign Affairs* (Godman 2014). The Indian Ocean ports of Gwadar in Pakistan, Hambantota in Sri Lanka and Chittagong in Bangladesh have all benefited from Chinese investment and account for 30 percent of global trade, according to Indian Ocean Rim Association.

Sri Lanka is a model for the latter part of this strategy. Sri Lanka, a key partner in China's Belt and Road initiative has been the recipient of large amounts of investment in infrastructure in recent years. In fact, China is Sri Lanka's biggest source of foreign direct investment (FDI) as well as providing development loans for projects such as the $500 million new Colombo Port Terminal, Hambantota Port, Sri Lanka's first four-lane expressway, and a new national theater, among others. These lucrative benefits for Sri Lanka have played a pivotal role in building the relationship.

The commitment from Sri Lanka in 2014 to join the Maritime Silk Road (MSR) indicates the proximity of the two states' strategic aspirations and is a reflection of the convergence of national interests. The MSR is a vital strategic project for China in the Indian Ocean, and will increase China's presence in South Asian shipping routes. Sri Lanka can be seen as a gateway port up the western coast of India and further west to Iran, a vital exporter of oil to China. The brand new port of Hambantota, 85 percent of it paid for with a Chinese loan, is located on the south of the island, historically not a traditional shipping route. However, it is the perfect location to meet the strategic objectives of the MSR. In an interview, Asanga Abeygoonasekara (2017) said that the island country's economic relationship with China was expected to be strengthened further with the Chinese economic zone proposed to be set up in Southern Sri Lanka and Sri Lanka's support for the Belt and Road initiative. Sri Lanka's relationship with China has seen a recent boom with the government stating that it aimed to attract more Chinese investments in order to strengthen its economy. China is currently Sri Lanka's largest foreign direct investor with investments worth $409 million (*Xinhua* 2016).

Admiral Wu Shengli, Commander of Chinese PLA Navy, put forward a new maritime security concept centered on "Common Security, Comprehensive Security, Cooperative Security and Continuous Security (4Cs) at the 21st International Seapower Symposium, in September 2014, from a perspective of jointly addressing global maritime security challenges (Zhang 2014). The MSR is therefore perceived as critical for Sri Lanka to become a leading player in the development of Indian Ocean trading ports, which China has more or less augmented itself. Sri Lanka also has an opportunity to build favorable ties with both the region's superpowers, India and China, as well as the emerging Southeast Asian nations.

Chinese influence in Sri Lanka is clearly growing, but without a doubt the relationship is not one-sided. The Sri Lankan government is fully in control of what is officially known as a "Strategic Cooperative Partnership." Sri Lanka itself is keen to project itself as the geographic center of the Indian Ocean. Former Sri Lankan Ambassador to China Nihal Rodrigo, in an interview, did not express concern over China's naval expansion and development of South Asian ports, but rather claimed that it "provides it (China) easier connectivity across the Indian Ocean which benefits South Asia." Both governments therefore have something to gain from Hamantota Port, described as one element of Sri Lanka's "five-hub" growth strategy, which aims to position and build the island as a global naval, aviation, commercial, energy, and knowledge center (Rodrigo 2017).

There is evidence to suggest that Colombo and Beijing now share policies on a whole range of issues, political and economic. This is in part a reflection of Chinese influence, but it is also attributable to Sri Lanka's ability to manipulate the relationship in its favor.

In April 2016, Sri Lanka officially lifted a hold on the Colombo Port City project, a $1.4 billion Chinese initiative to build a "mini-city" on reclaimed land at the country's capital. The project is the largest in Sri Lanka's history and falls under Beijing's Belt and Road and New Silk Road initiatives, meant not only to expand but also secure China's trade routes throughout Asia.

The controversy over the port city offers a taste of the potential consequences the One Belt initiative could bring: it has plunged Sri Lanka into debt. Interview of President Mathripala Sirisena to the *Hindu* in India, on November 11, 2016, "The port city agreement, when it was signed during President Rajapaksa's time, was contradictory to the constitutional provisions. No government in the past had signed such an agreement. We amended certain clauses of that agreement as the new government. In such an agreement, the importance of national security as well as regional security should be taken into consideration" (Sirisena 2016).

The Sri Lankan economy is reeling under the burden of heavy debt; despite this it will need more Chinese investment to revive it. Sri Lankan officials scrapped a controversial plan to give outright land ownership to China, saying they would instead offer the land on a 99-year lease (Rupasinghe 2016). Although China declined a debt for equity swap, their participation in Sri Lanka's infrastructure development has started. Colombo Port City project is expected to be given the necessary permissions and in fact, China has requested for 15,000 acres of land in Hambantota for the building of a massive, million-worker special economic zone. This idea seems to be gaining traction.[6]

Although Rajapakse was also criticized for pushing the country into a virtual debt trap with China, the bilateral relations are strong and resilient. The new regime of Sirisena closely scrutinized a host of Chinese projects for corruption as well as high interest rates being charged over $5 billion loans. In fact, the new government of President Maithripala Sirisena has relaxed ties with Beijing and moved closer to India. But the majority Buddhist island, which is home to some of the religion's most sacred sites, still depends on China for major development investment and loans.[7]

Sri Lanka's Buddhism and One China Policy: A Manifestation of Pragmatism

According to traditional Sri Lankan chronicles, Buddhism was introduced into Sri Lanka in the 3rd century BCE.[8] Sri Lanka has the longest continuous history of Buddhism of any Buddhist nation. Several Buddhist shrines were built and Buddhism has continued to thrive on the island.

---

[6]Sri Lanka's debt situation is severe. The country is currently in $58.3 billion debt to foreign financiers, and 95.4 percent of all government revenue is currently going toward paying back its loans. This means that out of every $100 that the government brings in only $4.60 is going toward essentials like education and public services. (Shepard 2016)

[7]He added that Sri Lanka has not changed its stance on its "One China" policy. "Sri Lanka is a traditional friendly neighbor of China's and the China–Sri Lanka relationship has always developed smoothly. Sri Lanka fully understands and respects China's concerns on the relevant issue. We appreciate the Sri Lankan position. We are willing to work together with Sri Lanka to constantly strengthen our traditional friendly partnership," Chinese Foreign Ministry spokeswoman Hua Chunying told a regular briefing in Beijing (PTI 2015).

[8]For several centuries Buddhism flourished in Ceylon. Travelers reported many thousands of monks ans magnificent temples. The Pali Canon was first written in Ceylon. In June 306 B.C. (i.e., 237 years after the demise of the Buddha), that Arhat Mahinda formally introduced Buddhism including the Tripitaka to Sri Lanka.

In the present population of Sri Lanka which is around 21 million, the Theravada Buddhists constitute around 70 percent of the population and all are Sinhalese.

Hindu, Islam, and Christianity are the other important religious minorities. Although Sri Lanka is not a Buddhist state, its 1978 Constitution, while assuring freedom of religion to all citizens, grants "foremost place" to Buddhism and declares it "the duty of the State to protect and foster the Buddhist Sasana (broad teachings of the Buddha)." Sri Lankan polity has sought to project itself as the guardian of Buddhism. Rather than upholding the peaceful core tenets of Buddhism, they have expressed their faith to the Buddhist clergy through generous grants for the renovation of Buddhist shrines and monasteries, or with lavish gifts to the *mahanayakes* (high priests) and other monks (Ramachandran 2013).

Buddhism has an influential presence in modern Sri Lanka. Buddhism in contemporary times has been influenced by the experiences of Sinhala Buddhist with colonialism from Europe, Christian missionaries, ideas and aspirations of gender equality, ethnic separatists and worldwide developmental and political organizations. Buddhism in modern Sri Lanka is a union of various, sometimes contradictory ideas and practices. Although for some people, Buddhism is a symbol of national unity and cultural heritage, for most Sinhala Buddhists, it is a combination of local tradition and a global religion, one that embeds in them a national identity while linking them to other Buddhist groups and movements around the world.

According to Nihal Rodrigo, Sri Lanka–China relations were initiated by the Chinese Buddhist Monk Fa Hsien, "who came all the way crossed India to also Sri Lanka and stayed for two years, speaking with our Buddhist monks; most of them because of their Buddhist scriptures they could manage some Pali. He is one of the earliest reporters of Sri Lanka of that time" (Rodrigo 2017). China–Sri Lanka relations in recent times have only strengthened.

> This is also evident because Sri Lanka has accorded top priority to its One China Policy. The earlier government of Rajapakse (2005–2015)

and the new government of Mathripala Sirisena (with effect from February 2015) affirms this commitment. The Tibetan leader, the Dalai Lama has never visited Sri Lanka. In fact, it is well known that even if Buddhist monks extend an invitation, the government might not grant a visa. "The Dalai Lama is very important. But the close relationship with China is more important," the official stated[9] (Aneez and Sirilal 2015). It is evident that whenever such a stand has been taken by the government, Chinese officials have lauded them. "Sri Lanka is a traditional friendly neighbor of China's, and the China–Sri Lanka relationship has always developed smoothly," said spokeswoman Hua Chunying during a briefing in Beijing. "Sri Lanka fully understands and respects China's concerns on the relevant issue" (Samaraweera 2016).

On the Tibet question and the recognition of the Dalai Lama, a Sri Lankan interviewee, Tammita Delgoda categorically asserted, "The Dalai Lama would be the nearest thing that we have to a Buddhist leader. Buddhism is very important in Sri Lanka. Despite this, Sri Lanka is the only Buddhist nation which has not invited the Dalai Lama, it will not go anywhere near the Dalai Lama" (Delgoda 2012).

Sri Lanka affirms its belief in the One China policy, and the Dalai Lama is restricted from addressing the Sinhalese Buddhists. Moreover, Sri Lanka is known for its independence and pragmatism in foreign policy, carefully avoiding any bilateral issue which may contain some semblance of distinct ideologies. Sri Lankan Buddhists have a homegrown firebrand strain of Buddhism, known as the Bodu Balasena (BBS). It is also not clearly known, except for some individual writings and assertions, that the minorities in Sri Lanka are being systematically eradicated by the BBS. This, obviously cannot be afforded by Sri Lanka as it seeks to portray itself as a peaceful Buddhist nation. It will also not be in the interest of Sri Lanka, to give impetus to the fundamentalist forces among the Buddhists, for the simple truism that China discourages any kind of religious

---

[9] http://www.reuters.com/article/us-sri-lanka-china-dalailama-idUSKBN0MT1K920150402

fanaticism. It can ill afford to let the soft power diplomacy whip up religious sentiments of any kind on its own land.

It is in this context that although the Dalai Lama has shown interest in visiting Sri Lanka, and the Sinhalese Buddhists also admire and respect the Tibetan leader, it is well known that the Sri Lankan government will never relent and has also never offered an explanation in public about its policy in dealing with the Dalai Lama.

China Studies in Sri Lanka

With the rapid development of East Asia and the rise of China at the global level, most countries of the world have realized the value of learning the Chinese language that has been described by the China studies experts as the first stage of inducing the interest in China studies. In the case of Sri Lanka, the interest in learning Chinese is growing due to several reasons including boosting Chinese investment in Sri Lanka as well as strengthening cultural ties between the two countries. At present the CRI Confucius Classroom at Lumbini College, Colombo, the Association for Sri Lanka–China Social and Cultural Cooperation and the Listeners Association of China Radio International in Sri Lanka are actively involved in running the Chinese language program. Since its inauguration in July 2007, CRI Confucius Classroom has been committed to providing Chinese language education service for Sri Lankan people and boosting the promotion of Chinese culture and bilateral cultural exchanges of the two countries (Sun and Liu 2012). The Confucius Classroom has opened several sessions of elementary, intermediate, and advanced Chinese courses and developed customized Chinese courses especially for local middle and primary schools, educational establishments, and commercial organizations. There is a Confucius Institute in Colombo University.

In May 2007, a Confucius Institute was established in the University of Kelaniya. The mission of the Confucius Institute, is to provide better awareness on Chinese language and its culture on undergraduates, as well as the general public.[10]

---

[10] http://units.kln.ac.lk/ccs/. Accessed on April 18, 2017.

The other institute which is involved in Chinese-language education is the Bandaranaike Centre for International Studies (BCIS) at Colombo. The institute offers Chinese-language courses at beginners, intermediate and advanced levels. Besides, it also undertakes research on China and has signed the Memorandum of Understanding (MoU) on Cooperation with the China Institute of International Studies in 2006. The BCIS also carries out exchange visits with scholars from the China Military Academy of Sciences, the China Institutes of Contemporary International Relations, the Beijing Foreign Studies University and the Shanghai Institute of International Studies. The Galle Dialogue, an annual conference series since 2010, organized by Sri Lanka's Ministry of Defence, focuses on themes of maritime security and the Indian Ocean. The theme for the 2016 conference was "Towards Maritime Partnerships" (Samaraweera 2016).

Among the notable think tanks in Sri Lanka is The Lakshman Kadirgamar Institute of International Relations and Strategic Studies (LKIIRSS), founded in 2006, is a multi-disciplinary research forum dedicated to analyzing Sri Lanka's strategic interests in the realm of international relations, within the contemporary domestic and global contexts. This institute functions as a forum for the generation of research and analysis, with a view to providing an input to national policy formulation (Abeysekara 2017).

The Regional Centre for Strategic Studies (RCSS) at Colombo too undertakes research and conduct workshops on China-related issues as part of research on regional studies. However, it is to be pointed out that China studies in Sri Lanka is at a nascent stage going step by step to become fully developed. According to Sinharaja Tammita-Delgoda, "China studies in Sri Lanka is developing as a knee jerk reaction. Sri Lanka has been a pro-west country for a long time, but at the same time it has a long friendship with China, and the commissioning of a port in Hambantota completely changed the pro-west orientation of Sri Lanka in favor of China" (Tammita-Delgoda 2012). China has been supporting various other projects as well and is now the largest donor and third largest trading partner of Sri Lanka. So, there is a strong consciousness of the value of China in Sri Lanka and with this the historical and cultural links are being forged successfully through the study centers.

Swaran Singh in his interview with Nihal Rodrigo sums up the extent of China studies in Sri Lanka when he says, "So it's interesting that China which is a very important country for Sri Lanka, you don't have so many good Sri Lankan China experts. But in China, you're saying China has smart experts on Sri Lanka" (Rodrigo 2017).

Conclusion

As articulated at the beginning of the chapter, the two countries in question, *viz.* Thailand and Sri Lanka have significant characteristics which bring them not only closer to China but also to one another. Despite their historical–cultural differences and geographical locations (with one sharing the continental shelf-based linkages with China and the other being traditionally in the ambit of India in South Asia), there are nonetheless similar effects of enhanced economic connectivity and shared Buddhist legacies on the perspective on China.

China–Thailand: Kith and Kin Relationship vs. Sri Lanka's State-led Relationship with China

It is very evident that the two countries of Thailand and Sri Lanka are very different in terms of their familiarity with the former having had the status of a vassal state, with Chinese settlers over centuries permeating Thai society very easily through language, identity, and cultural connections. It is well known that the Chinese settlers took on Thai names and adapted well into Thai society. Several generations of Chinese immigrants ensures that their cultural assimilation is complete.

The Sri Lankan people have no such common factors instilled through history or civilizational linkages. The Sinhalese have much more in common with India, as its closest neighbor in South Asia. Ties with Tamil Nadu in terms of language, cultural expressions, and affinity is more visible. With China, Sri Lanka's relations rest on the latter's geo-strategic significance in the Indian Ocean and as an important partner for China's BRI. People to people contacts are more recent and still evolving, with language being a significant barrier in bilateral relations. This also pertains to the demographic mix in Sri Lanka, where 12.6 percent of its population are Hindus (Viakram 2017).

China's Political Diplomacy and Influence: Winning Over the Leadership in Both Countries

China came to the rescue of Sri Lanka at the United Nations. When the US ended direct military aid in 2007 over Sri Lanka's deteriorating human rights record (a result of the wiping out of the LTTE), China stepped in and increased aid to nearly $1 billion (£690 million) to become the island's biggest donor, providing the latest weapons, including a free gift of six F7 fighter jets to the Sri Lankan air force. The proactive position of China prevented the UN Security Council from putting Sri Lanka on its agenda (Popham 2010). China's financial support even eclipsed Sri Lanka's biggest donor, Japan, and created a scenario to counter Western concerns about human rights (Manoharan 2016). China's zero tolerance toward extremist activities in Xinjiang in its own western region is well known.

Two factors explain why China has become Thailand's new best friend. First, Beijing's lack of criticism of political developments in the Kingdom. Second, the great attention China has given to Thailand's leaders. High level visits and side meetings between the two countries exceed those Thailand has with other countries. Thai Princess Sirindhorn visits China every year at the invitation of the Chinese government. Princess Chulabhorn is another frequent guest. China facilitated an ancestral visit by the former Thai Prime Ministers Thaksin and Yingluck Shinawatra in 2015, without antagonizing the Prayut Chan-o-cha government, or being heavily criticized by the Yellow Shirts. In contrast, Western leaders and diplomats have struggled in their interactions with the military government and the Pheu Thai party, and remind Thailand to uphold principles of liberal democracy. The Thai-Chinese relationship thus shows the strength of China's diplomacy. This has drawn Thailand toward China, even when it has not been in its own best interests (Chingchit 2016).

One China Policy: Thailand and Sri Lanka as Theravada Buddhist Nations

Regional integration in ASEAN mandates a unique role of Thailand, especially, within ASEAN as it has a large volume of trade, second only to Singapore. Thailand's importance for ASEAN is well known to China too, which ensures that the Thai polity is kept engaged, both through economic and security initiatives (Marwah 2016). Thailand is acutely sensitive to China's core interests and will not stake its relations with China on the issue of the Dalai Lama. Moreover, the Theravada Buddhists comprise the majority of the Buddhists in Thailand whose allegiance to the Dalai Lama is rarely an issue.

It is evident that Sri Lankan monks continue to meet the Dalai Lama in Delhi and in other places, but the State-led relationship with China is strong enough to prevent him from stepping into the country. Sri Lanka is not only conscious but also wary of China's wrath and will never breach this line of control. According to Nihal Rodrigo (2017), "Sri Lanka and China are firmly opposed to what China calls 'The Three Evils of terrorism, separatism and extremism'. There is close cooperation at the bilateral level as well as within regional and multilateral frameworks including at United Nations forums. Sri Lanka is a Dialogue Partner in the Shanghai Co-operation Organization (SCO). Defense cooperation with China, including military training and the supply of arms and other equipment have been of great value in Sri Lanka's decisive battle against the separatist terrorism." With respect to Taiwan, Sri Lanka has strongly supported the One China policy, and considered the territory as an integral part of the Peoples Republic. Sri Lanka has opposed all attempts by Taiwan to gain membership in international organizations composed of sovereign states (Rodrigo 2017).

China's Economic Diplomacy: Strategic Outreach of BRI

Development projects in Sri Lanka, including the Hambantota multi-purpose project, involve participation by the Chinese Government, companies, and corporate entities under different forms of management, the Chinese Export Import Bank and other groups. The Project Agreement, signed in 2007, and terms for repayment of its loan component are favorable to Sri Lanka and followed negotiations with the Chinese Government and the "advanced productive forces." At present, around 80 Chinese companies are also involved in various other Sri Lankan ventures and projects. Over 30 operate under special incentives provided by the Sri Lanka Board of Investment (BOI). Moreover, the people to people linkages between Sri Lanka and China have enhanced the inter-state relationship, through religious linkages, as well as through cultural interaction, tourism, educational, academic and technical exchanges. However, all is not well, mainly due to Sri Lanka's mounting debt burden and questions being raised about China's smart bid to push through investments and then converting its debt into equity.

Thailand too has been till 2014 maintaining a tightrope walk between its political ally, the US and China. However, since 2014, with the ousting of the Yingluck Shinawatra government, the country is growing closer to China. It is evident that Thailand–China relations will continue to thrive and prosper given Thailand's strategic location at the heart of mainland Southeast Asia and status as the region's second-largest economy. In fact, Thailand's position in the connectivity grid of Southeast Asia will ensure its place as the regional power in the sub-region of countries comprising Myanmar, Laos, Cambodia, and Thailand, regardless of the political situation (Denoon 2017: 232). Some issues however remain and stem from the question of adjacent and proximate positioning of China and have been discussed in the previous section.

In conclusion, to compare and contrast the two countries' interface with China, it would be appropriate to state that China studies have witnessed an ascendancy in both countries. While in Thailand, China looms large through language teaching, temples, festivals, people, business houses and China study centers, China studies in Sri Lanka are evolving gradually, backed by the political clout and economic space China has occupied in the past 10 years especially under the previous government of Rajapakse. It was his government which forged ties with China for the port and infrastructure projects. However, the present government of Maithripala Sirisena which came to power on the votes based on the previous government's heavy reliance on Beijing has now opted for a foreign policy that imbibes a balanced engagement with the US, India, and China (Balázs and Mendis 2017). This implies that China needs to be watchful of its economic positioning in Sri Lanka.

China, on its part, needs both Thailand and Sri Lanka for its BRI. Thailand is an integral component of its outreach to Southeast Asian nations and for ensuring that its core interests in ASEAN are not compromised. China's sensitivities and interests on land and sea are to be safeguarded by nations in its extended periphery — both big and small. To allude to an old saying in China "the fire burns high when everybody adds wood to it." Thus, both Thailand and Sri Lanka may be beneficiaries of a shared prosperity through reiterating their friendly and uncritical views of China.

References

Abeygoonasekara, Asanga. 2017. Interview to Prof. Swaran Singh on February 24.

Abeysekara, Asanga. 2017. Interview to Swaran Singh on February 24.

Andaya, Barbara Watson. 2014. Introduction to Southeast Asia: History, Geography, and Livelihood, www.asiasociety.org/education/introduction-southeast-asia. Accessed on February 21, 2017.

Aneez, Shihar and Ranga Sirilal. 2015. Sri Lanka Government Unlikely to Allow Dalai Lama Visit-Official, *Reuters* (April 2), http://www.reuters.com/article/us-sri-lanka-china-dalailama-idUSKBN0MT1K920150402. Accessed on June 26, 2017.

Balázs, Dániel and Patrick Mendis. 2017. Is China on the Road to International Isolation? *The Diplomat* (January 21, 2017), http://thediplomat.com/2017/01/is-china-on-the-road-to-international-isolation/. Accessed on June 26, 2017.

Baviera, Aileen P. S. 1999. China's Relations with Southeast Asia: Political Security and Economic Interests, Philippine-APEC Study Center Network Discussion Paper No. 99–17, Hilo, Hawaii, 24, 26. Accessed on March 1, 2015. https://hilo.hawaii.edu/uhh/faculty/tamvu/documents/baviera.pdf. Accessed on March 1, 2015.

Chachavalpongpun, Pavin. 2015. Thailand and China Build Ties of Convenience, *The Japan Times* (August 13), http://www.japantimes.co.jp/opinion/2015/08/13/commentary/world-commentary/thailand-china-build-ties-convenience/#.VlyEntIrLIV. Accessed on December 5, 2015.

Chingchit, Sasiwan. 2016. The Curious Case of Thai-Chinese Relations: Best Friends Forever? The Asia Foundation (March 30), http://asiafoundation.org/2016/03/30/the-curious-case-of-thai-chinese-relations-best-friends-forever/. Accessed on June 5, 2017.

Daily FT. 2015. Secure Seas Through Greater Maritime Cooperation-Challenges and Way Forward, http://galledialogue.lk/index.php?id=15#2015. Accessed on November 12, 2016.

Delgoda, Tammita. 2012. Interviewed by Dr. Sharad Soni on March 22.

Denoon, David B. H. (Eds.) 2017. *China, the United States, and the Future of Southeast Asia: U.S-China Relations* 2. New York: New York University Press.

Editorial. 2016. Our Bulldozers, Our Rules: China's Foreign Policy Could Reshape a Good Part of the World Economy (July 2), http://www.economist.com/news/china/21701505-chinas-foreign-policy-could-reshape-good-part-world-economy-our-bulldozers-our-rules. Accessed on March 10, 2017

Ehrlich, Richard S. 2011. China Comes to Thailand, *Asia Sentinel* (July 28) http://www.asiasentinel.com/econ-business/china-comes-to-thailand/. Accessed on March 10, 2015.

Forever Vagabond. 2016. The Real Threat to S'pore — Construction of Thai's Kra Canal Financed by China, *The Independent* (October 2), http://www.theindependent.sg/the-real-threat-to-spore-construction-of-thais-kra-canal-financed-by-china/. Accessed on 10 March, 2017.

Garver, John W. 1992. China and South Asia, *Annals of the American Academy of Political and Social Science* 519: 67–85.

Gethin, Rupert. 1998. *The Foundations of Buddhism.* Oxford: Opus Books, Oxford University Press http://www.ahandfulofleaves.org/documents/The%20Foundations%20of%20Buddhism_Gethin_1998.pdf. Accessed on April 21, 20147.

Globalsecurity.org. Year n.a. Thailand–China Relations. http://www.globalsecurity.org/military/world/thailand/forrel-prc.htm. Accessed on March 6, 2017.

Godman, Jack. 2014. Sri Lanka's Growing Links with China, *The Diplomat*, March 06, http://thediplomat.com/2014/03/sri-lankas-growing-links-with-china/. Accessed on April 7, 2017.

Goonatilake, Hema. 2010. Sri Lanka's role in the spread of Buddhism in South East Asia, *Sunday Times*, Sri Lanka, (June 20). http://www.sundaytimes.lk/100620/Plus/plus_16.html. Accessed on November 18, 2016. http://www.thehindu.com/opinion/interview/Solving-problems-of-Tamils-is-my-obligation-Sirisena/article16442765.ece. Accessed on April 7, 2017

Kataoka, Tatsuki. 2012. Religion as Non-religion: The Place of Chinese Temples in Phuket, Southern Thailand, *Southeast Asian Studies* 1(3): 461–485, https://englishkyoto-seas.org/wp-content/uploads/010305.pdf . Accessed on April 21, 2017.

Kataoka, Tatsuki. 2012. Religion as Non-religion: The Place of Chinese Temples in Phuket, Southern Thailand, *Southeast Asian Studies* 1(3): 461–485.

Kislenko, Arne. 2004. A Not So Silent Partner: Thailand's Role in Covert Operations, Counter-Insurgency, and the Wars in Indochina, *The Journal of Conflict Studies* 24(1): 64–96, https://journals.lib.unb.ca/index.php/jcs/article/view/292/465. Accessed on March 22, 2017.

Malik, and J. Mohan. 2001. South Asia in China's Foreign Relations, *Pacifica Review: Peace, Security & Global Change* 13(1): 73–90.

Manoharan, Priyakala. 2012. The Sri Lanka–China Relationship: A Print Media Analysis, Institute of Peace and Conflict Studies (June 4), http://www.ipcs.org/article/china/the-sri-lanka-china-relationship-a-print-media-analysis-3630.html. Accessed on April 19, 2017.

Marwah, Reena. 2016. Thailand's Increasing Closeness to China: What It Implies for ASEAN-Analysis, *Eurasia Review* (January 5), http://www.eurasiareview.com/05012016-thailands-increasing-closeness-to-china-what-it-implies-for-asean-analysis/. Accessed on April 18, 2017.

Popham, Peter. 2010. How Beijing Won Sri Lanka's Civil War, *The Independent* (May 22), http://www.independent.co.uk/news/world/asia/how-beijing-won-sri-lankas-civil-war-1980492.html. Accessed on April 19, 2017.

PTI. 2015. Maithripala Sirisena and an old friend of China: Xi Jinping, *The Economic News* (March 26), http://economictimes.indiatimes.com/articleshow/46701849.cms?utm_source=contentofinterest&utm_medium=text&utm_campaign=cppst. Accessed on June 7, 2017.

Ramachandran, Sudha. 2013. Sri Lanka's Muslims in the Cross Hairs, *The Diplomat* (September 11), http://thediplomat.com/2013/09/sri-lankas-muslims-in-the-cross-hairs/. Accessed on June 26, 2017.

Rodrigo, Nihal. 2017. Interview to Prof. Swaran Singh on February 25.

Rupasinghe, Wasantha. 2016. Sri Lankan President Maithripala Sirisena to Visit India in Delicate Balancing Act. *The Indian Express* (May 13), http://indianexpress.com/article/india/india-news-india/sri-lankan-president-maithripala-sirisena-to-visit-india-in-delicate-balancing-act-2798049/. Accessed on 7 April, 2017.

Samaraweera, Mangala. 2016. Remarks by Foreign Minister Mangala Samaraweera at Galle Dialogue 2016. Ministry of Foreign Affairs Sri Lanka, http://www.ibtimes.com/dalai-lama-sri-lanka-visit-china-ties-more-important-government-buddhist-leader-1869336. Accessed on June 26, 2017.

Sami, Shafi. 2012. Bangladesh: A Partner for Peace and Prosperity. In S. D. Muni and Tan Tai Yong (Eds.), *A Resurgent China: South Asian Perspectives*. New Delhi: Routledge, pp. 8–42.

Shepard, Wade. 2016. China Tells Sri Lanka: We Want Our Money, Not Your Empty Airport, *Forbes* (July 31), http://www.forbes.com/sites/wadeshepard/2016/07/31/china-to-sri-lanka-we-want-our-money-not-your-empty-airport/#7e3a8bb21169. Accessed on April 17, 2017.

Sirisena, Maithripala. 2016. Solving Problems of Tamils Is My Obligation, *The Hindu* (December 2).

Sun, Jiajia and Shuangyan Liu. 2012. CRI Confucius Classroom at Lumbini, Sri Lanka Holds Annual Commencement & Award Ceremony of 'My View of China' Essay Competition, *Hanban News* (May 3), http://english.hanban.org/article/2012-05/03/content_432435.htm. Accessed on April 18, 2017.

Sydney Southeast Asia Center. Year n.a. Our Research: Driving Research Excellence in Southeast Asia, http://sydney.edu.au/southeast-asia-centre/documents/pdf/auethavornpipat-ruji.pdf. Accessed on June 27, 2017.

Tammita-Delgoda, Sinharaja. 2012. Interview to Sharad Soni on March 22.

Vikram. 2017. A Closer Look at How Partition Changed Punjab's Religious Map, South Asia Blog, https://southasiablog.wordpress.com/category/demographics/. Accessed on April 29, 2017.

Winn, Patrick. 2010. Dalai Lama: Blackballed from Thailand, *Minn Post* (February 2), https://www.minnpost.com/global-post/2010/02/dalai-lama-blackballed-thailand. Accessed on June 8, 2017.

Women of China. 2014. Confucius Institute Inaugurated in Thailand's Khon Kaen University, (December 02), http://en.yibada.com/articles/8318/20141202/confucius-institute-inaugurated-in-thailands-khon-kaen-university.htm#ixzz4Pb6KO27b. Accessed on June 17, 2017.

Xinhua. 2016. Sri Lanka Should Maintain Strong Relations with China, U.S. to Win 'Trading Hub' Position, *Daily News* (November 30), http://dailynews.lk/2016/11/30/local/100671. Accessed on 7 April, 2017.

Yang, C. K. 1991. *Religion in Chinese Society: A Study of Contemporary Social Functions of Religion and Some of Their Historical Factors*. Taipei: SNC Publishing.

Zhang, Jianchang. 2014. Building Cooperation and Collaboration to Achieve Common Maritime Goals, http://galledialogue.lk/assets/files/2014/research_papers/building_cooperation_and_collaboration_to.pdf. Accessed on June 7, 2017.

Zhao, Yanrong. 2014. Confucius Institutes Extend Reach, (October 3), http://epaper.chinadailyasia.com/asia-weekly/article-3. Accessed on June 7, 2017.

9

Crafting a Bridge Role Through Chinese Studies Without Sinology: Lessons of South Asian Think Tanks for Singapore

Chih-yu Shih
Department of Political Science
National Taiwan University, Taiwan

Singapore arguably owns one of the world's best think tanks that focuses on Chinese affairs: the East Asian Institute (EAI). By comparison, South Asian countries look pale institutionally on policy analysis and Chinese affairs. Singapore distinguishes itself by its Chinese cultural background as well as English education. Together, the bilingual and multicultural characteristics of Singapore society enable a hybrid perspective that is difficult to emulate elsewhere. However, I will argue that political consideration and historical practices have jointly established a mode of analysis to do without the Chinese cultural sensibilities in Singapore's think-tank methodology. This methodological self-restraint has reached such an extent that the deliberately contrived technicality of the EAI operation has fixed its intellectual resources to an external position that is not significantly different from the analytical style of Nepali, Bangladeshi, or even Bhutanese in observing Chinese affairs. The latter faces the challenges of language and civilizational unfamiliarity with the Chinese culture and the Chinese people.

An Overlooked Comparative Perspective

Singapore, Nepal, and Bangladesh are comparable in (Zheng and Lye 2015, 46–47; Mitra 2013; PTI 2016; Kashinath 2016) one significant aspect. They each host more or less a wish or even a desire to be a bridge over the difference of China and its potential rival in India, the West, or both. Despite the practical unlikelihood of disregarding China's extreme alert at the cross-border activities of Tibetan priests, Bhutan may likewise have an unspoken wish to bridge the cultural distance between Tibet and the rest of the world. In addition, Singapore, Nepal, Bangladesh, and Bhutan are relatively small nations neighboring one or more major powers (Muni ND Yong 2012; Snedden 2016; Penjore 2014). Their value and image can be enhanced wherever they are able to provide a platform for the competing others to explore cooperation. For all the four nations, China appears to be in a common side of the gap to be bridged in order for China to better connect to another country.

Nonetheless, they are a number of variations. One example is that Singapore or Bangladesh does not share a border with China, whereas Nepal and Bhutan do, compelling India to consider China primarily as a competitor in the latter territories. In another example, India wields an overwhelming political influence in Nepal, Bhutan, and Bangladesh but significantly less influence in Singapore (Thapliyal 1998; Chowdhury 2013; Jain 1959; Singh and Syeda 2010). However, Singapore faces no less pressure from neighboring Muslim societies in Indonesia and Malaysia. Furthermore, Bhutan and Nepal are intrinsically a part of Tibetan issue because of vicinity and shared religiosity (Mathou 2014; Kumar 2010; Shneidermann 2013), but Bangladesh and Singapore are not, freeing the latter two from China's alert at separatist activities. Finally, Singapore's cultural familiarity with and ethnic proximity to China resembles its South Asian counterparts' cultural familiarity with India. Singapore enjoys an apparent advantage in understanding China.

Singapore and Bangladesh are distinct from each other, with China's significantly stronger cultural sensibilities toward the Chineseness of Singapore and the subsequent lessons drawn from Singapore's submission to Asian values and hierarchical governance as opposed to liberalism (Huei 2016). However, the EAI's cultural amnesia in the face of China renders its methodology as Bangladeshi or Nepali. Singapore and Nepal are different because the latter regards China as a leverage on India, whereas the former considers China as a force to be balanced by the US for China to be useful to Singapore (Roy 2005). The shared balancing perspective, albeit varied on China being a balancer or a target of balancing, offsets the relevance of cultural connection. Singapore's pragmatic approach to China has created a sense of relative deprivation among the Chinese (Zhang 2016), incurring anxiety toward Singapore's tendency toward the US. China's alienation from presumably Chinese Singapore contrasts China's liking of Nepal. The abortion of Chineseness, compared to the lack of it, poses a more serious challenge to China.

However, methodologically, if, for the sake of its ideological self-defense and political unity, Singapore consciously subdues its cultural connectivity to China so that it will have to rely on social science discourse to frame intelligence gathered from China (Yew 2017), then its presumably cultural sensitivity toward political and cultural nuances, which could have made the qualitative difference of Singapore's approach to China than the South Asian ones, will be no more than its capacity to gather quicker intelligence. Such a lost qualitative difference gives way to a quantitative phenomenon when culture does not play a role in the analysis. If Singapore can rely on recruiting Chinese nationals to gather intelligence (as if Chinese Singaporean were unable to gather), then the think tanks in South Asia could technically do the same. This comparison means that visits, consultations, and exchange of intelligence are the shared methods and civilizational stereotyping and national interest calculus from a perspective external to China make their shared epistemology. Relying on interviews of retired diplomats and think-tank experts, the chapter also discusses how bridging the differences for China would serve no function of bridging, wherever China is not interested in being bridged, other than producing or reproducing differences.

Singapore's Quest for Objectivism

Singapore strives for a multiple-bridge role between China and many parts of the world, which presumably include distinctively South Asia, Europe, and the US. China experts in other neighboring countries, which are relatively smaller than China, seem to share the same wish that their countries can be a bridge between China and primarily India. These experts come from Bangladesh, Bhutan, and Nepal. They have quite a different background than Singapore, as the latter has a very strong Sinological tradition among its Chinese population as well as intellectuals. Their own background varies to the extent that Bangladesh subscribes to Muslim rather than Buddhism as either Nepal or Bhutan does or to Confucianism that Singapore does more. In addition, India has a significantly stronger interest, influence, and intention in the three neighbors than China in its interaction with Singapore.

In fact, the strategic competition between China and India in Nepal and Bangladesh is conscious and conspicuous (Wang 2011; Rehman 2009; Pant 2007; Zhao 2007). This condition explains why some experts in those South Asian countries in between the two giants desire a bridge role to avoid the embarrassment of having to take side. The limitation on their capacity for such a bridge role is intellectual in the sense that their civilizational underpinning is more attached with India than China. However, being a bridge is still appropriate if the intention is to serve as a one-sided process that can make things that are Chinese better for the Indians to accept or more easily adjusted to the Indian context. Likewise, for Singapore to be a bridge primarily for China to better use things that are Western, it can well rely on its Sinological strength.

The ability to take advantage of Sinological resources engenders an agential subjectivity that is not registered in those think tanks that epistemologically adopt a perspective of China watching from the outside. This observation is made because Sinology provides a level of confidence that is not accessible to anyone else who considers themselves as a stranger who speculates on issues through pieces of evidence. By contrast, Sinologists are inclined to make judgments or learned guesses wherever insufficient intelligence is available because they are cognitively prepared to empathize with an internal Chinese standpoint (Shih, Chou, and Nguyen 2014; Tanaka 1993; Cohen 1984). If Nepali or Bangladeshi experts want to distance their Indian background to win trust from the Chinese side, then by renouncing the intellectual legacy embedded in any shared Indian worldview, they may appear more neutral in the view of the Chinese in the short run, while they would simultaneously lose their psychological preparedness to give lessons to an Indian audience or to translate to China regarding the expectation that is emerging from India for the Chinese side to consider.

Singapore has been deliberately doing this kind of self-renouncing after carefully considering its national interests. Singapore's best think tank on Chinese affairs, the EAI, evolves on the assumption that Singapore is both inside and outside of China, that is between East and West (Lim 2016: 29). This mindset is a sort of Sinological self-role expectation, as Sinologists are typically Europeans who are intellectually prepared to cross the civilizational divide. However, in practice, the Singaporean authorities have been alerted of Sinological components. These components mainly belong to a population that tends to romanticize their Chinese ethnicity. For a long time in Southeast Asia, during the Cold War, Chineseness connoted vulnerability to Chinese Communist infiltration and therefore posed a national security threat. In fact, the establishment of the EAI and its aftermath witnessed strong caution against Chineseness. Such caution, among other concerns (Silver 2005), led to the termination of the official sponsorship for Chinese language education in the country. As a result, the organization principle of the EAI has been self-quarantined to ensure the immunity of the population from any access to intelligence on China. This move means that Sinological resources available in the Chinese Singaporean community are completely unacceptable to the purpose of the EAI.

The EAI is not distinct from its South Asian counterpart, which is unfamiliar with the Chinese affairs, to the extent that Singapore is likewise a British colony that comfortably embraces its post-colonial connection with the West. This distinction is the manner in which

Singapore easily substitutes English for Chinese education in school. However, Singapore had quickly realized since the openness of China that a reconnection with China could be essential to Singapore's continuing welfare. For Singapore to benefit from the return of China to world capitalism, it has selected a bridge role for itself so that the world will come to Singapore to gain a professionally trustworthy access to China. This choice means that Singapore should gain credits to its objectivism by owning knowledge of all sides. Testifying quintessentially to this self-designated objectivist role, the EAI deliberately recruits Western-trained Chinese scholars who are methodologically rigorously Western and yet practically well-informed Chinese (Lim 2016).

Sinological resources readily available in Singapore have never made the consultant list. Rather, they remain at best half-institutional as scholars of Chinese humanities and novelists, dramatists, as well as poets who do receive little support and serve public teaching posts occasionally. (One typical example is Yoon Wah Wong (2012)). They contrarily find more systematic demand of service from neighboring Malaysia, where Chinese communities struggle with their own private effort to keep the Chinese cultural lineage alive. Veteran Chinese scholars whose childhood experienced the end of the anti-Japanese war find their history and values by no means inspiring for younger generations in Singapore but to a certain degree still triggering the sense of pride with the neighboring Chinese Malaysian population. (One typical example was Gwee Yee Hean (2010)). Similarly, Malaysian Chinese Sinologists who continue to observe the rise of China and readily provide the intellectual foundation for reconnection have little to do with Chinese studies by the mainstream indigenous academics. Thus, the organizational principle of the EAI simulates a South Asian kind of Chinese studies dispossessed of Sinological resources.

What would an agenda of Chinese studies dispossessed of Sinological underpinning look like? The South Asian neighbors of China offer the best case of comparison because they similarly can consider their own country to bridge the difference between China and India, with themselves being familiar with Indian intellectual traditions and political social conditions. This consideration is parallel to the EAI, at least in accordance with its organizational ideal, which values Western intellectual discourse to translate a locally sensitive intelligence gathered from Chinese sources. Granted that short-term employed Chinese scholars at the EAI are generally significantly better informed of Chinese affairs than international scholars, they suffer an epistemological eclipse familiar to their South Asian counterpart in the sense that they are only informants to a hosting institution that is self-quarantined outside of China and therefore is not an effective bridge for the Chinese side. This observation is apparently ironic for Singapore, which is presumably culturally capable of winning the trust of the Chinese side.

Reviewing the methodology of think-tank Chinese studies in the South Asian neighbors of China is useful in appreciating their style that the EAI unknowingly emulates and the Sinological lacuna that the EAI consciously makes itself suffer to enact its objectivist role. Considering the similar strategy adopted elsewhere in East Asia, especially in the communities that carry intensive Chineseness, cultural as well as ethnic, Singapore is not an exception. As two of the most recent examples, Taiwan and Hong Kong witnessed the rise of indigenous consciousness, ironically supported by their alien or post-colonial identity in relation to Japan and the UK, respectively, to resist connection with China. Nevertheless, such reconstruction of identity does not echo the survival strategy of Singapore where Chineseness threatens the neighbors in Malaysia and Indonesia more than the Singaporeans, while Chineseness would question the quest for a separatist statehood either in Taiwan or in Hong Kong. Nevertheless, Taiwan's think tanks likewise shy away from the rich Sinological resources available in the academic circle and turn to social science and strategic calculus in their studies on China.

Bridging the Differences Between India and China

What that makes Bangladesh or Nepal comparable to Singapore is a shared sense of being a bridge for China and its competitor. This comparison used to be a metaphor Taiwan had once adopted. This adoption was made at the time when the ruling Kuomintang (KMT) in Taiwan clearly would not be able to regain power in China, and yet the pressure for enhanced interaction between the two populations was mounting. In fact, even earlier than the realization that the KMT was not to strike back at the Chinese Communist Party, the Western social scientists used to consider Taiwan as a proxy for Chinese on the Chinese study agendas (Shih 2014). With the launch of the Cultural Revolution, the KMT grasped the opportunity to make Taiwan a bridge between Western modernity and Chinese tradition. However, this observation is an extremely awkward metaphor in the 21st century as contemporary political correctness conceived of any string of Chineseness anathema to the pursuit of Taiwan independence.

In comparison with the dwindling bridge-role conception in Taiwan, exchanges between China and its South Asian neighbors and the expectations to discover a deeper meaning in South Asian scholarship have been enhanced in the new century. The notion of "one belt, one road" is China's answer to such a quest for a deeper meaning. This intellectual reconstruction compels the South Asian neighbors to reflect on their self-identity, and they can do so in a rather smooth political atmosphere. China's political image in Bangladesh is consistently positive although China had sided with Pakistan during the independence war or vetoed Bangladesh's entry to the United Nations. China's socialist and revolutionary image inspired Bangladeshi intellectuals in the beginning. Its rising power and opportunity of a fast-growing economy in the 21st century has impressed its neighbor likewise turning development-driven. China's political relationship with Nepal has been particularly warm because of China's deliberate upbringing and a mutually appreciated Buddhist religiosity of the bilateral relationship. Even when the anti-Chinese activities have grown in the past decade because of the Tibetan issue, China has refrained from an interventionary move. No Chinese prime minister has failed to visit Nepal, including the cautious Wen Jiabao, who prudently urged his host to attend to the activities against China. Mohan Lohani (2012) notes the delicate interaction among India, China, and Nepal on the Tibetan issue:

> ...[W]ith India we share the same culture and language. Geographically, we are very close to the Eastern side of India and culturally too we have a lot in common. Moreover, Delhi is just an hour's flight away from Kathmandu, while to reach Beijing it takes at least five hours. Even for medical reasons, Nepalese fly to India for treatment. Quite a large number of Nepali students are studying in various Indian universities. Despite this, some politicians and scholars continue to look upon China as Nepal's reliable neighbor. We are close to the Tibet Autonomous Region of China. Tibet is a soft underbelly of China which becomes sensitive when Tibetan refugees engage in anti-China activities from Nepalese soil.

Nepal and Bangladesh are intensively connected to India in an all-round fashion, although the political ambivalence toward India is more than apparent. Unlike China's political innocence, the Indian influence in Nepal and Bangladesh has been excessively overwhelming to escape from an interventionist image and the resultant uneasiness among the Bangladeshi and Nepali interviewees. For example, a Nepali interviewee specifically complains about India for disrupting the political disintegration in the country (Ghimire 2016). Similarly, India has not hesitated to show its displeasure toward political situations of Bangladesh from time to time. All believe that India has its eyes on China while coping with Nepal and Bangladesh. This view makes China's seeming relaxation an even more suspicious tactic to lure its neighbors. Nevertheless, no intention exists to choose side in Nepal or Bangladesh, so the bridge-role looms plausible according to some of the local narrators.

Specific self-understanding that leads to a bridge or a middle role for Nepal is not uncommon among scholars as well as practitioners. To begin with, many China-related actors find the notion of triangular relationship very attractive. For example, Ramesh Nath Pandey (2012), former Foreign Minister of Nepal, specifically acknowledged, "We, in Nepal, see ourselves as a part of a large triangle" (Pandey 2012). He points to the reality that "Nepal has an open border with India and a very long border with China" (Pandey 2012). Therefore, he believes that "Nepal is in between India and China and will continue to be of strategic relevance both for India and China." Such a triangular conception is a harbinger for Hiranya Lal Shreshtha's analysis of "trilateral development" (Pandey 2012). He explains:

> Nepal desires a strong neighbor in the south as well as a strong neighbor in the north. It is our policy to support 'One China' policy. We do not want to annoy one neighbor against another. We want to be neutral and keep the two large neighbors, India and China, in harmony. This is in Nepal's interest ... In our opinion, since China is investing in other countries, also including India, this could be an important area for a trilateral partnership to emerge. So we need to take this through trilateral investment. (Pandey 2012)

The same triangular consciousness seems to be registered in the Chinese and Indian perspectives, rendering the bridge role even more plausible. Mohan Lohani (2012) cites Prime Minister Baburam Bhattarai, who believes that "instead of Nepal being a small yam, it can actually be [a] vibrant bridge between India and China." Lohani (2012) states:

> Nepal has a very long border with China and it has an open border with India, so Nepal is really sandwiched between these two big neighbors. However, Nepal has tried to keep a balanced relationship with both countries. Interestingly enough, we have been advised by Chinese leaders to maintain good relations with India. Similarly, when our Deputy Prime Minister was in India, he was advised by the Indian Prime Minister Dr. Manmohan Singh that Nepal should have good relations with China. With a population of less than 30 million, we are a small country yet of strategic importance for our two big neighbors. Their goodwill and friendly cooperation is vital to our progress and stability.

By comparison, the self-role conception for Bangladeshi intellectuals is less enthusiastic, if not inconsistent at all. In fact, suspicion toward Bangladesh's bridge role comes from the incapacity of the country to influence the two greater neighbors. For example, Ehsanul Haque (2016) believes that the course of India–China relations has its own path. However, as long as Bangladesh manages bilateral relationships well, some trickle-down effects are expected, as Humayun Kabir (2012) argues:

> Bangladesh not only believes that the Bangladesh–China relationship should be smooth but also believes that China should maintain a good relationship with other South Asian countries, including India. We don't want China and India to compete with each other because that itself works as a negative element for us. As we are thinking about Bangladesh in the 21st century, it can be a bridging nation in the region. For example, it can be a bridging nation between India and China. It can also be a bridging nation between South and South East Asia and also between South Asia and China. Bangladesh looks at itself as a bridging nation. It wants to maintain a good relationship with the new growth centers of Asia like India, China, and ASEAN. We believe that the Indo-Chinese relationship will make Bangladesh realize its larger objective of becoming a hub in the interregional collaboration.

Delwar Hossein (2016) is even more optimistic, provided that a more active role for Bangladesh in the global governance issues can be successful everywhere. In his portrayal of the future, he states:

> ...if you think the kind of relations Bangladesh has with India or with China, with more confidence and with more trust at some point of time, Bangladesh can play this role because our diplomacy has a track record and we have been playing a very active role in the least developed world and on the issues of climate change, global health. Bangladesh also took a very active role in the formation of South Asian Association for Regional Cooperation (SAARC) itself. It has a record of playing [an] active diplomatic role in regional and other frameworks. If India does not suspect Bangladesh's relations with China from [a] security or geo-political perspective, as I think this will be a fact very soon because the way our regimes are working focusing on Bangladesh's development, it

might become very clear to India and, of course, to China that Bangladesh doesn't pursue its geo-political interest by creating enmity or hostility between China and India. This is very important because India and China have to trust Bangladesh that it doesn't engage itself in the so called *realpolitik* game of using one great power against another. So there is an opportunity for Bangladesh because its foreign policy and discourse is moving towards the direction that Bangladesh feels that we need a strong South Asia under the leadership of India and we also need a strong Asia where China has its own strong role and India and other powers. The kind of vision which is working in the policy circle of Bangladesh and also among the people who are informed and aware of this, that kind of understanding will eventually help maintain some relations, some kind of informal role to reduce mutual mistrust between India and China.

A Chinese Bridge Without Sinology

A role of a bridge for two greater powers usually benefits from a kind of in-between consciousness. This in-between consciousness either makes one comfortable with both sides or enables one to be made comfortable to both sides so that the differences, misunderstandings, or collisions can be either dissolved in a mingling context or reinterpreted in an appreciative discourse (William and Oliver 2005; Johnson 2012; Casula 2009; Chellaney 2012; Duffy and Evans 1996). In other words, a bridge-role player can actively mediate between the two sides or passively accept its hybrid condition without feeling necessary to take side. The former is an interpreter state that breeds empathy toward each other. An interpreter state relies on the intellectual capacity of knowing the history, culture, contemporary situation of both sides, and strives to make things easier to understand for both. Its knowledge is civilizational to the extent that learning and assimilation are considered possible but not threatening. The latter resembles a buffer state whose survival requires the acceptance by both sides. A buffer state is territorially sandwiched, practically inconsistent, and intellectually tolerant. The interpreter and buffer states can be bridge-role players as long as all are conscious of their in-between position. Accordingly, a bridge role may have different versions and at the same time may have to compete with non-bridge roles (Kaya and Kentel 2005, Lesser 1994).

Bangladesh or Nepal is undoubtedly familiar with Indian cultures and practices. However, the same cannot be said about their understanding of China. With this imbalance in the level of familiarity, the bridge role is easier for one side to operate but not for the other. In the imbalanced condition, in-between consciousness is flawed because for both bridge-role players, China is more external than mutually constituted. Nepal is intellectually slightly more advantaged because of its shared belief in Buddhism with China. However, seeming shared religiosity does not contribute to the confidence in knowing China from an internal perspective. Nepali experts on China continue to lack a culturally sympathetic perspective to make studies of China as well as observed changes in China intellectually engaging, despite the acknowledged style of non-interventionism consistently demonstrated in China's Nepal policy.

Accordingly, one can derive four types of bridge roles from the South Asian experiences according to whether a bridge has a balanced relationality and whether a bridge is formed in an interpreter state or a buffer state. An interpreter state with a balanced in-between consciousness will be able to portray China and India in an appreciative narrative to each other. A buffer state with a balanced in-between consciousness can absorb the difference between China and India to alleviate the urgency to resolve it. On the one hand, the appreciation player and the absorption player are difficult for either Nepal or Bangladesh because they know significantly less about China; thus, India feels obliged to monitor China's involvement in Nepal and Bangladesh. On the other hand, China has significantly less intimacy with the two nations. The resulting expectation of them to comply with China's need is not strong or specific. By comparison, Singapore can fare well as a balanced interpreter state, given its Sinological resources and social and cultural connection to China (Lim 2016). Equally important is Singapore's knowledge of the Anglosphere, possession of trust by Western countries, and modernity of social life.

In-between consciousness that is imbalanced leads an interpreter state to rely on existing perspectives embedded in civilizational stereotyping, which emerges from religions such as Buddhism and Islam, ideology of socialism and capitalism, or even international politics of Cold War, China's rise, and global governance issues such as transnational waters. A buffer state that is imbalanced and tilted toward India would have to determine the things that China expects and wants from one's own nation so that one can endeavor to meet the expectation so that mutually acceptable and beneficial exchanges can take place (see Table 1). Take the Association for Southeast Asian Nations (ASEAN) for an example. All four bridge roles have been considered proper for the ASEAN in the literature. It could be an active but imbalanced bridge trying to connect to an isolated Communist state in Vietnam (Leifer 2013: 8–9). It could likewise be an active and balanced bridge trying to make an isolated Myanmar and the rest of the world feel more comfortable with each other (Fan 2013: 16). In contrast, the expectation of the ASEAN can be a passive and imbalanced bridge, aimed at introducing the regional resources to potential external investors (Yong 2014) or, alternatively, a passive and yet balanced player exemplified by the so-called ASEAN way (Majumdar 2015).

Nepal and Bangladesh can make an intelligence player to the extent that knowledge on China primarily comes from visits, statistics, exchange between think tanks, and encounters of travelers. According to Bhaskar Koirala (2016), on the one hand, Nepal does not own any expertise on Chinese poetry, calligraphy, classics, or painting. On the other hand, Nepal is also a plausible stereotyping player with its historical and religious background that contacts with the Chinese have constituted. If Singapore decides to purge

Table 1. Role-playing of a Bridge State

Identity \ Relationality	Balance	Imbalance
Interpreter state (active)	Producing appreciation	Incurring stereotypes
Buffer state (passive)	Absorbing differences	Gathering intelligence

Source: Author

Sinological resources from its intellectual repertoire, then its only function is to be an intelligence player as well.

Methodology Purged of Sinology

The methodology of those think tanks on Chinese affairs whose experts do not rely on Sinological resources is primarily composed of the methods of observation and gathering of intelligence, in addition to the stereotyping necessity in encountering an alien civilization. Observation can be physical as facilitated by visits, exchanges of views, living in the same neighborhood, and others. It can also be intellectual through the reading of statistics, reports, and analyses (Yew 2016). Where observation is most pertinent, events and daily lives can inform deeper structures or preferences that are not apparent without observation. The Nepali and Bangladeshi experts on China by and large are conscious of their best and most convenient methods to establish knowledge on China, which include visits, exchanges, and statistics. This is in line with Yew's observation of Singapore whose think tank "works produced in the 1990s read more like insider's account of the going-ons in China than scholarly analyses, relying heavily on personal experience, press sources and interpreting the speeches of political leaders" (Yew 2016, 12/24).

To physically observe and learn about China, one either traces the behavior of China during significant events or observes the way that the Chinese behave in person. Events could be those involving China or those taking place in the observers' surrounding. For the current generation of China experts, events mentioned by interviewees that inform the Chinese way of thinking during their career time usually include the border war between China and India in 1962, the pro-democracy movement of 1989, the NATO bombing of Chinese embassy in Belgrade, the clash of an American EP-3 reconnaissance aircraft with a Chinese J-8 fighter, the 2008 Beijing Olympics, and other events. The domestic events that repeatedly emerge in the Bangladeshi interviews include the independence war fought in 1971, the subsequent China's veto in the UN over the membership of Bangladesh through 1975, and the assassination of Sheikh Mujib in the same year. For Nepal, a common concern is Premier Wen Jiabao's visit to urge proper coping with anti-China activities rising in Nepal. The other is the transition from monarchy to democracy. In relation to this concern is the reference to India's intensive involvement in Nepal's domestic politics. All these events and issues lead concerned observers to draw impressions or expectations of China.

In addition to events, issue areas are relevant to the framing of analysis on China. One cross-board issue mentioned by almost all interviewees in Nepal and Bangladesh is China's dubious role in the SAARC. The level of China's participation can be in multilateral and bilateral issues, but each nation or even scholar can have a different perspective. With the competitive relationship between Pakistan and India, China's formal membership would mean a balancer against India. However, not a few local scholars wish to see China's full participation primarily to benefit from China's increasingly rich resources. In any case, event and issue areas incur analyses that position Bangladesh and Nepal in an outsider's perspective rather than an in-between player.

Civilizational and political dispositions affect China watching in a reversed manner. Instead of watching the practices to infer knowledge on China, civilizational and political dispositions guide the approach to China regarding the things to watch and the ways to answer. This observation is particularly pertinent in the case of Nepali Buddhism, which has extensive exchanges with Chinese Buddhism. Chinese visitors to Lumbini and investment in the infrastructure of the location to facilitate Chinese tourism testify to the significance of the shared religiosity between the two countries. The same claim is less credible for Bangladesh, which is Muslim in majority, despite the fact that passage of ancient Buddhism to China went through contemporary Bangladesh. Alternatively, the Bangladeshi perspective on China owes greatly to a romanticized image of anti-imperialism, which is so powerful that even China's siding with Pakistan during the independence war did not offset the positive feeling toward China among the Bangladeshi population. Unofficial diplomatic links were never really severed. In addition, later, the capitalist development in China has been likewise attractive to Bangladesh taking a similar re-orientation.

Nonetheless, positive disposition is not sufficient for good research. Methodologically, both South Asian countries rely on visits. Ramesh Nath Pandey (2012) specifically said that "for studying China, it is important that one visits China and that would be a great learning experience." As a great proportion of Nepali and Bangladeshi China experts come from the diplomatic circle, they benefit from their time of service in China to witness the development and observe the behavioral pattern and policy style of China as well as the personality of specific political leaders. Iftikhar-ul-Karim (2013) recalled his experience, stating that he "was surprised to say the least. We did not encounter any of the perceptions that we had of the Communist leaders of China." In another example, Humayun Kabir (2012) was similarly impressed upon hearing the Chinese counterpart to candidly "admi[t] that they did not know all the tricks to manage the unfolding tensions" on the South China Sea and the East China Sea. Ramesh Nath Pandey (2012) is able to portray Chou Enlai's humble character from their encounter. Furthermore, Harun ur Rashid (2013), who met with Mao Zedong before the Cultural Revolution, compares the leaders in person:

> I thought outwardly Mao Tse-tung looked like a primary school teacher very calm and composed. One could not ignore a big mole on his face. Little did I realize from his face that he was planning the so-called "Cultural Revolution" next year. Chou En-lai was smart and very alert. Marshal Chen Yi was a smiling diminutive figure with whom you could easily relate to and Chu The was a reserved person. There [were] hardly any cars on the main roads in Peking then and one could see people riding only cycles. We were taken to see a commune near Peking.

Academically, the visits have been and are increasingly emphasized. More students go to China for higher education. Interviewees mention that academic exchanges have been very helpful. Simply seeing is by itself a dramatic learning process compared with reading statistics and web news. Delwar Hossain (2016) finds that on the Internet, pieces of "information are not always correct. They don't give the right perspective." Harun ur Rashid (2013) and Iftikhar-ul-Karim (2013) gained inspiration from the condition of transportation that they witnessed and the change during the interlude to their later visits. The latter records:

> Tiananmen was a distant memory and the energy of frenetic economic activity was palpable everywhere. I remember in 1988 standing outside the Dayotai State Guesthouse for 40 minutes observing the cars on the road. I could hardly see 10 cars while the whole city it seemed was on bicycles and almost everyone wearing Mao suits. In 2002, the sight from the same complex of the guesthouse was completely different. Both sides of the road were full of cars and there was a traffic jam of 45 minutes, hardly any bicycle and no one in [a] Mao suit.

Changes are always most easy and important to watch whenever one visits China for a second time. These include "change in the life style of the people," according to Ramesh Nath Pandey (2012). He then discovers changes amid continuity by making a comment that China "had become more open" but "otherwise things were quite similar." Lailufar Yasmin (2016) similarly attends to changes. She ran into shy children being able to greet her in English under their parents' encouragement 10 years after her first visit, when no Chinese seemed interested in learning English at all. She tells why traveling and meeting with people are an essential method of China studies:

> And after going to China I gradually learnt that if you do not go to a country and mix with the people, you will have all sorts of wrong perceptions, and not only that you can have some of your perceptions actually confirmed. And you get to see them from a different light, that was the beginning of my love for China. I did lots of walking around on the roadside and streets, although I could not talk around much with the local people. Because whenever I would ask them a simple thing in English, they would stare at me and start laughing with an impression that she doesn't know Chinese. That made me think that they still think that they are the middle power, that they are the centre of the civilisation or centre of the earth. (Yasmin 2016)

Singaporean Think Tank in Comparison

With the extreme sensitivity of the Chinese identity issue ever since its independence from Malaysia, Singapore has endeavored to avoid becoming a Chinese nation. Socially, Chinese Singaporeans and Chinese Malaysians continue to stereotype "Xin-Ma huaren" (Chinese Singaporean and Malaysian) into a single group, which is a challenge to the nation building of Singapore regarding the boundary of its nationality. A few complications have evolved from Singapore's nation building process. To begin with, it must face the suspicious, if not inimical, atmosphere from neighboring Southeast Asian countries where ethnic Chinese make a significant portion of their population. It had to cope with communist infiltration during the Cold War as the majority of Singaporeans of earlier generations were patriotic Chinese. It had to gain support from the US to enhance its prestige among its neighbors. It had to maintain the loyalty of a quarter of non-Chinese citizens. All these moves point to a national grand strategy of distancing from China as well as Chinese cultural bearing. Consequently, the rich Sinological resources available among Chinese intellectuals have been kept away from the policy process.

Nevertheless, anticipating China's future rise, Lee Kwan Yew established the Institute of East Asian Philosophy in 1983 to study the role of Confucianism in economic development, which he found to be relevant in Japan's and Taiwan's success (Wong 2007). Such an institute was entirely subject to the control of the government. The influence of the civilian intellectuals was consciously excluded. In addition, the non-Chinese population would not feel alienated. The institute evolved into the East Asian Institute of Political Economy in 1990 to reflect the fast changes in China. It quickly turned into the EAI. The orientation of the EAI has been specifically non-Western and non-PRC so that the government can produce objective reports (Wong 2012). According to Wang Gengwu's (2007/2010) interview, the request is for the government to have accesses to the first hand and most recent development in China. To ensure this move, the report should be written in English, presented in social scientifically framed analysis, exempt from policy recommendations, immune from systematic influences of any particular source, and thus inclusive of as many perspectives as possible.

The above-mentioned last requirement makes recruitment of international scholars necessary. Wang Gengwu (2007/2010), the head of the EAI, reveals in his interview that such an objectivist policy is not intended to affect or lead the international views on China, but it should be available for all to use. He specifically mentions the interests of the Indian scholars in the EAI reports. To achieve such objectivity, John Wong, the former head of the research department, insists to read all drafts before their submission to the government to ensure that Chinese visiting analysts do not act defensively on behalf of China. Chinese sources are imperative, and yet the reports written by Chinese scholars are often methodologically flawed and full of political positions. Wong (2012) explains that it is the reason why he has been keen on recruiting short-run service of Western-trained Chinese scholars. By any standard, Sinological resources available among Chinese–Singaporean intellectuals are beyond remedy, given their use of Chinese language, potentially pro-China feeling, and lack of social science methodology.

In comparison with South Asian China experts, who grieve about the lack of access to Chinese humanities, the institutional philosophy of the EAI deliberately advises scholars to avoid connection to any Chineseness that is embedded in the humanities. The EAI could have found a learned audience and a rich repertoire of human capital otherwise but could have risked yielding on its pledge to objectivism. As it stands now, the EAI is institutionally and intellectually separate from the Chinese Singaporean population. In fact, Chinese Singaporean scholars live in an intellectually active environment. A cross-border Chinese intellectual community actually exists. Their research significantly involves Chinese identity, history of migration, and humanities, and many are creative writers themselves (Wong *et al.* 2015; Ngeow, Ling, and Fan 2014). They are China experts by any standard, as they read the Chinese literature, speak Chinese dialects, and follow Chinese affairs.

As the EAI renounces its candidacy for a culturally in-between observer, its bridge role loses credit to a degree. Watching China from a culturally estranged angle, upon the gathered information from Chinese scholars, and within a social scientific frame, the EAI could not interpret the Chinese affairs through the cultural lens. Therefore, its perspective is a kind of intelligence for a peculiar stranger struggling to make sense of Chinese phenomena. Methodologically, the EAI similarly relies on exchanges, visits, and interviews, although a larger scale and with a significantly better language skill than Bangladesh and Nepal. It has minimal interest in sharing Singapore's knowledge of the West with China institutionally despite retired EAI leaders including Goh Keng Swee and John Wong, who are busy advising Chinese governments of various levels everywhere. In other words, they are intellectually capable of playing the bridge role but institutionally and consciously do not. The institute is open to the sharing of its policy analyses with the rest of the world. However, this act is not unlike a translation aimed not at enlightening but at engendering a sense of familiarity among Anglophone readers with a subject above their head. No attempt is made to bring the Chinese perspective to the outside world. The EAI is a bridge that contributes not to mutual understanding but to Singapore's own identity as a site that treats differences as objectivism.

Conclusion: An Aborted Bridge Role

Does an intelligence player serve Singapore's interest or does its identity need better focus than, say, an appreciation player? Given that Singapore is not naturally an intelligence player with no appreciative knowledge of Chinese poetry, calligraphy, or painting, the self-quarantining of the EAI from these rich intellectual resources cannot easily erase the potential of cultural return. Such silenced potential could engender the anxiety toward the possibility of cultural reconnection and thus prompt the need to constantly stay alert at any such signs. Singapore's occasional tendency toward Washington or China's Southeast Asian rivals or criticism of Chinese affairs indicates the existence of such a desire for estrangement. Under this circumstance, the enactment of the bridge role at the same time alienates China from Singapore. As a result, Singapore's function as an intelligence state and its intended bridge role contradict each other. The estrangement of the Chinese population toward Singapore also harms Singapore's reputation as a bridge-role player, although its credits with China's rivals or with Singapore's Muslim neighbors can benefit.

China does not expect Nepal or Bangladesh to show sympathy toward its position to a level higher than allowed by the existing reciprocal relationships that it has earned through its anti-imperialist history, the Buddhist legacy, and the contemporary economic investment. However, China used to hold significantly higher expectation toward Singapore because of its cultural and ethnic Chineseness and, to a less extent, the demonstration effect of Singapore's exhibition of a successful authoritarian style of governing. Singapore's anti-Communist stance is not unlike Bangladesh's association with India during the independence war to the extent that China was not turned away from either country because of their political distance. In the case of Nepal, one could hardly imagine what would be left if the nation deliberately confined the Buddhist components in its bilateral relationship with China. Would China becoming a complete stranger win Nepal more credits with India and help Nepal's bridge role between India and China? Likely, this move would not. Alternatively, probably, would this reduce Nepal to an image of a puppet state of India?

Accordingly, the methodology of China studies can either reflect or incorporate an identity strategy. The methodology of Nepali and Bangladeshi experts combines a smaller extent of stereotyping, embedded in their Buddhist and political orientations, respectively, and a larger extent of intelligence, relying on visit, exchange, and statistics. For nations that are not balanced politically and culturally between China and India, for example, Nepal and Bangladesh, the methodology reflects the limitation of their tilted, although not always positive, relationship with India. Nevertheless, some intend to plan a bridge role for their nation in order for India and China to mutually appreciate each other slightly more and leave the bridge-role state to a peaceful environment. Neither Bangladesh nor Nepal can interpret China to India well, and both must struggle with their own understanding of China. Therefore, their bridge role is only possible as an imbalanced, absorption state. Such a bridge state serves to exempt India and China from urging for a solution to their contradictive positions. As a territorially and socially in-between site, Nepal could probably more effectively adopt the absorption approach in the long run.

Singapore's in-between identity is balanced between China and the West at large. However, Singapore chooses to turn imbalanced to cope with its own identity as well as its regional relationship. Therefore, Singapore's methodology of China studies incorporates a consciously contrived identity strategy. Nonetheless, Singapore could be a better intelligence state because its experts are capable of digesting intelligence more effectively and quickly. However, it has no disposition for conflict resolution. It does not attempt to make China better accepted by the West or make the West better accepted by China. It pursues a reputation that it handles China better on behalf of the West. However, it alienates China, so it loses empathy, intellectual appreciation, and the ability to serve the West in the long run. Nepal and Bangladesh are in a better position because they do not have to turn away from China culturally.

References

Bhaskar Koirala. 2016. Interviewed by Reena Marwah on September 16, http//politics.ntu.edu.tw/RAEC/comm2/Bhaskar%20K.pdf. Accessed on November 14, 2016.

Casula, Philipp P. 2009. Political and National Identity in Russia: Developments in Russian Political Thought in the 1990s. In Philipp Casula and Jeronim Perovi (Eds.), *Identities and Politics during the Putin Presidency: The Foundations of Russia' Stability*, 47–66,. Stuttgart: Ibidem Press.

Chellaney, Brahma. 2012. Rising Powers, Rising Tensions: The Troubled China–India Relationship. *SAIS Review of International Affairs* 32(2): 99–108.

Chowdhury, Mahfuzul H. 2013. Asymmetry in Indo-Bangladesh Relations. *Asian Affairs* 40(3): 83–103.

Cohen, Paul A. 1984. *Discovering History in China: American Historical Writing on the Recent Chinese Past.* New York: Columbia University Press.

Delwar Hossein. 2016. Interviewed by Sharad K Soni on March 24, http://politics.ntu.edu.tw/RAEC/comm2/Delwar%20Hossein.pdf. Accessed on November 14, 2016.

Duffy, Mary and Geoffrey Evans. 1996. Building Bridges? The Political Implications of Electoral Integration for Northern Ireland. *British Journal of Political Science* 26(1): 123–140.

Ehsanul Haque 2016. Interviewed by Sharad K Soni on March 24, http://politics.ntu.edu.tw/RAEC/comm2/Ehsanul%20Haque.pdf. Accessed on November 14, 2016.

Fan, Lilianne. 2013. Disaster as Opportunity? Building back Better in Aceh, Myanmar and Haiti. *HPG Working Paper* (November). London: Humanitarian Policy Group, Overseas Development Institute.

Gwee, Yee Hean. 2010. Interviewed by Chang-hong Chen at National Library of Singapore on April 10, transcribed by Ching-huan Su, http://politics.ntu.edu.tw/RAEC/comm2/InterviewSingapore0.pdf. Accessed November on 15, 2016.

Huei, Peh Shing. 2016. Commentary: The New Normal of Singapore's Relations with China. *Channel NewsAsia*, October 6, http://www.channelnewsasia.com/news/asiapacific/commentary-the-new-normal-of-singapore-s-relations-with-china/3184106.html. Accessed on November 16, 2016.

Humayun Kabir. 2012. Interviewed by Swaran Singh on March 1, http://politics.ntu.edu.tw/RAEC/comm2/InterviewB04.pdf. Accessed on November 17, 2016.

Jain, Girilal. 1959. *India Meets China in Nepal.* Bombay: Asia Publishing House.

Johnson, Nicole V. 2012. Turkish Reactions to the Arab Spring: Implications for United States Foreign Policy. *Global Security Studies* 3(4): 1–10.

Karim, Iftikhar-ul. 2013. Interviewed by Swaran Singh on March 2, http://politics.ntu.edu.tw/RAEC/comm2/InterviewB02.pdf. Accessed on November 16, 2016.

Kashinath, Prarthana. 2016. To Fend Off China, India Must Galvanize Ties With Bangladesh, *The Diplomat*, October 29. http://thediplomat.com/2016/10/to-fend-off-china-india-must-galvanize-ties-with-bangladesh/. Accessed on November 14, 2016.

Kaya, Ayhan and Ferhat Kentel. 2005. Euro-Turks: A Bridge or a Breach between Turkey and the European Union? A Comparative Study of French-Turks and German-Turks. *CEPS EU-Turkey Working Papers 14*, 1 January.

Kumar, Pranav. 2010. Sino-Bhutanese Relations: Under the Shadow of India-Bhutan Friendship. *China Report* 46(3): 243–252.

Leifer, Michael. 2013. *ASEAN and the Security of South-East Asia*. Oxon: Routledge.

Lesser, Ian O. 1994. *Bridge or Barrier? Turkey and the West After the Cold War*. R-4204-AF/A. Santa Monica, Calif.: Rand Arroyo Center.

Lim, Tai Wei. 2016. The Making of the East Asian Institute. In East Asian Institute (Ed.), *The East Asian Institute: A Goh Keng Swee Legacy*, 1–32. Singapore: World Scientific.

Lohani Mohan. 2012. Interviewed by Reena Marwah on January 26, http://politics.ntu.edu.tw/RAEC/comm2/InterviewN02.pdf. Accessed on November 16, 2016.

Majumdar, Munmun. 2015. The ASEAN Way of Conflict Management in the South China Sea. *Strategic Analysis* 39(1): 73–87.

Mathou, Thierry. 2004. Bhutan–China Relations: Towards a New Step in Himalayan Politics. Thimphu: Centre for Bhutan Studies, 388-411.

Mitra, Debamitra. 2013. Yam' Between Two Boulders: Re-Assessing India–Bhutan Relationship. *Jadavpur Journal of International Relations* (December 1) 17: 185–203.

Muni, S. D. and Yong, Tan Tai. 2012. *A Resurgent China: South Asian Perspectives*. New Delhi: Routledge.

Negow, Peter, Tek Soon Ling, and Pik Shy Fan. 2014. Pursuing Chinese Studies Amidst Identity Politics in Malaysia. *East Asia* 31(2): 103–122.

Pant, Harsh V. 2007. India in the Asia–Pacific: Rising Ambitions with an Eye on China. *Asia Pacific Review* 14(1): 54–71.

Penjore, Dorji. 2014. Security of Bhutan: Walking Between the Giants *Journal of Bhutan Studies* 10: 108–131.

PTI, 2016. Nepal Wants to Become Dynamic Bridge Between India, China: Prachanda. *Indian Express*, October 17, http://indianexpress.com/article/india/india-news-india/nepal-wants-to-become-dynamic-bridge-between-india-china-prachanda-3086434/. Accessed on November 12, 2016.

Pandey, Ramesh Nath. 2012. Interviewed by Reena Marwah on January 27. http://politics.ntu.edu.tw/RAEC/comm2/InterviewN03.pdf. Accessed on November 14, 2016.

Rashid Harun ur. 2013. Interviewed by Reena Marwah on March 2. http://politics.ntu.edu.tw/RAEC/comm2/InterviewB01.pdf. Accessed on November 14, 2016.

Rehman, Iskander. 2009. Keeping the Dragon at Bay: India's Counter-Containment of China. *Asian Security* 5(2): 114–143.

Roy, Denny. 2005. Southeast Asia and China: Balancing or Bandwagoning? *Contemporary Southeast Asia* 27(2): 305–322.

Shih, Chih-yu, Chih-chieh Chou, and Hoai Thu Nguyen. 2014. Two Intellectual Paths that Cross the Borders: Nguyen Huy Quy, Phan Van Cac, and Humanities in Vietnam's Chinese Studies. *East Asia* 31(2): 123–138.

Shneiderman, Sara B. 2013. Himalayan border citizens: Sovereignty and Mobility in the Nepal–Tibetan Autonomous Region (TAR) of China Border Zone. *Political Geography* 35: 25–36.

Silver, Rita Elaine. 2005. The Discourse of Linguistic Capital: Language and Economic Policy Planning in Singapore. *Language Policy* 4: 47–66.

Singh, Sinderpal and Syeda Sana Rahman. 2010. India–Singapore Relations: Constructing a "New" Bilateral Relationship. *Contemporary Southeast Asia* 32(1): 70–97.

Snedden, Christopher. 2016. *Shifting Geo-politics in the Greater South Asia Region*. Honolulu: Daniel K. Inouye Asia-Pacific Center for Security Studies.

Tanaka, Stefan. 1993. *Japan's Orient: Rendering Past into History*. Durham: Duke University Press.

Thapliyal, Sangeeta. 1998. *Mutual Security: The Case of India Nepal*. New Delhi: Spantech & Lancer.

Wallace, William and Tim Oliver. 2005. *In the Atlantic Alliance under Stress: US–European Relations After Iraq*. Cambridge: Cambridge University Press. pp. 152–176.

Wang, Gungwu. 2007/2010. Interviewed by Huifen Shen and Chang-hong Chen on September 25, October 1, 5, 2007 and January 14, February 25, March19, 2010, http://politics.ntu.edu.tw/RAEC/comm2/InterviewSGungwuW.pdf. Accessed on November 15, 2016.

Wang, Vincent Wei-cheng. 2011. "Chindia" or Rivalry? Rising China, Rising India, and Contending Perspectives on India-China Relations. *Asian Perspective* 35(3): 437–469.

Wong, John. 2012. *Goh Keng Swee and Chinese Studies in Singapore: From Confucianism to China Watching*. In Goh Keng Swee: A Legacy of Public

Service. In Chew Emrys and Kwa Chong Guan (Eds.), Singapore: World Scientific. pp. 245–277.

Wong, John. 2016. Interviewed by Chih-yu Shih, Chui-ling Shin, and Chang-hong Chen on November 5–9, http://politics.ntu.edu.tw/RAEC/comm2/InterviewSJohnWong.pdf. Accessed on November 15, 2016.

Wong, Sin Kiong, Ruixin Wang, Zhuo Wang and Shihlun Allen Chen. 2015. Producing and Reconstructing Knowledge on China in Singapore: Perspectives from the Academics and Mass Media. *Asian Ethnicity* 16(1): 8–27.

Wong, Yoon Wah, 2012. Interviewed and transcribed by Yiting Shen at Office of Associate Dean, Southern College (now Southern University College), Johor, Malaysia on March 26, http://politics.ntu.edu.tw/RAEC/comm2/InterviewSingapore1.pdf. Accessed November 15, 2016.

Yew, Chiew Ping. 2016. The Evolution of Contemporary China Studies in Singapore: From the Regional Cold War to the Present. *Journal of Chinese Political Science* 22(1): 135–158.

Yong, Cat. 2014. English Online Radio Station Durian ASEAN Launches for ASEAN. *Enterprise IT News.* March 10, http://www.enterpriseitnews.com.my/english-online-radio-station-durianasean-launches-targets-english-speaking-communities-in-asean/. Accessed on November 17, 2016.

Yubaraj Ghimire. 2016. Interviewed by Reena Marwah on September 17, http://politics.ntu.edu.tw/RAEC/comm2/Yubaraj%20Ghimire.pdf. Accessed on November 16, 2016.

Zhang, Feng. 2016. Start of China's Coercive Diplomacy towards Singapore. *The Straits Times* October 6, http://www.straitstimes.com/opinion/start-of-chinas-coercive-diplomacy-towards-singapore. Accessed on November 16, 2016.

Zhao, Hong. 2007. India and China: Rivals or Partners in Southeast Asia? *Contemporary Southeast Asia* 29(1): 121–142.

Zheng, Yongnian and Liang Fook Lye. 2015. *Singapore–China Relations: 50 Years.* Singapore: World Scientific.

10

South Asia's China Outlook: Reminiscing Through the Lens of Bangladesh and Nepal

Sharad K. Soni

Professor and Chairperson, Centre for Inner Asian Studies
School of International Studies
Jawaharlal Nehru University, New Delhi

In the 21st century, the rise of China is one of the most significant events in the world in general and Asia in particular. Not only an astounding economic growth but also rising diplomatic and political power provided China a much needed bulwark to play an indispensably important role in transforming the global geopolitical scenario. In the process, China's neighborhood policy has become a focused agenda given that it will have far-reaching regional and global significance, both economically and politically. What China is seeking by pursuing its neighborhood policy is to restore confidence in the regional neighborhood that China's rise is an opportunity not a threat. However, such policy in China's next door neighbor, South Asia, is more influenced by strategic concerns. No wonder then that China's rise has propelled its importance from that of a neighbor to a strategic partner, especially for the smaller countries in South Asia such as Bangladesh and Nepal. It is in this context that this chapter focuses on highlighting the image of China in South

Asia taking Bangladesh and Nepal as case studies. The chapter examines the approaches by which China is being studied in these two South Asian countries, both in terms of policy and knowledge, in a comparative perspective. While doing so it seeks to analyze the extent and pattern of China Studies in Bangladesh and Nepal. The two countries have established a few centers dealing with China Studies including the Confucius Institutes in order to understand and study not only Chinese foreign and security policies, but also Chinese economic advancement with a view to advocate greater economic and development cooperation between China and the South Asian region. These centers create tremendous scope for not only acquiring China knowledge but also studying China from different perspectives which could contribute to China policy-making at diplomatic level to benefit bilateral ties. The fact that China has no contentious issues affecting its bilateral relations with the two South Asian countries under discussion has also worked to its advantage. All this is aimed at strengthening China's South Asia policy to counter India's "Act East" policy, formerly known as "Look East" policy, i.e., as India tries to move eastwards to cultivate the countries of Southeast Asia, China is trying to move southwards to outflank India. So far as the identity strategy of Bangladesh and Nepal are concerned, there are differences in dealings with China and India between these two South Asian countries, which this chapter deals in depth. The objective is to gauge the potential of China Studies for engaging China effectively in South Asia and its strategic implications for Beijing's neighborhood policy. This may help explore several critical issues confronting the South Asian region as a whole.

Introduction

China and South Asia represent a unique example of the world's two ancient civilizations that have evolved at close proximity to each other over thousands of years. Rivers and mountains link China and South Asia in physical terms but the cultural and traditional links, particularly Buddhist linkages, are also interwoven in a wider context. The southern branch of the famous Silk Route that provided a series of trade routes serving as arteries for cultural transmission and interaction ran through the landmass of South Asia (Sami 2012:

16–17). Today in terms of geostrategic importance, South Asia ranks third after the Northeast and Southeast Asian regions in China's Asia policy in general and neighborhood policy in particular (Soni 2009: 255–256). What came to be known as "*zhoubian zhengce*" (periphery policy) or "*mulin zhengce*" (good-neighboring policy), Beijing's neighborhood policy aimed at establishing good relationships with neighbors in order to provide "China with a more secure environment in its periphery as a leverage to increase its influence in world affairs" (Zhao 2004: 259; Soni 2015: 176). In the past decade, fundamental changes that have been noticed in China's "periphery" policy point to the fact that the "periphery" has indeed become a primary concern for Beijing and that China's good neighbor approach has been to restore confidence in its regional neighborhood that its rise is an opportunity not a threat (Soni 2016: 146).

However, China's neighborhood policy in South Asia is more influenced by its military security concerns *vis-a`-vis* India or in other words geopolitical and geostrategic containment of India despite an increase in bilateral exchanges at the political, economic, military, and cultural levels. In the 21st century, China's growth trajectory in terms of its "rise" is one of the most significant events. With amazing economic growth coupled with rising diplomatic and political power, China has already been playing an important role in transforming the global geopolitical scenario and there is likelihood that Chinese power and influence will further increase in the years to come. The image of China rising, however, generates multi-sited reflections everywhere, inside and outside of China (Shih 2013: 18). That is why China's rise has catapulted its importance from that of a neighbor to a strategic partner, especially for the smaller countries belonging to South Asia. This paradigm shift in the way China is viewed in these South Asian countries, particularly Bangladesh and Nepal, has inevitably resulted in a transformation of the approach China is being studied, both in terms of policy and knowledge.

And herein the question arises if there is a way to distinguish between China policy and China knowledge in South Asian perspective. The answer lies into the fact that in South Asia knowledge of China always takes precedence to China policy because a particular country needs to be integrated culturally as well as academically in order to contribute to policymaking. What the policymakers initially fail to understand is understood by common people who go to China for study, business, and tourism purposes and in many cases they develop their academic and work relationships in addition to personal relationships that help strengthen bilateral ties from policy point of view. This is true to the cases of both Bangladesh and Nepal where China knowledge is also acquired by holding exchange programs and exhibitions on different aspects of China as part of China studies center's activities which create lot of scope to study China from IR perspective or economics perspective or international business perspective. This ultimately leads to contribute to China policymaking at a diplomatic level to the benefits of bilateral ties. It is, therefore, critical to examine how these two South Asian countries — Bangladesh and Nepal can effectively engage China in the days ahead.

It is against this background that this chapter focuses on South Asia's China outlook, but particularly from the comparative perspectives of Bangladesh and Nepal. While seeking to document the motivation for the initiation of China studies in these two South Asian countries, the endeavor is to compare the way China is being viewed by the two countries' China experts. While language teaching centers are being established to grasp China well, there is also a great interest in understanding China's trajectory of economic progress and expanding political significance not only as an Asian power but as a global leader. But in their identity strategy the two countries — Bangladesh and Nepal — differ in their viewpoints on China in very many ways that indeed are relevant to explaining their approaches to China. While Bangladesh demonstrates neutral posture in its dealings with China and India, Nepal outrightly displays pro-China approach in the same vein since it considers China a balance against India's influence in its internal affairs. Such differences in approaches to China between these two South Asian countries have motivated this chapter to address a few key questions as follows: How is China being studied in these two countries in order to form a firm opinion about viable bilateral engagements? What are the main issues that dominate Bangladesh–China and Nepal–China relations? Whether Bangladesh and Nepal look upon China as a partner in progress due to convergence of economic interests or other reasons? and whether Bangladesh and Nepal would prefer to pursue different approaches in dealing with China and India? Finally, the chapter also argues if Bangladesh and Nepal relate themselves to China as a source of support and comfort and if it is so, in what ways?

Understanding China Outlook Through China Studies in Bangladesh and Nepal

A well-known Indian analyst B. Raman explains, "the Chinese policy in the South Asian region has a mix of strategic and opportunistic dimensions — that is, working for carefully calculated long-term strategic objectives while not missing short and medium term opportunities that come its way" (Raman 2012). If he is to be believed, the response to Chinese policy from the South Asian countries has largely been in favor of both China and the individual country of South Asia like Bangladesh and Nepal as it has had direct bearing on their bilateral relationship. Keeping this in mind, China studies centers and institutes have been established in respective countries in order to undertake research on issues of mutual concerns as well as to complement each other on matters of policy initiatives favorable to bilateral ties. What is significant to be noted here is that the existence of China studies centers and institutes in these two South Asian countries is the latest development that came to the fore only in the new millennium. The comparative perceptions of the two countries about Chinese policy toward the region can be understood more substantially by looking into the aims and objectives as well as the focus areas of China studies centers, both in assumption and practice.

China Studies in Bangladesh

Bangladesh and China enjoy profound friendship which dates back to ancient time. In those days, Bangladesh was the region which had the closest communications with China in the entire subcontinent. However, Bangladesh–China relations did not start on friendly terms in the geopolitics of South Asia, especially in the context of 1971 war.

With the changes in domestic politics in 1975 Bangladesh's foreign policy priorities assumed a new dimension and Dhaka demonstrated remarkable maturity and pragmatism in taking initiatives to befriend China. Since China's recognition of Bangladesh in 1975, Beijing has remained a trusted partner in developing relationship with Dhaka taking into consideration the geopolitical configuration in South Asia (Yasmin 2009: 74). Keeping in mind that such considerations of South Asia can effectively engage China in the days ahead, Bangladesh Institute for Peace and Security Studies (BIPSS) formally launched the Bangladesh Centre for China studies (BCCS) in Dhaka on December 7, 2009 (BIPSS 2009). The new center, a specialized one established within the BIPSS framework, has a dedicated group of researchers who undertake research on various aspects related to China and Sino-Bangladesh relations.

The principal objective of BCCS is to understand and study Chinese foreign policy, to analyze Chinese security and also to study Chinese economic advancement with a view to advocate greater economic and development cooperation between Bangladesh and China as well as China and the greater South Asian region. The center also has partnership with think tanks and universities in China as well as other institutes elsewhere focusing on China. These include China Institute of International Studies, China Institute of Contemporary International Relations, Beijing Institute of International Strategic Studies, Shanghai Institute of International Affairs, and a host of Chinese friendship associations. The BCCS has been having bilateral seminars and workshops with these institutes at regular intervals. Professor Abdur Rob Khan of North South University who was earlier with BCCS says, "the interests of Chinese scholars in Bangladesh had both bilateral contents as well South Asian contents. But frankly speaking, the interests were mostly derivative of their interests in India" (Khan 2016). India factor, therefore, appears to be important to orient China's friendly views on Bangladesh, though Bangladesh cites internal economic situation as an important factor in forming its friendly views on China.

Another China studies center aimed at providing facilities of research and academic activities on China was established at the North South University campus in Dhaka. The future role of this center is to strengthen mutual bond and friendship between China and Bangladesh both at the state as well as individual levels. Similarly, a Confucius Institute at the North South University (NSU) in Dhaka was established on February 14, 2006 in accordance with the agreement signed with China's Yunnan University in November 2005. The objective is to promote the Chinese language in Bangladesh and further it all over South Asian region by means of approaching China, understanding China, and experiencing China. Besides, the institute makes efforts in strengthening the relationship between China and Bangladesh. Until recently, this was the only center of its kind in Bangladesh. Now they have opened another in Chittagong. They basically offer a certificate course/diploma in language and culture focusing on China. In the Confucius Institute, they have Chinese as well as Bangladeshi faculty. Khan remains amazed while explaining how excellently some of the Bangladeshi students perform on stage the different aspects of Chinese culture. "That shows their capability in terms of learning Chinese language, culture, etc." he adds (Khan 2016).

Further, in December 2013, a new center called East Asia Study Centre under the Faculty of Social Sciences of Dhaka University was opened of which Professor Delawar Hossein is the Founding Director. It focuses largely on Japan and China affairs so far as research and teaching are concerned. Since the Centre is at the very initial stage, Hossein is trying to create networks, pooling resources, involving more people, and interacting with Chinese and Japanese diplomats as well as academics, so that he could develop a focused research agenda. While this author was interviewing Hossein in Dhaka University, he made it clear that "the Center focuses more on political or economic security dimensions and less on cultural aspects" (Hossein 2016). So from that point of view, as he says, "we call it 'affairs'; China affairs, not China studies, so that we can focus more on political, social, and security phenomena which are very important for China's foreign policy." There is also a separate department of Chinese language within the Faculty of Languages in Dhaka University.

However, political scientists and scholars of area studies lament the low level of scholarship on Area studies in Bangladesh.

Ambassador Serajul Islam is currently the Chairman of the Centre for Foreign Affairs Studies, a Dhaka-based think tank working on issues related to foreign relations of Bangladesh. Speaking about China studies in Bangladesh Ambassador Islam says:

> The Chinese have been very clever in dealing with Bangladesh. They have trained many of our people in government in China, particularly in our armed forces who speak fluent Chinese. These days many students are also going to China to study. I don't know the exact number of students going to China but I think they are a good number. These people trained in China act in Bangladesh on behalf of China to further that country's interests in Bangladesh ... while Bangladesh has been overtly friendly with India, it is the Chinese who have increased the sale of their products to Bangladesh much more than India has because the people who have been trained in China act on their behalf in Bangladesh. (Islam 2012)

On the other hand, Hossein is of the opinion that,

> When it matters for research for knowing China more comprehensively, then we have serious shortage of academic programs on China. We don't have any separate academic program on China in the country which may deal with political, economic and cultural matters. What we offer in my department or other departments is only a coursework that a student can do on China. I think, we need to create opportunities for academic program on China and also for research on China, in particular what changes we see in Chinese foreign policy and Chinese development discourse. (Hossein 2016)

It seems that the government and higher education institutions in Bangladesh focus more on teaching as clearly demonstrated in the annual budgets. When there is a question of research, especially the research on China or Japan or East Asia, or India, Bangladesh has not yet developed such culture of funding. Yet, Professor Ehsanul Haque, Chairman at the Department of International Relations, University of Dhaka points out, "in South Asia China's cultural diplomacy is going to be very effective and it has, in fact, taken shape in our country because Chinese government is offering scholarship to Bangladeshi students" (Haque 2016). To be precise, cultural diplomacy is called soft diplomacy or using soft power, and by offering scholarship to Bangladeshi students China is using its soft power. Praising China for doing so, Haque is of the opinion that there is nothing wrong in China using its soft power in Bangladesh and that is going to be more effective than using other forms of power. He has following to say:

> ...there is an increasing level of interest among the Bangladeshi students to learn Chinese language. This is really positive thing that would help us to justify the issue of Chinese studies in Bangladesh. The other thing is that cultural diplomacy in our society is going to be more effective in the sense people are very receptive to such ideas. It means that you are having ties through cultural diplomacy and that is going to be a harmless kind of relationship. When you have military ties with China that causes concern in the minds of the people. When you have cultural relations with China, when you send people to China and Chinese people come to your country, these kinds of bilateral exchanges at the cultural level would certainly be very much helpful to both the countries having a sustainable relationship. [Hence,] cultural diplomacy has got its own power in Bangladesh. (Haque 2016)

Nevertheless, Professor Lailufar Yasmin of the Department of International Relations, University of Dhaka argues, "if China has to develop its soft power, it would be the first means and China needs to rely on the first means, i.e., to develop a full-fledged independent China studies centre" (Yasmin 2016). She stresses on developing an independent China studies center in Bangladesh which would have strong connections with China so that it could work exclusively on producing China knowledge and scholarship. This is so because without that there is no advancement in China policy. "We know from the development of Cold War politics that how America needed an intellectual basis for its advancement. So, China also needs to pursue it from that perspective" (Yasmin 2016). China experts in Bangladesh favor the launching of a Master's program on China studies, which can be taught from the social science perspective that can contribute to the domains of International Relations, Economics, and International Business in order to form opinion on policy matters conducive to Bangladesh–China relations. No wonder why social science approaches more easily attract Bangladeshi community as opposed to civilizational approach or policy approach.

China Studies in Nepal

Relations between Nepal and China are ancient, dating back to more than 2,000 years. The common mountains and rivers are manifestations of the age-old natural links between the two countries. The bilateral ties, ranging from the intimate cultural, historical, social, and spiritual links, have been continuously nurtured and promoted by Buddhism, which itself was expounded by Shakyamuni Gautam Buddha, who was born in 623 BC in Lumbini, a township in Rupendehi district of Nepal. Such a rich and varied historic and natural engagement between Nepal and China encouraged a group of 12 Nepalese intellectuals to envision the establishment and promotion of an organization in Nepal which would be focused specifically on China affairs and collaborative neighborly relations between Nepal and China. This group, which has Madan Regmi as the convener, initially designated the organization as China Study Centre (CSC) which came into existence in 1999 but in September 2006, it was supplemented with "Nepal" to express its geo-political locational identity.

According to Madan Regmi, the main focus of CSC-Nepal include promotion of understanding through exchange of research and study visits, interactions such as policy dialogue, seminars and conferences on identified themes, synthesis and dissemination of research and study results, and advancement of knowledge and informed resources base in the form of e-communication, library, documentation, publication, and consultation on strategic and developmental aspects of China and Nepal–China relations. Informing people about China to update and enhance their quality of understanding toward the neighboring country through publications in Nepali and English languages, is a core activity area of the

CSC-Nepal. The Center has also forged linkages and contacts with several organizations in China including Chinese Academy of Social Sciences (CASS), China Institutes of Contemporary International Relations (CICR), China Association for International Friendly Contact (CAIFC) and other institutions. Regmi, who himself is a writer and poet, believes that "cultural affinities can help enhance mutual understanding and collaborations" (Regmi 2012).

Informal and formal meetings take place between senior Chinese officials and scholars and the relevant CSC-Nepal officials and scholars to mutually enhance and strengthen information and knowledge-base of the respective institutions. The Centre has published books on China and South Asia, China's market economy, political history, statistical and general information. Two publications on *Social History of Tibet* and *Collected Works on China Studies* have been published in Nepali language. The Center's principal journal on Chinese studies known as *Friendship* contains articles on various topics of interests. The Center's another publication *Sadvaav* (in Nepali language) periodically features different aspects of current Chinese affairs. Its members regularly act as opinion educators through their writings and presentations in the media.

Other centers dealing with China studies in Nepal include the Centre for Nepal and Asian Studies (CNAS) at Tribhuwan University in Kathmandu. During the late 1980s the CNAS was very active in analyzing major developments in politics, economics, foreign and security policies of China along with many others publishing the annual *CNAS Year Review*. However, in the absence of support and encouragement from the state, the effort came to a standstill (Simkhada 2012: 158). Only recently there has been an urge to focus China has once again taken a front seat at the CNAS. There is also a Confucius Institute in Kathmandu University which was opened on June 13, 2007. The Confucius Institute works for promotion of Chinese culture and language in foreign countries through cooperation of local academic institutions. This institute at Kathmandu University is a high-level Chinese Language and Culture institution established in cooperation with Hebei University of Economics and Business with the ratification of Office of Chinese

Language Council International (KU 2007). This is also credited with being the first Confucius Institute in Nepal. On November 12, 2009, this Confucius Institute organized an orientation program on Chinese Language and Culture at Nepal Academy of Tourism and Hotel Management. During the occasion Dr. Li Wanxian, the Director of the institute, summarized the Chinese language course in three words: Membership, Scholarship and Friendship. According to him, "once the students opted for Chinese language program, they will become a member of Confucius Institute and take the responsibility learn Chinese well and get the scholarship for further study in China so as to make contribution to the friendship between China and Nepal" (KU 2009).

Two other universities have China studies centers which conduct seminars on China–Nepal relations from time to time. There are a few NGOs also which are involved in China studies, mainly on Chinese affairs. The CSC-Nepal has relations with the Institute of Strategic Studies in Islamabad, Pakistan as well. According to Hiranya Lal Shreshtha, "academically, China study is not yet openly developed in Nepal. The focus is mostly on China–Nepal bilateral relations. However, since China is now having an observer status in SAARC a new regional perspective on China studies in Nepal is emerging" (Shreshtha 2012). A different phenomenon has, though, occurred recently, i.e., Nepalese students are going to China for study but mostly in professional courses both for the short term as well as long-term durations. In addition, Beijing has already initiated an exchange of scholars program under which Nepalese scholars are invited to attend Chinese universities and think tanks to study which is an indicative of the fact that "China is trying to draw Nepal into becoming a strategic partner" (Tiwari 2013: 215–216).

What needs to be pointed out here is that like Bangladesh in Nepal too China studies has not yet developed from the social science perspective. Bhasker Koirala, who established a think tank, Nepal Institute of International and Strategic Studies and launched the China–India–Nepal trilateral cooperation in 2012, explains that there is hardly anyone who is pursuing China studies in Nepal in the social sciences and humanities (Koirala 2016). Most of the Nepalese students who are studying even in China, they are studying technical subjects like medicine, engineering, and so on. The students are going to China for study both on Chinese scholarships as well as under self finance schemes. Yubaraj Ghimire, a senior journalist who is currently Editor of *Annapurna Post*, a daily newspaper in Nepal, puts the figure of visiting Nepalese students to China for technical education as approximately 4,000. This is in addition to those who go to China to study language and culture. Ghimire is firm in his opinion when he says, "Now I will not be surprised if the future leadership of Nepal are the alumni of a Chinese college or University" (Ghimire 2016). Back in Nepal there is no source for funding to local think tanks which could develop expertise exclusively on China studies from social science, international relations or economy perspectives in order to contribute to Nepal's policymaking toward China. Even though China studies experts in Nepal are unanimous in their views that social science approaches more easily attract Nepalese community as opposed to civilizational approach or policy approach.

In both Bangladesh and Nepal, there is a clear understanding that the study of China and Chinese reflects the strategic choice of identity at various levels, and hence, the following paragraphs examine their respective identity strategy in order to highlight if they are pursuing a pro-China positioning, objectivism, or balance in the ongoing geostrategic scenario of South Asia where both China and India have important roles to play.

Issues Dominating Bangladesh–China and Nepal–China Relations

Bangladesh Perspective

Despite serious shortage of full-fledged academic programs on China studies, Bangladesh–China relations hold strategic importance at various levels because of two different historical reasons: (a) During 1971–1975 China was mostly known due to its opposition to Bangladesh Liberation War, and (b) In the post-1975 era China became popular in Bangladesh due to establishment of diplomatic relations between the two sides. During the period from 1976 to 1991 (Zia and Ershad regimes), there had been a deterioration in Bangladesh's relations with India, while China became a very important country. However, China policy of Bangladesh during this period was seen more of a choice by the military regimes to use it as a kind of balancer or a kind of support to deal with Bangladesh–India relations (Hossein 2016). After the restoration of democracy in Bangladesh in 1990, Bangladesh Nationalist Party (BNP) came to power by replacing the military regime in 1991 but it "followed the foreign policy of its military regimes, which were mostly based on pro-West, pro-Islamic world and pro-China determinants and were almost anti-Indian" (Bhardwaj 2005:45). In 1996, when Awami League (AL) came to power there was a paradigm shift in Bangladesh's China policy as the then Prime Minister Sheikh Hasina first visited China in 1997. But the AL not only pursued friendship with China it also improved bilateral relations with India, which is a kind of unique phenomenon in Bangladesh foreign policy today that reflects the country's identity strategy in its quest for objectivism. Nevertheless, China policy of Bangladesh has been quite consistent irrespective of any political parties or regimes ruling the country.

The issues that dominate the Bangladesh–China relations today include defense procurement, One Belt, One Road (OBOR), Economic benefit and SAARC. Haque (2016) points out that over the last two to three decades Bangladesh–China relationship is being assessed very much positively within the Bangladesh society which acknowledges the fact that China is a great power with enormous military supremacy. So, there is no reason to ignore China in Bangladesh's foreign policy. The foreign policymakers of Bangladesh also understand this fact, and they are now in favor of having more constructive relations with China which is certainly an important economic partner of Bangladesh. Besides, Dhaka receives most of its military hardware from China which is the only source of Bangladesh's defense procurement. Yet, "in the new context, Bangladesh's relations with China can be seen as an immature relationship; it needs much more scholarly attention from the academics in the country" (Haque 2016).

Regarding the role of Bangladesh if at all it wants to join the Chinese initiative of "One Belt, One Road" or the Silk Road Economic Belt and the Maritime Silk Road, the Bangladeshi experts have similar views when they say that any initiative from China for the development of the partner countries would be welcomed in the South Asia region. Hossain (2016) describes the OBOR as a kind of framework of China's current international relations. Stressing that it is indeed a package that China wants to promote basically for deeper relations with Bangladesh or with many Asian countries, he explains, "whether it is a 'Maritime Silk Road' or 'One Belt, One Road,' actually China thinks that their power projection and also the way they have developed their economy, they need to have more support and more market for their products and for their economic penetration" (Hossein 2016). Diplomatically also it is very important "because all big countries or great countries have kind of global ambition and for that matter China has global ambition or regional ambition," he says and adds "what we have learned from this is that every country in the world has its own ambitions, whether it is at sub-regional level or global level or regional level" (Hossein 2016). Although there is interest in OBOR because it will help Bangladesh in accessing other countries, joining this Chinese initiative seems to be taking time because, as Khan (2016) laments, "unfortunately there are no policies being written about this, that is a big lacuna in our research." Another view that there are some uncertainties in China's OBOR initiative, because things are not yet clear to the partner countries, has been elaborated by Haque (2016) who says the following:

> China has yet to make further clarification on this initiative, so, I think first of all Bangladesh government would be making a very careful assessment of the entire initiative and then it would be in a position to think about the possibility of joining this particular initiative...China really is guarded by financial trusts and we are living in a competitive world where interests compete with conflict.

So in this kind of situation, I think both the parties would certainly understand the importance of carrying out any initiative that benefits both of them…as long as Bangladesh's interests are preserved, Bangladesh has no reason to say no to this initiative.

About the economic benefits, it appears that given its power position in the world and its global and regional ambition it is very clear that China has economic, diplomatic, and security stakes, but Bangladesh in fact has its economic stake. That is what Hossein (2006) has to say, "When we have friendship with India, we don't feel our security or diplomacy is at stake. So, our's is basically economic. Our economy can benefit from close relations with China." Although India is also now gathering its economic strength, India has its own needs for infrastructure development and energy security as it is a huge country with a huge democracy. "It is not like China where the regime decides everything", says Hossein and adds that "India has different structure and has a different social system, so it needs its own development first. Country like Bangladesh can really benefit from India also, but China can invest." This is more so because moving out of Dhaka one can see how much need there is, roads and rivers are not in proper shape. "It is a kind of country of rivers, we have one of the finest river network systems but we don't have proper development. The rivers are drying, they are no longer rivers, they have become canals. It is really important for us to involve and get support from China and India for our economic development" (Hossein 2016).

On the trade front, earlier India was the largest trading partner of Bangladesh, now that has been replaced by China. Bangladesh's trade with China is expanding very rapidly, both in terms of absolute amount and percentage change among Bangladesh's top trade partners. Data from Export Promotion Bureau of Bangladesh confirms that the country's total merchandised export to China was US$808.14 million in 2015–2016, which had been merely US$319.66 million in 2010–2011. However, merchandised imports from China have been the highest for quite some time. The data of Bangladesh Bank shows that import from China was worth about US$9.8 billion in

2015–2016 as compared to US$5.9 billion in 2010–2011. The overall Bangladesh's trade with China is now about 26.5 percent of its total trade with the world, which is the highest with a growing trend. Chinese involvement in Bangladesh's two special economic zones (SEZs) and establishing a dedicated export processing zone (EPZ) for China may further help boost bilateral trade and increase Bangladesh's exports to the global market (Kabir 2016). Another important factor is China's involvement in Bangladesh's development including infrastructure. This is a new area which is expanding and where Bangladesh has to play a very delicate balancing terms of its relations with China and India (Khan 2016).

Since China has currently an observer status in the SAARC, it is also an issue if China should be given a membership of SAARC. Haque (2016) tries to be firm in his point of view saying, "at this moment, this won't be the right decision, because you have to understand reaction from other countries, especially reaction from India." According to him, China would be joining SAARC with its own agenda to have more access to South Asia, so when China gets more access to South Asia through SAARC that would give some sort of legitimacy to China's playing some sort of role in any kind of South Asian situation. If China continues its activities in the South China Sea that is also an issue for Bangladesh to think about. "China is flexing its muscle in the South China Sea and you cannot unrelate this with China's behavior in the South Asian region. If you look at China's behavior from that perspective, China could be seen as a country which has a tendency to dominate the South Asian region through its entry into SAARC" (Haque 2016).

Yasmin (2016) too dismisses the idea of giving China a membership of SAARC "because every individual organization has its own pulse and feel and South Asia was built with the idea that it is a common platform for all South Asian countries." According to her, "even the inclusion of Afghanistan in the SAARC was a bit farfetched. In South Asia, India, Pakistan, Nepal, Sri Lanka, Bangladesh, Bhutan, Maldives, the kind of culture that we have, Afghanistan does not fit into that, and then China is being talked about." She argues that "we have to understand what the criterion of defining a member country is. If it is common culture, China is not there, if it is geographical contiguity, China is not there, and by definition if we have China, then why not Myanmar because it is at our doorstep connected to both India and Bangladesh. And then with Myanmar, there are a lot of other countries which are connected." Her views have been supported by Hossein (2016) who makes it clear, "it is not wise to make China a member of SAARC now." He does not favor even the idea of creating observer status within SAARC mainly because SAARC has a lot to do internally to become a credible organization. He contends that "if you invite more burdens on your shoulder then you will just be an ineffective and SAARC has become like this, which has not even been able to formulate a proper mechanism to involve observers. In every Summit, observers come and speak and that's all. This is what the situation is now." In comparison to ASEAN and its structure, SAARC is far from the reality as the local Bangladeshi opinion demonstrates.

Nepal Perspective

Nepal considers its geopolitical situation as a buffer state between India and China. In its foreign policy, Nepal in the early part of the 20th century looked upon China as a balance to threats to its integrity from the British power in India. During the British rule in India Nepal managed to retain its autonomy, though the British were able to achieve whatever they wanted to within the Himalayan region (Pemble 1971: 68). Primarily, China's interest in Nepal has always been tied to its geopolitical concerns over the security of Tibet, which has been dominated by China since 1950 (Patel 2013: 42). At that time Nepal emerged as a forum for anti-China activities as thousands of Tibetan refugees trekked to Nepal through the Nepal–Tibet border. Faced with an uprising by the Tibetans during the 1950s (Soni and Marwah 2011: 289), China was keen to establish friendly relations with Nepal, which finally culminated in the establishment of diplomatic relations between the two sides on August 1, 1955. The period from 1955 and beyond saw China improving its position in Nepal through various diplomatic initiatives including exchanges of delegations, personal visits as well as the grant of economic aid which was largely untied. China's interest in Nepal was also due to the latter's strategic importance so much so that Chinese Premier Zhou Enlai visited Kathmandu in early 1957, thus giving high level attention to relations with Nepal (Tiwari 2013: 209). However, in the post-1958 period Nepal–China relations deteriorated especially because of Chinese claims to Mount Everest. The first anti-Chinese demonstration in the history of Nepal was organized in Kathmandu on April 21, 1960. In the same year in June, Chinese troops intruded into the northwest of Nepal which further escalated tensions. It was during this period that the B.P. Koirala government drew closer to India. The following decade of the 1970s witnessed the improved relations between Nepal and China and Chinese diplomacy was well regulated so that Nepal would not allow anti-Chinese activities on its soil. Since the 1980s Beijing has avoided involvement, or interference, in a country's internal affairs, but the growing importance of Nepal for managing Tibet cannot be understated (Ranade 2014).

China has been continuously concerned about the activities of Tibetans in Nepal ever since the Beijing Olympics of 2008. To reward Nepal for ensuring that Tibetans protests and activities are thoroughly scrutinized and Beijing is kept well aware, China has enhanced the amount of untied foreign aid and assistance to Nepal in addition to boosting economic and trade ties. China has also intensified its engagement policies including a "soft" diplomatic program using people-to-people contacts, cultural ties, student scholarships, and enlarged aid flows (Patel 2013: 42). There has been a growth in Chinese investment in Nepal's strategically important infrastructure, including airports and highways. By 2012–2013, 575 Chinese companies had received approval from the department of industry for FDI. Huawei and ZTE already have a monopoly in the telecom infrastructure sector and this has provided a tremendous fillip to Chinese language teaching. Tourism-related sectors are other areas of China's interest. Negotiations are also underway for direct flights between China and Nepal by a fourth Chinese airline and China has agreed to give Nepal a concessional loan for the purchase of six aircraft. While the increasing number of Chinese tourists to Nepal would be a major economic incentive, it would also give Beijing additional leverage over Nepal. Chinese travel agencies do bring tourists to the Kathmandu valley and to places like Lo Manthang in Upper Mustang (Ranade 2014). Nepal has also been assured that the development of the western province of China would benefit Nepal. This refers to the south-westerly branch of the old "Silk Road," now known as the Bangladesh–China–India–Myanmar (BCIM) economic corridor. In addition, China also agreed to consider Nepal's request for extending the 1,200 km. Qinghai–Lhasa–Shigatse railway to Kathmandu (Ranade 2014). On the issue of Nepal joining the OBOR, Nepal has shown some interest, but a formal position has not yet been spelled out. It seems that Nepal's decision on joining the OBOR will largely depend on how Nepal and China move forward in their relations. Ghimire (2016), however, believes, "Nepal will feel comfortable if such a deal has only developmental significance, not a strategic one."

The pro-China tilt of Nepal increased after Pushpa Kamal Dahal, popularly known as Prachanda assumed the position of Prime Ministership in August 2008.[1] In order to balance India's influence in Nepal's internal politics, the latter received advice from China on the drafting of its Constitution through the Maoist leaders. Beijing, on its part, remained concerned that provinces based on the issue of ethnicity would complicate matters for China and hence, guided Nepalese leaders to limit the number of provinces for improved governance. From the Chinese point of view, any instability in Nepal will have adverse consequences for Tibetan Autonomous Region. Not only that but also China is an important neighbor and critical to Nepal's development as Ghimire (2016) believes, but he adds, "We need to look into Nepal–China relations in different contexts": (a) The two countries have border relations, there are 15 or 16 districts out of 75 in Nepal which share the border with Tibet. There has been a very old trade relation and a kind of civilizational relation between the two countries and (b) the two countries share a diplomatic relation which has completed six decades now without major complications ever coming in the way. His explanation indi-

---

[1] He was the Prime Minister of Nepal from August 2008 to May 2009. In August 2016 he was elected for a second time and has been serving as Prime Minister since then.

cates that China throughout has been respected by Nepal as he stresses on the following:

> Despite being so big and powerful, China has chosen to remain a distant rather a non-interfering player. It does not interfere in Nepal's internal politics. The other issues in which China behaves differently from most other stakeholder powers/countries is that it acts only through the government, does not support anti-government or anti-State forces. That has been China's visible policy in Nepal so far. But, China despite maintaining distance from Nepal's internal politics, all these years, especially in the post-2006 period when Nepal went through major political changes, I would call it "radical changes", China has come much closer. (Ghimire 2016)

Another dominant issue is the Tibet factor in China–Nepal relations. It is, therefore, important here to understand the presence of Tibetans in Nepal. According to the CTA household questionnaire, there were 13,720 Tibetan residents in Nepal in 1998, and according to the UNHCR statistical yearbook 2007, the number had increased to 20,184 in 2006 (Marwah and Soni 2010: 266). Initially, there was no restriction on the number of refugees granted asylum in Nepal as Nepal's approach to Tibetan refugees was to integrate them into the economic life of the country, especially in the 1990s. The Tibetan community developed its own economic capabilities, especially with the introduction of the carpet industry and with support from foreign donors. However, it is no surprise that the flow of Tibetan refugees into Nepal declined significantly since China tightened border controls in the wake of the March 2008 protests (Marwah and Soni 2010: 267). In October 2013, after Beijing placed new emphasis on pursuing its policy for the conduct of relations toward its neighbors, or what Chinese analysts call "peripheral diplomacy," Nepal's importance has grown. Beijing has also broadened the scope of its political interactions mainly due to unsettled domestic political situation in Nepal which has pushed China to find new ways in order to intensify its influence in that country.

Security concerns, however, continue to be among the principal motivating factors, with Beijing extremely wary that Tibetans settled in Nepal could involve themselves in what it perceives as "anti-China" activities. China also remains apprehensive that Nepal, which has a 1,400-km border with the Tibet Autonomous Region (TAR), could be used as a springboard by "hostile powers" to provoke unrest in Tibet (Ranade 2014). However, as Ghimire (2016) takes stock of the situation, Tibetan people in Nepal by and large do realize that there are certain issues they have to be very clear about: Nepal has a large number of Mahayana Buddhists practicing under Tibetan Gurus. They are revered and respected in Nepal and in Kathmandu. So, those 20,000 people with Tibetan identity cards understand the sensitivity of the relations and China's intolerance toward any anti-Chinese activity in Nepal. At the same time Nepal is also a democracy which is directly involved with the right issues and in the name of right, a large number of Western NGOs, donors, and INGOs are present who provoke. But China has been ensured that there would be no uprising against China in Nepal. "Nepal would be bound to honor its assurance to China that its territory will not be allowed to be used against China" (Ghimire 2016) with China using its "soft" power and also "state" power changes are visible in Nepal on the issue of Tibetans. On an average, 2,000 people used to come to Nepal from Tibet each year earlier, now it is far less than 200 every year due to Chinese restrictions on the movement of Tibetans. In addition, with China opening up and given freedom of religion, there are people practicing Buddhism openly and they are maintaining cordial relations with the monasteries in Nepal. That may also have been one of the reasons affecting the number of Tibetans moving to Nepal. There is no doubt that "Nepal is trying to redefine its role in the Himalayas and finds China a ready partner… [and to] assuage the Chinese concerns, Nepal has followed the One China Policy and also does not allow Tibetans to engage in political protests from its territory" (Thapliyal 2017: 52).

Quest for Objectivism: Bangladesh's Identity Strategy Toward China and India

In its quest for objectivism the identity strategy of Bangladesh in dealing with China and India has been to demonstrate a neutral posture, especially in the post-Cold War period. Bangladesh has a record of playing active diplomatic role in regional and other framework. The dominant view in Bangladesh is that if India and China do not suspect their relations with Bangladesh in geopolitical and security perspectives, it might become very clear to both India and China that Bangladesh does not pursue its geopolitical interest by creating enmity or hostility between China and India. Hossein (2016) argues, "This is very important because India and China have to trust Bangladesh that it does not engage itself in the so called *realpolitik* game of using one great power against another." This can also be treated as an opportunity for Bangladesh to show its identity strategy at a time when its foreign policy and discourse is moving toward such direction where "Bangladesh feels that it needs a strong South Asia under the leadership of India and a strong Asia where China has its own strong role to play along with India and other powers" (Hossein 2016). At the same time, others contend that Bangladesh–India relationship is much more important than the Bangladesh–China relationship because of the geopolitical location of Bangladesh and the significant role that India plays in Bangladesh's foreign policy calculation. The contention is based on the following point of view:

> There is no denying of the fact that whichever party is in power in the country, they cannot ignore India in the foreign policy of Bangladesh. Simultaneously China is equally important to Bangladesh ... So, both are important. But ... to give more importance to one, I would certainly say Bangladesh-India relationship is more important. This is a reality. (Haque 2016)

However, there is still another view backed by Ambassador Islam (2012) who says, "the Chinese deal with Bangladesh as a nation unlike the Indians who play politics with us favoring the Awami League (AL) against the Bangladesh Nationalist Party (BNP)." Even, the assumption in India that the Awami League is pro-India and BNP is anti-India is "fallacious" and can be termed as "an inward-looking approach to international relations" (Bhardwaj 2003: 275). The fact remains that "both of them espouse neither pro-Indian nor anti-Indian machinations ... [and] attitude [of the two parties] towards India is governed by domestic compulsions and tactics to secure a modicum of regime security" (Bhardwaj 2003: 275).

Notwithstanding such diverse views, the fact remains that today Bangladesh is maintaining very friendly relations with both India and China. The regime is actually maintaining the same policy and objective approach toward the two major powers. Bangladesh now has a need for FDI and a support for infrastructural changes. It has some mega projects like deep sea port, metro railways, and energy projects. Moreover, it has to develop its infrastructure because the economy has grown so much so that it is now the 33rd largest economy in the world. Population has also increased and so the demand. Since more people are becoming part of middle class they have new kinds of demand and consumption, and hence Bangladesh needs more support from other countries. In such a situation, "China remains to be a very important partner and, of course, India too. It is not only geopolitical compulsions but also more of economic compulsions for Bangladesh" (Hossein 2016).

The matrix of China–Bangladesh relations infuses numerous avenues, ranging from strategic to commercial, from energy security to infrastructural. Chinese ventures into infrastructure building and port development are designed to strengthen Beijing's vision for a maritime corridor extending from the South China Sea to the Indian Ocean passing through the Bay of Bengal. This corridor will help resolve the Malacca Dilemma by pledging lesser reliance on the narrow Malacca Straits which witnesses transit of 80 percent of China's oil supplies (Masood 2015). In this context, China is helping to develop the Chittagong port along the coast of Bangladesh. On the other hand, India has also been pursued by Bangladesh to contribute to the development of Chittagong port, in addition to developing a deep sea port at Sonadia Island near Cox's Bazar. China, however, is already involved in the Sonadia port development project which would serve China as a crucial hub in its "string of pearls" strategy (Kashinath 2016). It indicates that Bangladesh needs both the Chinese and Indian help but not their influence, and hence seeks to counterbalance either country's ambitions to ensure equilibrium or for that matter objectivism in its foreign policy (Masood 2015).

Bangladesh also plays a key role in the development of connectivity of Northeast India. In this regard India's "Act East" policy, formerly known as "Look East" policy is very important for both India and Bangladesh. "When India was pursuing its Look East policy, it was isolating Bangladesh," Hossein (2016) stressed, "India should actually focus on Bangladesh first, because the main purpose is to improve North East India which cannot achieve results just by focusing on South East Asia." Due to its geographical proximity Bangladesh can contribute a lot by offering its market, capital investment and other things in the development of Northeast India's internal infrastructure and basic industrialization. In this sense, Bangladesh is a crucial part of India's "Act East" policy. "With Bangladesh India could actually pursue its 'Act East' policy properly" (Hossein 2016) as "neglecting Bangla State can give room to China to exercise monopoly in the strategic and commercial arenas" (Masood 2015).

China as a Balance Against India: Nepal's Identity Strategy

Nepal's identity strategy, particularly in the post-2008 period, lies in considering China as a balance against India, and hence it has adopted a pro-China approach. From the Nepalese point of view, Ghimire (2016) makes it clear that the degree and pace of proximity between Nepal and China during the tenure of KP Oli[2] as Prime Minister was unusual phase in the context of Nepal–India and Nepal–China relations. According to him, "Nepal–India relations almost hit at its Nadir. A blockade by India at a time when Nepal was reeling under impact of devastating earthquake was unimaginable. This diplomatic exercise by India as far as Nepalese are concerned, was absolutely devoid of human element. Any trouble between Nepal and India was sorted out in the past. But this one particular instance has left a deep anger and suspicion about the Indian attitude in the Nepalese mind. Oli perhaps treated it a bit differently, and secured China's commitment to come in Nepal's aid." The local views subscribe to a completely favorable approach to China pointing that it is very important for Nepal to engage with China in a

---

[2] He served as Prime Minister of Nepal from October 2015 to August 2016.

robust way both for Nepal's own development as well as for the regional development, regional peace, and regional stability. Agreeing to such views Koirala (2016) finds that China understands not only the sensitivity of the Chinese engagement with Nepal but also the relationship Nepal shares with India.

For the long time, India enjoyed almost exclusive influence in Nepal. However, in the last decade, mainly after the abolition of monarchy in 2008, other international players, especially China, have increased their influence in Nepal. "It began with India dictating political change and agenda in 2006. India began decisively influencing internal politics, peace process and the Constitution making process and rallied international forces behind it," explains Ghimire (2016) and adds, "China's enhanced presence should not be seen in isolation. This may be in pursuit of its own policy but also largely in response to the larger international or its competitors' presence in Nepal." Since then Chinese diplomacy in Nepal has shifted from "quiet diplomacy" to "vocal diplomacy" (Bhattarai 2017). China has also been taking increasing interest in Nepal's internal politics in addition to giving a new shape to bilateral military relations.

In December 2016, China's People's Liberation Army (PLA) announced its plan to hold the first-ever joint military exercise with Nepal which the latter accepted. This has been the first indication that Nepal is willing to change its military relationship with India. "India wants to maintain Nepal as its 'sphere of influence,' while China wants to increase its clout" and that "India sees China's growing influence in Nepal as not only related to trade and commerce, but a part of China's larger strategy to encircle it in South Asia" (Bhattarai 2017). Whatever may be the interpretations, Nepal appears to be favoring China outrightly over India, particularly after Kathmandu promulgated its constitution in 2015. Interaction and exchanges between Nepal and China significantly improved thereafter. The tensions between Nepal and India provided room for China to increase its influence in all areas of Nepal, including in politics and economy which is attested by the fact that during his tenure "KP Oli signed a trade and transit agreement with China, ending India's monopoly on Nepal's external trade" (Bhattarai 2017). In the long run, "India will not find it easy to deter Nepal from developing infrastructural links with China," and that "China was a variable in India's relations with Nepal and it would continue to be so, with active involvement through trade and economic links" (Thapliyal 2017: 52). Yet, under the current Nepal PM Pushpa Kamal Dahal India "seeks to put a rocky patch in relations with Nepal during the tenure of KP Oli behind it and look forward to a new chapter" (Parashar 2016). But it remains to be seen if Nepal could ever perform a balancing act between India and China rather than taking a pro-China positioning to balance India.

Conclusion

The evolution of China studies in South Asia did not take place in a vacuum, rather the two-pronged motivating factors, i.e., China's South Asia policy and the response to that policy from the South Asian countries, especially the smaller ones, including Bangladesh and Nepal, worked in consonance to realize this. What really has been noticed is that China's perceptions of a "peaceful periphery" as a prerequisite for its domestic development have come to dominate the PRC's post-1978 South Asia policy, which in later years also took into consideration India's "rise" factor (Rajan 2011). However, both in Bangladesh and Nepal, China studies are in a nascent stage. The people we interviewed in the two countries were very much clear on their opinion when they said that if China was to develop its soft power, China studies would be the first means and hence there is a need to develop devoted China studies centers. Indications were also high that there should be an independent China studies center which would have strong connections with China and that it would also work toward developing academic scholarship from the social science perspective. This is so because social science approaches more easily attract both the Bangladeshi and Nepalese communities as opposed to civilizational approach or policy approach so far as China studies in South Asia is concerned.

In comparative perspective both Bangladesh and Nepal differ in their approaches toward China and India when their identity strategies come to the fore. While Bangladesh seeks objectivism and adopts a neutral posture in dealing with China and India, Nepal pursues a pro-China approach by considering China a balance against India. However, Bangladesh and Nepal relate themselves to China as a source of support and comfort for their respective needs. Today Bangladesh–China relations have improved in certain areas like trade and defense, though a new dimension which is expanding is China's involvement in Bangladesh's development including infrastructure. But this is one particular area where Bangladesh has to play a very delicate balancing terms of its relations with India. On the other hand, China remains to be a significant player in Nepal due to the extent of bilateral ties being forged through both economic assistance and political engagement. Yet, academic inputs to impact policymaking in order to boost relations with China are lacking both in Bangladesh and Nepal. Analysts believe that Bangladesh and Nepal need to look at their relations with China and India on equal footing and work toward culminating them in strong diplomatic, strategic and trade relations. However, "these ventures must be carried out in an environment that acknowledges multipolarity in South Asia" (Masood 2015). This will help India and China to rise as complementary partners in the Asian century.

Acknowledgment

The author is grateful to Professor Chih-yu Shih of National Taiwan University for his comments and suggestions that helped improve the draft version of this chapter.

References

Bangladesh Institute for Peace and Security Studies. 2009. Bangladesh Centre for China Studies (BCCS) formally launched, http://bipss.org.bd/index.php?option=com_content&view=article&id=290:bangladesh-centre-for-china-studies-bccs-formally-launched&catid=9&Itemid=688. Accessed on June 28, 2017.

Bhardwaj, Sanjay. 2003. Bangladesh Foreign Policy vis-a-vis India. *Strategic Analyses* 27(2): 263–278.

Bhardwaj, Sanjay. 2005. Bangladesh at 35: Internal Dynamics and External Linkages. *Journal of International Affairs* 9(1–2): 43–54.

Bhattarai, Kamal Dev. 2017. India and China's Tug of War Over Nepal, *The Diplomat* (6 January), http://thediplomat.com/2017/01/india-and-chinas-tug-of-war-over-nepal/. Accessed on July 10, 2017.

Ghimire, Yubaraj. 2016. Interview by Reena Marwah for China Studies in South Asia Project.

Haque, Ehsanul. 2016. Interview by Sharad K Soni for China Studies in South Asia Project.

Hossein, Delwar. 2016. Interview by Sharad K Soni for China Studies in South Asia Project.

Islam, Serajul. 2012. Interview by Reena Marwah for China Studies in South Asia Project.

Kabir, Mahfuz. 2016. Expanding the Bangladesh-China trade frontier (10 October), http://www.thedailystar.net/op-ed/politics/expanding-the-bangladesh-china-trade-frontier-1296583. Accessed on July 8, 2017.

Kathmandu University (KU). 2007. Confucius Institute at KU, http://www.ku.edu.np/ci/index.php?go=home. Accessed on July 5, 2017.

Kathmandu University (KU). 2009. Opening Ceremony of the Chinese Language Course, http://www.ku.edu.np/ci/index.php?go=nathm. Accessed on July 5, 2017.

Kashinath, Prarthana. 2016. To Fend Off China, India Must Galvanize Ties With Bangladesh, *The Diplomat* (29 October), http://thediplomat.com/2016/10/to-fend-off-china-india-must-galvanize-ties-with-bangladesh/. Accessed on July 10, 2017.

Khan, Abdur Rob. 2016. Interview by Reena Marwah for China Studies in South Asia Project.

Koirala, Bhasker. 2016. Interview by Reena Marwah for China Studies in South Asia Project.

Marwah, Reena and Soni, Sharad K. 2010. Tibetans in South Asia: A Research Note. *Asian Ethnicity* 11(2): 263–268.

Masood, Asma. 2015. India–Bangladesh–China Relations: A Complex Triangle, *Myanmar Business Today* (30 March), 3(13), http://www.mmbiztoday.com/articles/india-bangladesh-china-relations-complex-triangle. Accessed on July 10, 2017.

Patel, Dharmesh. The Entangled Triangle of Nepal, India and China. *Culture Mandala: Bulletin of the Centre for East-West Cultural and Economic Studies* 10(2): 41–44.

Parashar, Sachin. 2016. Nepal–China Military Drill Worries India, *The Times of India* (27 December), http://timesofindia.indiatimes.com/india/

nepal-china-military-drill-worries-india/articleshow/56191873.cms. Accessed on July 10, 2017.
Pemble, John. 1971. *The Invasion of Nepal: John Company at War*, London: Constable and Co. Ltd.
Rajan, D. S. 2011. China and South Asia — An Indian Perspective, *C3S Paper* 723 (25 January), http://www.c3sindia.org/india/2099. Accessed on July 7, 2017.
Raman, B. 2012. China's Strategic Eggs in South Asia, *South Asia Analysis Group*, Paper no. 4595 (12 July), http://www.southasiaanalysis.org/%5Cpapers46%5Cpaper4595.html. Accessed on July 7, 2017.
Ranade, Jayadeva. 2014. Chinese Tilt to Indo-Nepal Axis, *The New Indian Express* (18 February), http://www.pressreader.com/india/the-new-indian-express/20140218/281951720720865. Accessed on July 7, 2017.
Regmi, Madan. 2012. Interview by Sharad Soni for China Studies in South Asia Project.
Sami, C.M. Shafi. 2012. Bangladesh: A Partner for Peace and Prosperity. In S.D. Muni and Tan Tai Yong (Eds.), *A Resurgent China: South Asian Perspectives*. New Delhi: Routledge, pp. 8–42.
Shih, Chih-yu. 2013. China Rise Syndromes? Drafting National Schools of International Relations in Asia, *Intercultural Communication Studies* 22(1): 9–25.
Shreshtha, Hiranya Lal. 2012. Interview by Sharad K Soni for China Studies in South Asia Project.
Simkhada, Shambhu Ram. 2012. Nepal: A Benign Neighbourhood. In S.D. Muni and Tan Tai Yong (Eds.), *A Resurgent China: South Asian Perspectives*. New Delhi: Routledge, pp. 145–175.
Soni, Sharad K. 2016. Buddhist Influence on China Studies in Mongolia: Exploring the Mongol-China-Tibet Linkages In Prapin Manomaivibool and Chih-Yu Shih (Eds.), *Understanding 21st Century China in Buddhist Asia: History, Modernity and International Relations*, Bangkok: Asia Research Centre, Chulalongkorn University, pp. 157–181.
Soni, Sharad K. 2016. Sino-Mongolian Relations in the Twenty-First Century: The Inner Mongolia Factor. In Michael Clarke and Douglas Smith (Eds.), *China's Frontier Regions: Ethnicity, Economic Integration and Foreign Relations*, London and New York: I. B. Tauris, pp. 140–170.
Soni, Sharad K. 2009. China's Periphery Policy: Implications for Sino-Mongolian Relations, *India Quarterly* 65(3): 251–269.

Soni, Sharad K and Marwah, Reena. 2011. Tibet as a Factor Impacting China Studies in India, *Asian Ethnicity* 12(3): 285–299.
Thapliyal, Sangeeta. 2017. Nepal's Trans-Himalayan Linkages with China, *Scholar Warrior*, Spring 46–54, http://www.claws.in/images/journals_doc/945177134_06_chap.pdf. Accessed on July 9, 2017.
Tiwari, Chitra K. 2013. China–Nepal Border: Potential Hot Spot?. In Bruce A. Elleman, Stephen Kotkin, and Clive Schofield (Eds.), *Beijing's Power and China's Borders: Twenty Neighbors in Asia*. New Delhi: Pentagon Press, pp. 205–217.
Yasmin, Lailufar. 2016. Interview by Reena Marwah for China Studies in South Asia Project.
Yasmin, Lailufar. 2009. Bangladesh-China Relations: Some Perspectives, *Himalayan and Central Asian Studies* 13(4): 74–78.
Zhao, Suisheng. 2004. The Making of China's Periphery Policy. In Suisheng Zhao (Ed.), *Chinese Foreign Policy: Pragmatism and Strategic Behavior*. Armonk: M.E. Sharpe, pp. 256–275.

Part IV

External Perspectives

11

An American Perspective on Vietnam's Sinology

James A. Anderson
Department of History
University of North Carolina at Greensboro, United States

"Mountains and rivers have demarcated the border [of our country]. The customs of the North [China] and the South [Viet Nam] are also different. We find [in antiquity] that the Triệu, the Đinh, the Lý, and Trần [dynasties] built our country. Alongside the Han, Tang Song, and Yuan [dynasties], the rulers [of our dynasties] ruled as emperors over their own part [of the world represented by the North and the South]."[1]

Nguyễn Trãi 阮廌 (1428) "The Great Declaration of the Wu's (China's) Pacification"

Many Vietnamese Sinologists in the modern era have sought in their research to explore a cultural "common ground" in the Sino-Vietnamese relationship while also highlighting political differences between the Chinese and Vietnamese states. Modern Vietnamese Sinology shares a general similarity with Vietnamese and Chinese traditional scholarship, in which "learning from antiquity" was paramount and the Chinese writing system was the tool for acquiring

---
[1] Translation from Wolters and Reynolds (2008: 209).

this learning. Language is the key to understanding elements of the shared Sino-Vietnamese tradition, as well as an important tool for distinguishing the strong differences between Vietnamese and Chinese societies. The premodern Vietnamese political elite generally read this scholarship with a practical interest in learning from the day-to-day statecraft of the past.

Even with this general link to traditional scholarship, modern Vietnamese Sinologists have faced unique challenges in their own times. The generation of Vietnamese scholars who received their formal education before 1975 were affected by the social upheaval of wartime, particularly for those scholars educated during the 1960s–1970s. Regarding the community of scholars trained after 1975, one will also note how renewed global linkages eventually shaped their scholarly methods and interests. This post-1975 generation was initially confronted with economic hardships, as well as the effects of the US-led embargo and cold relations with China in the aftermath of the 1979 border conflict. These factors limited scholarly contacts throughout the early 1990s. However, shortly after diplomatic relations with the PRC improved, members of this younger generation interacted more frequently with their Chinese counterparts as visiting scholars at PRC universities or as participants in international conferences. They also participated in other Sinology-focused academic exchanges hosted in Hong Kong, Taiwan, and overseas at various institutions in the West. The focus on Chinese language study remained important, but many scholars in the younger generation were required to develop a more varied set of research skills to address the questions posed by the Vietnamese government agencies that supported their research. In more recent years engagement with Western scholarship has become a significant factor in Vietnamese academic circles. This chapter also examines the differences between scholars who work in the formal academic institutions and those who choose for a variety of reasons to work outside "the Academy."

The chapter ends with the conclusion that Modern Vietnamese Sinology requires a more diverse set of academic skills, but that language training remains a central expectation. An admiration for China as a subject of study, tempered by an effort to maintain the historical distinctions that separate Vietnam from China, is apparent in the work of most of the Vietnamese scholarship examined here. Vietnamese Sinologists continue to seek a separate path for Vietnam as the country navigates its own journey into the future through the same waters as its large northern neighbor.

Introduction

An American perspective on Vietnam's Sinology first and foremost requires the re-education of the researcher to rid oneself of the historical myopia many Americans suffer from when confronted with the long, complex relationship between China and Vietnam. As a Westerner studying the history of Sino-Vietnamese relations, I decided early on to turn my focus away from the short period of the US involvement in Vietnam toward the much more significant premodern era of Sino-Vietnamese interactions. More recently I have been fascinated with the nearly 1,000-year-long period, during which political elite serving northern ("Chinese") regimes and southern ("Vietnamese") courts located in the Red (Hồng) River Delta have engaged one another through the medium of Sinitic script. I would argue that the literary conventions and philosophical schools of thought circulated between China and Vietnam through the Chinese character-based writing system and shared by a unified Sino-Vietnamese scholarly tradition provided a strong foundation for modern-day Vietnamese Sinological study, as evidenced by an analysis of the interviews with scholars conducted for this chapter.

Language training in both literary and modern Chinese is the key to understanding elements of the shared Sino-Vietnamese tradition, as well as an important tool for distinguishing the strong differences between Vietnamese and Chinese societies. While John Phan has argued effectively for the emergence of a distinct Vietnamese vernacular in the 10th-century period of political independence, the written language of political elite remained character-based.² Throughout the premodern period, through diplomatic communication, imperial edicts, official memorials and court chronicles, and private writing, scholars participated in a *Guwen*-centered (Cổ văn 古文) textual community that shaped the images they circulated about both China and Vietnam. Even after the development of the Vietnamese demotic script Chữ nôm 字喃, descriptions of Sino-Vietnamese cultural differences were communicated through a writing system, which initially took shape in societies located on the central plain (*zhongyuan* 中原) of North China. Although there now exists some debate about the actual geographical references to "North" and "South" in Nguyễn Trãi's famous declaration cited above following Ming's defeat by Lê Lợi (1385–1433) and his followers, centuries of Vietnamese scholars have accepted that training in the Confucian classics and deep knowledge of ancient Chinese history have produced the basic textual context required to construct a separate historical and cultural identity for the society that emerged on the Red River Delta and over time extended itself as modern Vietnam. Modern Vietnamese Sinology requires a more diverse set of academic skills, but language training remains a central expectation.

This chapter is divided into the following themes. First, I set the stage for modern Vietnamese Sinology by reviewing the communities and the difference between Vietnamese and Chinese traditional scholarship. I then discuss the generation of Vietnamese Sinologists, who received their initial training in the period before national reunification in 1975. I will then compare this early generation with the community of scholars trained after 1975, and note how the global linkages of this newer generation have shaped their scholarly

---

²Referring to the region of northern upland and lowland Vietnam in the 10th century, Phan argued for "the existence of a local dialect of Middle Chinese, its obsolescence in favor of Proto-Viet–Muong, and the eventual emergence of a new language from among the hybridized dialects that followed," a linguistic transformation that accompanied the political separation of the polity located in the Red (Hồng) River Delta from the Southern Han regime (see Phan, 2010).

methods and interests. I then examine the differences between scholars who work in the formal academic institutions and those who choose for a variety of reasons to work outside "the Academy." I will conclude with some notes on the future of Vietnamese scholarship on China.

Commonalities and Differences Between Vietnamese and Chinese Traditional Scholarship

Since premodern times there have existed commonalities and differences between Vietnamese and Chinese traditional scholarship. Premodern Vietnamese annalist histories did not appear until the 14th century, and compilers of these court-based histories largely followed the examples of their Chinese counterparts. The most prominent Vietnamese text describing Sino-Việt relations in the 10th and 11th centuries is the *Đại Việt Sử Ký Toàn Thư* 大越史記全書 (DVSKTT), compiled in 1479 under the direction of Ngô Sĩ Liên 吳士連 (fl. 1442–1479). This Vietnamese history was written a century after one of its main sources was compiled, the no longer extant text *Đại Việt sử ký* of Lê Văn Hưu 黎文修 (1230–1322), which was completed in 1272. This history was commissioned by the Trần emperor to express the independent nature of the Việt kingdom, in the shadow of its looming northern neighbor. Lê Văn Hưu's account recorded the history of the Việt kingdom through the end of the Lê Dynasty in 1224. Lê Văn Hưu's reasons for composing his history would have seemed familiar to his Chinese contemporaries. He sought to instruct and admonish the Trần court through lessons drawn from the past. Tales of strong and weak rulers, capable and inferior court advisors were all included in Lê Văn Hưu's work to remind contemporary leaders of paths to take and decisions to contemplate. The Trần court's reason for ordering Lê Văn Hưu to compile his history of the region was likely to bolster claims of autonomy by the Trần court in the face of growing aggression from the North. Such a detailed record of a long-standing independent Vietnamese state provided a source of strength for Trần envoys, who could insist that Vietnam's tributary relationship with China had historically made room for the region's *de facto* independence.

Lê Tắc's 14th-century history *An Nam chí lược* 安南志略 created a "common ground" that could be found among the scholarly communities that considered "learning from antiquity" to be paramount and took the medium of the Chinese writing system as the tool for acquiring this learning (Anderson 2001). Lê Văn Hưu would have certainly understood Lê Tắc's use of antiquity to provide examples for contemporary rulers and their learned advisors to follow. However, Lê Tắc's work would have also resonated with Chinese scholars who made the difficult decision to serve under a "conquest dynasty." Many officials from the former Song court withdrew from service rather than serving in the government of the conquering Mongols, and many other officials used their Confucian idealism as a reason to emulate this group. As Lê Tắc might have argued, someone still need to step forward in service, and such assistance was certainly required to maintain stability and coherence in the Sino-Viet tributary relationship.

Due to the fact that the 15th-century Vietnamese chronicler Ngô Sĩ Liên also used as his historiographical model the work of the Song scholar, Sima Guang 司馬光 (1019–1086), the DVSKTT text contains many stylistic characteristics of earlier Chinese works. Much of the terminology from the DVSKTT was borrowed from Sima Guang's *Comprehensive Mirror in Aid of Governance* (*Zizhi Tongjian* 資治通鑑). However, Ngô Sĩ Liên wrote with a somewhat different purpose, and searched for more concrete examples to illustrate his points. The political elite generally read this history with a practical interest in learning from the day-to-day statecraft of the past. The "moralizing vocabulary of the Confucian cannon," a prominent feature of most Chinese historical writing after the rise of Neo-Confucianism was not so highly visible in Vietnamese writing (Wolters 1986). O.W. Wolters writes that "the texts (of Vietnamese history) were not read in order to study a 'Confucianist' ideology. Instead, they would have been seen as resembling an encyclopedia of recorded wisdom that the Vietnamese could consult in ways that seemed relevant in reorganizing specific situations, such as an imperial succession, and the specific measures that those situations seemed to require" (Wolters 1979). Alexander Woodside (1988) argued the same point when the Nguyễn linked its imperial legitimacy to state-building efforts, in which its Confucian-trained elite relied on "the Chinese model." A similar use of China's past to provide guidance for Vietnam's future appears in the work of modern Vietnamese Sinologists, including older scholars such as Nguyễn Quang Hồng and younger scholars such as Phùng Thị Huệ, who indicated in her interview that she wishes to combines research on modern Chinese political policy with a research interest in Ancient Chinese political philosophy to understand China's recent successes and failures better and what these same factors could mean for similar developments in Vietnam.

The Pre-1975 Generation of Vietnamese Sinologists

The generation of Vietnamese scholars who received their formal education before 1975 were shaped by the social upheaval around them. This distinction was most dramatic for those educated during the 1960s–1970s period. The physical dislocation of many individuals in this generation and the large number that ended their careers working outside of formal academic institutions are both distinguishing features of a group of Sinologists. The First Indochina War (1946–1954) and then the American War (late 1950s–1975) made sustained study in one location difficult, scattered, or made major archival connections inaccessible, and disrupted the institutional linkages between centers of learning located in northern and southern Vietnam. Through all this turmoil, this generation of scholars either worked with the support of smaller communities of like-minded researchers or found state-sponsored support for training and research in the PRC through Beijing's alliance with the DRV.

Cao Tự Thanh, the pen name of Cao Văn Dũng since April 1975, is a good example of a scholar, whose early training prepared him for a career of working among Sino-Vietnamese literature, but whose later experiences would shape his working life and his relationship with the formal institutions of Vietnamese Sinology. Cao Tự Thanh was born in 1955 in Saigon, but he received his formal training in

Sino-Nôm studies in the North, graduating from the Department of Philology at Hà Nội University in 1977. Cao Tự Thanh's retirement from the Long An Provincial Bureau of Culture and Information in 1990 at the age of 35 caused the scholar to leave his formal instruction support behind at an early age. He has since then made a living privately as a translator of numerous works of popular fiction, including romance fiction and juvenile literature, as well as translations of short studies of traditional Chinese culture aimed at a general readership. Prior to retiring from the Bureau of Culture and Information, in addition to translations of Chinese literary classics, he translated, annotated, and edited the collected work of prominent scholars from the Nguyễn period including the southern Vietnamese anti-colonial poet Nguyễn Đình Chiểu 阮廷沼 (1822–1888). Cao Tự Thanh has also contributed works of Sinological scholarship to his field, including studies of Sino-Nôm literature of Vietnam's southern region (Nam Bộ) and a translation of the modern Chinese intellectual Hu Shi's 胡適 (1891–1962) *The Development of the Logical Method in Ancient China*. In his interview, Cao Tự Thanh argues that his work in China studies reached beyond literature to include premodern ("feudal") history, culture, and society.

Nguyễn Tôn Nhan is another good representative of this early generation, who made a living in tumultuous times. He is from a family of scholars with a grandfather, who failed the final regional civil service examination (Thi hương) offered by the Nguyễn court in the North in 1915 and returned to his home village in Hải Dương to work as a tutor of Sino-Nôm literature for the rest of his life. In 1954, his family left the North to resettle in Gia Định, close to the metropolitan center of Saigon. He studied Chinese literature and history in a self-guided and unstructured fashion for most of his youth, although he received guidance from both Professors Bửu Cầm and Nghiêm Toản at the Saigon School of Arts and Sciences (Trường Văn Khoa Sài Gòn). Nguyễn Tôn Nhan did not enter an institutional setting for his research, but continued to make an early living primarily from his translations of Chinese classic Daoist texts and work on other Sino-Vietnamese reference works. Even under these fairly austere conditions he managed to make a living. Nguyễn

Tôn Nhan professed in his interview a great affinity for the figures from China's ancient past, particularly the poets of the Tang and Song period, mirroring the type of connection that the traditional scholar elite noted in their own work. In his translations, he is in dialogue with earlier Vietnamese translators of these texts, in particular the translation of the 8th-century edition of Zhuangzi 莊子, subtitled the "True Scripture of Southern Florescence" (*Nan Hua Jing* 諵譁經) by Nguyễn Duy Cần. Nguyễn Tôn Nhan's edition is expanded and completely annotated, a sign of the careful scholarship practiced in Vietnamese academic circles in more recent years.

Nguyễn Tôn Nhan's interest in the ritual aspects of Confucianism has been a major factor in his work's enduring popularity. He refers to Trần Trọng Kim (1883–1953), the well-known scholar of premodern Vietnamese history and Sino-Vietnamese cultural exchange, whose work has enjoyed widespread contemporary popularity, despite his service in the Japanese-led collaborationist regime at the end of WWII. The historiographical perspective of Trần Trọng Kim and Vietnamese researchers of his era remained close to the orthodox histories presented in court chronicles of premodern Vietnamese dynasties, and so their presentation of Confucian values remained in the realm of political and intellectual history. Nguyễn Tôn Nhan's work on Confucianism highlights the religious qualities of the texts he translates and analyzes, bringing a new dimension to the works, which appeal to a modern readership searching for a new value in the study of Confucian ideas. Treating Confucianism as a religious tradition also reflects Nguyễn Tôn Nhan's inclination toward incorporating the approaches of social history in his research.

Phạm Thị Hảo, one of the few women included among these interviews, is an example of the earlier generation of Sinologists, coming from a scholar-elite family from the northern province of Nam Định. Her grandfather participated in the provincial civil service exams, and her father was a teacher of both Chinese and modern Vietnamese language. Phạm Thị Hảo received her initial training in Sinology through a DRV-sponsored program in 1951 at the Nanning University of Foreign Languages (Guangxi Nanning Waiyu Daxue 廣西南寧外語大學), where she studied Chinese literature and linguistics, eventually becoming an instructor for overseas Vietnamese students at the same institution. She later received a position at the Hanoi University of Pedagogy (Trường Đại Học Sư Phạm Hà Nội), where she remained until 1976, at which point she continued her career at the HCM City University of Pedagogy, eventually becoming the Chair of the Department of Philology until her retirement in 1987. Her research interests range from pedagogical materials to traditional and modern Chinese literature. Her exposure at a young age to Chinese literature instilled in her a love for Chinese fiction, both prose and poetry. Her publications have ranged from textbooks on modern Chinese and classical Chinese grammar, a translation of the famous modern Chinese author Lu Xun's *Wild Grass* (*Ye Cao* 野草), to a more recent effort to translate and annotate a large portion of the Chinese classic *The Book of Songs* (*Shijing* 詩經).

While teaching at the Hanoi University of Pedagogy, Phạm Thị Hảo worked with a number of prominent Vietnamese Sinologists, who would comprise a specific School of China studies from this early era DRV rule, including Lê Thước (1891–1975), Phạm Phú Tiệt, Cao Xuân Huy (1900–1983), Nguyễn Kỳ Nam, Đỗ Ngọc Toại, Đào Phương Bình, Phạm Thiều (1904–1986), and Hoàng Thúc Trâm (1902–1977). The Institute of Han-Nôm Studies (Viện Nghiên Cứu Hán Nôm) provided an institutional center for this community of scholars, but their appointment were located at institutions throughout Hanoi and, after 1975, in Saigon as well. Phạm Thị Hảo notes in her interview that these scholars encouraged her love for both ancient Chinese literature and the corpus of imperial period Vietnamese literature originally written in Classical Chinese. Phạm Thị Hảo in her interview divides the pre-1975 world of Vietnamese Sinology into the Northern School and the Southern School. From her perspective, the first modern generations of the Northern School, including the scholars Đặng Đức Siêu, Nguyễn Ngọc San, Phan Hữu Nghệ, and Phan Văn Các, received their Sinological training in the People's Republic of China. She also includes a first modern generation of the Southern School, which included Nguyễn Tri Tài and Nguyễn Khuê.

The Post-1975 Generation of Scholars

The generation of scholars who received training and began their careers after national reunification in 1975 faced very different challenges from the early generation of Sinologists. In a time of relative peace, this post-1975 generation was still confronted with economic hardship, as well as the effects of the US-led embargo and cold relations with China in the aftermath of the 1979 border conflict that limited scholarly contacts throughout the early 1990s. Shortly after diplomatic relations with the PRC improved, members of this younger generation interacted more frequently with their Chinese counterparts as visiting scholars at PRC universities or as participants in international conferences. They participated in other Sinological academic exchanges hosted in Hong Kong, Taiwan, and overseas at various institutions in the West. The new era of openness resulted in the circulation of new primary sources and data sources from abroad, including new theoretical approaches introduced in Western scholarly circles. At the same time, Vietnamese governmental agencies sought input from academicians on policy issues associated with Sino-Vietnamese relations, causing research in the social sciences to receive a greater emphasis. The focus on language study was not displaced by these new concerns, but many scholars in the younger generation were required to develop a more varied set of research skills to address the new questions their government patrons asked of them.

Members of this younger generation arrived at their positions from various paths of life. Phùng Thị Huệ noted in her interview that her route to researching China was not a straight line. In high school she loved literature, but she did not like studying Chinese. However by the time she joined college, Phùng Thị Huệ had developed an interest and she graduated from the Department of Chinese. She attended graduate school from 1978 to 1981, where she specialized in Han Nôm studies. At about the time of her graduation the Vietnam Academy of Social Sciences (Viện Hàn lâm Khoa học xã hội Việt Nam) started a Chinese research group (Viện Nghiên cứu Trung quốc) and in 1983 she took a position at VASS, where she remains to this day. She noted in her interview that most of her research time is spent addressing issues of interest to her institute and, I would extrapolate, the government agencies that VASS advises. Phùng Thị Huệ noted that China studies today are conducted for the benefit of maintaining friendly bilateral relations, and that her effort serves the Foreign Service and the research community in equal parts. In a modern sense, Phùng Thị Huệ's work resembles the efforts of Vietnamese court officials in the premodern period, seeking to understand China with the goal of smoothing out various aspects of the Sino-Vietnamese relationship.

Other younger scholars contribute to this aim to better bilateral Sino-Vietnamese relations through their research, even if their own research inclinations would proceed in a different direction. Nguyễn Thị Thu Phương began her studies with a strong interest in literature, but found in her career that her research would be guided by the dictates of her institution. One of the youngest scholars included in this study, Nguyễn Thị Thu Phương studied in the Department of Literature as an undergraduate at National Hanoi University from 1991 to 1995, and between 1997 and 2004 she received her Master's and doctorate degrees studied at VASS in the Institute of Literature. From 2001 to 2002 she was a visiting scholar in Guangxi, and in 2003 she visited sites in Hangzhou to gather information and to conduct interviews with Chinese experts. Although Nguyễn Thị Thu Phương considers her greatest achievement to have been the publication of her book *The Song Ci Poetry of Su Dongpo* (宋詞 蘇東波), she has not been able to continue to follow her own interest of writing more on this subject. She notes in her interview that her interests and the research requests of the Institute differ greatly, but she hopes in the future to be able to conduct studies according to her own interests.

"Academy" vs. "Non-academy" Scholars

As noted earlier, Vietnamese Sinology comprises scholars working inside and outside of formal academic institutions, and their institutional affiliation has an impact on the opinions of the current states of China studies in Vietnam. Cao Tự Thanh's relatively early departure from formal academic circles and state-supported research may explain his ambivalence regarding the current state of Chinese history taught in the Vietnamese educational system, which he termed "very poor, biased and outdated (*rất nghèo nàn, phiến diện và lạc hậu*)." His perspective is one of a scholar working outside "the system." He is not responsible for the public ramifications of his work, other than his desire to make a living by generating popular interest through his publications. Another scholar working outside of academia Nguyễn Tôn Nhan's description of working with publishers through advances on a book contract over two to three years is a dramatically different relationship than the academy-bound Vietnamese Sinologists have with their institutional patrons. Nguyễn Tôn Nhan has this arrangement because, he argues, his publishers trust his judgment in these larger scholarly projects. He also appears to have flexibility in his approach to the subject matters that the instructional scholars do not possess, and Nguyễn Tôn Nhan's close relationship with his publishers is another striking difference.

Phạm Thị Hảo is a strong example of an institutional scholar, who managed to make a career of teaching and writing with full support of the Vietnamese state. Her outlook on the field is very positive, although she is also concerned about the Chinese language training of future generations of Vietnamese scholars. The younger Sinologists included here, Phùng Thị Huệ and Nguyễn Thị Thu Phương, have strong institutional affiliations as state employees of VASS, and they both are optimistic that greater engagement with foreign intellectual currents will bring future benefits to Vietnamese Sinological research. For all three of these scholars, their stable careers in the Academy provide benefits, while their positions also require that they follow the research needs of their institutions. And of all the scholars examined in this study, the research profiles of Phùng Thị Huệ and Nguyễn Thị Thu Phương are most closely aligned with the current trends in modern Sino-Vietnamese relations.

The Future of Vietnamese Scholarship on China

Cao Tự Thanh does not have a good opinion of contemporary Vietnamese scholarship on China, blaming an overreliance on Western scholarly influences and a lack of rigorous Chinese language training for diluting Vietnamese scholars' abilities to study China in a perceptive and systematic manner. His pessimism is shared by some of the other researchers, but there appears to be a generational divide in opinion. Another scholar of the older generation, Nguyễn Tôn Nhan is enthusiastic about the future of his own efforts to preserve the Sino-Vietnamese literary tradition for a new generation of readers through his translation projects; however, his positive outlook is somewhat tempered by the more sober opinions of the younger Vietnamese Sinologists. Phạm Thị Hảo argues that the latest generation of Vietnamese Sinologists benefit from opportunities to study abroad, but that the ability to read texts in literary Chinese has now diminished. Common to many generations of classically-trained scholars, Phạm Thị Hảo has hope for what future researchers may gain but concern for the loss of rigor in text-based training, at which traditional scholars had once excelled.

Younger scholars are more optimistic, and as for the value of Western scholarship on China specifically, these younger Sinologists have a variety of opinions. Western funding agencies now play a part of supporting some Vietnamese scholars, which is a significant departure from the recent past. When asked about funding for her current research, Phùng Thị Huệ replied that a small part of funding had been provided by the Ford Foundation, another part by Japan, but that the majority of her research is funded by the Vietnamese government. Even with the Western funding she noted that she had limited contact with Western China scholars, while she maintained numerous contacts among Chinese scholars. However, Phùng Thị Huệ does assert that her study of China involves a combination of methodologies, and that she incorporates many Western ideas and methods because the quality of Western research on China is very high. Therefore, while personal engagement with Western scholars may be limited (although there are many Vietnamese scholars spending long periods overseas), engagement with Western scholarship has become a significant factor in Vietnamese academic circles.

Considering future Vietnamese research on China, Nguyễn Thị Thu Phương reflects on this question at length. She contends that in the future Vietnamese research will be more comprehensive because many more Vietnamese Sinologists will have the opportunity to study overseas. As a result, their scholarly views will be more objective because Vietnamese Sinologist will begin to see their subject matter from many perspectives rather than from a single viewpoint. Nguyễn Thị Thu Phương argues that Vietnamese scholarship on China was once narrowly focused and subjective because the earlier generation of Sinologists were influenced by their own experience in studying China. Moreover, the older generation's limited ability in foreign languages restricted their use of Western scholarship on China. Therefore, past Vietnamese Sinological scholarship was not nearly as objective as future scholarship will be. Nguyễn Thị Thu Phương contends that Vietnamese scholars of China may be constrained in their research in terms of the subject matter, but in the future they will be able to demonstrate their independent thinking and logical thinking in their research.

Concluding Thoughts

For Vietnamese Sinologists working in the modern era, this search for a "common ground" in the Sino-Vietnamese relationship while simultaneously seeking difference continues to be important. The Han Nôm scholar Professor Nguyễn Quang Hồng indicated in his interview that there is still utility in studying the Chinese model. As he noted, "Studying China from Viet Nam can be difficult, but one must show courage ... The Vietnamese show such bravery, because they must ... many East Asian countries benefited from (Chinese) learning, but (China) is not Viet Nam ... There were so many Chinese people, who came here to help the people of Viet Nam win national independence. So, for China, first of all we give our respect, we learn and study, we immerse ourselves (in the study of China), but we have to find the differences ... That's always true." This admiration for China as a subject of study while maintaining the historical and cultural distinctions that separate Vietnam from China appear to animate all the scholars examined here. Vietnamese Sinologists will continue to seek a separate path for Vietnam as the country navigates its own journey into the future through the same waters as its large northern neighbor.

References

Anderson, James A. 2001. The ANCL as Common Ground: Le Tac's Private History and its Sino-Vietnamese Audience. Boston: American Historical Association's 115th Annual Meeting, January 4–7.

Phan, John D. 2010. Re-imagining Annam: A Preliminary Look at the Languages of the Northern, Vietnamese Plains at the Turn of the 1st Millennium, *China Southern Diaspora Studies* 4: 3–24.

Wolters, Oliver William. 1979. Historians and Emperors in Vietnam and China: Comments Arising out of Le Van Huu's History, Presented to the Tran court in 1272. *Perceptions of the Past in Southeast Asia*, edited by Anthony Reid and David Marr, p. 84. Singapore: Heinemann Educational Books Ltd.

Wolters, Oliver William. 1986. Possibilities for a Reading of the 1293–1357 Period in the Vietnamese Annals. In Marr, David G. and A.C. Milner (Eds.), *Southeast Asia in the 9th to 14th Centuries*, p. 372. Cambridge: Cambridge University Press.

Wolters, O. W. and Craig J. Reynolds. 2008. *Early Southeast Asia: Selected Essays*. Ithaca, New York: Southeast Asia Program, Cornell University.

Woodside, Alexander. 1988. *Vietnam and the Chinese Model: A Comparative Study of Vietnamese and Chinese Government in the First Half of the Nineteenth Century*. Cambridge: Harvard University Press.

12

The Knowledge of Vietnamese Intellectual Class to China: Focusing on the Seventeen Vietnamese Scholars Interviewed by National Taiwan University

Xiangdong Yu*
Vietnamese Studies Institute, Zhengzhou University, Collaborative Innovation Center for Territorial Sovereignty and Maritime Rights

Sijia Cheng*
School of History, Zhengzhou University

Vietnam as a neighboring country of China has the tradition of studying and researching China since ancient times, and thus gradually forming the Vietnamese intellectual class' knowledge on China. The Vietnamese intellectual class' knowledge on

---

*Xiangdong Yu is Professor at the School of the Marxism Studies in Zhengzhou University, and also heads the Vietnamese Studies Institute at the Zhengzhou University. He is the author of *Vietnam* (1998) and of numerous works on Vietnamese history. His email address is yuxd@zzu.edu.cn. Sijia Cheng is a doctoral candidate at the School of History in Zhengzhou University. His email address is chengsj89@126.com.

China has abundant connotations, including both the knowledge and understanding of China, knowledge and understanding of Vietnam, Vietnamese people, and even the world with China as the media. From the perspectives of history and culture, Vietnamese intellectual class' knowledge on China was formed during the long-term contacts between China and Vietnam, and was also influenced by the then existing Han culture in Vietnam, Western education's development in modern times, and Vietnamese scholars who went to China to study from the 1950s to 1970s. The contemporary Vietnamese intellectual class, especially those who are engaged in China research, may be classified into three basic types, which are North Vietnamese intellectuals group, South Vietnamese intellectuals group, and the new generation of intellectuals after reunification. They acquired their knowledge on China through various means and under different conditions. Vietnamese intellectual class' knowledge and view on China not only helped Vietnam to know and understand China, but also to understand ancient Vietnam's traditional history and culture, and discuss the social problems and further enrich Vietnam's treasure house of knowledge.

Sinology, or China Studies, is a subject of much importance to current Vietnam, and there are quite a few scholars engaged in China studies both in the government and among the people. These scholars' knowledge on China could influence both the current development of the Sino-Vietnamese relations and the political, economic, cultural, and social aspects of Vietnam. The study project "Epistemologies for Thinking China" carried out by the Department of Political Science of National Taiwan University includes oral interviews with 25 scholars who are engaged in China studies. The Vietnamese intellectual class' way to access Chinese knowledge and their learning on China could be learned to some extent through 17 interviews out of the 25 interviews.[1] With the invitation from Professor Shi Zhiyu of NTU, the author intends to use these oral historical materials, combined with the history and current status between China and Vietnam, to discuss the Vietnamese intellectual class' knowledge on China, and the view of China formed during the process.

---

[1] For all the 17 interviews, please visit http://politics.ntu.edu.tw/RAEC/act02.php.

Connotation of Vietnamese Intellectual Class' Knowledge on China

When foreign intellectual class' knowledge on China is mentioned, we first think about Western scholars, mainly Western sinologists' understanding and research on China. Their knowledge on China, basically speaking, is knowledge and understanding from an international point of view. Compared with Western sinologists, since Vietnam is bordering southern China, Vietnamese intellectual class' knowledge on China has more abundant connotations. Specifically, it mainly consists of the following aspects.

First, knowledge and understanding on China itself. Due to the very close historical and cultural origins between China and Vietnam, Vietnamese people's, especially those of the intellectual class, knowledge on China date back many years, and many contemporary Vietnamese scholars think, "In Vietnam, people's research on Sinology started from the time when their ancestors first made contacts with China" (Pan 2005). Vietnamese intellectual class' knowledge and understanding on China itself includes abundant content, with both unique knowledge and understanding of traditional Chinese history and culture, and the continuous study on the development path and mode explored by China since modern times. Just judging from the 17 interviewed scholars, their understanding and research on China itself involve Chinese philology, linguistics, literature, history, religious study, traditional thoughts and culture, socialism theories with Chinese characteristics, and the practice and experience of contemporary China's development, almost covering the history and culture of China from ancient times to the present day.

Second, knowledge and understanding on Vietnam and Vietnamese people from the Chinese perspective. Vietnamese intellectual class' knowledge on China does not only include comprehensive understanding and grasp of Chinese tradition and reality but also the knowledge and understanding on Vietnam and Vietnamese people from the Chinese perspective. For example, a Vietnamese scholar's knowledge on China from Qin dynasty to

Tang dynasty is not only an understanding of ancient China but also an understanding of ancient Vietnam, which was under the jurisdiction of the Chinese county back then. Vietnam's officially edited history books, *Dai Viet Su Ky Toan Thu* and *Kham Định Viet Su Thong Giam Cuong Mục*, when editing their unofficial records of history, heavily referenced and quoted records of ancient Vietnam in Chinese history books. Just as Lv Shipeng depicted in *Vietnam Under Chinese Jurisdiction Period*: "relationship between China and Vietnam has endured over two thousand years, as Chinese nation and Vietnamese nation were under the same political administration for over half the time, so in politic, the first thousand years is already indispensable"(Lu 1977); Vietnamese scholars' research on China's opening up and reform and socialism theories with Chinese characteristics is not restricted to the knowledge and understanding of contemporary China, and it includes a lesson for the ongoing opening up and reform in Vietnam. Professor Xiangdong Yu once said, "Vietnam pays great attention to learning from the experience of China's opening up and reform, and published many books regarding China's opening up and reform, and the most important book should be the Vietnamese version of Volume III of *The Selected Works of Deng Xiaoping* published in the early period of 90s of the 20th Century" (Yu 2016).

Third, knowledge and understanding of the world with China as the media. Vietnamese intellectual class' knowledge on China does not only include the knowledge and understanding of China, Vietnam, and Vietnamese people but also knowledge and understanding of the world acquired with China as the media. It is widely known that due to geological and traffic restrictions, ancient Vietnam's knowledge of the world was extremely limited. Except for the understanding of a few neighboring countries (such as Champa Kingdom) and trading countries (such as Japan), its basic knowledge and understanding of the world is acquired with the help of China as the media. Specifically speaking, first, Vietnamese governing class took ancient China's knowledge and understanding generally, and viewed and treated foreign countries (except China) based on Chinese traditional perspective and China's outlook on foreign countries, and Ly Van Phuc even proposed "the idea of Chinese and foreign countries should only be sought in articles and formalities," and "if Vietnam should be foreign, I don't know what else is Chinese" (Ly 2011: 235); second, Vietnam also learned about other countries and the world by sending envoys to China to communicate with envoys of other countries, for example, in Ming and Qing dynasties, Vietnamese envoys in China often communicated with Korean envoys through writings and poems. During the Wanli period of the Ming dynasty, Vietnamese envoy Phung Khac Khoan and Korean envoy Li Suiguang's exchange of writings and poems strengthened the relationship between the two countries; third, through its long-term communication with China, Vietnam also tried to learn more about the world and understand modern science by importing and reading varied Chinese books. The famous Vietnamese scholar of the 18th century, the "knowledgeable" Le Quy Don read a few Chinese books written by missionaries such as Matteo Ricci, Ferdinand Verbiest, and Giulio Aleni during his tenure as an envoy in the Qing dynasty and gained knowledge regarding the Western contemporary cultural and modern science, thus further expanding Vietnam's knowledge about the world (Yu, 2000; Yu, 2009).

The Influencing Factors of Vietnamese Intellectual Class' Knowledge on China

The Long History of Contact and Communication Between China and Vietnam

The contact and communication between China and Vietnam date back several centuries. As early as the pre-Qin period, there has been scattered description of the legendary figures, such as Shen Nung, Zhuan Xu, Yao, Shun, and Yu, and places far south as Jiaozhi. The *Shangshu Dazhuan* even recorded that Yue Shang once gifted a *Phasianus colchicus* to the Zhou Dynasty (Institute of History, Chinese Academy of Social Sciences 1982). At the very first year of the early

Han Dynasty, the present-day northern part of Vietnam was included into the territory of the feudal Chinese dynasty. From then onward, Vietnam entered the provincial era, and for more than a thousand years, the Chinese culture spread in Vietnam, the contact and communication between the Chinese and Vietnamese increased, and the knowledge about each other also increased.

From the time Dinh Bo Linh introduced sovereignty in Vietnam in 968 AD, to the following dynasties of Dinh Dynasty, early Lê Dynasty, Ly Dynasty, Tran Dynasty, later Lê Dynasty, etc., the feudal dynasties of Vietnam have kept a close suzerain–vassal relationship with China. In the meantime, the Vietnamese culture, consciousness of independence, and nationalism kept developing. From considering China as a closely related part of Vietnam to gradually realizing the distinction between China on the north and Vietnam, the Vietnamese formed the idea of a clearly independent consciousness. Ly Thuong Kiet of the Ly Dynasty thought it was destined that the land and sea of Vietnam should be ruled by their own king. Later Nguyen Trai of the Lê Dynasty claimed that since Vietnam and China have different geography and customs, they should rule their own countries in "*Pingwu Dagao*" (Ngo *et al.* 1984b). From then on, the Vietnamese people gradually began to view and study China from the perspective of a foreign country. Meanwhile, since Vietnam has been influenced by the Chinese culture for over a thousand years, the Vietnamese scholars during the feudal period continued to take inspiration from China to learn and mimic, and transcend and accept Chinese culture unconsciously, based on which they developed their own national culture.

Since the middle of the 19th century, both China and Vietnam suffered invasions by the Western imperial countries and faced similar national crises and revolutionary tasks. Therefore, the connection between these two countries developed further, and Vietnam looked up to China for modern Western ideas and Marxism. Many influential Vietnamese ideologists, reformers, and revolutionists, such as Phan Boi Chau, Dang Huy Tru, and Ho Chi Minh, came to China to seek a solution to save their country (Yu 2000). After the victory of the Vietnam in August Revolution in 1945 and the foundation of the

People's Republic of China in 1949, China and Vietnam continued their friendly relationship for a period, and China's influence over Vietnam became even stronger. More Vietnamese scholars focused on China and gained actual knowledge on China, and therefore formed a new understanding of China against the backdrop of a new era.

Ubiquitous Han Culture in Vietnam Society

Historical development has continuity and heritage, and the form and development of culture show distinct legacy in both the countries. Vietnamese's knowledge on China originated a long time back and therein many think patterns and specific contents are practiced till now. Thus, the modern Vietnamese intellectual class' knowledge on China has a close tie with the social and cultural environment of Vietnam.

Vietnam is a key member of the ancient East Asian Han Cultural Circle, and the Chinese Han culture has a huge impact on Vietnam's society. American scholar Alexander Barton Woodside said, "For a period of two thousand years or even longer, Vietnam, Korea, Japan and China are key members of the ancient East Asian culture" (Woodside, 1971). The footprints of the influence of China's Han culture are everywhere throughout the ancient society of Vietnam: In politics, the rulers of Vietnam have learned ideas from China's traditional political system and the Confucius' political ideas, so as to establish their own country system; in diplomacy, Vietnam has kept a suzerain–vassal relationship with China for a long time, and has established a sub-suzerain–vassal relationship with itself as the center (Dai Kelai 2004); in education, Vietnam has set up official and private schools just like China, and has imported Chinese books in huge volumes, and generally follows the ideas of Confucianism, Buddhism, and Taoism.

The use of Chinese characters has a huge impact. Irrespective of the time period, i.e., when China had direct jurisdiction over Vietnam or the period when Vietnam established independent dynasties and kept a suzerain–vassal relationship with China,

Chinese characters have always been used as official characters in Vietnam. Historical books and literature works written in Chinese character are far more than those written in Nom character. Today, the Latinized Quoc Ngu character has still retained a lot of Chinese–Vietnamese characters. For Vietnamese scholars who want to dive deep into their history and directly inherit the essence of traditional culture, one important prerequisite is the understanding of the Chinese character and language in order to improve the ability to use them. Meanwhile, it is also an important prerequisite for the Vietnamese scholars to directly acquire Chinese knowledge.

The knowledge of all the 17 Vietnamese scholars about China seems to have been affected by the Han Culture that continues to exist in the Vietnam society. Nine of these scholars[2] come from traditional Vietnamese families who have mastered Chinese characters and Chinese culture, which they learnt from their grandfather and father since childhood, so as to facilitate their study about China and formed a basis for the formation of their China view. For example, Nguyen Phuc Buu-Cam was born into a royal family of the Nguyen Dynasty, and his great-grandfather was the famous Prince Tuy-ly Nguyen Phuc Mien Trinh. Mien Trinh was the son of Vua Minh Mạng, who was famous for his poems and literature. Buu-Cam's parents are also famous writers and poets, and being born into such a family, Buu-Cam learned Chinese characters from childhood and was greatly affected by the Chinese culture[3]; or Phong Van Giao, whose father was also a Confucian knew the teachings of Chinese characters. Van Giao learned Chinese characters and culture from childhood, and thus was provided with great understanding of Chinese characters and poems even before he went to China for study.[4]

---

[2] They are Ly Viet Dung 李越勇, Tran Tuan Man 陈俊敏, He Jianxing 何健行, Phan Van Coc 潘文阁, Dang Vu Khieu 邓武跳, Nguyen Phuc Buu-Cam 阮福宝琴、阮奎, Pham Thi Hao 范氏好, Nguyen Ton Nhan 阮孙颜. For their interviews, see http://politics.ntu.edu.tw/RAEC/act 02.php. Accessed on January 18, 2016.
[3] For detailed accounts, see the Interview of Hán Nôm expert Buu-Cam at http://politics.ntu.edu.tw/RAEC/act02.php. Accessed on January 18, 2016.
[4] Pham's interview transcript at http://politics.ntu.edu.tw/RAEC/act02.php. Accessed January 18, 2016.

The Impact of Western Education on Vietnam Development from Modern Times

Since the independence of Vietnam from China in 968, the education system of Vietnam learned a great deal from China. In 1070, Ly Thanh-tong built Confucius temples and statues of sages like Confucius and Duke of Zhou, offered sacrifices to gods and ancestors in each season, and ordered the prince to learn more about Chinese (Ngo *et al.* 1984a). Professor He Chengxuan thinks, "this is the start of Confucianism being taught in Vietnam and Confucius being idolized" (He 2000). In 1075, under the supervision of Ly Nhan-tong, the son of Ly Thanh-tong, the first imperial examination in Vietnam was held, and Le Van Thinh qualified and was selected to serve as the king (Ngo *et al.* 1984a). In the following year, "the imperial college was established and civil officials were selected from scholars" (Phan 1884). From then onward, traditional Confucianism education and the imperial examination system were gradually established and extended to modern times.

In modern times, the French colonial authority started to introduce Western education in Vietnam due to the need of colonial rule. From 1861, the French colonial authority established a cathedral school, Ba Da Loc, in southern Vietnam to implement bilingual education in French and Vietnamese (Xu 1992). Till the promulgation of the Public Education Act in 1917, Vietnam had a basically complete Western education system, thus allowing Western education to rise in Vietnam (Chen 2005). Even after France's withdrawal from Vietnam, the education system established by the French continued to exist and was inherited by the southern Vietnam government.

The Western education brought in by the French colonial authority is in essence a colonial education or assimilation education, and it aims to abolish the Chinese and Nom characters used by the Vietnamese and implement French and Quoc Ngu characters, so as to cut off the ties between Vietnamese people and their traditional history and culture as well as the Han culture. Their main objective was to train the France-loving force and local administration people, and reinforce the colonial rule over Vietnam. But the ties between Vietnam and China and the influence of Han culture are so deep that they cannot be easily cut off. *Nan Feng* magazine, funded and established by the French colonial authority, always kept a Chinese column, and articles in it were printed in Chinese, Quoc Ngu character and French.

Objectively speaking, the Western education introduced by France led to the trend of modern education development, and it provided a chance for Vietnam people to detach from the traditional Confucianism or Han Culture and acquire a modern education system, and also enabled Vietnamese scholars to understand Vietnam and China from Western perspective and method. Nine of the seventeen scholars interviewed[5] clearly show that they have received French education in their early years. Western education and Western knowledge system also affected their knowledge about China to some extent. For example, Nguyen Van Hong reckons, "To study China, one cannot totally follow the Chinese perspective, but should also talk about China from a Western perspective."[6] According to Dang Vu Khieu, he had already read the French translated *Sishu Wujing* before he went to China to study Chinese language, and this provided a certain basis for later studies about China, and especially Confucianism.[7]

Impact of Going to China to Study from the 1950s to Early 1970s

From 1950s to early 1970s, relations between Vietnam and Chinese communist parties were close. China had provided massive aid to the Vietnamese people during the First Indochina War and the Vietnam War. During this period, many Vietnamese students went to China

---

[5]The nine scholars are Ly Viet Dung 李越勇, Huynh Minh Duc 黄明德, Tran tuan Man 陈俊敏, Nguyen Van Hong 阮文鸿, Nguyen Bang Tuong 阮鹏翔 Dang Vu Khieu 邓武跳, Nguyen Phuc Buu Cam 阮福宝琴, Nguyen Khue 阮奎和, and Nguyen Ton Nhan 阮孙颜. Accessed on January 18, 2016.

[6]For his interview, see http://politics.ntu.edu.tw/RAEC/act02.php. Accessed on January 18, 2016.

[7]For his interview, see http://politics.ntu.edu.tw/RAEC/act02.php. Accessed on January 18, 2016.

for further studies, and they can basically be divided into three categories: first, Vietnamese cadre students who studied in Party School of the Central Committee of CPC and military academies, and there are more than a thousand Vietnamese cadre students who went to China for further studies within 15 years of the establishment of diplomatic relationship (Guo 1992); second, Vietnamese students who went to Guangxi to study Chinese language in two talent-training schools located in Nanning and Guilin. From 1951 to 1955, these schools had trained more than a thousand talents from Vietnam (Huang *et al.* 1986); third, Vietnamese high school graduates who went to Chinese colleges for studies, and there were more than 2,000 such students who went to China for studies within 15 years of the foundation of the PRC (Huang *et al.* 1986). Beside those students, many Vietnamese technicians and workers came to China for training. Among the 17 interviewed Vietnamese scholars, 8 scholars[8] came to China during this period. For example, Dang Vu Khieu belongs to the first category, and he came to Party School of the Central Committee of CPC[9] to study as a cadre from 1954 to 1956, and he recalls one of his fellow students becoming a vice premier of Vietnam in later years.[10] Ho Si Hiep belongs to the second category. He came to Nanning talent-training school to study Chinese language and literature, and then he went back to Vietnam and worked as a college teacher[11]; the other six scholars, Tran Xuan De, Nguyen Huy Quy, Phan Van Cac, Nguyen Van Hong, Nguyen Bang Tuong and Pham Thi Hao, basically belong to the third cate-

---

[8]The eight scholars are Tran Xuan De 陈春提, Ho Sy Hiep 胡仕协, Nguyen Huy Quy阮辉贵, Phan Van Coc 潘文阁, Nguyen Van Hong 阮文鸿, Nguyen Bang Tuong 阮鹏翔, Dang Vu Khieu 邓武跳和, and Pham Thi Hao 范氏好. For their oral history interviews, see http://politics.ntu.edu.tw/RAEC/act 02.php. Accessed on January 18, 2016.

[9]The Institute of Marx and Lenin mentioned in Dang Vu Khieu's interview was the former name of Central Chinese Communist Party School.

[10]For Dang's interview, see http://politics.ntu.edu.tw/RAEC(Dai/act02.php. Accessed on January 18, 2016.

[11]See the interview at http://politics.ntu.edu.tw/RAEC/act02.php. Accessed January 18, 2016.

gory. They first came to Chinese or Vietnamese language school or training facilities to study Chinese language, and later came to Chinese universities like Peking University, Shandong University and Nanjing University for study.[12] Most of these scholars returned to Vietnam after completing their education, and began to engage in study related to China. The experience of studying in China has a certain influence on their studies related to China, and it even affects the Vietnamese students they teach.

There are many factors affecting all the 17 interviewed Vietnamese scholars' knowledge on China. Here factors of history and culture are the basis, and Western education and the experience of studying in China provided study method and knowledge system different from traditional knowledge. But what finally facilitated or decided Vietnamese intellectuals class' knowledge on China are Vietnamese national awareness, national concept, and national thinking mode with Vietnamese characteristics.

Basic Types of Vietnamese China-studying Intellectual Class

Since the August Revolution in 1945, the history of Vietnam took a new path (Dai and Yu 1988). In the historical course that followed, two great historical events, namely secession and reunification, had a profound impact on the country and its people. First, with the achievement of the Geneva Agreement, Vietnam was divided into two rally regions with 17th parallel as the border, and gradually Vietnam was divided and governed separately by the North and the South (Shi 1993). In the following 20 years, Vietnam was divided into two parts, and the South and North belongs to two international factions that have opposite ideologies and opposing attitude, respectively. Second, in April 1976 after reunification, Vietnam held a nationwide general election and produced a unified Congress. From the end of June to the beginning of July, the unified Congress held a meeting in Hanoi and declared the reunification of the North and the South, and

---

[12] See their interviews at http://politics.ntu.edu.tw/RAEC/act02.php. Accessed January 18, 2016.

changed the name of the country to the Socialist Republic of Vietnam to end the secession (Liang and Liang 2007).

These two historical events also affected the Vietnamese intellectuals group. The split of north and south brought distinctive difference inside the Vietnamese intellectuals group, and academic style and knowledge system with different features were formed. The reunification of north and south allowed the intellectual classes from both sides to merge, and thus cultivated a new generation of Vietnamese intellectuals group against a unified background. Under such a grand background, Vietnamese intellectuals group who studied China consisted of three groups: the first one was the North Vietnamese Intellectuals Group established before 1976, which was mainly affected by Soviet and Chinese ideologies; the second one is the South Vietnamese Intellectuals Group also established before 1976, which was mainly affected by tradition and Western knowledge system; the third one is the new generation of intellectuals group formed in 1976 after the reunification, and it gradually connected with the world after the innovation and opening up. A brief description and analysis of this situation is hereby made describing the conditions of the 17 Vietnamese scholars.

North Vietnamese Intellectuals Group

Eight scholars out of the 17 interviewed for this study belong to the North Vietnamese Intellectuals Group. They are Tran Xuan De, Ho Si Hiep, Nguyen Huy Quy, Phan Van Cac, Nguyen Van Hong, Nguyen Bang Tuong, Dang Vu Khieu, and Pham Thi Hao. All of them were educated and nurtured in North Vietnam and later went on to study in China. Thus, they have an emotional attachment toward Chinese studies and have developed a relatively convenient way of studying China and relying on Chinese study results and methods. They have a certain sense of identification with Chinese culture, and they have their own opinions on many ancient and modern aspects related to their knowledge about China. Their knowledge system about China mainly consists of the following aspects.

First, knowledge and study on Chinese characters and language. These eight scholars have studied in China, so they learned Chinese characters and language systematically, and some of them are still engaged in the study on Chinese characters and language even after going back to Vietnam, for example, Phan Van Cac, who translated many Chinese literature into Vietnamese, has his own opinion on Chinese characters, and thinks, "Chinese character is different from the phonetic character, and it doesn't change with the development and change of pronunciation, so it's easy for Chinese people to understand their ancient character, and thus inherit the history and culture of China."[13]

Second, knowledge and study on Chinese literature. Nearly all of these scholars have varied study interests in Chinese literature, for example, Tran Xuan De's study on Chinese literature covered both the ancient and modern times, which includes legends such as *The Book of Songs* and *The Songs of Chu* of the pre-Qin era and literature works of Lu Xun, Guo Moruo, Xu Zhimo, Wen Yiduo among others.[14] Another example is scholar Ho Si Hiep, who did an in-depth study on the Tang poetry generally liked by Vietnamese people, and both his Master's and doctorate theses involved the study on Du Fu's poems.[15]

Third, knowledge and study on Confucianism, Buddhism, and Taoism thoughts. They all have varied degrees of knowledge and dealt with both Chinese and Vietnamese Confucianism, Buddhism, and Taoism thoughts. For example, Dang Vu Khieu during his interview mentioned that Chinese Confucianism, Buddhism, and Taoism all have the same origin, and he compared this with the theory that Confucianism, Buddhism, and Taoism have a common source as claimed by Vietnamese scholars.[16] Nguyen Bang Tuong combined

---

[13] See Pham's interview at http://politics.ntu.edu.tw/RAEC/act02.php. Accessed on January 18, 2016.

[14] See Tran's interview at http://politics.ntu.edu.tw/RAEC/act 02.php. Accessed on January 18, 2016.

[15] See Ho's interview at http://politics.ntu.edu.tw/RAEC/act02.php. Accessed on January 18, 2016.

[16] See Dang's interview at http://politics.ntu.edu.tw/RAEC/act02.php. Accessed on January 18, 2016.

the Chinese Confucian thoughts and Ho Chi Minh's thoughts together for the study, and he thinks Ho Chi Minh thoughts contain many essences of the Confucian thoughts.[17]

Fourth, knowledge and study on Chinese history. Vietnamese intellectual class' knowledge and study on Chinese history mainly focus on traditional history. For example, Dang Vu Khieu once mentioned in his interview that his study on Chinese ancient historical works such as Confucius's *Chunqun* and Si Maqian's *Shiji* were actually aimed to review the tradition of Vietnam ancient history, so as to understand the historical origin of Le Van Huu's *Dai Viet Su Ky* and Ngo Si Lien's *Dai Viet Su Ky Toan Thu*.[18]

Finally, knowledge and understanding on socialist theory with Chinese characteristics and the development of modern China and its experience. Since currently both Vietnam and China are socialist states, and are conducting similar reform and opening up policy, therefore innovation and development of socialist theory with Chinese characteristics and the practice and experience of China's economy and society construction have always been the focus of Vietnam's academic circles. Vietnam established a research institute on China in Vietnam Academy of Social Sciences in 1993, and the institution publishes a magazine called "*Chinese Studies Review*." This institution is the most important Chinese studies institution in Vietnam (Pan 2005), and it mainly focuses on the study of modern China, and Nguyen Huy Quy was once the Director of the institution and Chief Editor of the magazine as well.[19] Scholars from other institutions, like Nguyen Van Hong, Nguyen Bang Tuong, and Dang Vu Khieu conducted varied degrees of study on socialism with Chinese characteristics and modern China's development.

---

[17] See Bang Tuong Nguyen's interview at http://politics.ntu.edu.tw/RAEC/act02.php. Accessed on January 18, 2016.
[18] His interview at http://politics.ntu.edu.tw/RAEC/act02.php. Accessed on January 18, 2016.
[19] See Nguyen Huy Quy's interview at http://politics.ntu.edu.tw/RAEC/act02.php. Accessed on January 18, 2016.

South Vietnamese Intellectuals Group

Six of the 17 Vietnamese scholars belong to the South Vietnamese Intellectuals Group. They are Ly Viet Dung, Huynh Minh Duc, Tran Tuan Man, Nguyen Phuc Buu Cam, Nguyen Khue, and Nguyen Ton Nhan. Compared with northern scholars, their life experiences are varied. Most of them received traditional Sinology education from their families, and later engaged in China studies because they selected related majors for study, or got influenced by religions like Buddhism, or were forced to make a living by it. Southern scholars mainly focus on ancient China.

Their knowledge on China mainly consists of the following aspects: first, study on Chinese literature, like translation and introduction of Chinese ancient literatures. For example, Ly Viet Dung has translated Pu Songling's (a litterateur of Qing Dynasty) *Liaozhai Zhiyi*, and compared it with the Vietnamese novel *Truyen Ki Man Luc*.[20] Nguyen Phuc Buu Cam mainly studies *The Book of Songs* and Bai Jun-Yi's *Pipaxing*.[21] Huynh Minh Duc, who has knowledge on modern Chinese literature studied modern Chinese scholars like Hu Shi and Liang Qichao, and his Master's thesis was titled "Hu Shi and Chinese New Vernacular Literature Campaign."[22] The second aspect includes study on thoughts of Chinese Confucianism, Buddhism, and Taoism. All the six scholars are interested in Confucianism thoughts. Nguyen Phuc Buu Cam published *Chinese Philosophy Under Song Regime: Essay on Philosophy* in his early years, and Tran Trong Kim wrote a preface for his book.[23] Ly Viet Dung and Tran Tuan Man believe in Buddhism, and have translated many Chinese Buddhism works, and compared Chinese Buddhism with

---

[20] Ly's interview is available at http://politics.ntu.edu.tw/RAEC/act02.php. Accessed on January 18, 2016.

[21] Buu's interview is available at http://politics.ntu.edu.tw/RAEC/act02.php. Accessed on January 18, 2016.

[22] See Huynh Minh Duc interview at http://politics.ntu.edu.tw/RAEC/act02.php. Accessed on January 18, 2016.

[23] For Buu Cam's interview, see http://politics.ntu.edu.tw/RAEC/act02.php. Accessed on January 18, 2016.

Vietnamese Buddhism. Nguyen Ton Nhan became interested in Taoism when hiding at home trying to avoid military service. He went to study Taoism theory and Taoism.[24] Third, knowledge and study on Chinese history. Similar to northern scholars, southern scholars also show keen interest in Chinese traditional history, and their main aim is to serve Vietnamese history. Nguyen Phuc Buu Cam said, "if one does not understand and examine Sinology documents, it will be difficult to study the ancient Vietnamese books written in Chinese," and "Study on Chinese history is to clarify our historical documents issue."[25] Finally, some of the southern scholars also have certain knowledge on Chinese ancient medicine. For example, Huynh Minh Duc thinks Chinese medicine is the root of ancient Chinese culture, and he has translated 12 traditional Chinese medicine books like *Shang Han Lun* and *Huangdi Neijing*.[26]

The New Generation of Intellectuals Group after Reunification

Of the 17 interviewed Vietnamese scholars, only Cao Tu Thanh and Phung Thi Hue belong to this group. One of them comes from the south and studies Chinese literature, history and culture, and the other comes for the north and studies social problems of modern China and socialism with Chinese characteristics, and these two have their specific views on China.

The two scholars' knowledge on China mainly relates to two aspects: first, knowledge and study on Chinese literature. Cao Tu Thanh studied Hán Nôm in college and received education on ancient Chinese language. However, from his translation pieces it is evident that he is not only interested in ancient Chinese literary works, such as *Liaozhai Zhiyi* and *Zi Bu Yu*, but also modern Chinese works, especially the popular literature liked by Vietnamese people.

---

[24] For Nguyen Ton Nhan's interview, see http://politics.ntu.edu.tw/RAEC/act02.php. Accessed on January 18, 2016.

[25] For Buu Cam's interview, see http://politics.ntu.edu.tw/RAEC/act02.php. Accessed on January 18, 2016.

[26] For Huynh's interview, see http://politics.ntu.edu.tw/RAEC/act02.php. Accessed on January 18, 2016.

He has also translated many influential Kuang Fu stories, such as Jin Yong's *Legend of the Condor Heroes* and *Lu Ding Ji*.[27] Second, knowledge and study on modern China. Phung Thi Hue is a scholar engaged in the study on modern China, and she works at the Institute of the Chinese Studies at Vietnam Academy of Social Sciences. She has many contacts in the Chinese academic circle and with scholars, and has a good understanding of the Chinese language. During the period that Nguyen Huy Quy and Do Tien Sam run the institution, she was the Chief Editor of the magazine *Chinese Studies Review*. She mainly studies Deng Xiaoping's socialist theory with Chinese characteristics, social problems in modern China's development, and economic relations between Vietnam and Taiwan.[28] Through the analysis of these two scholars of the new generation, we could clearly tell that northern and southern scholars rely more on traditions, where their knowledge on China shows more reality and utility.

The new generation of Vietnamese scholars engaged in China studies mainly consists of scholars educated after reunification, and also young scholars who went to China or Western countries to study and then came back home after Vietnam's innovation and opening up. Their knowledge on China has a wider perspective, and they have solid understanding of relative theory and new knowledge structure. These new generation of Vietnamese scholars are the main force of China studies in Vietnam. This study plan of the National Taiwan University mainly focuses on some famous scholars, but not the young generation of scholars. In fact, there are other scholars who were educated in Vietnam and who showed great promise in the 1980s and 1990s, such as Nguyen Kim Shan, engaged in Confucianism study, and Nguyen Tai Dong, engaged in Eastern philosophy study, and they have many academic results and promising academic development.

---

[27] For Cao's interview, see http://politics.ntu.edu.tw/RAEC/act 02.php. Accessed on January 18, 2016.
[28] See Phung Thi Hue's interview at http://politics.ntu.edu.tw/RAEC/act 02.php Access January 18, 2016.

Conclusion

Many of the Vietnamese scholars studying China have profound knowledge, an insightful foundation, myriad results and have greatly contributed to Vietnamese academic circle. Their knowledge on China has a major influence on Vietnamese authority and people. Many of them show more identification to Chinese culture and hope the friendly relation between China and Vietnam continues. The scholars that the author was acquainted with, like Tran Nghia, Hoang Van Lau, Dinh Van Minh, and Nguyen Chi Sach, all have made contributions to the cultural communication between China and Vietnam. As Vietnamese scholars, the China study they engaged, their knowledge on China, and especially their China views are part of the Vietnamese cultural system and are influenced by the Vietnamese culture, thinking characteristics, and methods.

Historically, Vietnam's feudal emperors and officials once regarded China as a respectful "governing country," and a "model" to imitate, and their dialect must include Chinese. Meanwhile, they often emphasized on their own features and differences, and even surpassed China. Professor Ching Ho Chen once pointed out that there are some disagreeable traits in the Vietnamese cultural thoughts (Chen 1992). In the 19th century, Nguyen dynasty prospered with marked developments in culture and education, and showed great promise in poetry. The dynasty saw famous scholars like Nguyen Van Sieu and Gao Ba Quat, and there were royal members of the Nguyen dynasty who were famous for their poems, like Prince Cong Shan and Prince Tuy-ly. Therefore, there it is said, "Nguyen Van Sieu and Cao Ba Quat's articles could be compared with those of the Xi Han dynasty, and Prince Cong Shan and Prince Tuy-ly's poems could be compared with Tangshi." For this reason, some Vietnamese scholars think it showed some unacceptable pride. The inherited national thoughts influence many even today and affect the views of Vietnamese intellectuals engaged in Chinese studies.

Vietnamese intellectual class' knowledge and view on China not only help Vietnam to know and understand China but also to understand ancient Vietnam's traditional history and culture, as well as discuss the social problems and enrich the treasure house of knowledge. The China view of Vietnamese intellectuals' class is an issue that needs to be studied in-depth in the future. In fact, when looked at from another perspective, the Chinese intellectuals' class' knowledge and views on Vietnam are also issues that needs to be studied in detail, and require criticism and must be transcendent, thereby helping people of these two countries to better understand and communicate with each other.

References

Chen, Jinhe 陈荆和. 1992. *Danan shilu yu Ruanchao zhuben* 〈大南实录〉与阮朝硃本 [The Veritable Records of the Great Nam and the Imperial Archives of the Nguyen Dynasty]. *Newsletter of the Chinese Association for Southeast Asian Studies*, 1(4): 53–54. Translated by Ta Na 塔娜译.

Chen, Li. 陈立 2005. *Lun Faguo zhimin tongzhi xia de Yuenan jiaoyu* 论法国殖民统治下的越南教育 [On the Education Policy in Vietnam under the French Colonial Rule]. *World History* 5: 67–76.

Dai, Kelai 戴可来. 2004. *Lüelun gudai Zhongguo yu Yuenan zhijian de zongfan guanxi* 略论古代中国与越南之间的宗藩关系 [A Brief Thesis on the Ancient Suzerain–Vassal Relationship of China and Vietnam]. *History and Geography of Chinese Frontiers* 2: 115–120.

Dai, Kelai and Yu, Xiangdong (Eds.) 戴可来、于向东主编. 1988. *Yuenan* 越南 [Vietnam]. Nanning: Guangxi People's Press.

Guo, Ming (Ed.) 郭明主编. 1992. *Zhong Yue guanxi yanbian sishinian* 中越关系演变四十年 [The Forty-year Evolution of Sino-Vietnamese Relations], p. 59. Nanning: Guanxi People's press.

He Chengxuan 何成轩. 2000. *Ruxue nanchuanshi* 儒学南传史 [The Southbound History of Confucian Scholarship], p. 337. Beijing: Beijing University.

Huang Guoan *et al.* 黄国安等. 1986. *ZhongYue guanxishi jianbian* 中越关系史简编 [An Abridged History of Sino-Vietnamese Relations], p. 200. Nanning: Guangxi People's Press.

Institute of History, Chinese Academy of Social Sciences (Ed.) 中国社会科学院历史研究所《古代中越关系史资料选编》编辑组. 1982. *Gudai ZhongYue guanxishi ziliao xuanbian* 古代中越关系史资料选编 [Selected Literature of Ancient History of Sino-Vietnamese Relation Institute of History], p. 2. Beijing: Chinese Social Science Press.

Liang, Yingming and Liang, Zhiming 梁英明, 梁志明. 2007. *Dongnanya jinxiandaishi (xiace)* 东南亚近现代史（下册）[Modern History of Southeast Asia (lower volume)], p. 666. Beijing: Kunlun Press.

Lu, Shi-peng 吕世朋. 1977. *Bei shu shiqi de yuenan* 北属时期的越南 [*Vietnam during China's Reign*], p. 2. New Taipei City: Huashi Press.

Ly, Van Phuc 李文馥. 2011. "YiBian," 夷辨 [Alien Agency], in Yi-yuan CHEN 陈益源 (Ed.), *Yuenan han ji wenxian shulun* 越南汉籍文献述论 [*A Review of Vietnam's Chinese Literature*], p. 235. Beijing: Zhonghua Book Company 中华书局.

Ngo, Si Lien *et al.* 吴士连、范公著、黎僖等著，陈荆和. 1984a. *DaYue Shiji quanshu (shang) benji juan san* 大越史记全书（上）本纪卷三 [Complete Book of the History of the Great Việt (the upper volume), Chronicle of Emperors 3], p. 249. Tokyo: Tokyo Daigaku Toyo Bunka Kenkyujo.

Ngo, Si Lien *et al.* 吴士连、范公著、黎僖等著，陈荆和. 1984b. *DaYue Shiji quanshu (shang) benji juan san* 大越史记全书（上）本纪卷三 [Complete Book of the History of the Great Việt (the upper volume), Chronicle of Emperors 3], pp. 248, 254. Tokyo: Tokyo Daigaku Toyo Bunka Kenkyujo.

Pan, Jin-e 潘金娥. 2005. *Yuenan Zhongguoxue yanjiu de fazhan licheng yu xianzhuang* 越南中国学研究的发展历程与现状 [The Progress and Present Conditions of Chinese Studies in Vietnam]. *Social Sciences Overseas* 4: 24–27.

Phan, Thanh Gial *et al.* (Eds.) 潘清简等著. 1884. *Qinding Yueshi tongjian gangmu zhengbian juan san* 钦定越史通鉴纲目 正编卷三 [Khâm Định Việt Sử Thông Giám Cương Mục, Volume 3]. *The National Library of Vietnam*, Edn. No. R. 594: 38.

Shi Yinhong 时殷弘. 1993. *Meiguo zai Yuenan de ganshe yu zhanzheng (1954–1968)* 美国在越南的干涉与战争（1954–1968）[American Intervention and War in Vietnam, 1954–1968], p. 2. Beijing: World Knowledge Press.

Woodside, Alexander Barton. 1971. *Vietnam and the Chinese Model*, p. 7. Massachusetts: Harvard University Press Cambridge.

Xu Shaoli 徐绍丽 1992. *Faguo zhiminzhuyizhe zai Yuenan tuixing de jiaoyu zhengce* 法国殖民主义者在越南推行的教育政策 [Education Policy Administrated by the French Colonial Authorities in Vietnam]. *Newsletter of Chinese Association for Southeast Asian Studies* 1: 15.

Yu, Xiangdong (Ed.) 于向东主编 2000. *Dongfang zhuming zhexuejia pingzhuan Yuenan juan* 东方著名哲学家评传·越南卷 [Autobiography of Renown Oriental Philosophers: The Vietnamese Volume], p. 192. Jinan: Shangdong People's Press.

Yu, Xiangdong. 2009. *Shi lun shiba shiji yuenan xuezhe li guichun de shijieguan* 试论18世纪越南学者黎贵惇的世界观 [On the World View of Le Quy Don: A Vietnamese Scholar in the 18th Century] *Studies of Philosophy* 哲学研究 11: 113–118.

Yu, Xiangdong 于向东. 2016. *Cong zhongguo shijiao huiwang yuenan gexin 30 nian* 从中国视角回望越南革新30年 [Rethinking Vietnam's Innovation for 30 Years from the Perspective of China], *Global Times* 环球时报, February 1, 7th Edition.

13

Post-Chineseness, Sinology, and Vietnam's Approach to China

Chih-yu Shih
Department of Political Science
National Taiwan University, Taiwan

The notion of post-Chineseness is enlisted to analyze Vietnamese Sinology as a comparative agenda. Post-Chineseness refers to the cultural preparation and the political process of mutual acknowledgment among those who consider one another sharing (some kind of) Chineseness, practically defined according to the context and its trajectories, at each time and each site. Chineseness can thus have various, if not entirely irrelevant, meanings. Vietnamese Sinologists have relied on different kinds of post-Chineseness to make sense of their relationship with the encountered Chinese to select and determine the mode of self-understanding, the purpose and a strategy to reconnect, and the normative criterion to assess and manage the relationship. Chinese Vietnamese are significantly less than Chinese Southeast Asia elsewhere in number. However, the history of Vietnam is considerably closer to China than those of Korea and Japan are, in terms of the length of merger. The post-Chineseness of Vietnamese scholarship therefore complicates its role identity *vis-à-vis* China, intellectually as well as practically.

Introduction

Defining China or Chinese is an impossible mission, and the validity of this statement becomes apparent if one recollects the intellectual histories of China studies, Chinese studies, and Sinology, which have, respectively, produced scholarship on China, Chinese people, and Chinese civilization. Nevertheless, borrowing the notion of family resemblance from Ludwig Wittgenstein (1986: 31), one still finds that scholars can practically identify their research scope despite their incapacity to reach any consensual definition. Such practical Chineseness hints at socially recognizable traits and turns Chineseness into a role identity instead of an involuntary, fixed, or shared quality, innate as well as acquired. Chineseness accordingly carries expectations that impose a duty to perform either on those who strive for recognition of their Chineseness by others or on those whom others recognize as owners of Chineseness.

Studies on China, Chinese people, and Chinese civilization together make Chineseness an epistemologically plausible and discursively expressible identity. To the extent that it is impossible to monopolize its substance, it attains the characteristics of a social role. Given that roles can be denied or claimed in contradiction to expectations, owning Chineseness necessarily involves a political process that has contextual behavioral and policy implications. Thus, a Sinologist may have studied Chinese topics so extensively and intensively that his or her intellectual capacity and psychological capacity to take the role-identity of Chineseness can be much stronger and even more willingly than the people he or she studies, obscuring the distinction between Sinologists and the Chinese they study. As a result, all can potentially speak and act in the capacity, or on behalf, of Chinese as long as one can convincingly perform the duty expected of such a role in its context. Post-Chineseness is the concept that characterizes the indefinite practicality of Chineseness as a role-identity.

Post-Chineseness refers to the cultural preparation and the political process of mutual acknowledgment among those who consider one another sharing (some kind of) Chineseness, practically defined according to the context and its trajectories, each time and each site. Chineseness can thus have various, if not entirely irrelevant, meanings. For example, Chineseness in the Confucian Northeast Asia may indicate one's degree of cultural centrality (Shih 2010: 537–560), whereas it mainly triggers the politics of differentiation in postcolonial Southeast Asia (Wang 2002). Centrality implies a shared quality among a set of population, a proportion of which may have a higher degree of centrality than others. By contrast, the politics of differentiation in Southeast Asia rejects it. In Hong Kong and Taiwan, for example, Chineseness may bifurcate into pursuits of both ethnic difference and cultural centrality because of the mixed post-colonial culture bred by Japan and Confucianism introduced by generations of migrants. Chineseness can likewise negatively include those who strive to achieve non-Chinese identities through the same process of mutuality, constituting a dyadic contrast. In other words, post-Chineseness refers to the intellectual capacity of people to use the cultural resources in their reach for reconnecting with one another as Chinese.

An example of post-Chineseness is given to illustrate what it means. If ancestor worship is considered Chinese, then the people who are able and willing to recognize Chineseness in one another by their shared learning, practice, or teaching of ancestor worship are exercising a vague kind of Confucian Chineseness. Similarly, those who deny Chineseness while practicing ancestor worship can likewise be exhibiting Chineseness in the sense that they deliberately distinguish the non-Chinese nuances of their ritual from that of others who are allegedly Chinese. The behavioral and policy implications of this particular example include a will to connect, or disconnect, with a separate Chinese population to reconcile a dispute, grasp an opportunity, trigger sympathy in an incident, and fulfill self-enhancement, among others. They try forging a sense of greater self, which is defined by a perceived common ancestor.

Post-Chineseness in Vietnam is distinctive because of (1) the long history of the political merger between Vietnam and dynastic China, (2) the shared religious and cultural beliefs of the Vietnamese with the Chinese, and (3) the recurrent migration as well as the resultant kinship across contemporary borders. Vietnamese intellectuals have relied on different kinds of post-Chineseness to make sense of their relationship with the encountered Chinese to select and determine the mode of self-understanding, the purpose and a strategy to reconnect, and the normative criterion to assess and manage the relationship. Chinese Vietnamese are significantly less than Chinese Malaysian, Thai, and Indonesians in number. The history of Vietnam is considerably closer to that of China than those of Korea and Japan in terms of the length of merger. The post-Chineseness of Vietnam therefore complicates its role-taking *vis-à-vis* China, intellectually as well as practically.

Crafting the Post-Chineseness Agenda

Post-Chineseness thus has no definitive content or scope, even if all who own a certain kind of Chineseness ostensibly have to share post-Chineseness. Self-identified Chinese are those who share different Chineseness with different other self-identified Chinese in context. As a result, Chineseness is more a processual notion than a substantive one; however, it still appears definitively in the context in which two can recognize in each other a shared Chinese feature. Thus, all Chinese have to be post-Chinese because they uniquely share something with different Chinese, but no such Chineseness can be shared by all. Given that owning or losing Chineseness have equal likelihoods, someone not considered Chinese elsewhere is potentially an owner of Chineseness as long as such recognition of him or her assuming Chineseness is mutually agreeable.

A Tibetan, a Taiwanese, or a Chinese Malaysian can similarly claim post-Chineseness where they achieve mutual recognition with someone else even if the Tibetan, the Taiwanese, or the Chinese Malaysian culture may not be shared by others who claim being Chinese. They are in between different identities and images to the extent that their mutually recognized Chineseness only partially constitutes their selfhood. They can also claim that the Chineseness they own is not shareable with others not living and growing up in the same geo-cultural background; therefore, Tibetans, Taiwanese, and Chinese Malaysians are arguably different. They cannot recognize in each other any familiar Chineseness, each having evolved on a peculiar trajectory. This kind of differentiated Chineseness denies any other self-claimed Chinese belonging to their group and makes their own a kind of culturally isolated Chineseness.

Ironically, if they insist being non-Chinese outsiders, as many Tibetans, Taiwanese, and Malaysian Chinese are inclined to do, they are still entitled to a kind of epistemological Chineseness informed by their own civilization or methodology, which enables them to recognize, understand, and connect with the Chinese people who may or may not see Chineseness in Tibetans, Taiwanese, and Malaysian Chinese. To claim a complete distinction, they must know what Chineseness represents and show how their respective Chineseness is unique. This intellectual capacity to know Chineseness is the basis to achieve reconnection if so desired in a different context.

In a nutshell, post-Chineseness describes how a China scholar strategically positions himself or herself through scholarship on China so that the relationship between his or her community and China is intellectually sensible.

Altercasting Embedded in Post-Chineseness

Post-Chineseness, which is registered in the cultural preparation for, and the process of, reconnecting any two populations considered owning Chineseness, is inevitably altercasting as well as reflexive altercasting (Epstein 2012: 135–145; Wehner 2015: 435–455). Altercasting occurs when a Chinese group incurs a particular component of its alleged Chineseness, which the alter-Chinese group is perceived to share by the former; consequently, the latter is obliged to respond positively to the former. The alter group's obligation to respond reflects the role expectation imposed on it. However, even if practiced by the same group, the alleged Chineseness can be different in accordance with the context of the encounter. For those who espouse "the Chinese Dream," which eyes on Chinese Southeast Asian as same Chinese, for example, food or Chinese language of

Chinese Malaysians could represent their Chineseness; thus, Chinese Malaysians are expected to eat rice together and speak Mandarin. By contrast, as neither the food nor use of Mandarin applies to the Tibetans, suffering from the same British imperialism could be a trigger. This imposes an obligation on the Tibetan population to embrace Chinese nationalism.

Reflexive altercasting emerges when an actor relies on the strategic use of Chinese cultural resources to meet what is perceived to be the alter group's role expectations of him or her. For example, a Tibetan who desires an educational opportunity may stress his or her Chinese citizenship and proficiency in Mandarin. Alternatively, he or she could pledge opposition to Tibetan independence for the sake of national unity. This strategic role-taking might have an acculturation effect; however, it does not take away his or her intellectual capacity to revert in another future context. Reflexive altercasting for a self-regarded non-Chinese group works in the opposite. For example, the same Tibetan group who promotes Tibetan independence would deliberately abort the duty of national integration imposed by the Chinese. Those who belong to this group could walk out to join Dharamsara or insist on the superiority of religion over politics. Reflexive altercasting in the last example proceeds to counter-altercasting, which generates the self-role expectation that the Chinese authorities would punish it.

The pressure on self-altercasting is particularly strong for actors looking for recognition for their Chineseness. When one declares the ownership of Chineseness shared by a Chinese alter group, one's identity of being Chinese comes from an internal perspective of the imagined scope of Chineseness and is called an insider's Chineseness. Failure to win recognition would challenge one's identity of being an insider. For those acting in the name of a weaker national actor surrounding China, their endeavor to reconnect with the Chinese would primarily require them to achieve recognition instead of providing recognition. This mechanism necessitates self-altercasting among those who see themselves as owners of Chineseness because they need to meet the role expectations of their Chinese alter group. In Vietnam, for example, many Sinologists believe that understanding the Chinese culture is essential to the understanding of the Vietnamese culture.[1] Being an insider in the Chinese culture thus enhances the appreciation for Vietnamese culture and consequently promotes self-respect, according to this view.

By contrast, for surrounding national actors whose identity is internally determined by their fellow citizens, their identity rests on the sense of difference from China. This kind of Chineseness is an outsider's Chineseness. Asserting and basing their own identity on their knowledge of what differs from China, these actors' ownership of Chineseness is generally contradicting. Such Chineseness cannot be rewarding to their self-understanding or even confirmed at all, unless their Chinese counterpart would act in a manner consistent with their expectations. The Chinese alter group is expected to avoid treating them as either Chinese overseas or Chinese culture subscribers. Altercasting is essential to an outsider's identity-based Chineseness. For the outsider Vietnam, China could represent an achiever to emulate, an interest seeker to avoid, or a growing power to defend, among others. Vietnam's national identity comes primarily from deliberately excluding the perceived cultural components that they share with China.

Between being an insider and being an outsider, a hybrid identity of being both an insider and an outsider exists. This hybrid identity requires support from both the Chinese alter group to recognize one's Chineseness and one's own group to partially achieve an identity of being non-Chinese. Consciously being not entirely Chinese, in-between actors identify with the role of being owners of Chineseness. The role is a component of the identity. In other words, the role substitutes for the identity to a certain extent so that an actor can deal with the Chinese as belonging to the same group. However, no role-playing is present when the alter group is not considered Chinese. Whether the role consciousness more strongly faces the Chinese alter group than the non-Chinese alter group is contingent. In the case of Chinese Vietnamese, one could more strongly identify with Chineseness to reconnect with the Chinese motherland during a political crisis in Vietnam. In this case, reflexive altercasting would

---

[1] A sentiment revealed in the oral history of a good number of Senior Sinologists, to be discussed later.

be dominant to achieve recognition from the Chinese alter group. Alternatively, the Chinese role consciousness for Vietnamese Sinologists could be stronger when facing Chinese counterparts so as to achieve equal status. In this case, altercasting instead of self-altercasting is the appropriate pattern because Vietnamese Sinologists would offer lessons about Vietnamese deviations for the uninformed Chinese Sinologists to learn.

Memory vs Resource in Role Identity

Whether or not one assumes an insider's perspective and strive to gain recognition from the Chinese alter group is often an acculturated decision, which is almost intuitive although mutable. One's cultural memory acquired through socialization prepares one to accept what is immediately rational for one to position one's cultural self (Assmann 2011: 210–224; Erll 2011). Under the influence of cultural memory, the decision on one's cultural position is not one's own choice. Nonetheless, it is a kind of choice for two reasons. First, the decision on one's position has to be a choice collectively made by the earlier generations and taught to the contemporary members to reflect the evolutionary wisdom. Second, re-socialization in consideration of new evolutionary pressures eventually facilitates a change in cultural memory, that is, everyone participates in adjusting the cultural memory. Cultural memory prompts an intuitive and emotional reaction to achieve a purpose constituting post-Chinese identities.

What action to take with one's position and/or what position to take with one's action are questions on using cultural resources instead of cultural memory. The selection of the cultural resources to use depends on how one conceptualizes the Chinese alter group, being a constant process of becoming or a discernable scope of being. In this regard, two approaches that parallel the division between humanities and social sciences decompose the strategic practices of post-Chineseness into temporal Chineseness and spatial Chineseness. Temporal Chineseness, defined as Chineseness that has an evolutionary trajectory under constant reconstruction, relies on the knowledge of the history and philosophy of the alter group to be able to empathize with the emotional and epistemological characteristics of this group. Spatial Chineseness, defined as Chineseness that has a discernable scope, is based on the combination of structural, comparative, and local intelligence; this combination is independent of the intervention of alternative emotions or epistemology already adopted by Vietnamese observers.

The process of becoming embodies temporal Chineseness, which one can trace through a significantly broader and longer trajectory from the past. Three types of temporal Chineseness emerge according to the self-positioning of one's role identity. The first is "cultural Chineseness," in which members belonging to the same Chinese group share a cultural identity because they live together long enough to understand the relationships, issues, and emotions of one another in ways that out-group members cannot fully appreciate. The second type, "Sinological Chineseness" possesses culturally in-between perspectives of both China and Vietnam so as to eloquently translate and make sense of both sides. The third type, "civilizational Chinese" presupposes mutually estranging ontological identities between China and Vietnam, as an out-group, and allows the latter to learn, assess, and handle Chinese identities.

Spatial Chineseness exists in its being and is defined by the corresponding site and prevailing conditions. Spatial Chineseness requires an objective scope so that one can gather intelligence to speculate its conditions as well as behavioral pattern. No pressure exists to attribute Chineseness to knowledge revealing the past. As temporal Chineseness, spatial Chineseness has three types according to the positions of Vietnamese observers. "Experiential Chineseness" speaks of an in-group self-consciousness resulting from living together with a recognizable Chinese group, with concomitant consensual role obligations. An actor possessing "ethnic Chineseness" usually shows less Chineseness in front of a Chinese alter group, tends toward self-altercasting to win respect, and demonstrates less Vietnamese characteristics in front of their fellow citizens to enable self-altercasting in another direction. "Scientific Chineseness" demonstrates one's knowledge of the Chinese alter group, such that

Table 1. Post-Chineseness Divided into Scholars as Subjects and China/Chinese as Objects

Memory Resource	Subjects Inside (Role)	Subjects Between (Role-Identity)	Subjects Outside (Identity)
Temporal object	Cultural Self-altercasting	Sinological altercasting	Civilizational altercasting
Spatial object	Experiential Self-altercasting	Ethnic Self-altercasting	Scientific/Policy altercasting

Source: Author.

objectively analyzing a Chinese alter group and epistemologically distancing it from one's own group simultaneously testify to the identity of an external collector of Chineseness (see Table 1).

Altercasting and Vietnam's Practices of Post-Chineseness

Vietnamese who perceive Vietnam or Vietnamese as Chinese are not usually considered relevant. However, the succeeding discussion shows that Vietnamese intellectuals who grew up in a Chinese cultural environment, owing to their family traditions, are prepared to view the Chinese alter group at times to be within the boundary of a greater self, which simultaneously includes their own. This leads to either cultural Chineseness or experiential Chineseness. In case the Vietnamese group is consciously outside, the resources for it to reconnect with the Chinese alter group include civilizational Chineseness and scientific Chineseness, depending on whether the enlisted identity of the Chinese alter group is considered a process of becoming or a scope of being. A process of becoming incurs the subjective attitude toward an exotic civilization, historiography, or ideology. A process of being involves the objective analysis abiding by Vietnam's interests. In case both Chineseness and Vietnamese characteristics constitute the Vietnamese identity that is in between, the cultural resources include either Sinological Chineseness, which translates meanings for both sides, or ethnic Chineseness, which strives for recognition from both sides.

For Vietnamese intellectuals and people who perceive Vietnam as an insider, consciously or not so consciously, they apply cultural norms to either assess China and its performance or reflect on their own problems in the form of self-criticism, i.e., reflexive altercasting. Criticism is significantly more powerful than assuming an outsider's position because Vietnam's criticism, regardless of its correctness in the eyes of China, can reveal the weakness of Chineseness, which an outsider can rarely do. The pressure of reflexive altercasting is reduced whenever one's position is supported by the knowledge of actors, both inside and outside. One owns an in-between kind of Chineseness that neither side does. However, when an actor self-positioning in between the insider and the outsider ends up in a situation in which both sides can claim knowledge of one's identity, e.g., ethnic Chineseness, he or she is reduced by both sides altercasting the one that owns no discourse in the middle.

Altercasting and Civilizational Chineseness

Vietnamese who apply Vietnam's perceived civilizational standards to identify, evaluate, and absorb Chinese civilizations, specifically from the perspective of differentiation are exercising civilizational Chineseness. Differences constitute the civilizational identity of Vietnam that forms Vietnam's distinctive identity. Themes that emancipate, demonize, romanticize, patronize, historicize, or merely relativize China illustrate this type. Under civilizational Chineseness, learning from Chinese experiences shows no signs of assimilation. The Vietnamese geo-culture, evolving out of the local history as well as indigenous religions, will undergird such civilizational borrowing. Confucianism, Daoism, and even Buddhism are first assimilated into or transformed by indigenous cults. Civilizational Chineseness stresses two distinctive trajectories — China and Vietnam, intertwining but independent.[2] The purpose of owning civilizational Chineseness is to separate it from Vietnamese identity.

---

[2] Oral history of Phan Van Cac, http://politics.ntu.edu.tw/RAEC/comm2/vietnam_04.doc. Accessed on March 11, 2017.

Altercasting leads to the expectations of China refraining from enlisting civilizational resources to restore the metaphors of Middle Kingdom or All-Under Heaven during the time of its rise to major power. China should not act as the sole origin of Vietnamese civilization or consider Vietnam a student exclusive of the Chinese cultural sphere. China should not expect Vietnam to exchange political favors for China's beneficial treatments that grow out of China's expanding scale of economy. China should instead maintain its role as just another civilization with a different past and future to be liked or disliked. Civilizational Chineseness motivates Vietnam to assert civilizational uniqueness. Civilizational Chineseness could lead to soft resistance of Vietnam by restricting the spread of Chinese civilizational commerce in Vietnam. Intellectual narratives could alert nationals to the arrogance or misinterpretation of Vietnam's civilizational history in Chinese discourses.

The Vietnamese society is inclined to watch and assess China, positively and negatively alike. Web information about China typically receives more frequent hits.[3] If this curiosity originates from a sense of a distinctive perspective, it represents civilizational Chineseness. For example, the curiosity toward Vietnam's path to Marxism is normally accompanied by a comparison with the Chinese path.[4] This comparative consciousness is keenly applied to the quest for Vietnam's history of philosophy, widely acknowledged to be heavily grounded on Chinese philosophies. Mutual learning indicates civilizational Chineseness. In fact, Chinese students in Vietnam have been observed to learn better than other foreign students.[5] Nevertheless, a veteran suggests that Taiwanese are better Sinologists because of their Chinese background reveals Vietnam's external position.[6] Another veteran opines that the more one knows about China, the more one appreciates how different from China Vietnam

---

[3] Nguyen Huy Hoang enlightens me on this phenomenon.
[4] Oral history of Nguyen Bang Tuong, http://politics.ntu.edu.tw/RAEC/comm2/vietnam_05.doc. Accessed on March 11, 2017.
[5] I benefit from an interview with Tran Thuy Anh on this particular reflection.
[6] Oral history of Ly Viet Dung at http://politics.ntu.edu.tw/RAEC/comm2/interviewV%20Ly%20Viet%20Dung.pdf. Accessed on March 11, 2017.

is.⁷ However, this does not preclude Confucianism or Sinology from being a universal value, according to yet another learned scholar.⁸

One interviewee expresses the view of instrumental Confucianism, whereby people access Confucianism with different calculi of interest. Although they share Confucianism and other cultural traditions with the Chinese, Vietnamese who hold a negative attitude toward China exhibit a clearly opposing attitude. One explanation is that Chinese embrace a strong Han-centric sensibility.⁹ This triggers Vietnamese nationalism, sometimes to the extent of people refusing to learn the Chinese language.¹⁰ When the political atmosphere becomes extreme, the studies of China and Sinology can be entirely halted. Although most people clearly distinguish the Chinese people from the Chinese government, alienation from the Chinese government can be considerably intense that many Vietnamese allegedly remain constantly alerted by any move the Chinese government is taking.

Altercasting and Scientific Chineseness

Vietnamese scholars who rely on a presumably objective scale or policy agenda to study an alter Chinese group as a discernible site or body that others can describe, explain, and compare are exercising scientific Chineseness. Institutionalists, Marxists, as well as think-tank analysts illustrate this type. Scientific Chineseness treats China as conditions of capacity, demographics, social structure, and policy orientation that Vietnam has to cope with. Scientific scholarship allows Vietnam to contribute to China studies because of Vietnam's empathetic capacity to compare, supported by sited intelligence, familiarity with Confucianism and Daoism, alliance experiences, war history, the same system of party-state, common Russian pedagogy, and the Chinese language skill. Unique, if not

---

⁷Oral history of Phan Van Cac.
⁸Oral history of Le Huy Tieu at http://politics.ntu.edu.tw/RAEC/comm2/interviewV%20Le%20Huy%20Tieu.pdf. Accessed on March 11, 2017.
⁹Oral history of Le Huy Tieu.
¹⁰I am indebted to Vu Duoan Luan on this observation.

more comprehensive, China expertise in Vietnam results in a peculiar kind of comparative studies, in which the approach to Chineseness is universally applicable.

Altercasting leads to the expectations that the same values and rationality that Vietnam considers common and normal have to constitute Chineseness. The strategic implication is the presentation of a non-distinctive China ready to cope with Vietnam through power play, exchange of interests, or monopoly of influence.[11] China is expected to be perceived in Vietnam only as strategic opportunities or threats, resulting in a bilateral relationship plagued by uncertainty, mistrust, and competition. China is expected to oppose the multilateral as well as global intervention in their bilateral interaction. Vietnam expects China's policy to be carrot and stick. In scientific Chineseness, Vietnamese detect the calculus of China's national interest.

Most forms of scientific Chineseness treat China's behavior as composed of characteristics that everyone else similarly owns or understands. However, Vietnamese scholars do not adopt this prevailing perspective. Internally, these sporadic scientific identities analyze Chinese leadership style.[12] Externally, they regard China as a player of international politics facing Vietnam, which prefer a multilateral over a bilateral frame when dealing with China. A major component that influences Vietnam's self-identity is the reference to China as a big nation to the effect that an asymmetric relational constitutes Vietnam's nationhood. Vietnam expects China's expansion, but Vietnam has no intention of confronting China or expectation that the ASEAN could stop China.[13] Neither will Vietnam's alliance with either the US or Japan, if successful, be against China nor will Vietnam romanticize China's historical support for Vietnam with the belief that China did what was best for China's own interests. In general, though, Vietnamese Sinologists are not enthusiastic in owning this kind of scientific Chineseness, which other nations can easily own.

---

[11] I am indebted to Nguyen Tran Tien on this reflection.
[12] I am indebted to Nguyen Huy Hoang on this observation.
[13] I am likewise indebted to Nguyen Huy Hoang on this observation.

Scientific Chineseness actually features alienation from classic Chinese studies. During the time of confrontation, Sinologists left their agenda behind and switched to other subjects.[14] Consequently, knowledge about China originated primarily from Russian materials. Scientific Chineseness about China minimally required peculiar Vietnamese perspectives to make sense. During the Vietnam–China rift, more general subjects substituted for Chinese learning: philosophy and Marxism on one side, and Vietnamese culture and the Russian language on the other. Western China studies flourished and appeared to study China objectively; thus, one's knowledge of China does not have to depend on the Chinese literature.[15]

Altercasting and Sinological Chineseness

Vietnamese scholars who can describe and explain the different functions and values of the Chinese and Vietnamese cultural beliefs to the members of each group are practicing Sinological Chineseness. Non-Chinese Confucians in general and Church Sinologists in particular illustrate this type. Sinological Chineseness in Vietnam stresses the need to have a deep understanding of China so that Vietnam can learn from China what is useful and deal with China without the support of a third party. Such learning comes from empathy, or even sympathy, rather than uninformed romanticizing dominant in civilizational Chineseness.[16] Sinological Chineseness identifies Vietnam as assuming the role of an intellectual who knows the social, political, and psychological difficulties that Chinese leaders suffer and reads with confidence between the lines the policy messages from China. Owning Sinological Chineseness is therefore accompanied by a duty of double-sided communication, including uncritically showing the negative side of China.

Altercasting leads to the expectations that China and Vietnam will be reciprocal, willing to share, and appreciative of each other's

---

[14] Oral history of Nguyen Huy Quy. http://politics.ntu.edu.tw/RAEC/comm2/vietnam_03.doc. Accessed on March 11, 2017.
[15] Oral history of Phan Van Cac.
[16] Nguyen Van Hong shares his own reflection with me in an interview.

relationship. Once the interpretation of one party's consideration is revealed to the other party, the latter has the role obligation to show sympathy and patience. During difficult negotiations, China is obliged to prevent the situation from escalating into an irrevocable level. China is also expected to exert patience and accept a non-solution as a solution in a kingly manner, which has been preached and praised in Sinological classics as well among their contemporary disciples.

Sinologists are emotionally involved in their works of translation.[17] Good translations of the Buddhist texts, literary pieces, scenes, and philosophies are essential to the learning of Chinese culture.[18] Some Sinologists have never been to China but can develop deep empathy toward the Han characters through the texts. Others are worried, though, that isolated translators could miss the needed touch in their translation because they fail to capture the spirit of the time due to their lack of living experiences in China. For example, a student of "The Forbidden Female" expounds the challenge of translating the contemporary novel to convey the triad of a universal human rights message, a gender equality message, and the reform and openness message.[19] The exact choice of Vietnamese words to convey the delicate messages and the flow of the episodes presuppose an intricate appreciation of the Chinese narratives.[20] Overall, Sinological Chineseness encourages a general sense of duty to both their political leaders and school children. Sinologists intend that their leaders understand China correctly and their pedagogy enriches the curriculum so that reading about China in Vietnam can avoid an inherent bias caused by a short-term rift.[21]

---

[17] Oral history of Nguyen Ton Nhan, http://politics.ntu.edu.tw/RAEC/comm2/interview%20VN%20NGUYEN%20TON%20NHAN%20CH.pdf. Accessed on March 11, 2017.
[18] Oral history of Hồ Sĩ Hiệp, http://politics.ntu.edu.tw/RAEC/comm2/interviewV%20Ho%20Si%20Hiep.pdf. Accessed on March 11, 2017.
[19] Oral history of Pham Thi Hao, http://politics.ntu.edu.tw/RAEC/comm2/interview%20VN%20PHAM%20THI%20HAO%20CH.pdf. Accessed on March 11, 2017.
[20] *Ibid.*
[21] Oral history of Pham Tu Chau, http://politics.ntu.edu.tw/RAEC/comm2/interviewV%20Pahm%20Tu%20Chau%20Chinese.pdf. Accessed on March 11, 2017.

Sinologists are used to the suspicion that they are overly pro-China during Vietnam–China conflicts.[22] From the point of view of Sinologists, they explain this image to their profound knowledge of China. According to a think-tank scholar, recommendations of Sinological Chineseness can sometimes be acceptable to the government.[23] A well-trained Sinologist learns Chinese classics by heart that they reflect humanities in them. Sinology enables one to transcend mundane affairs and regard wars as only transient phenomena. An interviewee finds himself in complete agreement with a Chinese counterpart on the assessment that China and Vietnam have no good reason to fight.[24] Well-equipped scholars can not only translate texts, i.e., Buddhist and Confucian texts and literary pieces but also convey the spirit so that each party is able to appreciate the mood and the temper of the other party. For example, a veteran discovers an either–or mentality plaguing both parties. This mentality is caused by a shared style of nationalism — either to praise the other side to the extreme or to despise it to the extreme.[25] Nevertheless, most Sinologists seem to believe that the Han culture features open-mindedness.

Self-Altercasting and Ethnic Chineseness

Vietnamese who can describe and explain the different functions and values of the nuanced ways of life embedded in a certain cultural or geographical space that overlaps with a discernible Han Chinese domain are practicing ethnic Chineseness. Han or other ethnic Chineseness in Vietnam or on the borders that are capable of communicating with both Vietnam and China, as well as within their own groups, illustrates this type. Ethnic Chineseness is strong among those Chinese Vietnamese who escaped at the end of the Vietnam War to live abroad. It is equally evident among the Kinh population

---

[22] Pham Quang Minh shares this general impression with me in an interview.
[23] Phung Thi Hue shares her experiences with me in an interview.
[24] Nguyen Van Hong enlightens me on this particular reflection in an interview.
[25] Oral history of Nguyen Van Hong.

in Guangxi, China. Others, who are neither Han nor Kinh but nonetheless on the borders, such as certain divisions of the Yao people, travel culturally in between, too. The ethnic Chineseness of these populations, whose densities are high within a territorial scope, can be more evident in case they adopt distinctive religions, dialects, diets, and clothes, making their difference a political statement of identity.

The identity of ethnic Chineseness is necessarily hybrid and can easily cause a misunderstanding or stereotyping from either Chinese or Vietnamese. The life task resulting from ethnic Chineseness is for the population or its sympathetic scholars to remain acceptable to both sides and therefore impose on their members a certain pressure to shift and adapt in accordance with the context. Confrontation between China and Vietnam is their nightmare.[26] Self-altercasting is a survival skill. However, self-altercasting can lead to different strategies, with some simulating the same identities in compliance with their Chinese or Vietnamese counterpart, whereas others resisting it to establish a social space to which they are entitled.

Vietnamese Chinese are called Kinh, many of whom reside in Guangxi — the three islands outside the city of Fangcheng. The Kinh population speaks both Chinese and Vietnamese. A good number of them make a living by daily crossing the River of Beilun to the city of Mong Cai (or Mangjie) on the Vietnamese side, where gambling is allowed. Interviewees take the identity of Chinese despite their Kinh status that will link them to the major nationality of Vietnam. However, in their work, they primarily receive and entertain Han tourists from China. A particular nostalgia for Mao Zedong–Ho Chi Minh friendship sweeps over the three islands. On the one hand, the Kinh community is disposed to their Chinese citizenship to avoid historical discrimination inflicted by the Han population. On the other hand, they act superior to the Vietnamese. Numerous legends relate the contribution made by the early Kinh generations to the Chinese nation building. This population complains about the

---

[26] Oral history of Ha Kien Hanh, http://politics.ntu.edu.tw/RAEC/comm2/vietnam_13.pdf. Accessed on March 12, 2017.

Vietnamese policy, which allegedly aggravates the relationship between both sides during the border clashes. Resistance to China is rare among the contemporary Kinh population.

By contrast, few signs of resistance among the Chinese Vietnamese have been evident. First, during the Civil War, Chinese Vietnamese in the south dreaded the conscription by the Saigon authorities to fight the North. The aftermath of the unification in 1975 is the large outflow of Chinese Vietnamese to escape the communist rule.[27] Some of the migrants who have settled in the US have continued to hope that the US would support the democratization of Vietnam. On the contrary, Chinese Vietnamese staying in Vietnam rather have an isolated mentality.[28] They have resented the public-sanctioned certificate for those who speak the second language because they consider Chinese being their mother language.[29] Chinese Vietnamese in general are fond of Ho Chi Minh. They show a significant support for nation building in Vietnam.[30] Their operating languages are Chinese dialects, which are different from Mandarin. Chinese consciousness,[31] together with support for Vietnamese nationalism, produces a hybrid identity with uncertainty as well as incapacity in gaining the recognition from either Chinese or Vietnamese in-group members.

Self-Altercasting and Experiential Chineseness

Scholars who mingle with a self-identified Chinese population within a discernible boundary long enough to present, explain, and interpret Chinese lives from the sited viewpoint are practicing experiential Chineseness. Anthropologists, travelers, and migrant scholars illustrate this type, as well as people living in regions that do

---

[27] Pham Quang Minh enlightens me on the situation of this period.
[28] My impression is indebted to Dao Thi Tam Khann's research experiences.
[29] Oral history of Nguyen Van Khang, http://politics.ntu.edu.tw/RAEC/comm2/InterviewV%20Nguyen%20Van%20Khang%20Chinese%201.pdf. Accessed on March 12, 2017.
[30] Oral history of Ha Kien Hanh.
[31] Oral history of Ly Viet Dung.

not distinguish the two peoples,[32] in historical official families running a Chinese lifestyle,[33] and in circles in which intensive intermingling occurs.[34] The Chinese lifestyle includes both traditional and socialist lifestyles, resulting in the intuition that their experiences are mutually exchangeable.[35] Experiential Chineseness enables people to view China as their own group and willingly conform to the norms and institutions practiced by the Chinese population. However, a hatred may arise during conflicts with China given that Chinese are presumably like one's own folks; thus, a strong sense of relative disappointment is felt.[36]

Self-altercasting to fulfill the role of being Chinese-like and practicing certain lifestyles does not negate one's self-awareness of being Vietnamese. The pressure to retain the familiar in-group recognition from the Chinese population sharing the same life experiences and values induces the anxiety of being associated with the different lifestyle adopted by Vietnamese elsewhere. Confrontation between the Chinese and the Vietnamese immediately causes a twist of identity, in which Vietnam, rather than China, appears to be more culpable. Self-altercasting leads to the mitigation of the conflict happening in high politics and the expectation that the conflict will inevitably pass.[37] An expectation that the Vietnamese side would concede also exists. Under experiential Chineseness, anything that happens to China is considered likely to happen to Vietnam.

Experiential Chineseness comes most naturally in the family, neighborhood, and school as seniors exhibit an unreserved practice

---

[32] Oral history of Nguyen Bang Tuong.
[33] Oral history of Pham Thi Hao as well as that of Tran Tuan Man, http://politics.ntu.edu.tw/RAEC/comm2/InterviewV%20Tran%20Tuan%20Man.pdf. Accessed on March 12, 2017.
[34] Phung Thi Huy shares her son's learning experiences in China being positive, for example.
[35] Oral history of Ly Viet Dung.
[36] I am indebted to Pham Quang Minh on the affect of disloyalty and betrayal directed at Vietnam among Chinese.
[37] Pham Quang Minh agrees that confrontations are by all means transient from the Vietnamese perspectives.

of Chinese culture and religion for the younger generations to emulate.[38] Many Vietnamese Sinologists could recollect certain family traditions. Some of these traditions have proceeded from the past imperial officialdom, usually from a grandparent wholeheartedly engrossed in Confucian teachings as well as the classic literature.[39] Fathers are even more important if they have been determined Sinologists.[40] Teachers are equally important in some cases because they reinforce the interest and aptitude of a traditionally grown child for Sinological scholarship.[41] With an embedded childhood, some Sinologists carry on their studies all by themselves outside the formal curricula. They are naturally self-disciplined that they could continue a tradition they gradually consciously represent in their selfhood. This family tradition may at times include the legendary incidents of historical fights with China as if the wars have been family feuds not to be considered alarming, as civilizational or scientific Chineseness would assume.

Beyond the intellectual dimension, experiential Chineseness is present among the rank-and-file who are exposed to Chinese soap operas, movies, and novels that carry logics and values familiar to the Vietnamese audience who automatically accepts Chinese narratives as its own.[42] In fact, Chinese narratives easily attract Vietnamese viewers exactly because the lifestyle, rhetoric, and social relations all echo the Vietnamese experiences.[43] Vietnamese who mingle with

---

[38] Oral history of Vu Khieu, http://politics.ntu.edu.tw/RAEC/comm2/vietnam_07ch.pdf. Also see oral history of Nguyen Van Khang, http://politics.ntu.edu.tw/RAEC/comm2/InterviewV%20Nguyen%20Van%20Khang%20Chinese%201.pdf. Both accessed on March 12, 2017. In addition, one anonymous interviewee says that her experiences living in the border area since childhood make no distinction between the two people except in the language they each use.

[39] Oral history of Tran Le Bao as well as that of Nguyen Khue, http://politics.ntu.edu.tw/RAEC/comm2/interview%20VN%20NGUYEN%20KHUE%20ch.pdf. Accessed on March 12, 2017.

[40] Oral history of Nguyen Huy Quy as well as that of Phan Van Cac.

[41] Oral history of Nguyen Ton Nhan.

[42] Oral history of Tran Xuan De, http://politics.ntu.edu.tw/RAEC/comm2/InterviewV%20Tran%20Xuan%20De.pdf. Accessed on March 12, 2017.

[43] I am indebted to both Tran Hoang Quan Nguyen Tran Tien on this observation.

the Chinese population in their neighborhood or during their study in China similarly and typically have the sense of difference in national identity, having been desensitized at the basic levels.[44] The linguistic and cultural environments that enable the Vietnamese to transcend the sentiment that nationalism easily monopolizes are the major facilitators of mutual empathy.[45] However, presumably in-group Chinese who deviate from expected pattern or the consensual reality deny the value of Vietnamese members and cause anxiety as well as retaliation.

Self-Altercasting and Cultural Chineseness

Scholars who study or practice Confucianism or any other perceived Chinese cultural, religious, or political belief system in their lives and apply this belief system to their understanding of Chinese phenomena are practicing cultural Chineseness. Cultural Chineseness forms a certain imagined mutuality exclusively between Vietnamese and Chinese.[46] It enables people to take advantage of the classic wisdom accumulated in the shared cultural memory confidently and comfortably. Cultural Chineseness is more intensive than experiential Chineseness to the extent that the former develops from a long-time association and familiarity with Chinese discourses and therefore is more appreciative than the latter's mere practice of the same lifestyle, which does not necessarily reach the intellectual level. Compared with Sinological Chineseness, which introduces China to Vietnam, cultural Chineseness focuses on Vietnam's self-enhancement.[47] It can facilitate a powerful criticism of China by appealing to the values and norms to which China presumably subscribes. It can even serve as a

---

[44] Oral history of Le Huy Thieu, http://politics.ntu.edu.tw/RAEC/comm2/InterviewV%20Le%20Huy%20Tieu%20Chinese.pdf. Accessed on March 12, 2017.

[45] Hoang Thu Anh enlightens me on the impression that Vietnamese easily distinguish the Chinese people from the Chinese government and understand that the desire to control Vietnam is primarily a government policy.

[46] More than that between China and any other country according to Ho Si Hiep, see his Oral history.

[47] Oral history of Vu Khieu.

methodology of how to search and use Chinese beliefs that are not immediately available.[48]

Looking for clues from Chinese examples on how to deal with a similar situation exemplifies a kind of self-altercasting.[49] Chinese examples are intuitively relevant as if the success and failure of the Chinese similarly reproducible in Vietnam once the same response to a similar situation is attempted (Nam 2014: 139–156). Moreover, an understanding of the Chinese culture is believed to be functional to the understanding of the Vietnamese culture,[50] as if the cultures of both sides are the same despite the fact that Vietnam is a different country with a distinctive past,[51] that is, how one understands Vietnam would be a matter of how one understands China.[52] A sense of self-altercasting similarly exists in the criticism of China, as if criticizing China is tantamount to self-criticism.[53]

Vietnamese Han Nom characters have set the foundation of cultural Chineseness.[54] They not only allow the Vietnamese literati to comprehend and teach Chinese classics and Chinese thoughts but also leave a tradition of poetry that prompts a number of Vietnamese Sinologists to declare their superior grasp of Chinese culture compared with their Japanese and Korean counterparts (Nguyen and Phan 2014: 123–138). The Nom system provides a specific methodology for a senior to assess how well the younger generations have preserved their own culture.[55] In addition, Buddhist beliefs

---

[48] Oral history of Nguyen Bang Tuong.
[49] Sinology enables one to understand modern nationalism and the thought of Ho Chi Minh. See oral history of Nguyen Van Hong.
[50] Oral history of Buu Cam, http://politics.ntu.edu.tw/RAEC/comm2/interview%20VN%20BUU%20CAM%20ch.pdf. Accessed on March 12, 2017.
[51] Oral history of Pham Tu Chau.
[52] Oral history of Cao Tu Thanh, http://politics.ntu.edu.tw/RAEC/comm2/interview%20VN%20CAO%20TU%20THANH%20ch.pdf. Accessed on March 12, 2017.
[53] So, China assessed by democracy and peace is harbinger for Vietnam assessed by the same criteria. See oral history of Tran Le Bao.
[54] Oral history of Nguyen Van Khan.
[55] Strongly emphasized by many Sinologists, for examples, see oral history interviews of Tran Le Bao, Nguyen Ton Nhan, and Pham Thi Hao.

comprise another powerful foundation of cultural Chineseness as renowned Vietnamese priests may travel to serve temples in Guangxi. The argument that keeping rather than averting cultural Chineseness is the key to Vietnam's own cultural subjectivity simply means that the Vietnamese culture is heavily indebted to the Chinese culture.[56] Appreciation for one's culture is how self-respect evolves[57]; thus, the appreciating the Chinese cultural legacy is how Vietnam can develop cultural dignity.[58]

Vietnam has to protect cultural Chineseness not merely because of self-respect and self-confidence. Cultural Chineseness is also Vietnam's proud intellectual capacity to read between the lines the mind of the Chinese leader given the similar cultural calculi of both cultures. In addition, Vietnam is able to see the moral problem of the Chinese leadership precisely because Vietnam is aware of how China violates its own cultural norms or alleged behavioral patterns.[59] Vietnamese intellectuals and political leaders know how not to abandon their moral ground and yet cope with the encroaching China on the rise by relying on both their shared cultural pattern and political party system.[60] All these Chinese norms are simultaneously Vietnamese norms and patterns. A veteran goes as far as suggesting that Vietnam is the little brother who occasionally fails to address the need for saving the face of the big brother in accordance with their shared system of propriety.[61] Another veteran who frequently contributes to opinion columns in newspapers under a pen name explains that he decided to use the pen name lest his real name should embarrass his Chinese counterpart with whom he has had a long relationship.[62]

---

[56] Oral history of Phan Van Cac as well as that of Vu Khieu.
[57] Oral history of Tran Xuan De.
[58] Oral history of Tran Tuan Man as well as that of Nguyen Khue, who expresses pride and satisfaction in becoming a Sinologist.
[59] I am indebted to Nguyen Huy Hoang on this reflection.
[60] I am indebted to Tran Viet Thai on this reflection.
[61] I am indebted to Nguyen Tran Tien who shares the brotherhood analogy given by his father.
[62] The anonymous interviewee uses "PGS TS Tran Le" as pen name.

Mixed Chineseness and Policy Implications

The capacity for fluidity, embedded in complex cultural memory and history, in terms of self-positioning between an in-group identity and an out-group identity suggests that human decisions ultimately produce the act of positioning. Individuals owning Sinological Chineseness always have the potential to shift toward the position of an outsider who subsequently yields Confucian standards for Western realism when assessing China's Vietnam policy and preparing for realignment in international politics. As a result of the shift, the role-identity of Sinological Chineseness originating from the duty of translating between Chinese and Vietnamese evolves into a unilateral identity of Scientific Chineseness defined by the necessity to manage China. Furthermore, someone owning ethnic Chineseness to meet the expectations of both Chinese and Vietnamese may revert to the role of a cultural successor of Confucianism and enter a high profile demanding the reconstitution of Vietnamese identity with a clearer respect for Chinese legacy. Another plausible scenario is having some individuals initially feeling comfortable with undistinguishing Vietnamese and Chinese ways of life under the condition of experiential Chineseness; they could support civilizational distinction, which exposes the negative image of Chineseness, if Vietnam has been the sole successor of a moral culture, which China aborts.

The volatile nature of owning Chineseness inevitably prompts uncertainties in policy. The coexistence of different kinds of Chineseness is the norm and the spirit of the new century. Accordingly, a South Vietnamese veteran's use of traditional Chinese characters, which seemingly convey a pro-Taiwan disposition to ethnic Chineseness, may succeed in cultural Chineseness due to its efficiency in linking Han Nom and the Chinese classics. Accordingly, cycles, as methodology, fare better than a typical evolutionary or linear historiography. Cycles of cooperation, teaching and learning, realignment, suppression, sharing, and aversion, combined with a variety of emotional characteristics, such as opportunism, enthusiasm, anxiety, anger, happiness, and hatred, demand an epistemology not obstructed by linearity, consistency, structure, or parsimony.

A quote from a Sinologist veteran who strives to surpass making an impossible choice could be a good harbinger for the coming age of mixed Chineseness:

> Zen scholars in Vietnam often advocate the difference between Vietnamese and Chinese Zen, pointing to the former's national spirit and its perseverant continuity. For my own taking, this is wrong. Zen is no more than just Zen. Vietnamese Zen and Chinese Zen are identical. The national soul is a matter of historiography. For example, [Emperor] Trần Nhân Tông [(1258–1308)], who led troops to fight Mongolian invaders, was a historical character. Do not confuse his two roles. The role of emperor obliged him to fight. The other role as a Buddha required him to follow religious practices. His leadership in fighting was not derived from being a Buddha. One could not argue in his case that the Vietnamese Buddha was [a] nationalist. Do not mix two roles in order to reflect one's own desire for national independence and autonomy. Zen is most alerted at dichotomy… Zen is a spirit of selflessness. How can Zen promote self-independence? Vietnamese scholars commit the habit of reading the patriotic spirit and the love for the Mother Nature into Zen, but people of all other countries also love their countries and the Mother Nature.[63]

References

Assmann, Aleida. 2006. Memory, Individual and Collective. In E. Goodin and C. Tilly (Eds.), *The Oxford Handbook of Contextual Political Analysis*, pp. 210–224. Oxford: Oxford University Press.

Epstein, Charlotte. 2012. Stop Telling Us How to Behave: Socialization or Infantilization. *International Studies Perspectives* 13(2): 135–145.

Erll, Astrid. 2011. *Memory in Culture*. London: Palgrave Macmillan.

Nam, Nguyen. 2014. A Local History of Vientamese Sinology in Early Twentieth Century Annam — the Case of the Bulletin Du học báo 遊學報. *East Asia* 31(2): 139–156.

Nguyen, Huy Quy and Phan, Van Cac. 2014. Humanities in Vietnam's Chinese Studies. *East Asia* 31(2): 123–138.

---

[63] From oral history of Tran Tuan Man.

Shih, Chih-yu. 2010. The West That Is Not in the West: Identifying the Self in Oriental Modernity. *Cambridge Review of International Affairs* 23: 537–560.
Wang, Gungwu. 2002. *The Chinese Overseas: From Earthbound China to the Quest for Autonomy.* Cambridge: Harvard University Press.
Wehner, Leslie E. 2015. Role Expectations as Foreign Policy: South American Secondary Powers' Expectations of Brazil as a Regional Power. *Foreign Policy Analysis* 11(4): 435–455.
Wittgenstein Ludwig. 1986. *Philosophical Investigation.* p. 31. Translated by G. E. M. Anscombe. Oxford: Basil Blackwell Ltd.

Web References

Buu, Cam. Year n.a. Oral History. Department of Political Science, National Taiwan University, The Research and Educational Center For China Studies and Cross Taiwan-Strait Relations, http://politics.ntu.edu.tw/RAEC/comm2/interview%20VN%20BUU%20CAM%20ch.pdf. Accessed on March 12, 2017.

Cao, Tu Thanh. Year n.a. Oral History. Department of Political Science, National Taiwan University, The Research and Educational Center For China Studies and Cross Taiwan-Strait Relations, http://politics.ntu.edu.tw/RAEC/comm2/interview%20VN%20CAO%20TU%20THANH%20ch.pdf. Accessed on March 12, 2017.

Ha, Kien Hanh. Year n.a. Oral History. Department of Political Science, National Taiwan University, The Research and Educational Center For China Studies and Cross Taiwan-Strait Relations. 2017, http://politics.ntu.edu.tw/RAEC/comm2/vietnam_13.pdf. Accessed on March 12, 2017.

Ho, Si Hiep. Year n.a. Oral History. Department of Political Science, National Taiwan University, The Research and Educational Center For China Studies and Cross Taiwan-Strait Relations, http://politics.ntu.edu.tw/RAEC/comm2/interviewV%20Ho%20Si%20Hiep.pdf. Accessed on March 11, 2017.

Le, Huy Thieu. Year n.a. Oral History. Department of Political Science, National Taiwan University, The Research and Educational Center For China Studies and Cross Taiwan-Strait Relations, http://politics.ntu.edu.tw/RAEC/comm2/InterviewV%20Le%20Huy%20Tieu%20Chinese.pdf. Accessed on March 12, 2017.

Ly Viet Dung. Year n.a. Oral History. Department of Political Science, National Taiwan University, The Research and Educational Center For

China Studies and Cross Taiwan-Strait Relations, http://politics.ntu.edu.tw/RAEC/comm2/interviewV%20Ly%20Viet%20Dung.pdf. Accessed on March 11, 2017.

Nguyen, Bang Tuong. Year n.a. Oral History. Department of Political Science, National Taiwan University, The Research and Educational Center For China Studies and Cross Taiwan-Strait Relations, http://politics.ntu.edu.tw/RAEC/comm2/vietnam_05.doc. Accessed on March 11, 2017.

Nguyen, Huy Quy. Year n.a. Oral History. Department of Political Science, National Taiwan University, The Research and Educational Center For China Studies and Cross Taiwan-Strait Relations, http://politics.ntu.edu.tw/RAEC/comm2/vietnam_03.doc. Accessed on March 11, 2017.

Nguyen, Khue. Year n.a. Oral History. Department of Political Science, National Taiwan University, The Research and Educational Center For China Studies and Cross Taiwan-Strait Relations, http://politics.ntu.edu.tw/RAEC/comm2/interview%20VN%20NGUYEN%20KHUE%20ch.pdf. Accessed on March 12, 2017.

Nguyen, Ton Nhan. Year n.a. Oral History. Department of Political Science, National Taiwan University, The Research and Educational Center For China Studies and Cross Taiwan-Strait Relations, http://politics.ntu.edu.tw/RAEC/comm2/interview%20VN%20NGUYEN%20TON%20NHAN%20CH.pdf. Accessed on March 11, 2017.

Nguyen, Van Khang. Year n.a. Oral History. Department of Political Science, National Taiwan University, The Research and Educational Center For China Studies and Cross Taiwan-Strait Relations, http://politics.ntu.edu.tw/RAEC/comm2/interview%20VN%20NGUYEN%20TON%20NHAN%20ch.pdf. Accessed on March 12, 2017.

Pham, Thi Hao. Year n.a. Oral History. Department of Political Science, National Taiwan University, The Research and Educational Center For China Studies and Cross Taiwan-Strait Relations, http://politics.ntu.edu.tw/RAEC/comm2/interview%20VN%20PHAM%20THI%20HAO%20CH.pdf. Accessed on March 11, 2017.

Pham, Tu Chau. Year n.a. Oral History. Department of Political Science, National Taiwan University, The Research and Educational Center For China Studies and Cross Taiwan-Strait Relations, http://politics.ntu.edu.tw/RAEC/comm2/interviewV%20Pahm%20Tu%20Chau%20Chinese.pdf. Accessed on March 11, 2017.

Phan, Van Cac. Year n.a. Oral History. Department of Political Science, National Taiwan University, The Research and Educational Center For China Studies and Cross Taiwan-Strait Relations, http://politics.ntu.edu.tw/RAEC/comm2/vietnam_04.doc. Accessed on March 11, 2017.

Tran Xuan De. Year n.a. Oral History. Department of Political Science, National Taiwan University, The Research and Educational Center For China Studies and Cross Taiwan-Strait Relations, http://politics.ntu.edu.tw/RAEC/comm2/InterviewV%20Tran%20Xuan%20De.pdf. Accessed on March 12, 2017.

Tran, Le Bao. Year n.a. Oral History. Department of Political Science, National Taiwan University, The Research and Educational Center For China Studies and Cross Taiwan-Strait Relations, http://politics.ntu.edu.tw/RAEC/comm2/InterviewV%20Tran%20Le%20Bao%20Chinese.pdf. Accessed on March 12, 2017.

Tran, Tuan Man. Year n.a. Oral History. Department of Political Science, National Taiwan University, The Research and Educational Center For China Studies and Cross Taiwan-Strait Relations, http://politics.ntu.edu.tw/RAEC/comm2/InterviewV%20Tran%20Tuan%20Man.pdf. Accessed on March 12, 2017.

Vu, Khieu. Year n.a. Oral History. Department of Political Science, National Taiwan University, The Research and Educational Center For China Studies and Cross Taiwan-Strait Relations, http://politics.ntu.edu.tw/RAEC/comm2/vietnam_07ch.pdf. Accessed on March 12, 2017.